Containing Balkan Nationalism

RELIGION AND GLOBAL POLITICS

SERIES EDITOR
John L. Esposito

University Professor and Director
Prince Alwaleed Bin Talal Center for Muslim-Christian Understanding
Georgetown University

ISLAMIC LEVIATHAN
Islam and the Making of State Power
Seyyed Vali Reza Nasr

RACHID GHANNOUCHI
A Democrat Within Islamism
Azzam S. Tamimi

BALKAN IDOLS
Religion and Nationalism in Yugoslav States
Vjekoslav Perica

ISLAMIC POLITICAL IDENTITY IN TURKEY
M. Hakan Yavuz

RELIGION AND POLITICS IN POST-COMMUNIST ROMANIA
Lavinia Stan and Lucian Turcescu

PIETY AND POLITICS
Islamism in Contemporary Malaysia
Joseph Chinyong Liow

TERROR IN THE LAND OF THE HOLY SPIRIT
Guatemala under General Efrain Rios Montt, 1982–1983
Virginia Garrard-Burnett

IN THE HOUSE OF WAR
Dutch Islam Observed
Sam Cherribi

BEING YOUNG AND MUSLIM
New Cultural Politics in the Global South and North
Asef Bayat and Linda Herrera

CHURCH, STATE, AND DEMOCRACY IN EXPANDING EUROPE
Lavinia Stan and Lucian Turcescu

THE HEADSCARF CONTROVERSY
Secularism and Freedom of Religion
Hilal Elver

THE HOUSE OF SERVICE
The Gülen Movement and Islam's Third Way
David Tittensor

MAPPING THE LEGAL BOUNDARIES OF BELONGING
Religion and Multiculturalism from Israel to Canada
Edited by René Provost

RELIGIOUS SECULARITY
A Theological Challenge to the Islamic State
Naser Ghobadzadeh

THE MIDDLE PATH OF MODERATION IN ISLAM
The Qur'ānic Principle of Wasaṭiyyah
Mohammad Hashim Kamali

CONTAINING BALKAN NATIONALISM
Imperial Russia and Ottoman Christians, 1856–1914
Denis Vovchenko

Containing Balkan Nationalism

Imperial Russia and Ottoman Christians, 1856–1914

DENIS VOVCHENKO

OXFORD
UNIVERSITY PRESS

OXFORD
UNIVERSITY PRESS

Oxford University Press is a department of the University of Oxford. It furthers
the University's objective of excellence in research, scholarship, and education
by publishing worldwide. Oxford is a registered trade mark of Oxford University
Press in the UK and certain other countries.

Published in the United States of America by Oxford University Press
198 Madison Avenue, New York, NY 10016, United States of America.

© Oxford University Press 2016

Library of Congress Cataloging-in-Publication Data
Names: Vovchenko, Denis.
Title: Containing Balkan nationalism : imperial Russia and Ottoman
Christians, 1856–1914 / Denis Vovchenko.
Description: New York, NY : Oxford University Press, [2016] | Includes index.
Identifiers: LCCN 2015050170 | ISBN 9780190276676 (hardback : alk. paper)
Subjects: LCSH: Russia—Relations—Balkan Peninsula. | Balkan
Peninsula—Relations—Russia. | Turkey—Relations—Balkan Peninsula. |
Balkan Peninsula—Relations—Turkey. | Balkan Peninsula—Ethnic
relations—History—19th century. | Balkan Peninsula—Ethnic
relations—History—20th century. | Nationalism—Balkan
Peninsula—History. | Christianity and politics—Balkan
Peninsula—History. | Eastern churches—Balkan Peninsula—History. |
Religious minorities—Balkan Peninsula—History. | BISAC: HISTORY / Europe /
Eastern. | HISTORY / Military / World War I.
Classification: LCC DR38.3.R8 V68 2016 | DDC 949.6/038—dc23 LC record available
at http://lccn.loc.gov/2015050170

1 3 5 7 9 8 6 4 2
Printed by Sheridan Books, Inc., United States of America

To my wife

Contents

Preface

I SHOULD ADD a note on historical dates, geographical names, and terms. Throughout the period under investigation, all Orthodox lands relied on the Julian Calendar (also known as the Old Calendar), which was twelve days behind the Gregorian Calendar in the nineteenth century. Unless otherwise noted, the dates in the book will reflect that usage. I tried to follow the same principle with place names. That is why I use "Constantinople" instead of "Istanbul" or "Philippoupolis" instead of "Plovdiv." Generally, for majority-Slavic northern Balkan provinces, I used common Serbian and Bulgarian names rather than archaic Greek terms, for example, "Sliven" instead of "Silimnos." I followed conventional usage of key historical terms and names, for example, "Russo-Turkish War" instead of "Russo-Ottoman War." For the most part, I have transliterated modern Greek, Slavic, and Turkish names according to the Library of Congress System. Unless indicated otherwise, all translations are my own. Below are the most important abbreviations.

GARF	(State Archive of the Russian Federation, Moscow)
RGVIA	(Russian State Military History Archive, Moscow)
RGALI	(Russian State Archive for Literature and Art, Moscow)
AVPRI	(Russian Imperial Foreign Policy Archive, Moscow)
OPI GIM	(Manuscript Division of the State Historical Museum, Moscow)
OR RGB	(Russian State Library Manuscript Division, Moscow)
RGIA	(Russian State Historical Archive, St Petersburg)
OR RGPB	(Russian State Public Library, Manuscript Division, St Petersburg)
AYE	(Greek Foreign Ministry Archive, Athens)
ELIA	(Greek Archive for History and Literature, Athens)
AEP	(the Archive of the Ecumenical Patriarchate, Istanbul)

Acknowledgments

THIS BOOK HAD its start as my doctoral dissertation. First of all, I am grateful to all my professors at the University of Minnesota, who trained me as a historian and introduced to me some key political science concepts and models. My advisor, Theofanis G. Stavrou, has truly changed my life. He inspired me to pursue this particular topic and to concentrate on Greek-Russian relations. He put together a wonderful dissertation committee including Drs. Ron Aminzade, Caesar Farah, John Kim Munholland, and Martin Sampson. Thanks to Kyria Freda Stavrou and Soterios G. Stavrou, my wife and I quickly overcame the culture shock when we moved from Russia to Minnesota. The pride that my wife and parents felt for me helped me persevere through many years of coursework in Moscow and Minneapolis.

The University of Minnesota also funded most of my dissertation research in the Russian archives with the Dunn Peace Fellowship, the Graduate School Thesis Research Grant, and the History Department Thomas S. Noonan Fellowship. My research in Greece was made possible by the Allison F. Frantz Fellowship sponsored by the American School of Classical Studies at Athens. Dr. Maria Georgopoulou and her amazing staff went out of the way to make me feel comfortable in the stacks of the Gennadius Library in 2006 and 2007. For several months, Loring Hall became a home away from home for me and my wife.

Northeastern State University in Tahlequah had enough faith in me to give me a job and to sponsor two of my summer trips through the Faculty Research Council in 2009 and 2010. The College of Liberal Arts at NSU facilitated another research trip when it matched the Oklahoma Humanities Council Summer Research Grant in the summer of 2013. The fellowship from the American Research Institute in Turkey enabled me not only to improve my Turkish-language skills but also to access the archive of the Patriarchate of Constantinople where Father Vissarion, Kyrios Kostas, and Kyrios Petros opened my eyes to the past and present of the Orthodox community in Istanbul.

On many occasions, I found in Ada Dialla, Iannis Karras, and Andreas Sideris a living example of how to connect Greek and Russian cultures. It was a great relief when Kyria Efthimia Papaspirou quickly gave her permission to publish some rare posters I photographed at the Greek Historical Museum. Under Alla Vladimirovna Rudenko, the reading room of the Russian Imperial Foreign Policy Archive became a very welcoming place to me and other researchers. Nina Ivanovna Abdulaieva was very patient with me when I began exploring the holdings of the State Archive of the Russian Federation.

I am enormously grateful to the editors and the anonymous readers at Oxford University Press for their valuable feedback. My colleagues are a community of teacher-scholars who created a healthy intellectual environment at NSU and encouraged me to keep improving my manuscript. Brad Agnew and Norm Carlisle made extremely useful comments after reading my introduction. Sylvia Nitti helped me modify Map 4.1 and deal with the challenges of Greek handwriting. A special thanks goes to Donna Graham and Misti Hanrahan, who have turned the Interlibrary Loan into an indispensable service and tirelessly request dauntingly exotic materials for me.

Containing Balkan Nationalism

Introduction

THE BALKANS HAD long fascinated the political imagination of Russian commentators of all ideological stripes. Reporting on the Balkan Wars of 1912–1913 for a Kiev newspaper, Leon Trotsky wrote, "The effects of the war demonstrate only too clearly to the Balkan nations and first of all to Serbia that they can exist only in a permanent economic and political federation."[1] Unlike Trotsky, most Russian scholars and journalists who were interested in the Balkans tended to be on the right wing of the political spectrum. They saw Russia as part and parcel of a Balkan federation—a vision rooted in a long history of messianic imperialism. Several months before the Russo-Turkish War of 1877–1878, Fyodor Dostoevsky justified Russia's right to take possession of Constantinople "as the leader, protector, and guardian of Orthodox Christianity—the role it was destined to play since Ivan III who had elevated the double-headed eagle of Tsargrad over Russia's ancient symbols." Only that kind of claim would be acceptable to both Balkan Slavs and Greeks, divided by ethnicity but united in faith.[2]

A future union of Russia and Balkan Christians was not always imagined on the ruins of the Ottoman Empire. Some advocated including Turkey into a Balkan federation. Still, the words of Trotsky and Dostoevsky capture the many tensions that developed in contemporary views on Russian cultural identity and foreign policy at the turn of the twentieth century. Secular nationalism was violently redrawing the map of Europe throughout the 1800s: Italy and Germany became unified and the new nation-states of Greece, Serbia, Montenegro, Rumania, and Bulgaria emerged from the slow breakup of the

1. Trotsky, Leon, "Serbia v siluetakh," in Andrei Shemiakin, ed., *Russkiie o Serbii i serbakh* (St. Petersburg: Aleteia, 2006), p. 522. Unless otherwise noted, all translations into English are mine.

2. Dostoevsky, Fyodor, "Dnevnik pisatelia. 1876," in *Dnevnik pisatelia* (Moscow: Institut russkoi tsivilizatsii, 2010), p. 376.

Ottoman Empire. The debates about the significance of Russia's connection to the Balkans reflected and to some extent even shaped the efforts of Russian, Ottoman, Greek, Bulgarian, and Serbian statesmen and prelates to adapt the newly politicized concept of ethnicity to existing religious and dynastic structures.

The Bulgarian Church Question was one of those issues facing the political and religious leaders in Eastern Europe. My book focuses on the consequences of the Bulgarian movement for independence of their national church from the Ecumenical Patriarchate of Constantinople between 1856 and 1914. The story goes back to 1453 when the Ottoman Turks had completed their conquest of the Christian Balkan kingdoms and the Byzantine Empire with the storming of Constantinople. By the early 1500s, they had conquered the Arab Muslim states and taken control of what is today the Middle East. With their capital in Constantinople, the Ottomans chose the Patriarch of that city as the head of all Orthodox Christian churches in their domains. As the only official mediator between the Orthodox Christians and the Ottoman government, he was thus responsible for collecting taxes, administering justice, and maintaining schools and charities. The Patriarchate of Constantinople used its position to absorb the previously autonomous Bulgarian and Serbian churches and to acquire great influence over the elections of chief prelates in ancient patriarchates of Alexandria, Jerusalem, and Antioch.[3]

Already in the 1500s, ethnic Greeks or Hellenized locals had occupied key positions in all Ottoman dioceses and introduced Greek as the language of liturgy and instruction at urban schools.[4] Some middle-class non-Greek Christians, especially lower-level clerics, increasingly resented this domination and their discontent crystallized in the mid-1800s with a new ideology of nationalism, which explicitly gave political significance to cultural distinctions.[5] In the aftermath of the French Revolution, the idea of national sovereignty challenged the rule of divinely ordained kings. All that was solid was melting in the air in the 1800s despite the best efforts of conservative and

3. Runciman, Steven, *The Great Church in Captivity* (Cambridge: Cambridge University Press, 1968), pp. 165–185; Haddad, Robert, *Syrian Christians in a Muslim Society: An Interpretation* (Princeton: Princeton University Press, 1970), pp. 63–64.

4. Hopkins, James Lindsay, *The Bulgarian Orthodox Church: A Socio-Historical Analysis of the Evolving Relationship Between Church, Nation, and State in Bulgaria* (Boulder: East European Monographs, distributed by Columbia University Press, New York, 2009), pp. 56–57.

5. Genchev, Nikolai, *The Bulgarian National Revival Period* (Sofia: Sofia Press, 1977), pp. 36–41.

legitimist monarchs of the post-Napoleonic Holy Alliance and the Concert of Europe to maintain the status quo.[6]

In the Ottoman Empire, nationalism first developed among the Christians, who unlike the Muslims had maintained closer contacts with Europe. From 1821 to 1830, the Greeks rebelled against the Ottoman sultan and created a tiny but ambitious national kingdom in parts of mainland Greece. It then sought to expand its influence in the Ottoman Balkans and the Middle East through the ethnically Greek leadership of the Patriarchate of Constantinople.[7] This aggressive irredentist policy further politicized the ethnic divisions within Orthodox Christian communities. In reaction, prosperous Bulgarian merchant and craft guilds in Constantinople and Philippoupolis (modern Plovdiv) became the core of an emerging Bulgarian nationalist movement directed against the Patriarchate of Constantinople.[8]

The movement violated the principles of the Orthodox Church because it rejected precise territorial boundaries and aimed at incorporating all Slavic-speaking Christians into its future church, thereby tearing apart mixed Greek-Bulgarian-Serbian communities. Independent church status meant legal and cultural autonomy within the Islamic structure of the Ottoman Empire, which recognized religious minorities rather than ethnic ones. With that in mind, Bulgarian nationalist leaders appealed to the Ottoman government directly but also attempted to enlist the support of the European Great Powers.[9]

---

6. Schroeder, Paul, "The 19th-Century International System: Changes in the Structure," *World Politics*, 39, 1 (October 1986): 1–26.

7. Skopetea, Elli, *To "protypo vasileio" kai i Megali Idea: Opseis tou ethnikou provlimatos stin Ellada, 1830–1880* (Athens: Polytypo, 1988); Grishina, Ritta, "Fenomen Bolgarskoi Pravoslavnoi Tserkvi (1870–1940e gg)," in *Chelovek na Balkanakh: Sotsiokulturnye izmeneniia protsessa modernizatsii (seredina XIX v—seredina XX v)* (St. Petersburg: Aletheia, 2007), p. 228.

8. Mazhdrakova-Chavdarova, Ogniana, "Bulgarskoto natsionalno predstavitelstvo—idei i opiti za suzdavaneto my (40-te–60-te godini na XIX vek)," *Istoricheskii Pregled*, 49, 4–5 (1993): 21–54.

9. Clarke, James, *Bible Societies, American Missionaries & the National Revival of Bulgaria* (New York: Arno Press and New York Times, 1971); Clarke, James F., "Protestantism and the Church Question in 1861," in Hupchick, Dennis, ed., *The Pen & the Sword: Studies in Bulgarian History by James F.Clarke* (Boulder: East European Monographs. Distributed by Columbia University Press, New York, 1988), pp. 328–344; Merdzanov, Ivan, "Die Habsburgermonarchie und die katholischen Missionen in den Bulgarischen Landen im 18. –19. Jh.," *Bulgarian Historical Review*, 2 (1994): 31–59; Genchev, Nikolai, "Frantsia i Bulgaro-Grutskite tsurkovni otnoshenia prez 50–70-te godini na XIX v.," *Istoricheski Pregled*, 32, 4 (1976): 31–56; Genov, Rumen, "Bulgarskoto tsurkovno-natsionalno dvizhenie v kraia na 60-te godini na XIX v. prez pogleda na angliiskata diplomatsia," *Istoricheskii Pregled*, 42, 5 (1986): 73–77.

As the only major Orthodox Christian state, Russia was the obvious country for Bulgarian nationalists to turn to. Traditionally, however, the Russian
tsars backed the Patriarchate of Constantinople as the institutional bedrock of
their influence in the so- called Christian East—the Russian term for the area
populated by Orthodox Christians of the Ottoman Empire.[10]

In February 1870, the Bulgarian church was established by the Sultan's
decree as the "Exarchate" without the consent of the Patriarchate. The inability to reach a compromise on the issue of jurisdictional and territorial delimitation of mixed Greek-Slavic areas led to the convening of the Local Council
of Ottoman Christian Orthodox churches in September of 1872. The Council
proclaimed as schismatics the Bulgarian church movement leaders and those
affiliated with them for having brought *phyletismos* or ethnonational divisions
into the Church. This Schism accelerated the ongoing splintering of the
previously united Ottoman Christian community and led to a series of local
armed conflicts in Ottoman Macedonia and Thrace, which would ultimately
snowball into the Balkan Wars of 1912–1913 and influence the alignments of
the Balkan states in World War One.[11]

Research Objectives

I will demonstrate that Russian intellectuals and diplomatic, military, and
ecclesiastical agents especially on the higher level tirelessly worked with the
Ottoman government, rival churches, and various European diplomats to reconcile the parties of the conflict based on the preservation of the overarch-
ing Orthodox Christian identity and the institution of the Patriarchate. This
experience will help direct today's international efforts aimed at containing
ethnic nationalism and associated conflict in divided societies by promoting
federative and power-sharing arrangements based on existing traditions and
structures.

Clearly, Russian officials and commentators were motivated by the need
to restore the unity of their traditional clientele in a geopolitically strategic
area. At the same time, many of them argued that the Patriarchate was more
consistent with the religious and dynastic foundations of both the Ottoman
and Russian Empires than was the ethnocentric Bulgarian Church. For the

---

10. Trubetskoi, Grigorii, "Rossia i Vselenskaia patriarkhia posle Krymskoi voiny (1856–
1860)," *Vestnik Evropy*, 4 (1902): 549–592; 5 (1902): 5–51; and 6 (1902): 469–507.

11. Stavrianos, Leften, "L'Institution de l'Exarcat Bulgare: Son influence sur les relations
inter-Balkaniques," *Les Balkans*, 11 (1939): 56–69; Aarbakke, Vemund, *Ethnic Rivalry and
the Quest for Macedonia, 1870–1913* (Boulder: East European Monographs. Distributed by
Columbia University Press, New York, 2003).

Russians, patching up Greco-Slavic family feuds would stabilize the Ottoman Empire, increase Russian influence, and empower Christian minorities in regard to the Muslim majority and the centralizing Ottoman policies. Responding to this strong political and cultural demand, scholars, clerics, and journalists in Orthodox Christian centers in Russia and the Balkans modernized the meaning of the Christian East as a source of new supranational alternatives to Western-inspired secular nationalism.

Furthermore, my analysis of various abortive and successful attempts to defuse ethnonationalism inside Ottoman Christian minority institutions may offer another perspective on "consociationalism" or power-sharing facilitated by external involvement such as diplomacy, direct military occupation, international supervision of local police forces, and the press. The efforts of the Ottoman authorities, Russian and Balkan diplomats, intellectuals, and prelates often converged to strengthen the Orthodox Christian identity shared by all parties to the conflict as the basis for territorial and hierarchical church autonomy. Although the Bulgarian church was primarily ethnically based, from the viewpoint of both the theocratic Ottoman state and canon law, it had to remain part of the Orthodox minority led by the Patriarchate of Constantinople if it wanted to operate legally.

Elements of democratic governance also developed in this process of adapting traditional institutions to the challenge of nationalism. The arrangements hammered out by the Ottoman government and Russian diplomats and ecclesiastics enabled the followers of the Patriarchate of Constantinople and the Bulgarian church movement to elect their representatives to communal councils on the local and imperial levels. Their lay members were instrumental in the selection of the bishops assigned to their dioceses. The main difficulty was to move both parties to agree on the territorial jurisdiction of each church and on the respective ethnic minority rights within predominantly Slavic and Greek-speaking Balkan dioceses.

Mapping the Literature, Staking Out the Argument

My research contributes to the discussion of several important issues in European and Middle Eastern history. To encourage interdisciplinary dialogue, I will draw on political science models of resolution and management of conflicts caused or exacerbated by irredentism. Specifically, I will apply the concepts of federation and power-sharing to make sense of various Russian initiatives to prevent internal and external nationalist agitation from destroying the Patriarchate of Constantinople.

The book relies on a variety of archival and published sources from Russia, Greece, Turkey, and Bulgaria to shed more light on the murky waters of the Eastern Question. This curious name refers to the problem of Ottoman decline and uncertainty over the future control of lands stretching from the Danube to the Tigris and Euphrates. Historians have usually discussed the Eastern Question as a purely diplomatic issue involving the European Great Powers and the newly established small but rapacious Balkan nation-states from the late 1700s to the end of the Great War.[12]

My analysis will help broaden the horizons of the Eastern Question by examining the extremely creative clash of modern and traditional paradigms that affected not just politics and institutions but also popular loyalties and identities at the time. As such, my book will be part of the study of the enormously rich cultural aspects of the rivalry over the influence on the Balkans and the Middle East started by Theofanis Stavrou.[13]

Within this historiography of the Eastern Question, my book is the first one to examine the Bulgarian Church Question in its entirety rather than

---

12. Key works include Macfie, A. L., *The Eastern Question, 1774–1923* (London and New York: Longman, 1996); Goldfrank, David, *The Origins of the Crimean War* (London and New York: Longman, 1994); Jelavich, Barbara, *Russia's Balkan Entanglements, 1806–1914* (Cambridge and New York: Cambridge University Press, 1991); Schoellgen, Gregor, *Imperialismus und Gleichgewicht: Deutschland, England und die orientalische Frage 1871–1914* (Munich: R. Oldenbourg Verlag, 1984); Rossos, Andrew, *Russia and the Balkans: Inter-Balkan Rivalries and Russian Foreign Policy, 1908–1914* (Toronto and Buffalo: University of Toronto Press, 1981); Millman, Richard, *Britain and the Eastern Question, 1875–78* (Oxford: Oxford University Press, 1979); Georgiev, Vladimir et al., eds., *Vostochnyi vopros vo vneshnei politike Rossii (konets XVIII–nachalo XXv.)* (Moscow: Nauka, 1978); Jelavich, Charles and Barbara, *The Establishment of the Balkan National States, 1804–1920* (Seattle: University of Washington Press, 1977); Kofos, Evangelos, *Greece and the Eastern Crisis, 1875–1878* (Thessaloniki: Institute for Balkan Studies, 1975); Schroeder, Paul, *Austria, Great Britain, and the Crimean War: The Destruction of the European Concert* (Ithaca: Cornell University Press, 1972); Anderson, M. S., *The Eastern Question, 1774–1923: A Study in International Relations* (New York: St. Martin's Press, 1966); Jelavich, Charles, *Tsarist Russia & Balkan Nationalism: Russian Influence in the Internal Affairs of Bulgaria & Serbia, 1879–1886* (Berkeley and Los Angeles: University of California Press, 1958); Taylor, A. J. P., *The Struggle for Mastery in Europe, 1848–1918* (Oxford: Oxford University Press, 1956); Temperley, Harold, *England and the Near East* (London and New York: Longman, 1936); Driault, Edouard, *La Question D'orient depuis ses origines jusqu'à la Paix De Sèvres* (Paris, 1921).

13. Stavrou, Theofanis, *Russian Interests in Palestine, 1882–1914: A Study of Religious and Educational Enterprise* (Thessaloniki: Institute for Balkan Studies, 1963); Batalden, Stephen, *Catherine II's Greek Prelate: Eugenios Voulgaris in Russia, 1771–1806* (Boulder: East European Monographs; New York: Distributed by Columbia University Press, 1982); Bruess, Gregory, *Religion, Identity and Empire: A Greek Archbishop in the Russia of Catherine the Great* (Boulder: East European Monographs; New York: Distributed by Columbia University Press, 1997); Prousis, Theophilus, *Russian Society and the Greek Revolution* (DeKalb: Northern Illinois University Press, 1994); Dialla, Anta, *E Rosia Apenanti sta Valkania: Ideologia kai Politike sto Devtero Miso tou 19ou Aiona* (Athens: Alexandreia, 2009).

in its separate stages.[14] The existing scholarly literature on the Bulgarian Church Question has added greatly to our knowledge of its major events and developments. But it suffers from a teleological reading of local Balkan and general European history. Whether in its nationalistic or less partisan form, it privileges Bulgarian or Greek or Serbian nationalists over the allegedly outdated religious and dynastic alternatives.

Most scholarly studies on this topic are deterministic narratives explaining how Ottoman Christian provinces and their populations came to be partitioned and nationalized by 1912–1922, with the focus mainly on which irredentist movement was gaining the upper hand at a given time. They hardly ever discuss the possibility of containing Balkan nationalism outside or within traditional Ottoman institutions, thereby giving short shrift to efforts to propose a supra-nationalist alternative. Nationalist historians have generally dominated the field, repeatedly presenting the typically primordialist account of eternal nations acting as sleeping beauties until the late 1700s when they suddenly began to "awaken" from Ottoman slumber and stupor. This "revival" naturally led to national "liberation" struggles of varying degrees of intensity and the gradual but inexorable "unification" of "unredeemed brethren" with their "homelands."[15]

Turkish academics turn this argument on its head by reversing the heroes and villains. They tend to portray Ottoman Christians generally and the Greek-dominated Patriarchate of Constantinople specifically as ungrateful and even treacherous subjects who supposedly rejected the blessings of Ottoman tolerance and kept hatching up conspiracies to restore the medieval kingdoms that were smashed by the early Ottoman sultans. Those intrigues

---

14. Bondareva, Victoria, *Bolgarskii Ekzarkhat v 1878–1897 godakh* (unpublished Ph.D. dissertation. Krasnodar: Kuban State University, 2006); Aarbakke, Vemund, *Ethnic Rivalry and the Quest for Macedonia, 1870–1913* (Boulder: East European Monographs; New York: Distributed by Columbia University, 2003); Lange-Akhund, Nadine, *The Macedonian Question, 1893–1908, from Western Sources* (Boulder: East European Monographs; New York: Distributed by Columbia University, 1998); Markova, Zina, *Bulgarskata ekzarkhia, 1870–1879* (Sofia: Bulgarian Academy of Sciences, 1989).

15. See for example Papaconstantinou, Michael, "The Struggle of Hellenism over Macedonia," *Balkan Studies*, 1 (1960): 129–142; Pundeff, Marin, "Bulgarian Nationalism," in Sugar, Peter, and Lederer, Ivo, eds., *Nationalism in Eastern Europe* (Seattle: University of Washington Press, 1969), pp. 93–98; Nikov, Petur, *Vuzrazhdane na bulgarskiia narod: Tsurkovnonatsionalni borbi i postizhenia* (Sofia: Nauka i Izkustvo, 1971 [1929]); Dakin, Douglas, *The Unification of Greece, 1770–1923* (New York: St. Martin's Press, 1972); Vakalopoulos, Konstantinos, *O Voreios Ellinismos kata ten proime fase tou Makedonikou Agona (1878–1894)* (Thessaloniki: Institute for Balkan Studies, 1983); Vakalopoulos, Konstantinos, *Modern History of Macedonia, 1830–1912: From the Birth of the Greek State until the Liberation* (Thessaloniki: Barbounakis, 1988).

and rebellions invited interventions of power-hungry European empires and, in the view of Turkish scholars, became the single most important cause of Ottoman collapse.[16]

Many contemporary Balkan historians began to consciously distance themselves from the nationalist narrative enshrined in the works of their college professors and in the high school textbooks they had been raised on. Instead, they subscribe to "constructivism"—a dominant trend in nationalism studies.[17] In the constructivist line of reasoning, starting in the late 1700s, the Enlightenment notion of popular sovereignty politicized ethnic distinctions thus encouraging novel and even unprecedented claims by groups previously with little political power. Moreover, educated elites, often for selfish socioeconomic reasons, invented or imagined the idea of supposedly eternal nations and imposed it on the rest of their unsuspecting societies through control of the print media and, if lucky, of the government.

Having rejected primordialism, the constructivists produced their own anachronistic historical lens with their bias in favor of modernization theory. They share the assumption that secularism and industrialization inevitably supersede "pre-modern" cultural and socioeconomic structures. Thus, the most recent Greek scholarly works paint a picture of an unavoidable takeover of the Patriarchate of Constantinople by the brand new Western ideology of nationalism. Established Ottoman Christian lay and clerical leaders somehow forgot about their vested institutional and economic interests. They inexplicably succumbed to the irresistible calls of homegrown and foreign-based nationalist sirens and pied pipers whom they blindly followed all the way to the destruction of the Ottoman Empire. Although a radical departure from Greek nationalist historiography, the constructivist study by Paraskevas Matalas is limited to the pre-1872 period and is fundamentally handicapped by the absence of sources from the Patriarchate of Constantinople and Russia.[18]

In contrast, the book by Dimitris Stamatopoulos is well-attuned to the complex and often contradictory interplay of nationalist, religious, and

---

16. Sofuoglu, Adnan, *Fener Rum Patrikhanesi ve Siyasi Faaliyetleri* (Istanbul: Turan Yayincilik, 1996), pp. 18–29; Alkan, Hakan, *Fener Rum Patrikhanesi: Uluslararasi Iliskiler Acisindan Bir Yaklasim* (Istanbul: Gunce, 1999), pp. 43–45; Atalay, Bulent, *Fener Rum Patrikhanesi'nin Siyasi Faaliyetleri (1908–1923)* (Istanbul: TATAV, 2001), p. 5.

17. Hobsbawm, Eric, *Nations and Nationalism since 1780: Programme, Myth, Reality* (Cambridge: Cambridge University Press, 1990).

18. Matalas, Paraskeuas, *Ethnos kai Orthodoxia: Hoi Peripeteies Mias Scheses: Apo to 'Helladiko' sto Voulgariko Schisma* (Herakleio: University of Crete Press, 2002).

imperial identities pervading the efforts of the Patriarchate to strengthen its legitimacy and influence in the face of the new challenges of lay-dominated mass politics. But in the end, Stamatopoulos portrays the Patriarchate as gradually losing its traditional ecumenical role and inexorably adopting Greek nationalism. This unwarranted conclusion is due to the chronological limits (1873) and lack of Russian sources. As a result, Stamatopoulos insufficiently appreciates the staying power of what I would call "Pan-Orthodoxy"— the principle of Orthodox unity in Russia's foreign policy and in its educated society.[19]

Unlike Stamatopoulos, Paschalis Kitromilides argues in favor of a more dynamic and multilinear relationship between the Patriarchate and Greek nationalism. When the Bulgarian church movement divided Christian Orthodox communities after 1856, many bishops in Ottoman Thrace and Macedonia reacted by turning to Greek nationalism and seeking the support of local Greek diplomatic representatives. But their superiors in Constantinople and pro-Ottoman lay leaders sought to stop or even reverse the process of nationalization taking place on the provincial level. In contrast, the Russian Church was allegedly promoting "active nationalist strategies" in the Balkan Orthodox churches. The last point is clearly an oversimplification on the part of Kitromilides due to the lack of Russian sources.[20]

The most recent Bulgarian book on the Bulgarian church movement does not go beyond 1870 and discusses the Russian role based only on published and secondary sources rather than on archival sources.[21] Other Bulgarian scholars began to question the modern ethnocentric logic of the Bulgarian Church, which never intended to include non-Orthodox Bulgarian speakers. Its leading Russian-educated prelates and the Ottoman institutional framework combined to maintain a distance between the Bulgarian Exarchate and Bulgarian state-sponsored irredentism.[22]

---

19. Stamatopoulos, Demetris, *Metarrythmisi kai Ekkosmikevsi: Pros Mia Anasynthesi tis Istorias tou Oikoumenikou Patriarheiou ton 19o aiona* (Athens: Aleksandreia, 2003).

20. Kitromilides, Paschalis, "The Ecumenical Patriarchate," in Leustean, Lucian, ed., *Orthodox Christianity and Nationalism in Nineteenth-Century Southeastern Europe* (New York: Fordham University Press, 2014), pp. 23–26.

21. Boneva, Vera, *Bulgarskoto tsukovnonatsionalno dvizhenie, 1856–1870* (Sofia: Za bukvite–O pismenekh, 2010).

22. Kalkandjieva, Daniela, "The Bulgarian Orthodox Church at the Crossroads: Between Nationalism and Pluralism," in Krawchuk, Andrii, and Bremer, Thomas, eds., *Eastern Orthodox Encounters of Identity and Otherness: Values, Self-Definition, and Dialogue,* (New York: Palgrave-McMillan, 2014), pp. 54–55.

On the other hand, the literature that does focus on the Russian role is often written from the Bulgarian perspective,[23] or tends to reduce complex attitudes and reactions to the Bulgarian Question to the supposedly unstoppable rise of Pan-Slav sympathies in Russian diplomacy and educated society.[24] I will put in the foreground resistance to nationalism in the political and intellectual responses to the Bulgarian Church Question, using fresh methodology and hitherto untapped archival materials and neglected published sources.[25]

Russia's defeat in the Crimean War (1853–1856) led to sweeping socioeconomic reforms and provoked intense reexamination of cultural and political certainties.[26] In the post-Crimean context, Bulgarian appeals for support to Russian diplomats and publicists helped politicize earlier Romantic Slavophile ideas of cultural affinity and uniqueness of Russia, Orthodox Christians, and Slavs. Bulgarian nationalists began posing as Russia's unredeemed blood brothers victimized not only by the Ottoman Turks but also by their fellow Orthodox Greeks. Bulgarian activists were instrumental in inspiring Pan-Slav organizations first in Moscow and then in St. Petersburg and other major cities.[27]

---

23. Khevrolina, Victoria, *Rossiiskii diplomat graf Nikolai Pavlovich Ignatiev* (Moscow: Russian Academy of Sciences, 2004); Kiril, *Graf N. P. Ignatiev i Bulgarskiat tserkoven vopros: Izsledovane i dokumenti* (Sofia: Sinodalno Izdatelstvo, 1958); Markova, Zina, "Russia and the Bulgarian-Greek Church Question in the Seventies of the 19th Century," *Etudes Historiques*, 11 (1983): 159–187.

24. Kitromilides, Pashalis, "The Ecumenical Patriarchate," p. 19; Stamatopoulos, Dimitris, "The Orthodox Church of Greece," in Leustean, Lucian, ed., *Orthodox Christianity and Nationalism in Nineteenth-Century Southeastern Europe* (New York: Fordham University Press, 2014), p. 53; Sinno, Abdel-Raouf, "Pan-Slawismus und Pan-Orthodoxie als Instrumente der Russischen Politik im Osmanischen Reich," *Welt des Islams*, 28 (1988): 537–558; Liluashvili, Kukuri, *Natsionalno-osvoboditelnaia borba bolgarskogo naroda protiv fanariotskogo iga i Rossia* (Tbilisi: University of Tbilisi Press, 1978); Meininger, Thomas, *Ignatiev & the Establishment of the Bulgarian Exarchate (1864–1872)* (Madison: University of Wisconsin Press, 1970).

25. Lora Gerd's work on Russia's involvement in the Bulgarian Church Question skillfully weaves together archival and published Russian, Bulgarian, and Greek sources but doesn't relate them to the discussion of modernity or ethnic conflict management—"Rossia i greko-bolgarskii tserkovnyi vopros v 80–90-e gody XIX veka," in *Konstantinopol i Peterburg: Tserkovnaia politika Rossii na Pravoslavnom Vostoke (1878–1898)* (Moscow: Indrik, 2006), pp. 225–308; "Rossiia i greko-bolgarskii tserkovnyi vopros v nachale XX v.," in *Konstantinopolskii Patriarkhat i Rossiia, 1901–1914* (Moscow: Indrik, 2014), pp. 136–179.

26. Maiorova, Olga, "Searching for a New Language of Collective Self: The Symbolism of Russian National Belonging during and after the Crimean War," *Ab Imperio*, 4 (2006): 187–222.

27. Nikitin, Sergei, "Iuzhnoslavianskie sviazi russkoi periodicheskoi pechati v 60-e gody XIX veka," *Uchenyie zapiski Instituta Slavianovedeniia*, 6 (1952): 89–154; Nikitin, Sergei, *Ocherki po istorii iuzhnykh slavian i russko-balkanskikh sviazei v 50–70e gody XIX veka* (Moscow: Nauka, 1970).

This pro-Bulgarian agitation created special dilemmas not only for Russia's longstanding religion-based foreign policy in the Christian East and but also for its cultural identity. Language and religion are central for any national self-image, but even the most chauvinistic Russians in and outside government circles never clearly defined Russianness but professing Orthodoxy was assumed to be its main component at the turn of the twentieth century.[28]

The debate about Russia's relation to its coreligionists abroad spilled over into the pages of Russia's main newspapers, church periodicals, travelogues, scholarly journals, and confidential government papers. The issue involved the Greeks, who were the founding members of the Orthodox family, and Bulgarian Slavs, who were kinsmen to the Russians. The Russians then were forced to clarify for themselves the relative significance of faith and blood. Dressed in modern garb, the ideal of Orthodox unity and Russian messianism consistently trumped ethnocentrism in the minds of the supporters of Pan-Slavism, Pan-Orthodoxy, and the Greco-Slavic world.

. That polemic affected Russian officials in St. Petersburg and in the Ottoman Empire but the main Russian policy consistently promoted Orthodox unity throughout this period. It made sense strategically as both a Russian asset in its imperialist rivalry with the other Great Powers and as a valuable resource for the local Greco-Slavic Christian minorities in the Ottoman society where the majority and the rulers defined themselves in Islamic terms. Similarly, the Russian government prudently continued to rely on established autonomous religious institutions to administer its Muslim population in spite of nationalistic calls for implementing assimilation programs.[29]

I will argue that cultural responses to the Bulgarian Church Question included not only Pan-Slavism and Pan-Orthodoxy but also Greco-Slavism. They never superseded one another but coexisted in a fruitful tension and competition.[30] All three visions clashed over how to reconcile the traditional legitimacy of religious and imperial dynastic institutions and legitimation with the new secular ethnonationalism. Pan-Slavism has been much

---

28. Weeks, Theodore, *Nation and State in Late Imperial Russia: Nationalism and Russification on the Western Frontier, 1863–1914* (DeKalb: Northern Illinois University Press, 1996), pp. 30–32, 68.

29. Crews, Robert, *For Prophet and Tsar: Islam and Empire in Russia and Central Asia* (Cambridge, MA: Harvard University Press, 2009), pp. 294–299.

30. Lora Gerd charts a progression of dominant ideologies starting from Pan-Slavism of the 1850s and 1860s to "imperial nationalism" and "Neo-Byzantinism" of the late 1800s in *Russian Policy in the Orthodox East: The Patriarchate of Constantinople (1878–1914)* (Warsaw and Berlin: De Gruyter Open, 2015), p. X.

understudied[31] and treated as a purely ethnic "conservative" ideology.[32] Pan-Orthodoxy and Greco-Slavism are virtually terra incognita in the uncharted waters of the scholarly literature.[33]

These competing visions ultimately aimed to create a Russian-centered non-Western civilization based on reformulated Orthodox Christian cultural and political connections. Although these views rejected liberal or socialist Progress, they should be seen as modern because they were invented intellectual constructs. In addition, they advocated unprecedented geopolitical changes, emphasized ethnic categories, and consciously used the concept of cultural-historical type to decenter Western civilization.[34]

What do other academics and foreign policy practitioners have to gain from solving these fascinating history's mysteries of these exotic Eastern locales? By highlighting the continued political and cultural significance and the adaptability of religious institutions and identities, my book challenges the dominant analytical social science paradigm. As in historical studies, it is widely accepted in political science literature that national identity and the nation-state are key elements of modernity and as such they inevitably assign traditional religious and dynastic institutions to the garbage heap of history.[35] For example, the most respected and regularly reprinted general Balkan history textbook describes the entire nineteenth century as "the Age of Nationalism."[36]

---

31. Zlatar, Zdenko, "Pan-Slavism: A Review of the Literature," *Canadian Review of Studies in Nationalism*, 17, 1–2 (1990): 1–17.

32. Jersild, Austin, *Orientalism and Empire: North Caucasus Mountain Peoples and the Georgian Frontier, 1845–1917* (Montreal, Kingston, London, Ithaca: McGill-Queen's University Press, 2002), pp. 133–135.

33. Pan-Orthodoxy is discussed but not conceptualized in reference to Konstantin Leontiev's views—Zhukov, Konstantin, *Vostochnyi vopros v istoriosofskoi kontseptsii K. N. Leontieva* (Saint Petersburg: Aleteiia, 2005); Andronov, Iu. V., Miachin, A. G., Shiriniants, A. A., *Russkaia sotsialno-politicheskaia mysl' XIX-nachala XX veka: K. N. Leontiev* (Moscow: Knizhnyi dom Universitet, 2000); Nelson, Dale, *Konstantin Leontiev and the Orthodox East* (unpublished Ph.D. dissertation. Minneapolis: University of Minnesota, 1977); Lukashevich, Stephen, *Konstantin Leontev, 1831–1891: A Study in Russian "Heroic Vitalism"* (New York, Pageant Press, 1967).

34. Vovchenko, Denis, "Modernizing Orthodoxy: Russia and the Christian East (1856–1914)," *Journal of the History of Ideas*, 73, 2 (April 2012): 295–317.

35. Anderson, Benedict, *Imagined Communities: Reflections on the Origins and Spread of Nationalism* (London: Verso, 1991); Gellner, Ernest, *Nations and Nationalism* (Ithaca: Cornell University Press, 1983); Weber, Eugen, *Peasants into Frenchmen: Modernization of Rural France, 1870–1914* (Stanford: Stanford University Press, 1976).

36. Stavrianos, Leften, *The Balkans since 1453* (New York: New York University Press, 2000 [1958]), pp. 215–412.

Explicitly or implicitly most social scientists justify the breakup of ethnically and religiously diverse dynastic empires as well as resulting conflicts as objectively progressive developments. I will argue that despite the appeal of nationalism as part of Western modernity in the late nineteenth century the Christian Orthodox centers in the Ottoman Empire, the Russian Empire, Greece, Bulgaria, and Serbia formulated and promoted supranational ideologies and public policies directed at containing nationalism within existing structures in Eastern Europe up to the First World War.

Recently, there has been some interest in resistance to nationalism. Even in modern nation-states such as Croatia, the Catholic Church and the European Union were able to project an alternative supranational identity that helped the country avoid sliding into a fascist state in the aftermath of the Yugoslav wars of the early 1990s.[37]

There are even more reasons to doubt the inevitability of the triumph of nineteenth-century nationalist movements inside multiethnic and multiconfessional empires. The leaders of those movements did not have the resources of nation-states or modern mass media at their disposal. They did receive support from the self-proclaimed homeland states of Greece, Bulgaria, and Serbia but the bureaucratic machinery of nascent Balkan nation-states was not available to them in Ottoman provinces. Most people do not usually embrace nationalism without the experience of state-controlled propaganda, schools, police, and armies.

On the other hand, the nationalists' opponent, the Patriarchate of Constantinople, could count on the appeal of the authority of tradition among the largely illiterate and ethnically mixed Balkan Christian villagers. The patriarchs could also obtain significant Russian diplomatic and financial support. Just like other empires, the Ottoman Empire was built on conquest and domination by the center over the periphery. Since the beginning of their expansion in the 1300s, the Ottomans declared that their true faith had enabled them to wrest control of parts of Europe, the Middle East, and Africa from both infidel kings and less pious Islamic potentates. While their Muslim subjects faced no legal discrimination, Jews and Christians were treated as second-class citizens much like the racial divisions in twentieth-century Western "bifurcated" colonial states.[38]

---

37. Bellamy, Alex, *The Formation of Croatian National Identity: A Centuries-Old Dream?* (Manchester: Manchester University Press, 2003), p. 183.

38. Mamdani, Mahmood, *Citizens and Subjects: Contemporary Africa and the Legacy of Late Colonialism* (Princeton: Princeton University Press, 1996).

However, foreign rulers like the Ottomans are often accepted if they provide such collective goods as security and prosperity. Another attraction of
the Ottoman system was indirect rule. Ironically, the more the Ottomans centralized their government, the weaker they became.[39] The Romanov dynasty
used the institutions of local autonomy even more successfully to win the
hearts and minds of its largest religious minority.[40] Between 1856 and 1914,
most Russian policymakers did not seek to destroy the Ottoman Empire but
aimed to turn it into a federated structure with significant rights for provinces and religious minorities. Far from being a foreign import, that agenda
echoed the views of many Christian and Muslim interest groups especially in
the last decade before 1914.[41]

After the disturbing genocides and ethnic cleansings of the twentieth
century, historians are turning a more sympathetic eye to the experience
of multiethnic religious and dynastic empires.[42] Some argue that without
the preventable and contingent outbreaks of the Balkan Wars and the First
World War, the Ottoman, Habsburg, and Russian Empires may not have been
doomed to disintegrate, as it turned out, into fractious nation-states.[43]

Political scientists, however, seem to be oblivious to this changing
wind in historical studies. The chasm between our disciplines naturally
limits the prescriptions they can offer to resolve today's tensions and conflicts. My book may help bridge the gap between the disciplines by offering a fresh cultural and institutional perspective. There is a consensus

---

39. Hechter, Michael, *Alien Rule* (New York: Cambridge University Press, 2013), pp. 2,
55–60.

40. Crews, *For Prophet and Tsar*, pp. 353–355.

41. Sean McMeekin's *The Russian Origins of the First World War* made the case for Russian
aggressive designs in the Near East but his book met with a lot of criticism such as Bobroff,
Ronald, *Revolutionary Russia*, 26, 1 (June 2013): 82–84.

42. Todorova, Maria, *Imagining the Balkans* (New York: Oxford University Press, 2009),
p. 187; Streusand, Douglas, *Islamic Gunpowder Empires: Ottomans, Safavids, and Mughals*
(Boulder: Westview Press, 2011), p. 2.

43. Mazower, Mark, *The Balkans: A Short History* (New York: Modern Library, 2000),
p. 115; Crews, *For Prophet and Tsar*, p. 355; Keyder, Caglar, "The Ottoman Empire," Hagen
von, Mark, "The Russian Empire," in Barkey, Karen, and von Hagen, Mark, eds., *After
Empire: Multiethnic Societies and Nation-Building: The Soviet Union and the Russian, Ottoman,
and Habsburg Empires* (Boulder: Westview Press, 1997), pp. 30–44; 58–72. In that volume,
there is less optimism about Austria-Hungary but Joachim Remak was more positive: see
his "Healthy Invalid: How Doomed the Habsburg Empire?," *Journal of Modern History*, 41,
2 (June 1969): 127–143. Pieter Judson has recently made a powerful argument against exag-
gerating the strength of nationalist movements in *Guardians of the Nation: Activists on the
Language Frontiers of Imperial Austria* (Cambridge, MA: Harvard University Press, 2006).

within political science that minority rights[44] secured in the mechanisms of power-sharing and federation are the best ways to promote peace in ethnically divided societies.[45] While recognizing the great potential of communal autonomy and power allocation, scholars note the dangerous tendency of those institutions to perpetuate ethnic divisions and prevent cross-ethnic integration.[46]

Some have gone even further and pointed to a disheartening paradox. On the one hand, federations can provide enough institutional carrots to keep minorities from breaking away. But at the same time, any meaningful autonomy creates more opportunities for secessionism.[47] This problem is especially acute if there is an irredentist dynamic in place, which tends to spike to dangerous levels when the host state provokes a minority to seek support in an adjacent homeland where its kinsmen are in the majority. If a homeland pays excessive attention to "unredeemed brethren" across the border, this can also trigger suspicion and even repression of a troublesome minority by the host state.[48] Many commentators expected irredentist conflicts to intensify in the aftermath of the Soviet collapse,[49] as did indeed occur in the dissolution of Yugoslavia,[50] and in anticipation of

---

44. Peleg, Ilan, *Democratizing the Hegemonic State: Political Transformation in the Age of Identity* (Cambridge: Cambridge University Press, 2007), p. 19.

45. Hechter, Michael, *Containing Nationalism* (Oxford and New York: Oxford University Press, 2000), pp. 134–159.

46. Lake, David A., and Rothchild, Donald, "Containing Fear: the Origins and Management of Ethnic Conflict," in Brown, Michael E., Cote, Owen R. Jr., Lynn-Jones, Sean M., and Miller, Steven E., eds., *Nationalism and Ethnic Conflict* (Cambridge, MA: MIT Press, 1997), p. 115; Byman, Daniel, *Keeping the Peace: Lasting Solutions to Ethnic Conflicts* (Baltimore and London: John Hopkins University Press, 2002), pp. 148–152.

47. Kymlicka, Will, "Is Federalism a Viable Alternative to Secession?," in Lehning, Percy, ed., *Theories of Secession* (London and New York: Routledge, 1998), pp. 111–150.

48. Weiner, Myron, "The Macedonian Syndrome: A Historical Model of International Relations and Political Development," *World Politics*, 23 (July 1971): 665–683; Carment, David, "The International Dimensions of Ethnic Conflict: Concepts, Indicators, and Theory," *Journal of Peace Research*, 30, 2 (1993): 137–150.

49. Chazan, Naomi, *Irredentism and International Politics* (Boulder and London: Lynne Rienner and Adamantine Press, 1991).

50. Ambrosio, Thomas, *Irredentism: Ethnic Conflict and International Politics* (Westport and London: Praeger; 2001); Brown, Michael, ed., *Ethnic Conflict and International Security* (Princeton: Princeton University Press, 1993); Gagnon, V. P., "Ethnic Nationalism and International Conflict: The Case of Serbia," *International Security*, 21, 2 (2006): 130–166.

the specter of "Weimar Russia"[51] made more relevant during the ongoing crisis in Ukraine.[52]

Furthermore, modern analysts despair of any real possibility of diminishing the potentially disruptive political role of ethnicity[53] and of promoting supra-ethnic identities[54] because they focus on the implementation of often well-intentioned but artificial frameworks and limit themselves to drawing on a small selection of case studies over the last thirty years or so. Traditional religious and dynastic identities and institutions provide a shared cultural and institutional space which can be a more promising start for developing more organic power-sharing arrangements to accommodate newly politicized ethnic divisions. My account of past efforts to achieve exactly that is a reminder of their potential relevance, which has largely been ignored in the prevailing literature on conflict prevention, resolution, and management.

Structure

This book is organized chronologically into seven chapters. The first chapter provides background on the status of religious minorities in Islamic states with special emphasis on the situation of Orthodox Christians in the Ottoman Empire before the Crimean War (1853–1856). It also explains how after 1453 the Russian imperial government and society developed the political and cultural traditions of protection and sponsorship of their coreligionists in the Balkans and the Middle East who were primarily represented by the Patriarchate of Constantinople.

The second chapter focuses on how the Ottoman government, the Patriarchate, and Russian policymakers and publicists responded to the Bulgarian church movement at its initial stage from 1853 to 1861. This movement became possible in 1856 as part of the secularizing Ottoman reforms

51. Brubaker, Rogers, *Nationalism Reframed: Nationhood and the National Question in the New Europe* (New York: Cambridge University Press, 1996), pp. 107–147; Saideman, Steven, and Ayres, William, *For Kin or Country: Xenophobia, Nationalism, and War* (New York: Columbia University Press, 2008).

52. Saideman, Steven, and Ayres, William, "For Kin or Country: Why the Crimea Crisis Is Not about a Greater Russia Project," *Washington Post* (6 March 2014). http://www.washingtonpost.com/blogs/monkey-cage/wp/2014/03/06/for-kin-or-country-why-the-crimea-crisis-is-not-about-a-greater-russia-project/. Retrieved 30 July 2015.

53. Hale, Henry, *The Foundations of Ethnic Politics: Separatism of States and Nations in Eurasia and the World* (Cambridge: Cambridge University Press, 2008), p. 262.

54. Esman, Milton J., *An Introduction to Ethnic Conflict* (Cambridge: Polity, 2004), p. 190.

known as Tanzimat. These reforms included attempts to promote the legal equality of all Ottoman subjects irrespective of their creed and to strengthen the lay element over the religious hierarchy in the Muslim, Christian, and Jewish communities. Russian diplomats and to a lesser extent even prelates supported those Ottoman reforms because they hoped that greater representation and the resulting influence of the lay elite on the finances and on high clergy elections would encourage the Bulgarian nationalist leaders to drop their plans of breaking from the Patriarchate of Constantinople.

Chapters 3 through 6 discuss the consequences of the separation of the Bulgarian nationalist movement from the reformed institutions of the Patriarchate in 1860. To found their own legitimate institutions, the Bulgarian church movement attempted to enlist the support of the Ottoman government, of Russian diplomats and publicists, and of Western diplomats and missionaries. The movement's feverish agitation led to polemics about whether Russia was a modern nation-state and a potential nucleus of a future Pan-Slav union or was rather a multinational empire with dynastic and religious foundations. Russian diplomatic, military, and ecclesiastical officials answered that question in their efforts to return the breakaway Bulgarian groups back into the fold of the Patriarchate based on mutual concessions.

As I will show, the Russians relied on diplomacy, interchurch relations, and the print media to interact with rival churches, the Ottoman government, and European diplomats both before and after 1870, when the Bulgarian Exarchate was established by the Sultan's decree without the consent of the Patriarchate. During the Russo-Turkish War of 1877–1878, Russia's direct military occupation of Ottoman Bulgarian lands provided additional leverage in dealing with the Bulgarian Church Question. Military agents would also play an important role during the reorganization of the courts and the gendarmerie in Ottoman Balkan provinces supervised by European officers from 1903 to 1908.

For most of this period, the Ottoman government, depending on the personality of four successive sultans, remained more or less committed to the Tanzimat reforms. Ottoman policymakers often used divide-and-rule tactics to weaken non-Muslim minorities. The political context changed with the military coup of 1908 led by Westernizing army officers who forced Sultan Abdulhamid II to move from autocracy to a constitutional monarchy. The resulting Young Turk government greatly accelerated the pace of modernizing reforms. Their increasingly centralizing and assimilationist policies quickly antagonized non-Turkish groups who began to successfully cooperate with each other through participation in parliamentary politics. Russian diplomats, bishops, and commentators took advantage of those new opportunities to promote reconciliation within the largest Christian minority in the Ottoman Empire up to its invasions by Balkan states in 1912.

The last chapter focuses on the changing Russian attitudes and policies towards Muslim Slavs in order to examine from a different perspective the relative importance of ethnicity and religion in the minds of Russian policy-makers, scholars, and journalists.

Russian Messianism in the Christian East (1453–1853)

IN MARCH OF 1556, Tsar Ivan IV, also known as Ivan the Terrible, granted the Serbian Hilandar Monastery on the Holy Mount Athos a plot of land with all necessary buildings in Moscow within a short walking distance from the Kremlin. Abbot Sylvester and his monks would be able to use that property to collect rent, church dues, alms, and donations. They needed this kind of financial support "because the sins of Christendom had multiplied and the infidel Turks took over not just their monastery but also the whole Serbian state." Although they were Ottoman subjects, Ivan the Terrible took pity on them "seeing their grief, oppressed status, humility, and supplication to Our government." In exchange, the Serbian monks would be eternally praying for the souls of Ivan's late grandfather, parents, and his whole family.[1]

This story captures the dynamic of Russia's relationship to Ottoman Christians before the age of Enlightenment and Romanticism. Ottoman institutions and Russian support were two main sources of Orthodox unity of ethnically diverse populations with a long history of internecine conflicts.

All roads lead to Rome. In our case they lead not to the banks of the Tiber River but rather to the shores of the Bosphorus—a place of exceptional natural beauty and a key strategic site at the intersection of trade routes between Europe and Asia, the Black Sea and the Mediterranean. That is where Emperor Constantine the Great moved the capital of the Empire after rejecting pagan gods and embracing Jesus Christ as his savior. Although some scholars doubt

---

1. Ivan IV to the Hilandar Monastery, March 1556, Dolgova, Svetlana et al., eds., *Moskva-Serbiia, Belgrad-Rossiia: Sbornik dokumentov i materialov.* Vol. 1 (Moscow and Belgrade: Arhiv Srbije, Glavnoie arhivnoie upravleniie, 2009), pp. 208–209.

the sincerity of his conversion, Constantine is considered a saint equal to the Apostles in both Catholic and Orthodox churches. In the spirit of Christian humility, he had the old Greek colony of Byzantium renamed after himself into Constantinople in 330 AD. That fresh start would allow "New Rome" to outlive the original one by almost one thousand years and to extend Roman influence among all kinds of barbarians who found themselves on the edges of or even deep inside imperial domains. After the fall of Constantinople in 1453, the specter of Rome had haunted Eastern Europe and eventually made Moscow its new home to fundamentally shape Russian foreign policy and cultural identity.

Byzantine Commonwealth in Eastern Europe

Constantinople struck the imagination of rank-and-file Slavs of Eastern Europe and still survives in some of their languages as the Imperial City or *Tsarigrad*. The native elites were even more fascinated with all things Byzantine. Up to the Age of the Crusades, the Eastern Roman Empire remained the most significant European political economic and cultural power. Tribal aristocracy eagerly sought commercial and dynastic ties to Constantinople to satisfy the growing appetite for luxury goods, fancy buildings, impressive fortresses, bridges, and education. The unrivaled prestige, beauty, and might of Constantine's New Rome appeared to be based on the protection of the Divine Wisdom and Mother of God herself.

Orthodox Christianity was by far the most important avenue of transmission of Greco-Roman art, literature, and law. The idea of divine right appealed to aspiring local monarchs with their centralizing agendas. Universal brotherhood of man attracted to the church those who felt mentally stifled by narrow-minded tribal paganism. The splendor of Orthodox Christian liturgy, chanting, icons, and mosaics as in the spectacular cathedral of Hagia Sophia won over the rest who had only a vague understanding of the message of the gospels.[2]

From the Byzantine perspective, religion justified the Roman idea of the universal empire and the Greek sense of superiority over the barbarians. The government in Constantinople sponsored missionary activities to render predatory pagan savages along the border less hostile. The most famous missionaries were saintly brothers Cyril and Methodius of Thessaloniki, whose father was probably a Byzantine governor of the city and their mother was of

---

2. Obolensky, Dmitri, *The Byzantine Commonwealth: Eastern Europe, 500–1453* (London: Weidenfeld and Nicholson, 1971), pp. 288–290.

Slavic background. They created the alphabet now known as Cyrillic to help translate the Scriptures and other kinds of church literature from Greek into Old Church Slavonic. In the 1800s, Russian Pan-Slavs would claim them as "the Enlighteners of Slavdom" commemorated to this day on May 11 in a special church service.[3] In 1992, the monument to Cyril and Methodius graced one of Moscow's central squares, which was renamed into the Slavic Square.

Christianized barbarian tribes became part of the *oecumene* or the Greco-Roman civilized world under the jurisdiction of the Ecumenical Patriarchate of Constantinople. They were considered as client states of the autocrat on the throne in Constantinople—*symmachoi* in Greek or *foederati* in Latin. As the guardian of the only correct or "Orthodox" form of Christianity and as the successor to St. Constantine, the Emperor was supposed to preserve the purity of faith and generally to help his Patriarch prepare true believers for the coming of Antichrist and the Final Judgment.[4]

Bishops sent from Constantinople to new barbarian dioceses were usually ethnically or culturally Greek and for all practical purposes served as local agents of the imperial government.[5] Aware of such dangerous implications of Orthodox Christianity, newly converted rulers of medieval Bulgaria, Serbia, and Kievan Rus demanded independence or autocephaly for their churches from the Patriarchate of Constantinople. With that goal in mind, Prince Yaroslav of Kiev raised the ecclesiastical status of his capital in 1037. Now it was the seat of the archbishop or metropolitan. Yaroslav also insisted on the appointment of that prelate from among his own subjects and on the canonization of Russian saints.[6]

Kievan Rus never seemed to have acknowledged universal political pretensions coming from Constantinople. They implicitly denied the continuity between the First and the Second Rome as they refused to call Byzantines "Romans." Instead, they referred to them as "Greeks" based on the main language of the Eastern Roman Empire.[7] Another grain of salt about the Byzantine right to world domination can be detected in the ways Russian

---

3. Petrovich, Michael Boro, *The Emergence of Russian Panslavism, 1856–1870* (Westport: Greenwood Publishers, 1985. First published: New York: Columbia University Press, 1956), pp. 87–88, 150.

4. Obolenskii, *The Byzantine Commonwealth*, pp. 272–276.

5. Likhachev, Dmitrii, *Natsionalnoie samosoznanie Drevnei Rusi* (Leningrad: Academy of Sciences, 1945), p. 18.

6. Ibid., pp. 19–20.

7. Franklin, Simon, "The Empire of the Rhomaioi as Viewed from Kievan Russia: Aspects of Byzantino-Russian Cultural Relations," *Byzantion*, 53, 3 (1983): 526.

compilations of Byzantine chronicles usually focused on religious developments and skipped secular history.[8]

In contrast to Kievan Rus, medieval Bulgaria could not ignore the claims
of the Eastern Roman Empire because they shared and contested long land
borders for centuries. To confirm their sovereign status, Bulgarian kings
forced the Patriarchate of Constantinople to recognize the Bulgarian Church
as a patriarchate in its own right in 929[9] and again in 1235.[10] At that same
time, changing political winds made the Russian Church more independent as well. In the 1240s, Batu Khan in the glorious tradition of Genghis
Khan, his grandfather, overran most Russian principalities, reaching as far
as Poland and Hungary. Although the ambitious conqueror pulled back to
the Volga area and Central Asia, divided Russian princes found themselves in
a tributary dependence on their Mongol suzerains for another two hundred
years as part of the khanate of the Golden Horde. To avoid diplomatic complications, the Patriarchate of Constantinople often preferred to appoint a native
Russian rather than a Roman subject to the post of the Metropolitan of Kiev.[11]

Even before the Mongol conquest, Kiev had lost its significance with the
fragmentation of Kievan Rus into several smaller powers in the manner of
other patrimonial states like the Carolingian Empire to its west. New emerging centers further north were more secure from Mongol raids and quickly
attracted migrants and refugees with the irresistible prospects of a more comfortable life. Starting as one such city, Moscow became more significant in
the early 1300s after one Metropolitan of Kiev took up residence there and
turned it into the ecclesiastical capital of all Russian lands.[12]

Seljuk and later Ottoman Turks posed an even more serious threat than
the Mongols to the heartland of the Orthodox Christian world. Their ambitions went beyond occasional raids and tribute collection. They involved
direct occupation, settlement, and establishment of Islamic rule.[13] The

---

8. Ibid., pp. 517–518.

9. Pundeff, Marin, "Bulgarian Nationalism," in Sugar, Peter, and Lederer, Ivo, eds.,
Nationalism in Eastern Europe (Seattle: University of Washington Press, 1969), p. 98.

10. Arnakis, George, "The Role of Religion in the Development of Balkan Nationalism,"
in Jelavich, Charles and Barbara, eds., *The Balkans in Transition* (Berkeley and Los
Angeles: University of California Press, 1963), p. 127.

11. Kartashev, Anton, *Ocherki po istorii russkoi tserkvi*. Vol. 1 (Saint Petersburg: Biblioglobus,
2004), p. 313.

12. Ibid., pp. 313–323.

13. Vryonis, Speros, "Nomadization and Islamization in Asia Minor," *Dumbarton Oaks
Papers*, 29 (1976): 41–71.

Byzantine Empire was in effect surrounded when the Ottoman conquest of the Balkans ended the independence of Serbia and Bulgaria in the aftermath of the epic battle on the Kosovo field in 1389. The Byzantine emperors saw no other choice but to turn again to the Latin West for help as Alexis Comnenus had done, sparking the First Crusade in 1095. Eastern Orthodox experience with the early Crusades was extremely bitter, especially after 1204 when the knights of the Fourth Crusade looted Constantinople instead of stemming the onslaught of Seljuk Turks and reconquering Jerusalem. They held the Byzantine capital for two generations, and seized many other Byzantine lands as their fiefs. There is still a saying in Greek: "The sword of the Turk is better than the bread of the Frank."[14]

The Russians took a similarly dim view of Catholicism following the attacks of Teutonic knights in the Baltic region and the Lithuanian conquest of most of former Kievan Rus in the 1200s and 1300s. Many highest church positions remained unfilled and "the common enemies of Christians like wolves began to snatch souls out of the hands of God." The Patriarchate had to send special envoys or "exarchs" there to restore a semblance of church organization there.[15]

Around 1400, the union of the Roman Catholic and Eastern Orthodox churches was seen as a precondition for the renewal of the controversial Crusading tradition. After several false starts, in 1438 and 1439 key prelates from all over the Christian world got together first in Ferrara and after a plague outbreak there in Florence. Orthodox hierarchs hoped to convince their Western counterparts to abandon the ideas and practices that were not sanctioned at the generally recognized seven Ecumenical Councils convened between 321 and 787: the emanation of the Holy Spirit from both the Father and the Son, the teaching of the Purgatory, the liturgical use of unleavened bread, etc.

After months of exasperating disputes, the Pope presented an ultimatum—the Eastern Orthodox should accept all Roman Catholic doctrines including the primacy of his office or leave empty-handed. More or less willingly, all Orthodox delegates including the ethnically Greek Metropolitan of Moscow Isidore signed the act of church union. Most lower-level Greek

---

14. Stavrianos, Leften, "The Influence of the West on the Balkans," in Jelavich, Charles and Barbara, eds., *The Balkans in Transition* (Berkeley and Los Angeles: University of California Press, 1963), p. 186.

15. "The Mission of Archbishop Mikhail of Bethlehem to Russia as a Patriarch's Exarch. Latin Proselytizing Activities. 1397," in Zisis, Theodoros, ed., *Konstantinoupoli kai Moskha* (Thessaloniki: Vryennios, 1989), p. 188.

clergy and commoners rejected the deal but the Byzantine government and the Patriarch of Constantinople were too desperate to follow the public opinion. However, Prince Vasilii of Moscow and Russian bishops refused to support the Byzantine policy line and went so far as to depose Isidore as a heretic and to exile him abroad. Russian uneasiness about such a bold stand they had taken and inevitable tension with the Eastern Roman leadership dissipated at the news of the fall of Constantinople to Sultan Mehmet II on 29 May 1453. It seemed that God turned away from the Second Rome for its betrayal of the only true Christian faith.[16]

Pax Ottomanica: The Bifurcated State of the Sultans at Its Height, 1453–1600

Istanbul's brand new 1453 Panorama Museum was built to celebrate the 660th anniversary of the major victory of the Crescent over the Cross and the Roman eagle. Its main display takes poetic license to reconstruct the drama of the final Ottoman bombardment and storming of Constantinople. This exhibit is only one of many ways in which the ruling AK Party noisily promotes the "Spirit of the Conquest" to present itself as a torchbearer of Ottoman legacy and to signal the demise of Turkish secularism.

As modern Turkish historians often like to stress, Mehmet II saved "the Eastern Christians from subjugation to the Roman Church" and granted the Patriarchate more power than the Byzantine emperors had ever done.[17] Since the sultans made Constantinople their capital (called interchangeably *Konstantiniye* or *Istanbul* in Turkish), they appointed the Patriarch of that city as the head of the whole Orthodox Christian *millet*, which literally means "nation." Curiously, non-Muslim communities indeed could be seen as former governments in captivity placed under the jurisdiction of the Ottoman Foreign Ministry with significant legal and cultural autonomy. As the only official mediator between Orthodox Christians and the Ottoman government (also known as the Sublime Porte), the Patriarch of Constantinople and the leading archbishops in the Synod of the Patriarchate assumed many worldly responsibilities such as collecting taxes, meting out justice, and maintaining schools. Motivated primarily by administrative efficiency, the Ecumenical Patriarchate incorporated the previously autonomous Bulgarian and Serbian

---

16. Kartashev, *Ocherki*, pp. 374–380.

17. Sofuoglu, Adnan, *Fener Rum Patrikhanesi ve Siyasi Faaliyetleri* (Istanbul: Turan Yayincilik, 1996), pp. 13–14.

churches, strengthened its control over the archbishoprics in vassal Danubian principalities of Wallachia and Moldavia, and acquired great influence over the elections of chief prelates in ancient patriarchates of Alexandria, Jerusalem, and Antioch. Naturally, small pockets of Sultan's Catholic subjects, mostly in Lebanon and Bosnia, were outside Patriarchate's jurisdiction.[18] Map 1.1 illustrates the vast extent of Ottoman domains around 1560.

There is a debate about whether the patriarchs of Constantinople can be seen as part of *askeri* or the ruling class. Technically, non-Muslims didn't belong there and the patriarchs were liable to the same punishments as any other infidel subject of the sultans. But the treatment of patriarchs in the ceremonial protocol of the Ottoman court, along with their functions and privileges, suggests that their rank was equivalent to that of vizier. Indeed, the patriarch was the only non-Muslim member of the Imperial Divan, which met inside the Topkapi Palace complex as shown in Figure 1.1.[19]

The patriarch and his agents were the only Christian Orthodox subjects to enjoy tax immunities and the rights to travel in Muslim clothes, bear weapons, and ride horses.[20] The patriarchs relied on the Ottoman law enforcement system to shepherd their flock. The black sheep among them were typically charged with "inciting insubordination, which made it impossible for local bishops to collect taxes and to perform religious rites." The incumbent patriarch would request that the troublemaker in question be arrested and sent to the galleys until "he corrects his behavior."[21] Given the extremely low life expectancy of galley slaves, it was in effect a death sentence.

Clearly, the patriarch's job entailed serious risks. If he were suspected of treason, the whole Orthodox community could suffer the consequences. Thus, Sultan Selim, nicknamed "the Grim" (r. 1512–1520), received information from his well-organized spy service about some anti-Ottoman conspiracies brewing in the Patriarchate. He presented his Orthodox subjects with a stark choice—accept Islam or leave Istanbul. All their churches would be turned into mosques. Those who refused to convert would be killed. Zenbelli

18. Runciman, Steven, *The Great Church in Captivity* (Cambridge: Cambridge University Press, 1968), pp. 165–185; Haddad, Robert, *Syrian Christians in a Muslim Society: An Interpretation* (Princeton: Princeton University Press, 1970).

19. Osmanagaoglu, Cihan, *1862 Rum Patrikligi Nizamati Cercevesinde Fener Rum Ortodoks Patrikhanesi* (Istanbul: Oniki Lehva, 2010), p. 4.

20. Alkan, Hakan, *Fener Rum Patrikhanesi: Uluslararasi Iliskiler Acisindan Bir Yaklasim* (Istanbul: Gunce, 1999), p. 38.

21. Patriarch Eremios III to the Sultan, 14 October 1719, Stainova, Mihaila, ed., "Des relations entre le Patriarcat Oecumenique et La Sublime Porte au commencement du XVIIIe siecle," *Balkan Studies*, 25, 2 (1984): 451–452.

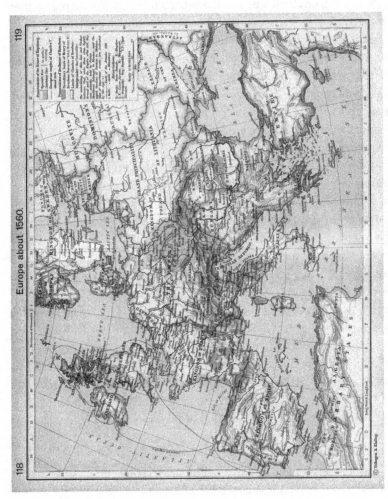

MAP 1.1 Europe, 1560. The University of Texas Map Collection. http://www.lib.utexas.edu/
maps/historical/history_balkans.html

FIGURE 1.1 Top Kapi Palace at the entrance to the Golden Horn harbor (personal photograph). The tall slender tower with a conical roof marks the pavilion where Divan sessions were held from the late 1400s to the mid-1600s.

Ali Cemali Efendi, the top Muslim cleric or *Seyhulislam*, initially authorized Selim's decision with a fatwa but then thought better of it. It went against the sharia since his late grandfather Mehmet II had granted the Orthodox subjects security of life and freedom of religion in a special decree. When Selim demanded a copy of the document, the Patriarch alleged that it had been destroyed in a fire. At this fateful moment, the Grand Vizier and the Sheyhulislam were able to find two or three old Janissaries who were in Mehmet II's army in 1453. Their testimony finally convinced Selim, which was, no doubt, a relief for the Patriarchate.[22] This story shows that in legal proceedings even a patriarch's words had to be confirmed by Muslim witnesses.

One way or another, ethnic Greeks or Hellenized locals gradually occupied key positions in all dioceses introducing Greek as the language of the liturgy and instruction at schools especially in urban areas where bishops resided.[23]

---

22. Atalay, Bulent, *Fener Rum Patrikhanesi'nin Siyasi Faaliyetleri (1908–1923)* (Istanbul: TATAV, 2001), pp. 5–6.

23. Hopkins, James Lindsay, *The Bulgarian Orthodox Church: A Socio-Historical Analysis of the Evolving Relationship Between Church, Nation, and State in Bulgaria* (Boulder: East European Monographs, distributed by Columbia University Press, NY, 2009), pp. 56–57.

Nationalist Bulgarian historians and the Western scholars under their influence had long argued that the Patriarchate, which was situated in the Phanar area of Constantinople, represented only Greek interests. According to this school of thought, the so-called Phanariotes alone managed to preserve a sense of ethnic self-identity through their links to such surviving Byzantine institutions as the Patriarchate. They also increased their clout through trade and diplomacy where they served as middlemen between the Ottomans and the rest of Europe.[24]

They allegedly refused to maintain Slavic heritage from Greek-dominated diocesan centers and siphoned off most local funds into their own coffers as well as the pockets of various Ottoman officials to pay for the debts resulting from regular bribes that had to be paid for all kinds of official business including confirmation of top church appointments. The gravest accusation is that Greek prelates destroyed Slavic books and monuments to erase their national memory.[25] But many modern Bulgarian scholars took issue with that traditional view and began to question the myth about the intentional Hellenization of Balkan Slavs by the Patriarchate in the Ottoman period. [26]

More or less benign neglect, the bureaucratic convenience of using one official language, and the understandable lack of Ottoman government support are more plausible reasons to account for the diminishing resources available to preserve both Slavic and Greek material culture. Coming from the long and glorious Greco-Roman tradition, ethnic Greeks had more trained personnel to fill higher ecclesiastical posts. The use of Greek in advanced urban schools also made sense because the literary languages of Balkan Slavs and Rumanian-speaking Wallachians and Moldavians were less established and prestigious. In fact, the role of Greek in the Ottoman Balkans and the Middle East could be compared to Latin in medieval Europe.[27]

But lower-level clergy was everywhere native born. Parish priests, abbots, and monks maintained a network of primary schools and used Old Church Slavonic in teaching, Divine Liturgy, and manuscript copying. Far from suppressing those traditional cultural pursuits, their Greek superiors typically tolerated and often even sponsored them contrary to the later claims of

---

24. Hupchik, Dennis, "Orthodoxy and Bulgarian Ethnic Awareness under Ottoman Rule, 1396–1762," *Nationalities Papers*, 21, 2 (Fall 1993): 76.

25. Ibid., p. 88.

26. Danova, Nadia, "Predstavata za 'Drugiia' na Balkanite: Obrazut na Gurka v bulgarskata knizhnina prez XV-sredata na XIX," *Istoricheskii Pregled*, 49, 6 (1993): 8.

27. Stavrianos, Leften, "Antecedents to the Balkan Revolutions of the Nineteenth Century," *Journal of Modern History*, 29, 4 (1957): 346.

Bulgarian nationalist activists.[28] Monasteries played a particularly prominent role in the survival of Balkan Slavic culture. Thanks to the Ottoman policies, they enjoyed tax immunity and economic autonomy. That is why they had the resources to train local parish priests, to maintain libraries, and to do research such as collecting folk songs, etc.[29]

Arab caliphs and Ottoman sultans had created institutions that depoliticized ethnicity and made religion the most meaningful form of identity. In the later and not necessarily servile words of the official historian and archivist of the Patriarchate, "the Bulgarian hatred of the Greeks disappeared because they had all been brought to the same level by the sultan's rule ... which made possible the coexistence of Orthodox Christian peoples previously consumed by unbrotherly hostility."[30] Christian unity is easier to achieve if enforced by law.

Indeed, all non-Muslims (known as *dhimmis* or *reaya*) were tolerated but second-class subjects. Actually, "reaya" means "slave" in Modern Greek but historical memory often overdramatizes the past. Non-Muslims were forbidden to bear arms, to follow the Muslim dress code, to ride horses, to walk on the footpath if Muslims were there, or testify in the sharia courts against Muslims, etc. Non-Muslims needed to pay a special tax for "protection" of their lives and property and to apply for a permission to build a new church or repair an old one.[31] But in the memorable phrase of historian Arthur Stanley Tritton, "the conduct of the rulers was often better than the law demanded." Although the position of *dhimmis* deteriorated from early to later centuries of Islam, Christians could sometimes be found in positions of authority over Muslims, and apostasy and relationships with Muslim women were not always punished by death.[32]

In the bustling Ottoman capital, discriminatory laws were often allowed to lapse but at times they were enforced with exemplary severity. In 1577, Sultan Murad III forbade Christians and Jews not just to dress in Muslim-style clothes but also to wear any expensive high-quality garments and shoes.

---

28. Markova, Zina, "Tserkovnata vlast i bulgarskiiat dukhoven zhivot prez XVIII i nachalnite desiateletiia na XIX vek," *Balkanistika*, 1 (1986): 194–197.

29. Osmanagaoglu, *1862 Rum Patrikligi Nizamati*, p. 181.

30. Gedeon, Manuel, ed., *Engrafa patriarhika kai synodika peri tou Voulgarikou zetematos (1852–1873)* (Constantinople: Patriarchal Publishing House, 1908), p. XXV.

31. Bosworth, C. E., "The Concept of Dhimma in Early Islam" in Braude, Benjamin, and Lewis, Bernard, eds., *Christians & Jews in the Ottoman Empire: The Functioning of a Plural Society*. Vol.1 (New York: Holmes & Meier Publishers, 1983), pp. 37–52.

32. Tritton, Arthur, *Caliphs and Their Non-Muslim Subjects: A Critical Study of the Pact of Umar* (London: Oxford University Press, 1930), pp. 231–232.

"If the authorities caught a Christian or a Jew wearing a silk belt, the belt would be confiscated and the guilty individual hauled before a judge and given bastinadoes."[33]

If we use the comparative lens, we can see that the model of a "bifurcated state" could apply to the Ottoman Empire with important qualifications. The term describes the functioning of a colonial state that gave full rights to white settlers and disenfranchised colonized natives.[34] In Islamic empires, religion played a role similar to that of race in Western colonies. But the boundary between first- and second-class subjects was easier to cross in Islamic empires— changing one's faith is usually less problematic than changing skin color.

How did it feel to be part of the Islamic majority? The revenue coming from state lands and the special taxes on the reaya were originally redistributed by the caliph among arms-bearing Muslim heads of households, a larger portion going to the needy. These social obligations of the state toward the Muslim community were recorded in the holy texts of Islam and the decrees of the Second Righteous Caliph Umar. To determine who was eligible for handouts from the public purse, Umar had the census taken to that effect thus setting an early precedent for the welfare state in the form of "military communism."[35]

Since there was no institutional mechanism of enforcing claims on the state, the caliphate's responsibility to the faithful became part of legitimating discourse with little substance. It often took some violent collective action as a food riot for common Muslims to receive relief in times of distress. The idea of state's dependence on the religious commandments and the consensus of the community survived to the Ottoman times. The Ottoman sultan, as any Islamic ruler, was supposed to see to the welfare of the Muslim community. Thus, there were mutually binding rules and claims we expect now as citizens. If the ruler violated the Islamic law, in theory he could be deposed. This happened many times in practice with enough elite and/or popular support especially in the eighteenth century, when the power of the Ottoman central government declined.[36]

Islamic notions of state and citizenship are strikingly similar to the modern concept of conservative communitarianism. They share emphasis

---

33. Boyar, Ebru, and Fleet, Kate, *A Social History of Ottoman Istanbul* (New York: Cambridge University Press, 2010), p. 177.

34. Mamdani, Mahmood, *Citizens and Subjects: Contemporary Africa and the Legacy of Late Colonialism* (Princeton: Princeton University Press, 1996), pp. 16–17.

35. Hitti, Philip, *A History of the Arabs* (New York: St. Martin's Press, 1970), pp. 169–177.

36. Salzman, Ariel, "Citizens in Search of a State: The Limits of Participation in the Late Ottoman Empire," in Hanagan, Michael, and Tilly, Charles, eds., *Extending Citizenship, Reconfiguring States* (Lanham, Boulder, New York, Oxford: Rowman & Littlefield, 1999), p. 40.

on organic values not tied to any institution of the civil society. They both stress "a return to community, religion, family" and "what in general might be called a culture of consensus." What was traditionally called the "outbursts of Islamic fanaticism" is similar to radical populism as expressions of "a moral voice" characteristic of conservative communitarianism. Likewise, both suffer "from a total neglect of democracy, being almost entirely a theory of citizenship as a self-empowering force."[37]

By modern standards, the Islamic treatment of minorities reminds of business protection rackets but in the unenlightened Middle Ages the Islamic policy toward "the people of the Book" compared favorably to mass forced conversion of pagan Saxons under Charlemagne, expulsions of Muslims and Jews from Spain at the time of Columbus (most of whom moved to the Ottoman Empire), the horror of the decades of the Wars of Religion that followed the Reformation, or the dragooning of Orthodox Christians into the union with the Catholic Church in the Polish-Lithuanian Commonwealth. The Greeks under Venetian and Genoese rule fared much worse than in the Ottoman-controlled parts because of heavier taxation, stricter regulation of commerce, lack of autonomous Orthodox Christian institutions, rigid feudal social divisions, and strong pressure to convert to Catholicism. In the 1500s and 1600s, Greek commoners on Cyprus, Crete, Chios, and smaller islands often welcomed the Ottomans as liberators who eliminated Italian overlords and post-Byzantine native aristocrats.[38]

In addition to day-to-day socioeconomic interactions, Ottoman Christians and Muslims rubbed shoulders and joined hands in Sufi lodges or *"tekke."* Intriguingly, that Ottoman Arab word was borrowed into Greek where it means "opium den." Some interesting substances may have been used to help some Sufis work themselves into the kind of physical and emotional state achieved by the famous Whirling Dervishes through dance.

Like Christian monasteries, the Sufi centers offered a possibility of a more direct mystical connection to God through some charismatic teacher or saint, who could be either living or dead. This unorthodox but exciting mix of popular pagan, Muslim, and Christian elements made Islam more acceptable and facilitated conversions.[39] A perplexed British traveler asked one such group

37. Delanty, Gerard, *Citizenship in a Global Age: Society, Culture, Politics* (Buckingham and Philadelphia: Open University Press, 2000), pp. 29–30.

38. Stavrianos, Leften, "Antecedents to the Balkan Revolutions of the Nineteenth Century," *Journal of Modern History*, 29, 4 (December 1957): 338.

39. Doja, Albert, "A Political History of Bektashism in Albania," *Totalitarian Movements and Political Religion*, 7, 1 (March 2006): 88–89.

whether they were truly Muslim. "So we are," they told her, "but of course we keep St. George's Day."[40]

In addition to conversion, Islam spread through waves of Turkish colonization especially in Bulgarian lands strategically adjacent to Constantinople. *Devshirme* or child levy was enforced longest again in Bulgarian lands from about 1400 to 1705. The best and the brightest boys were forcibly selected from Christian villages and raised as privileged slaves of the sultan with no other loyalties like family or region. They enjoyed great career opportunities as Janissaries in the army with a good chance of merit-based promotion all the way up to grand viziers.[41]

One famous example was Rustem Pasha. The rise of a boy from a Croatian backwater to the post of the governor of Diyarbakir was spectacular enough. But what followed next borders on a fairy tale. In 1539, Sultan Suleyman the Magnificent was giving him in marriage his favorite daughter Mihrimah, whom he had sired with his beloved Roxolana. Other courtiers envied Rustem's fortune and started circulating the rumor that he had leprosy. The palace doctors examined him and found lice, which, surprisingly, worked out to Rustem's advantage. If someone had lice, it was considered a positive proof of the absence of leprosy in Ottoman medical circles. This is how Rustem Pasha got a nickname "the louse of fortune." He became legendary for his enormous wealth he had amassed while serving as Grand Vizier twice from 1544 to 1553 and from 1555 to 1561. He used some of it to build one of Istanbul's most beautiful smaller mosques, whose tiled interior is decorated with stunning blue and red patterns. The structure itself was designed by Sinan—the most celebrated Ottoman architect and another famous product of the child levy system.[42]

Despite such success stories, *devshirme* is not remembered fondly in the Balkan historical memory. In a Nobel Prize-winning Serbian novel, we see Bosnian village boys taken from their families and put into baskets to be loaded on horses. One of them would grow up to become Grand Vizier Sokollu Mehmed Pasha but for the rest of his life he would be haunted by the memories of pain of separation from his family and discomfort of the long bumpy journey from Vishegrad to Constantinople. "Many parents had hidden their children in the forests, taught them how to appear half-witted, clothed them in rags and let them go filthy, to avoid the aga's attention."[43]

---

40. Mazower, *The Balkans*, p. 63.

41. Hupchik, "Orthodoxy," p. 77.

42. Sumner-Boyd, Hilary, and Freely, John, *Strolling Through Istanbul: The Classic Guide to the City*. Revised ed. (New York: Tauris Parke Paperbacks, 2012), p. 172.

43. Andrich, Ivo, *The Bridge on the Drina*, trans. Lovett F. Edwards (Chicago: University of Chicago Press, 1977), p. 24.

There were isolated cases of mass forced Islamization of whole communities but it never became a general Ottoman policy both because of relevant injunctions in the Quran and because of the natural reluctance to lose the sources of extra tax revenue. New Christian saints in the Ottoman period included very few martyrdoms caused by attempts at forced conversion.[44] In their vitae, there were many images of tolerant Turks such as governors and judges[45] despite the generally negative references to Muslims in popular culture as fanatical, violent, lazy, and sex-crazed.[46]

A Christian convert to Islam was considered a "Turk" even if he or she continued to speak Greek or Slavic.[47] Inevitably, negative ethnic stereotyping survived in Bulgarian folklore. There, the Greeks were almost as bad as the Turks—their treacherous policy was believed to cost Bulgarians their independence because it supposedly allowed the Ottomans to destroy rival Balkan Christian kingdoms one by one in the 1300s. One would think that lower-level non-Greek clergy had reasons to be unhappy about their hampered promotion prospects in the Greek-dominated Patriarchate of Constantinople. But most of the time, the literati tended to promote the idea of unity of all Christians in the face of Islam.[48] Even in the folk songs the main difference was based on religion and led to the strong emphasis against marriages with infidels.[49]

The Ottoman rule ended conflicts not just between the Byzantine Greeks and Bulgars but also between medieval Bulgaria and Serbia. With old political and cultural boundaries gone, a sense of mixed Slavic consciousness developed. Parish priests and influential monasteries also contributed to this process as the Bulgarians relied on the Old Church Slavonic liturgical books from the Serbian lands, where there was a stronger monastic tradition of manuscript revising and copying.[50]

In medieval Slavic usage, "Greek" was not a purely ethnic term but referred to all Byzantine subjects. [51] In the Christian Roman Empire, "Hellene"

---

44. Aretov, Nikolay, "The Abducted Faith and Bulgarian National Mythology," *Etudes Balkaniques*, 39, 2 (2003): 111.

45. Ibid., p. 119.

46. Angelov, Dimitur, "Bulgarinut v narodnite pesni ot turskogoto igo, samosoznanie i samochuvstvie," *Makedonski Pregled*, 16, 3 (1993): 33–34.

47. Gradeva, Rossitsa, "Turks and Bulgarians, Fourteenth to Eighteenth Centuries," *Journal of Mediterranean Studies*, 5, 2 (1995): 175.

48. Ibid., pp. 178–179.

49. Angelov, "Bulgarinut," p. 44.

50. Hupchik, "Orthodoxy," pp. 83–84.

51. Danova, "Predstavata," p. 9.

as the standard ancient and modern word for "Greek" came to mean "pagan." Normally, the Byzantines, especially outside the narrow circles of Renaissance-minded intellectuals, called themselves "Rhomioi"—Romans. In its Turkicised form "Rumlar," this name was applied to all Orthodox Christian subjects or *Rum milleti*. Even now it is used in Turkey and is differentiated from "Yunanlar" or Greek citizens, literally, "Ionians."[52]

Thus, Ottoman encounters and interactions between the Greeks and the Bulgarians toned down their ethnic differences although they did not reach the level of fusion as with the Serbs. They left each other a lot of loanwords that reflected extremely close connections based on the shared creed and the mixed urban craft guilds and rural communities.[53] Religion rather than any awareness of ethnic kinship was also behind the respect for Russia that had been growing since the fall of Constantinople in 1453. Many Balkan Slavs believed that deep devotion to the only true Christian faith made Muscovy the strongest Orthodox state and the only hope of liberation from the Turks.[54]

The Making of the Third Rome: Moscow's Irredentist Relationship to the Christian East, 1453–1800

These rather exaggerated notions reflected Russia's own self-understanding from the late 1400s. At the same time as Orthodox Christian kingdoms in southeastern Europe crumbled under the Ottoman onslaught, the princes of Moscow finally unified northeastern Russian lands and shook off their dependence on the Golden Horde, a Mongol successor state centered on the Volga area and Islamized since about the mid-1300s. Metropolitans of Moscow strongly encouraged secular rulers to defy infidel overlords in Crusading terms. In 1480, Muscovy became truly independent after rebuffing the last significant attempt of Khan Ahmad to enforce militarily his demand for annual tribute. The Russian Church likewise stopped appealing to the Patriarch of Constantinople for confirmation of the elections of the Archbishop of Moscow. Russian bishops felt that Byzantine purity of Orthodox faith had been tainted by the union with the Pope, short-lived as it was, and by the humiliation of subordination to the Muslim government.[55]

---

52. Xydis, Stephen, "Greek Nationalism," in Sugar, Peter, and Lederer, Ivo, eds., *Nationalism in Eastern Europe* (Seattle: University of Washington Press, 1969), pp. 210–211.

53. Danova, "Predstavata," p. 6.

54. Gradeva, Rossitsa, "Turks and Bulgarians Fourteenth to Eighteenth Centuries," *Journal of Mediterranean Studies*, 5, 2 (1995): 182.

55. Kartashev, *Ocherki*, pp. 394–395.

Now elected by Russian bishops, the Metropolitan of Moscow was confirmed by the prince reenacting the relationship that had existed between Eastern Roman emperors and patriarchs of Constantinople. Church and court circles produced texts that invited Moscow princes to assume the role of Byzantine emperors and to eventually liberate their fallen capital. Prince Ivan III acted on those assumptions in 1472 when he married Zoe Paleologus, the niece of the last Byzantine emperor. Western governments also acknowledged Muscovy's implicit claim on the lands of the former Byzantine Empire as they encouraged Russian princes to join various anti-Ottoman coalitions. Moscow rulers were in no rush to challenge the sultans militarily but starting with Ivan III they adopted the Byzantine double-headed eagle as their own emblem.[56]

Ivan IV, better known as Ivan the Terrible, cashed in on his grandfather's marriage to the Greek princess when he had himself crowned as the Tsar of Russia in 1547 at the age of 17. That title is a Russian variation on the word "Caesar." It referred to Byzantine emperors and after 1453 occasionally to Muscovite princes as they attempted to raise their office high above even the highest Russian nobility in their relentless centralization drive. Shortly after the Ottoman conquest of the Balkans, various Christian dignitaries also began to address Russian rulers as "tsars," asking for financial support of churches, monasteries, and subject Orthodox populations generally.

It was embarrassing for patriarchs of Constantinople to follow in the footsteps of lesser prelates to beg the Russians for money but it was desperately needed given the diminishing resources of the Orthodox *millet* and the debts incurred to bribe Ottoman officials and to run Christian community institutions on a day-to-day basis. They had to forget the century-long proud stance of the Russian Church that had in effect made itself independent of the Ecumenical Patriarchs in 1453. In exchange for a generous grant of alms, in 1562 the Patriarchate recognized Ivan IV as "Tsar and Sovereign of all Orthodox Christians east to west all the way to the Ocean" in the bloodline of Roman emperors.[57]

Ever since then, Ottoman Christian clerics like Serbian abbots of the St. Nicholas Monastery in Khopovo (Vojvodina) and of the Papracha Annunciation Monastery in their requests for aid favorably compared Russian tsars to famous Byzantine emperors such as Constantine the Great, Justinian

---

56. Kartashev, *Ocherki*, pp. 403–408.

57. Kapterev, Nikolai, *Kharakter otnoshenii Rossii k Pravoslavnomu Vostoku v XVI i XVII stoletiakh* (Sergiev Posad, 1914), pp. 26–29.

the Great, and Leo the Wise.[58] As "the sun and the first true pillar of the Orthodox faith," Tsar Mikhail I would not turn away from the needs of Archbishop Neofit, who had lost 4,000 silver pieces extorted by the Turks—they alleged that Neofit had been converting Muslims to Christianity.[59] Many Serbs, such as Archbishop Mikhail and his flock, felt under Ottoman rule like "sheep among wolves" and had no protector except the Lord, St. Nicholas, and Tsar Alexei I.[60] As "new Constantine of New Rome," Tsar Alexei was "the light of Orthodoxy shining across the world." He had also erected the true Cross to strengthen all the Orthodox Christians and "to defeat evil God-forsaken Hagarenes and other hostile nations (*iaziki*)."[61]

To use a political science term, we will see the emerging dynamic of irredentism—the discourse and policy of political incorporation of culturally related unredeemed populations. In more modern times, irredentism is usually ethnic such as in the Serbo-Croatian War of 1991 and some other Yugoslav wars. But the Islamist rhetoric, especially about liberating Palestine, sounds irredentist too.[62]

Patriarchs of Constantinople had much more difficulty recognizing the church of Moscow as a patriarchate in its own right. They understood that they would be much less needed and rewarded if the Russian tsars had a patriarch at home. But by 1587 enough political will and financial largesse convinced all four ancient patriarchs of Constantinople, Alexandria, Jerusalem, and Antioch that for Moscow to be the Third Rome it had to have both the tsar and the patriarch.[63]

To buttress Moscow's new ecumenical Pan-Orthodox significance, Russian tsars and patriarchs sought to amass as many holy relics of famous saints as possible. They either received them in exchange for alms or more often purchased them from their Ottoman coreligionists.[64] Although

58. Abbot Jeremiah to Tsar Mikhail I, 16 September 1638, *Moskva-Serbiia*, p. 235; Abbot of the Papracha Annunciation Monastery to Tsars Ivan V and Peter I, 8 September 1687, ibid., p. 340.

59. Abbot Stephen to Tsar Mikhail I, some time in 1640, ibid., p. 238.

60. Archbishop Mikhail of Kratovo to Tsar Alexei I, 26 December 1647, ibid., p. 263.

61. Abbot Neofit of the Serbian Ascension Studenitsa Monastery to Tsar Alexei I, 10 March 1662, ibid., p. 302.

62. Ambrosio, Thomas, *Irredentism: Ethnic Conflict and International Politics* (Westport and London: Praeger, 2001), p. 7; Brubaker, Rogers, *Nationalism Reframed: Nationhood and the National Question in the New Europe* (New York: Cambridge University Press, 1996), pp. 5–7.

63. Kapterev, *Kharakter*, pp. 35–37.

64. Ibid., pp. 72–74.

Russia was a relatively strong military and economic power in the 1500s and 1600s, its educational level was deplorable. The lack of proper educational system created a continuous demand for all sorts of experts but especially pressing was the need to revise and publish various religious and liturgical texts. Self-taught native editors were able to amass multiple manuscript copies of Old Church Slavonic books and found many differences in them. Although some taught themselves some Greek, often times they could not understand which Old Church Slavonic copy was a better translation of the Greek original. That is why the Russian government and the Patriarchate of Moscow often requested books and invited educated Greek monks to supervise those decades-long efforts to print a uniform body of reliable church literature.[65]

Education among Ottoman Christians lagged far behind the Scientific Revolution in Western Europe but there survived a rather sparse network of cathedral schools. They were supposed to be supported by local bishops and the Patriarchal School in Constantinople—the single college-level institution in the Empire. Eastern patriarchates were able to maintain some schools in Venetian-held Greek areas such as on Crete, which fell to the Ottomans only in 1669. The Ionian Islands would be part of the Most Serene Republic until its defeat at the hands of Napoleon. Many Greeks from Venetian areas studied at the Venetian-controlled and still essentially medieval scholastic University of Padua, where a few young Ottoman Christians pursued their education as well.[66]

There is a debate on the reasons for the extremely accelerated pace of top-down church reforms under Patriarch Nikon of Moscow (1652–1658). They were meant to bring even the minutest rituals into total conformity with Greek models (making the sign of the cross with three instead of two fingers, etc.). Some see this leap from gradual to radical Byzantinization of Russian church life as a function of Nikon's impetuous personality.[67]

Others stress the political motivation of the church reform that developed at exactly the same time as Eastern Ukraine, also known as "Little Russia," rose against its Polish Catholic government and became part of Muscovite Russia with significant local autonomy rights. Orthodox Christians in Poland were under the jurisdiction of the Patriarchate of Constantinople and their rituals were slightly different from those in Muscovy. Russian Tsar Alexei I, father

---

65. Kartashev, *Ocherki*, vol. 1, pp. 487–497; vol. 2, pp. 98–102.

66. Kraft, Ekkehard, *Moskaus Griechisches Jahrhundert: Russisch-Griechische Beziehungen und metabyzantinischer Einfluss, 1619–1694* (Stuttgart: Steiner, 1995), pp. 28–32.

67. Ibid., pp. 127.

of Peter the Great, supported Nikon's rapid Byzantinization of the Russian church because it suited his agenda to incorporate Ukraine into his domains.

Another reason Patriarch Nikon's often clumsy and repressive actions received vital government backing was the widely shared expectation in the East that the unification of Russia and Eastern Ukraine was only the first step to reclaiming the Byzantine Empire. As the Third Rome in theory, Muscovy could not be seen as different from its eastern brethren outwardly even at the cost of the internal schism known as the Old Belief, which persists until today.[68]

In addition to Greek letters, the Russian government also obtained valuable political information from alms seekers who were required to leave written accounts of their travel at the border checkpoint. Needy travelers were only too happy to supply intelligence about Ottoman and Polish lands they crossed in hopes of more generous handouts. Even after their return from Moscow, many of them became essentially Russian spies sending reports back to Moscow, again counting on a handsome payout. Since Muscovy did not have permanent embassies abroad until Peter the Great (1689–1725), occasional diplomats on mission in the Ottoman capital were actually required to consult the Patriarchate there. Obviously, Orthodox clerics ran a great risk with Ottoman authorities linking themselves so closely to a foreign government. Many lost their jobs and some their lives on His Majesty's secret service.[69]

One of them, Patriarch of Constantinople Parthenios III, apparently meant what he wrote to Tsar Mikhail Romanov in 1644: "God has given all Orthodox Christians Your sovereign and holy kingdom to console us, to protect us, to help us, to make us proud and strong."[70] In the Turkish historiography, Mehmet IV had Parthenios executed because he had developed papal pretensions interfering with purely political matters. Parthenios allegedly even admitted to having incited the Wallachian ruler Konstantin to revolt.[71] Disappointed with the Patriarchate, Mehmet IV decreed that new patriarchs be inaugurated in the presence not of the Sultan but merely of Grand Vizier at the Sublime Porte—the new seat of government outside the Top Kapi Palace, as shown in Figure 1.2.[72]

---

68. Kartashev, *Ocherki*, vol. 2, pp. 145, 152, 178.

69. Kapterev, *Kharakter*, pp. 277–308.

70. Ibid., p. 31.

71. Atalay, *Fener Rum Ortodoks*, p. 9.

72. Sofuoglu, *Fener Rum Patrikhanesi*, p. 17.

FIGURE 1.2 "The Sublime Porte" (Constantinople: Abdullah Freres, 1880–1900). Library of Congress Prints and Photographs Division, Reproduction Number: LC-USZ62-82347 LC-DIG-ppmsca-03794. Located outside the Top Kapi Palace complex across from the royal Gulhane Park, this building served as the seat of Ottoman government from the mid-1600s to the end of the First World War.

The hopes of Ottoman Christians were aroused by Ivan the Terrible's conquest of the successor states of the Golden Horde—the Muslim khanates of Kazan, Astrakhan, and Siberia in the mid- to late 1500s. Despite much talk and symbolism of the Third Rome, Moscow did not confront the Ottomans militarily until the war of 1677–1681, when they unsuccessfully tried to take Eastern Ukraine from Russia's still weak control.[73]

Ironically, the first time the Russian rulers felt audacious enough to openly recognize the irredentist role of liberators of the Christian East was when Tsarina Sophia and Peter the Great joined the papal-sponsored Holy League of Venice, Austria, and Poland from 1686 to 1700.[74] The decisive battle of that war was fought at the gates of Vienna. The Ottoman defeat

---

73. Kraft, *Moskaus*, pp. 84–85.

74. Kapterev, *Kharakter*, p. 379.

and the loss of Hungary clearly marked the beginning of Ottoman retreat and disintegration under the increasing pressure of covetous neighbors and internal uprisings.

But that was clear only in hindsight—the Ottomans still could and did wage successful wars of aggression. The mouth of the Don River –the main Russian territorial gain of those campaigns—was lost in 1711 when the Sublime Porte launched an attack in support of Sweden, which had been badly beaten by Peter the Great in the long "Great Northern War" of 1700–1721 for control of the southeastern Baltic Sea littoral. Although caught unprepared, Peter had a trump card or two up his sleeve. He received support from Dmitrie Cantemir, a ruler of the borderland Moldavian principality and a vassal of the Sultan. Setting a precedent for most other Russo-Turkish wars, Peter issued proclamations inciting Ottoman Christians to rebel and to support their Russian liberators. Although many were excited, only tough or foolhardy Slavic highlanders of Montenegro answered the call. But for the first and last time in the eighteenth century, the Russian forces were defeated not far from the Danube and Peter had to ask for peace.[75]

In the subsequent wars of 1735–1739 and especially of 1768–1774, the Russian government continued the tradition of irresponsibly inciting subject Christian populations to insurrection. Catherine II's proclamation called on "pious" "Orthodox Greek and Slavic nations" (narody) to join Russia's holy war against the oppressive infidel Hagarenes. Their treacherous government had itself started hostilities to support Catholic Poland because Russia demanded equal rights for Orthodox Christians there. Local Orthodox Christians were more numerous than the Hagarenes in the Balkans. It was time for them to join their Russian brothers in Christ to expel the infidels and to liberate with God's help Constantinople, "the capital of ancient Greek emperors."[76]

Catherine the Great's agents made empty promises of immense Russian armies coming soon to relieve local rebels. In 1771, the Russian Baltic squadron led by Alexei Orlov sailed into the Aegean and destroyed the Ottoman navy, but with very few marines it could not offer effective assistance to Greek auxiliaries in the Peloponnesus. Short of regular troops soon to be annihilated on the Danube, the Sublime Porte called on Muslim Albanian irregulars to deal with the problem. They were successful particularly in the

75. Sumner, Benedict, *Peter the Great and the Emergence of Russia* (New York: Collier Books, 1962), p. 75.

76. Catherine II to Balkan nations, 29 January 1769, *Moskva-Serbiia, Belgrad-Rossiia*, pp. 428–430.

task of wreaking havoc on the civilians, looting their homes and churches for months.[77]

The Treaty of Kuchuk Kaynarji, which ended that war, included the Ottoman pledge to pardon all local participants, but there was no oversight of how it was enforced. In other respects, the treaty was a great gain for Russia as the Sublime Porte acknowledged the humiliating loss of the northern part of the Black Sea coastline with the Crimea. It was the first majority Muslim Ottoman area to be conquered by a European power. In an effort to perhaps placate the Greeks and no doubt to economically develop newly annexed lands, Russian diplomats secured the important privilege of tariff-free passage through Ottoman waters to all ships flying the Russian flag.[78] The document also gave Russia certain narrow rights in relation to Ottoman Christians (specifically, those in Wallachia and Moldavia but also those serving an Orthodox church to be built in Constantinople) that later were used as pretexts to claim the irredentist role of protection of all of them.[79]

If the war of 1768–1774 was a war of necessity declared by the sultan on Russia, the next war of 1787–1792 was one of choice, although again technically started by the Porte. In 1782, Catherine discussed an alliance with Austria to destroy the Ottoman Empire and in a letter to Joseph II suggested a "Greek Project" of how to partition it. Austria would get the Western Balkans whereas its eastern part with Constantinople would be turned into a revived Byzantine Empire to serve as a buffer state under Russian protection. Because of less than stellar Austrian performance in the ensuing conflict, the allies failed to completely obliterate the Ottoman presence in Europe. In the future, Austrian policymakers would never agree on anything like that, preferring to keep the Ottomans weak rather than to risk making the Russians too strong.[80] Figure 1.3 is a contemporary British print that illustrates the complex political arrangements during that war.

The Russian victories also raised the hopes of many unredeemed Orthodox Christians for the coming liberation from the Ottomans. Those battles were usually fought on both sides of the Danube—in Rumanian-speaking Moldavia

---

77. Gritsopoulos, Tasos, *Ta Orlofika: I en Peloponniso epanastasis tou 1770 kai ta epakoloutha autis* (Athens: Mnemosyne, 1967).

78. Druzhinina, Elena, *Kuchuk-Kainardzhiiskii mir 1774 goda* (Moscow: AN SSSR, 1955).

79. Davison, Roderick, "'Russian Skill and Turkish Imbecility': The Treaty of Kuchuk Kainarji Reconsidered," *Slavic Review*, 35, 3 (September 1976): 482.

80. Roider, Karl, *Austria's Eastern Question, 1700–1790* (Princeton: Princeton University Press, 1982).

FIGURE 1.3 "The Christian Amazon, with her invincible target, Alias, the focus of genial rays, or Dian of the Rushes, to much [sic] for 300,000 Infidels" (London: J. Crawford, 24 October 1787). Library of Congress Prints and Photographs Division, Reproduction Number: LC-USZC4-6748. Joseph II of Austria hides behind Catherine II, who is battling Sultan Selim III with an apish Louis XVI and the King of Spain to his side.

and Wallachia and South Slavic lands. Bulgarian folklore developed a legend of Diado Ivan, Russian Grandpa Ivan, destined to make Balkan Christians free.[81] The Greeks also came up with a prophecy of a blond nation to come from the north to accomplish the same feat.[82]

The connection between Ottoman Christian prelates and the Russian government continued along traditional lines despite the profound Westernization of all areas of Russian life encouraged since Peter the Great. Meticulously planned St. Petersburg became the new capital and Russia's window on the West, but the country continued to be the Third Rome closely connected to the Christian East. Eastern patriarchs actually helped Tsar Peter complete the turn to absolutism on the model of England and the Lutheran states, where the monarch was officially in charge of the church.

---

81. Pundeff, "Bulgarian Nationalism," p. 105.

82. Xydis, "Greek Nationalism," p. 221.

There were also personal reasons for such a change—Moscow Patriarch Adrian as Nikon before him was leaning toward a theocracy as he vigorously insisted on the need for the government to consult the church as the voice of Christ. After Adrian's death, Peter put on hold the elections of his successor and decided to diminish the status of the Russian church and its potential as an autonomous source of opposition. The Patriarchate was to be transformed into a government agency: "the office of the Orthodox religion," also known as the Holy Synod. It consisted of a college of key Russian archbishops but at its head was Over-Procurator, an appointed lay official with a legal or military background. In 1723, Eastern patriarchs recognized the Holy Synod as the equivalent of the abolished Patriarchate of Moscow.[83]

As before, Ottoman Christian clerics begged Russian royalties for financial aid throughout the 1700s and 1800s. "With God's help and mercy," the Habsburg army temporarily "liberated" parts of Serbia including Belgrade by 1718. But this transition had created so many problems that only Peter the Great as "the light of the East" could help solve. The Turks, "the cursed tyrannical barbarians," had destroyed many churches including the Belgrade cathedral. The lack of liturgical books, vessels, and even vestments made it impossible to celebrate the Divine Liturgy. On the other hand, Habsburg-sponsored Catholic missionaries were winning over many naïve and ignorant people. Addressing all those pressing needs required not just money to rebuild churches but also sending two competent teachers to start a school for Orthodox priests.[84]

The positive economic impact of the Treaty of Kuchuk Kaynarji was even more important than generous financial aid in creating a Greek Ottoman bourgeoisie of sorts with significant power not just in Greek lands but in most cities of the Empire. Greek traders and shipowners from the Aegean islands of Spetses, Psari, and Ydra took advantage of the privilege of free passage through Turkish waters under the Russian flag. They made fortunes connecting new Russian Black Sea areas to Mediterranean markets and gained naval experience as they had to defend themselves against pirates. As a result of this traffic, a greater number of middle-class Greeks were exposed to Western intellectual developments than was the case before.[85] Not surprisingly, *Philike Hetaireia*, the main anti-Ottoman Greek conspiratorial network, was started

83. Sapozhnikov, Dmitrii, ed., *Pisma vostochnykh patriarkhov* (Simbirsk: Gubernskaia Uchenaia Arkhivnaia Kommisiia, 1898), pp. 5–6.

84. Archbishop Moisei of Belgrade to Emperor Peter I, 1 September 1718, *Moskva-Serbiia*, pp. 390–391.

85. Xydis, "Greek Nationalism," pp. 213–214.

by three Greek merchants in Odessa in 1804. They were moderately successful in setting up affiliated Masonic-style cells across the Greek lands mostly
because they falsely claimed to be acting in the name of the Russian tsar.[86]

Although Greek conspirators tried to exploit religion, their main motivation was Western-style nationalism. Not all Enlightenment *philosophes*
seduced by Friedrich II or Catherine II believed in popular sovereignty but
they all used nation as the main category of politics and culture. Language
was seen as central to any nation's existence and progress in the powerful
argument of Herder. Isolated intellectuals of subject Slavic nationalities in
Habsburg Austria began to politicize the ideas of Slavic cultural affinity. To
resist Germanization or Magyarization, they defended the value of Czech
and Slovak languages based on their connection to the great Slavic race, of
which "the Russian branch dominates the area between the Black Sea and
the Arctic Ocean ... explores the seas between Asia and America."[87] Since
the Renaissance, classical antiquity was assuming the status of the cradle of
Western civilization and educated Europeans encouraged Greek students and
immigrants to revive Greece from the Ottoman ashes. Adamantios Korais
was the most important Greek scholar of this group who spent most of his life
in Paris before and during the French Revolution.

His method did not include assassinating the sultan and his pashas but
consisted in editing and publishing ancient Greek texts in a more modern
adaptation. That translation was not into Greek spoken at the time but into a
strange artificial language that combined elements of Ancient and Modern
Greek. He coined a lot of words to purify the language of Turkish, Slavic, and
Italian loanwords that described post-classical realities. This wishful thinking of an armchair intellectual does not strike one as a very effective way
to change the world but it would do just that when the newly independent
Greek nation-state adopted Korais' program after 1830. In the late 1700s, the
Patriarchate of Constantinople opposed subversive Westernizers and pagan
worshipers like Korais. Their heady agitation for a new Hellenic dream could
provoke real Ottoman repression against the Orthodox *millet*. Philosophically,
the Enlightenment focus on nation and language left little meaningful space
for religion, which was often branded as "superstition."[88]

---

86. Arsh, Grigorii, *Eteristskoe dvizhenie v Rossii: Osvoboditelnaia borba grecheskogo naroda v nachale XIX veka i russko-grecheskie sviazi* (Moscow: Nauka, 1970).

87. Freidzon, Vladimir, "Predstavleniia i idei slavianskoi obshnosti v pervoi polovine XIX veka," *Voprosy Istorii*, 9 (1978): 64.

88. Gourgouris, Stathis, *Dream Nation: Enlightenment, Colonization, and the Institution of Modern Greece* (Stanford: Stanford University Press, 1996), pp. 90–100.

In contrast, most Turkish historians consider the Greeks of Constantinople and the Patriarchate in particular to be the main inspiration of nationalist separatism and even the leadership of the emerging Greek conspiratorial societies. Ottoman tolerance backfired: "the Orthodox (*Rumlar*) enjoyed independent religious life and institutions, independent courts and neighborhood administration, independent tax-collecting structures and schools, artistic and commercial life at the expense of the Ottoman nation." All that enabled the ungrateful Orthodox subjects to avoid assimilation into Turkish Muslim culture, to preserve their "folklore" and to nurture dreams of reviving the Byzantine Empire although the Ottoman government trusted them and did not discriminate between them and "its own children."[89] The Patriarchate went so far as to turn its monasteries over to the pirates.[90] Another Turkish tendency is to put much blame on European intervention: "initially, the relations between the Ottoman state and the minorities had been positive" before the 1700s when those false Christian friends began to interfere.[91]

"Russian propaganda" is emphasized in this context. As lesser causes of the Greek rebellion, there is a mention of the mistreatment of Christians by unruly Janissaries and all kinds of slurs that uneducated Muslims began to use against the Christians.[92] The still marginal group of Turkish historians echoes the views of their mainstream Balkan cousins—although some local priests and bishops were involved in anti-Ottoman conspiracies, the Patriarchate was not because the restoration of the Byzantine Empire would diminish its existing rights and privileges.[93]

Unlike their superiors, lower-level clergy had less to lose in terms of their status in the Ottoman system and were thus less immune to the exciting new ideology. Ironically, the seeds of nationalism cropped up in the ancient monasteries of the Holy Mount Athos—the most Pan-Orthodox place one can think of. From at least the 900s, it attracted monks from all over the Orthodox lands and eventually became organized into an autonomous republic. Although all communities were ethnically mixed, traditionally three of twenty monasteries were considered as Slavic—Russian St. Panteleimon's, Bulgarian Zografou, and Serbian Hilandar.

---

89. Sofuoglu, *Fener Rum Patrikhanesi*, pp. 19–21, 28.

90. Atalay, *Fener Rum Ortodoks*, p. 9.

91. Alkan, *Fener Rum Patrikhanesi*, p. 36.

92. Sofuoglu, *Fener Rum Patrikhanesi*, p. 33; Alkan, *Fener Rum Patrikhanesi*, p. 48.

93. Osmanagaoglu, Cihan, *1862 Rum Patrikligi Nizamati Cercevesinde Fener Rum Ortodoks Patrikhanesi* (Istanbul: Oniki Lehva, 2010), p. 107.

In the 1760s, Greek and Serbian monks of the Hilandar monastery apparently displayed a shocking level of nationalistic arrogance. In 1762, in response to the boastful ethnocentrism of his brothers in Christ, Bulgarian Father Paisii wrote "A Slavic-Bulgarian History" reminding his kinsmen of political and cultural glory of medieval Bulgarian kingdoms. His book could enjoy only limited success as it circulated mostly among Bulgarian clerics only in manuscript copies until its first publication in 1844.[94]

Late-eighteenth-century politicization of the concept of ethnicity began to affect the Russian educated society and bureaucratic mind as well. That agonizing process started as a "compensatory nationalism"—an instinctive reaction to the overwhelming flood of Western influence unleashed by Peter the Great. Then its intense search for suitably glorious Russian folklore and history went with the Western Romantic flows.[95]

In the 1700s, Russian diplomatic memos occasionally detailed by name Christian Balkan peoples. Proclamations spread by Catherine the Great's agents in Slavic areas reminded local Christians of "the bonds of faith and blood" to incite them to rise in support of Russian armies. But the main emphasis was on supraethnic religious bonds. In the Danubian theater of the war of 1768–1774, the Russian command formed a volunteer unit of about 3,000 Greeks, Serbs, and Bulgarians.[96] Most of such auxiliaries were of little practical military value as they primarily consisted of Balkan brigands who were attracted by the prospect of booty and were naturally ill-disposed to follow orders.[97]

In May 1803, Alexander I's foreign minister Prince Adam Chartoryiski, himself ethnically Polish, proposed to partition the Ottoman Balkans into separate states. In contrast to Catherine's "Greek Project," in this case the irredentist rationale was not historical or religious but ethnic. The new liberated states would be connected to Russia through "the identity of religion and origin" to remain under the tutelage of the Russian ruler as "the Emperor or Protector of the Slavs of the East."[98] Before the right set of circumstances

---

94. Pundeff, "Bulgarian Nationalism," pp. 101–103.

95. Rogger, Hans, National Consciousness in Eighteenth-Century Russia (Cambridge, MA: Harvard University Press, 1960), pp. 156–172.

96. Dojnov, Stefan, "La Russie et le movement de liberation nationale bulgare au XVIIIme siècle," Etudes Historiques, 12 (1984): 44–45.

97. Ibid., p. 48.

98. Quoted in Sugar, Peter, "The Southern Slav Image of Russia in the Nineteenth Century," Journal of Central European Affairs, 21, 3 (1959): 45.

emerged, that memo would be an irrelevant fantasy, much like the run-of-the-mill outpouring of war plans in modern defense departments.

Russia's Ottoman Dilemma: Partition or Preservation (1804–1853)

Major revolts against the sultans were never caused by small coteries of conspiring middle-class nationalists. Religion remained the most important category in the Ottoman bifurcated state, where even wealthier Christians were legally and politically disadvantaged in regard to their Muslim fellow countrymen. But this situation prevailed for centuries without any dangerous Christian uprisings as long as the Sublime Porte was able to maintain domestic order and promote imperial expansion. Since the late 1600s, crushing victories of the European powers exposed Ottoman weakness. Throughout the 1700s, the sultans kept losing control of their own provinces as ambitious governors, who had risen from among local landholders, distanced themselves from the government in Istanbul to style themselves as feudal lords. As in the European Dark Ages, they cared only for their own domains and enjoyed raiding neighboring areas.[99]

Strangely enough, they appealed to Western novelists—Alexander Dumas romanticized one of them, Ali Pasha of Yannina, in his famous *Count of Monte Cristo*. Sultans Selim III (r. 1789–1808) and Mahmud II (1808–1839) tried to reverse those centrifugal tendencies and even looked to the West, especially Revolutionary and Napoleonic France, as a model. Selim III came to power the year of the French Revolution and attempted to substitute a drilled conscript army for the Janissary troops, which had degenerated from an elite corps of professional Islamized Christian slave soldiers into a voluntary useless but privileged all-Muslim militia. Those reforms provoked a reaction led by Muslim clerics who accused Selim III of being a crypto-infidel. But to non-Muslim minorities he did not appear as a Westernizer. Selim III made dress codes more strict—yellow turbans and shoes for Muslims, red hats and shoes for Armenians, black for Orthodox Christians, and blue for Jews. No one was to dress extravagantly or "above their station" but non-Muslims were punished more harshly. Like Caliph Harun al Rashid of *The Arabian Nights*, Selim III occasionally toured the streets of his capital in disguise. Once he came across a lavishly attired Orthodox Christian and "he had the man killed on the spot."[100]

---

99. Davison, Roderic, *The Reform in the Ottoman Empire, 1856–1876* (Princeton: Princeton University Press, 1963), p. 18.

100. Boyar and Fleet, *A Social History of Ottoman Istanbul*, pp. 178–180.

In the meantime, provincial lords continued their depredations unchecked. Pasvanoglu Osman Pasha inherited from his father the governorship of Vidin—a Danube fortress in today's Bulgaria. He often sent his raiding parties to Moldavia, Wallachia, the Sofia province, and the Belgrade district. Haci Mustafa Pasha of Belgrade was a decent governor for a change, loyal to the sultan, and genuinely concerned with the welfare of the people under his jurisdiction. He was affectionately called "the Serbian mother." He despaired of any possibility to stop the devastation visited on his province by Pasvanoglu as his garrison was small and sultan's punitive expeditions against Pasvanoglu were more or less miserable failures. That is why, at the suggestion of local Serb notables, Mustafa Pasha broke with the fundamental Islamic law and not just allowed all able-bodied Christians to arm themselves but actually required them to do so in 1799, despite the opposition of local Muslim clerics.[101]

In the late fall of 1801, Pasvanoglu's agents stirred up the revolt among the Janissaries in Belgrade itself that killed Mustafa Pasha and unleashed a reign of terror in the Belgrade area. In 1804, the Christian militia and the Muslims loyal to the Sultan had enough of lawlessness and joined forces in a revolt against the mob rule by the Janissaries run wild. What started as a social protest changed into a Christian secessionist movement under the impact of the Russo-Turkish War of 1806–1812.[102]

It is worth taking a step back and bringing insights from political science to better understand this case because many later Balkan uprisings would be similar. The Serbs were driven not just by desperation and the survival instinct. The sense of injustice also played a significant part. Previously supported by the Belgrade governor, the rebels saw the mob rule as abnormal and unacceptable. Total hopelessness and frustration (also known as "total deprivation") usually lead to resignation to one's fate. Whenever people perceive a gap between reality and their higher expectations, this feeling of "relative deprivation" motivates them to rebel to achieve better prospects.[103]

The First Serbian Uprising (1804–1813) created a dynamic that would be repeated in the subsequent development of the Eastern Question. A native insurgency would expose conflicting agendas of the European powers in the "Near East"—a traditional term for the Balkans and the Middle East. In that case,

---

101. Zens, Robert, "Pasvanoglu Osman Pasha and the Pashalik of Belgrade, 1791–1807," *International Journal of Turkish Studies*, 8, 1–2 (2002): 95–100.

102. Ibid., pp. 102–103.

103. Gurr, Ted, *Why Men Rebel* (Princeton: Princeton University Press, 1970), p. 24.

at first, Austria and Russia wanted to have nothing to do with the revolt but had to take action when Napoleon's insatiable appetite for world domination drew France into the Balkans and ignited imperial rivalry. The Russian Foreign Ministry was alarmed at the Serbian requests for Austrian mediation between the rebels and the Sublime Porte. "This circumstance could not fail to attract the attention of His Majesty who is particularly favorable to the fate of this co-ethnic nation (*edinoplemennoi natsii*) and is willing to secure their future prosperity." With this fear of losing the Serbs to Austria came the instruction to the Russian diplomats to avoid the impression of being indifferent to their plight.[104]

Orthodox South Slavs at this time themselves often used the idea of ethnic affinity with the Russians to ask for special protection of the "Russian sovereign and the most gracious protector of Orthodox Christians especially of those of the same ethnicity and language."[105] Serb rebel leaders increasingly tried to monopolize that niche referring to the tsar as "the only earthly helper, protector, and father" as well as "the consolation and pride of all Slavs."[106] Although their shared religion remained the main reference point, the distrust of Ottoman Greeks occasionally made itself felt. When asking the Russian government to accept Serbia as a Russian protectorate, the Serb leaders mentioned several conditions—no land grants in Serbia for any landlord, no extension of serfdom, and the ban on ethnic Greeks holding any military or civilian office.[107]

Eventually, the Sultan became Napoleon's junior ally to reconquer the Black Sea areas lost to Catherine II. In the ensuing war of 1806–1812, Russia discovered the strategic value of the Serbian rebels, and in the peace treaty of Bucharest Tsar Alexander I forced the Sublime Porte to give pardon and territorial autonomy to them. It was the first time that any Balkan ethnic group was mentioned by name in an international treaty albeit still in the context of the Russian traditional protection of Ottoman Christians.[108]

The uprising in Greece also grew from provincial separatism. The Famous Ali Pasha of Yannina had been a de facto ruler of Albania and northern Greece

---

104. A. A. Chartoryiskii to A. A. Jerve, 18 September 1804, Nikitin, Sergei, Chubrilovich, Vaso et al., eds., *Pervoie Serbskoie Vosstanie 1804–1813 gg i Rossiia*. Vol. 1. *1804–1807* (Moscow: Nauka, 1980), pp. 50–51.

105. Herzegovinian delegates to I. P. Miletich, 24 September 1804, ibid., p. 52.

106. Georgiii Petrovich et al. to Alexander I, 1 May 1805, ibid., p. 112.

107. Negotiations between Karageorgii and F. O. Paulucci, 28 June 1807, ibid., p. 386.

108. Meriage, Lawrence, "The First Serbian Uprising (1804–1813) and the Nineteenth-Century Origins of the Eastern Question," *Slavic Review*, 37, 3 (September 1978): 439.

since 1787. By 1819, reformist Sultan Mahmud II (1808–1839) considered him-self strong enough to reassert centralized control over those areas. During the two-year-long struggle for survival, Ali Pasha encouraged Greek conspirators to organize a revolt in the Peloponnesus to divert some government troops from the north.[109]

The international environment at the time could not be very favorable to the two-pronged Greek rebellion of February and March of 1821 started in Moldavia-Wallachia and the Peloponnesus. By the late 1700s, the Ottoman Empire had become one of England's main markets. Other European powers followed suit. No wonder most of them were increasingly interested in pre-serving the territorial integrity of the still vast realm of the sultans to secure their exports and investments (see Map 1.2).[110]

Furthermore, the predatory nature of eighteenth-century balance-of-power politics had been made even worse in the Revolutionary and Napoleonic Wars, where France sought to dominate the entire continent. Tired of constant insecurity, the Great Powers transformed the system of international relations. During the talks in Vienna (November 1814–June 1815), they agreed on the key principles of the European Concert—to respect the existing borders, to prevent miscommunication, and to settle differ-ences at periodic diplomatic congresses. To sanction those brand new good neighbor policies, Russia, Prussia, and Austria (with the United Kingdom and France abstaining) formed the Holy Alliance, which lasted from 1815 to 1848. The so-called Vienna System was able to minimize the relatively brief shocks of the Crimean War and of German and Italian unifications to hold out until about 1900, when the new quest for European domination began.[111]

Given this background, the European Great Powers initially treated the Greek revolt as an illegitimate insurrection although the Ottoman Empire had not been included into the Concert of Europe. When the Greek rebels appealed to the Christian powers for help, their timing could not have been worse—at that same moment, the European monarchs with their foreign ministers were discussing at the Congress of Laibach (today's Ljubljana) the

109. Skiotis, Dennis, "The Greek Revolution: Ali Pasha's Last Gamble," in Diamandouros, Nikiforos, Anton, John, Petropulos, John, and Topping, Peter, eds., *Hellenism and the First Greek War of Liberation (1821–1830): Continuity and Change* (Thessaloniki: Institute for Balkan Studies, 1976), pp. 97–109.

110. Stavrianos, Leften, *Balkan Federation: A History of the Movement toward Balkan Unity in Modern Times* (Hamden: Archon Books, 1964), pp. 14–15.

111. Schroeder, Paul, "19th Century International System: Changes in the Structure," *World Politics*, 39, 1 (October 1986): 12–13.

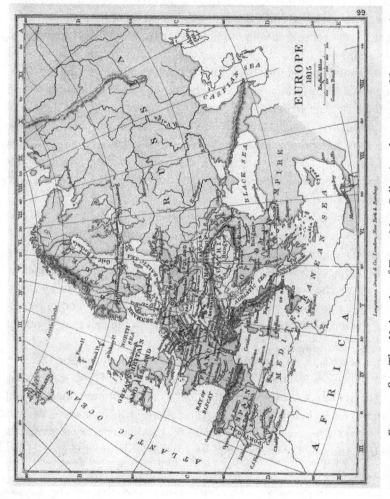

MAP 1.2 Europe, 1815. The University of Texas Map Collection. http://www.lib.utexas.edu/
maps/historical/history_balkans.html

need to intervene to suppress revolutionary unrest in another sovereign country if general peace were endangered.[112]

Even the execution of Patriarch Gregory V and several other metropolitans was not shocking enough to European leaders. In the generally accepted view, the Patriarch was merely a scapegoat. Before and during the Greek War of Independence, he condemned the followers of secular Enlightenment and revolutionaries.[113] Not surprisingly, the Turkish historians have a different opinion. Some maintain that his execution was intended not so much to punish a traitor but to deter European powers from inciting Orthodox Christians to rebellion.[114] Most Turkish historians are convinced that Gregory V was indeed the mastermind behind the Greek Uprising and even confessed his guilt in writing to the investigators. That is why he fully deserved to be hanged from the gate of the Patriarchate in his liturgical vestments on Easter Sunday of 1821. His body was dragged along the streets, mutilated, and thrown into the Golden Horn harbor to be picked up by a Greek ship bound for the Russian port of Odessa.[115] The main gate of the Patriarchate of Constantinople has been shut and locked to commemorate the hanging of Gregory V on Easter Sunday of 1821 as shown in Figure 1.4.

Things could have been worse—Mahmud II's initial reaction to the news of the Greek Uprising was to order the extermination of all Orthodox Christians. He quickly changed his mind and mercifully decided to bring only the ringleaders to justice. Dr. Sofuoglu argues that the atrocities committed by the Greek rebels in the Peloponnesus deserve to be called a genocide—they massacred thousands of Muslims, young and old, committing the most heinous crimes like "cutting open the bellies of pregnant Turkish women."[116]

Three years later the Ottomans proved unable to suppress the insurrection. The Greek cause found sympathy among educated Europeans—many sent donations and some restless souls such as Lord Byron went there to fight and often to die for it. Even the US government seriously considered intervening to help the Greek rebels. It took some cool heads to reject such proposals in the US Congress. For one of them, Representative John Randolph, "it was

---

112. Shparo, Olga, *Osvobozhdeniie Gretsii i Rossiia, 1821–1829* (Moscow: Mysl, 1965), p. 54.

113. Kitromilides, Paschalis, "The Ecumenical Patriarchate," in Leustean, Lucian, ed., *Orthodox Christianity and Nationalism in Nineteenth-Century Southeastern Europe* (New York: Fordham University Press, 2014), pp. 27–28.

114. Osmanagaoglu, *1862 Rum Patrikligi Nizamati*, p. 107.

115. Alkan, *Fener Rum Patrikhanesi*, p. 49; Atalay, *Fener Rum Ortodoks*, p. 10.

116. Sofuoglu, *Fener Rum Patrikhanesi*, pp. 47–51.

FIGURE I.4 The shut and locked main gate of the Patriarchate of Constantinople (personal photograph). Visitors need to use a side door.

a difficult and an invidious task to stem the torrent of public sentiment when all the generous feelings of the human heart were appealed to." He had to remind of the obvious logistical difficulties of sending supplies overseas and of the risk of war, which the heavily indebted young republic simply could not afford.[117]

Whereas Philhellenism in Western Europe and North America electrified the liberal segments of the public, in Russia the Greek cause found support among the conservatives as well. They saw in them not only the hapless descendants of Homer and Plato but fellow Orthodox Christians who had traditionally enjoyed Russian protection.[118]

Whether the Greek rebels were perceived in ethnic or religious terms, the agitation reinforced the image of Balkan coreligionists as powerless victims waiting for Russian saviors. Thus, Greece was allegorically portrayed as an

117. "John Randolph's Opposition to Daniel Webster's Resolution," January 1824, Hadzidimitriou, Constantine, ed., *"Founded on Freedom and Virtue": Documents Illustrating the Impact in the United States of the Greek War of Independence, 1821–1829* (New York and Athens: Anthony D. Caratzas, 2002), pp. 241–242.

118. Prousis, Theophilus, *Russian Society and the Greek Revolution* (DeKalb: Northern Illinois University Press, 1994), pp. 55–104.

almost naked helpless woman threatened by a heavily armed Turk.[119] In 1824, in this pro-Greek and pro-Christian environment, Alexander I of Russia was ready to depart from the legitimist principles. Shortly before his death, he proposed to create three semi-autonomous principalities out of Greek lands under the suzerainty of the Sultan.[120]

Very reluctantly, England, France, and Russia intervened essentially because of humanitarian reasons and the public outcry to prevent the total destruction of the Peloponnesus. In 1827, their joint squadrons destroyed the combined Ottoman-Egyptian navy in the Battle of Navarino. From 1828 to 1829, Russia alone waged a war with the Ottomans, but it was not a Crusade to reclaim the Byzantine Empire. Russia's much more limited goals were to reopen its vital Black Sea trade, to achieve narrowly defined territorial gains, to reassert Serbian autonomy, and to extract the same status for Greece. After Russia's victory, the other Great Powers upgraded that autonomy to independence at the London conference in 1830, creating a small Greece barely half today's size.[121]

Still, this unlikely success of Greek rebels would inspire many subsequent uprisings led by desperate conspiratorial nationalist groups without a wide social base. Their only plan and hope would be to provoke Ottoman repressions and reprisals in order to generate European public sympathy and to bring about foreign intervention. The most notable examples are the uprisings on Crete the 1860s and 1890s and in Bosnia-Herzegovina in the 1860s and 1870s, the April Uprising in Bulgaria in 1876, and the Ilinden Uprising in Macedonia in 1903.

After the volcanic eruption of the "Greek Question" was over by 1830, the Powers showed their commitment to preserving the Ottoman Empire. The reluctance of the Concert of Europe in the beginning of the whole issue proved fully justified at its end. The new Kingdom of Greece quickly became a factor of instability in the area. Even the foreign king the Great Powers imposed on Greece could not keep Greek irredentism in check—Othon I of the Catholic Bavarian dynasty was too young at first and then too eager to be a popular ruler from 1832 to 1862. Both England and Russia had to work

---

119. Dostian, Irina, *Russkaia obshchestvennaia mysl i balknaskie narody: Ot Radishcheva do Dekabristov* (Moscow: Nauka, 1980), pp. 130–131.

120. Bitis, Alexander, *Russia and the Eastern Question: Army, Government, and Society, 1815–1833* (Oxford, New York: Oxford University Press, 2006), p. 163.

121. Frary, Lucien, *Russia and Independent Greece: Politics, Religion, and Print Culture (1833–1844)* (unpublished Ph.D. dissertation, University of Minnesota, Minneapolis, 2003), pp. 38–39.

together to suppress Greece's voracious appetite for expansion into Ottoman borderlands in the 1830s and 1840s.[122]

Another reason the Russians were increasingly disappointed with Greece was its iconoclastic religious reform. Echoing Adamantios Korais' ideas, Theocletos Pharmakidis argued that Greece had won its independence not only from the Sultan but also from his henchman ensconced on the throne of the Patriarchate of Constantinople. Like Korais, Pharmakidis saw continued dependence of the Orthodox Church in Greece on the Patriarchate as an infringement of Greek sovereignty. In addition to being a stooge of Oriental despots, the Patriarchate was also a traditional channel of Russian influence. To the liberals like Pharmakidis, Russia was an embodiment of reactionary absolutist monarchism and the main pillar of post-Napoleonic Restoration.

If left unchecked, the Patriarchate could use its bishops in Greece to put all sorts of political and cultural obstacles in its path to Enlightenment. Trained at the University of Goettingen, Pharmakidis had absorbed German Protestantism and won the favor of Georg von Maurer, the regent during King Othon I's minority (1833–1835). The two men pressured the Greek bishops to sign the declaration of church independence in 1833. Greek historians often see it as the first triumph of ethnonationalism over canon law that emboldened the leaders of the nascent Bulgarian church movement.[123]

The document cited the earlier Russian precedent to establish the Holy Synod as the governing body of the Church of Greece. Although ostensibly based on the Russian model, the Greek church reform was a victory for pro-British and pro-French circles.[124] Indeed, the Russian ambassador did not attend the ceremony to celebrate the establishment of the Church of Greece and the inauguration of the Holy Synod on 27 July 1833. The main nineteenth-century Russian authority on the Church of Greece took an issue with the analogy made by Pharmakidis. The creation of the Moscow Patriarchate in 1588 was not a unilateral action but a product of negotiations with the Patriarchate of Constantinople.[125] It seemed that reborn Greece quickly forgot

---

122. Rall, Hans, "Griechenland zwischen Russland und dem ubrigen Europa: Die 'Grosse Idee' der Griechen zwischen 1847 und 1859," *Saeculum*, 18, 1–2 (1967): 169.

123. Papadopoulos, Chrysostomos, *Historia tes Ekklesias tes Hellados*. Vol. 1 (Athens: P. A. Petrakou, 1920), pp. 444–446.

124. Stamatopoulos, Dimitris, "The Orthodox Church of Greece," in Leustean, Lucian, ed., *Orthodox Christianity and Nationalism in Nineteenth-Century Southeastern Europe* (New York: Fordham University Press, 2014), pp. 34–35.

125. Kurganov, Fedor, *Ustroistvo upravleniia v Tserkvi Korolevstva Grecheskogo* (Kazan: Kazan Theological Academy Press, 1872), pp. 125, 149.

about the sacrifices Russia had made for its freedom. The perception of ingratitude would repeatedly poison Russia's relations with all Balkan Christian nation-states later in the 1800s.

The Revolution of 1843 (a military coup to be exact) would introduce the Constitution of 1843 and a change of guard at the top of the Greek ruling class. But even with that shake-up and a lot of Russian mediation, the Greek government would take nine more years to normalize the status of its church through negotiations with the Patriarchate.[126]

The more Tsar Nicholas I (1825–1855) reflected on the twin forces of nationalism and revolution in the "Greek affair," the more disgusted he was with it.[127] His own reign began with the Decembrist Revolt, whose leaders sought to abolish or limit absolute monarchy in the name of popular sovereignty. Their concept of the nation was civic and territorial although they were going to encourage ethnic and religious minorities to assimilate into the Russian culture over time.[128]

The suppression of the Decembrist Revolt had not put to rest the spirit of nationalism, which continued to stir opposition to Nicholas I's autocracy. Inspired by German Romanticism, the growing Slavophile ("Slav-loving") movement did not advocate liberal revolutions but an independent public sphere to create an authentic national culture and "a moral regeneration" of Russia. To accomplish those noble goals, they promoted "spiritual enlightenment" embodied in the Byzantine Fathers of the Orthodox Church and the pristine faith of the simple Russian folk.[129] Although they idealized the Christian character of the peasant commune among various Slavic groups, the leading Slavophiles such as Alexei Khomiakov and Ivan Kireevskii were not very interested in the Russian messianic role in the Near East or messy Balkan politics of the day.[130]

Greek and Serbian irredentist ideology and policies served as models for other Balkan nation-states that emerged from the Ottoman breakup later in

---

126. Frazee, Charles, *The Orthodox Church and Independent Greece, 1821–1852* (London: Cambridge University Press, 1969), pp. 171–195.

127. Frary, *Russia and Independent Greece*, pp. 30–32.

128. Rabow-Edling, Susanna, "The Decembrists and the Concept of a Civic Nation," *Nationalities Papers*, 35, 2 (May 2007): 374.

129. Rabow-Edling, Susanna, "The Political Significance of Cultural Nationalism: The Slavophiles and Their Notion of a Russian Enlightenment," *Nationalities Papers*, 32, 2 (June 2004): 448–449.

130. Petrovich, *The Emergence of Russian Panslavism, 1856–1870*, pp. 32–60; Stykalin, Alexander, "Russkii slavianofil serediny XIX veka o zarubezhnykh slavianakh (putevye zapiski, V. A. Panova)," *Sovetskoe Slavinovedenie*, 1 (January 1999): 94–100.

the 1800s. Like Adamantios Korais, the Greek nationalists originally focused on reviving classical Greece including its language. This cult of dead pagans was promoted in new Greece geographically limited mostly to Attica and Peloponnesus—the heart of ancient Hellas. This façade of Hellenism was no mere flight of fancy but the main strategy of proving the new state's right to exist in the eyes of Europe. Some critics, such as the German ethnographer Jakob Fallmerayer, argued that various Slavic and Turkish admixtures had so heavily contaminated the blood and the language of contemporary Greeks that they had no right to claim any direct link to Leonidas, Themistocles, Plato, Aristotle, etc. To prove Fallmerayer wrong, Greek officials, journalists, and scholars joined hands to find and invent evidence of unbroken cultural connections between ancient and modern Greeks.

To complicate those strenuous efforts, most Greeks at the time called themselves not Hellenes but *Rhomioi* or "Romans." Their self-image and worldview were rooted in a living Byzantine legacy whose ties to other Balkan peoples and Russia clashed with modern ethnocentric Greek nationalism. Bringing together the two strands of Greek culture was an urgent intellectual task and it is not fully accomplished even today.[131]

The political expression of this attempted reconciliation was the *Megale Idea* or Great Idea—the dream of restoring not the Athenian Empire of Pericles or Greater Macedonia of Alexander but actually the Byzantine Empire of Constantine and Justinian. This version of irredentism remained the main government ideology to the end of the First World War. It was formulated in 1844 among intelligentsia and bourgeois members of the bureaucracy born outside the borders of new and small Greece. For them it was a matter of job security whether all ethnic Greeks were considered as part of the nation or not. Representing the tiny Greek Kingdom as the nucleus of the future empire justified endless government expenditure with many opportunities for embezzlement. Larger landowners and traders also liked the Idea because it allowed indefinite postponement of solving the problem of inequality between rich and poor.[132] This kind of social imperialism would also inspire later irredentism of other Balkan nation-states.

In addition to social tensions, the Greek political system was also in turmoil. England, France, and Russia imposed a monarchy on the newborn state and picked a king they could agree on. It was the Bavarian prince Otto who

---

131. Herzfeld, Michael, *Ours Once More: Folklore, Ideology, and the Making of Modern Greece* (New York: Pella, 1986), pp. 24–52.

132. Andreopoulos, George, "State and Irredentism: Some Reflexions on the Case of Greece," *Historical Journal*, 24, 4 (December 1981): 953.

brought a lot of German advisers and mercenaries to help him plant the seeds of European civilization on the rough stones of Attica and the Peloponnesus. The military coup of 1843 forced him to send most of the foreigners out and to share power with the Greek elites represented by government officials and members of parliament.[133]

The mainstream (which meant censored) Russian press at the time had little faith in the native ability to develop effective modern institutions in Greece.[134] As in regard to Serbia and later Balkan nation-states, there were good reasons for such doubts. Throughout the 1800s, Greece consistently failed the Weberian test of any real government—achieving the monopoly on the legitimate use of violence. The Greek authorities did not have the means to disarm and to disband brigand bands. Instead, they had to include them into armed forces as clients into patronage networks and to pay them for protection against themselves.[135] The bandits were also the main agents of the Great Idea occasionally sent into neighboring Ottoman areas to foment rebellion there. In addition to keeping away some troublesome elements, this strategy provided the Greek leadership with a degree of deniability, thereby avoiding the risk of an open conflict with the Sultan as well as of European economic and political sanctions.[136]

At the same time, the Ottoman Empire was not doing much better than Greece and was quickly earning the later title of the "Sick Man of Europe." Emboldened by his destruction of Ali Pasha of Yannina in 1822 and of the Janissary Corps in 1826, Sultan Mahmud II unsuccessfully tried to discipline another provincial feudal lord, Mehmet Ali of Egypt. Instead, the Egyptian army overran Syria, defeated an Ottoman army, and advanced to Istanbul. Mahmud II concluded a defensive alliance with Russia. Tsar Nicholas I landed a large force for the defense of the capital and deterred the imminent Egyptian takeover.[137] In 1839, the Ottoman forces tried to recapture Syria but

133. Frary, Lucien, *Russia and Independent Greece: Politics, Religion, and Print Culture (1833–1844)* (unpublished Ph.D. dissertation, Minneapolis: University of Minnesota, 2003), 293–294.

134. Theodorou, Theodoros, "E Rosia kai e epanstase tes 3es Septemvriou 1843," *Valkanika Symmeikta*, 4 (1992): 89.

135. Batalas, Achilles, "Send a Thief to Catch a Thief: State-Building and Employment of Irregular Armed Forces in Mid-Nineteenth Century Greece," in Davis, Diane, and Pereira, Anthony, *Irregular Armed Forces and Their Role in Politics and State-Formation* (Cambridge: Cambridge University Press, 2003), p. 150.

136. Koliopoulos, John, "Brigandage and Irredentism in Nineteenth Century Greece," *European History Quarterly*, 19, 2 (1989): 193–228.

137. Georgiev, Vladimir, Kiniapina, Nina et al., eds., *Vostochnyi vopros vo vneshnei politike Rossii, konets XVIII—nachalo XX vekov* (Moscow: Nauka, 1978), pp. 119.

lost disastrously both on land and at sea, which may have precipitated the death of Sultan Mahmud II several days later. The European powers again saved the empire when English and Austrian naval squadrons forced the Egyptians to pull back home.

In exchange for this crucial assistance in 1839, the Western powers, especially England, pressured the new sixteen-year-old Sultan Abdulmecid I and the small group of reformist bureaucrats to issue the Gulhane Edict introducing the long period of secularizing reforms known as Tanzimat. It continued one way or another until the collapse of the Ottoman Empire in 1918. The goal was to strengthen the empire internally by increasing administrative efficiency and defusing the explosiveness of age-old religious divisions inherent in any Islamic bifurcated state. The Ottoman central government highly publicized its mostly bona fide efforts to promote respect for life, property, and equality of all subjects, especially in the areas where European consuls were stationed.[138]

But local Muslims often reacted angrily to the growing erosion of their traditionally privileged status and increasing interference of outside powers on behalf of Ottoman Christians after 1839. Making a virtue out of necessity, the Sublime Porte reminded their population and foreign observers of traditional Ottoman benevolence and tolerance toward non-Muslims going back to the conquest of Constantinople in 1453. But the authorities did not get too upset when somebody (often Christian girls) disappeared after refusing to embrace Islam or going back on conversions made under duress.[139]

Another reason Ottoman reformers emphasized their continued commitment to ancient autonomy of non-Muslim groups was to put to rest the concerns of Christian prelates. If everyone was to be equal, then the Christian clergy would have to share with laity their control of tax collection, allocation of resources, adjudication of disputes, and family law. On the other hand, although all non-Muslims were inferior to Muslims, the Orthodox *millet* was considered more prestigious than the Armenian and Jewish *millets* in the Ottoman pecking order.[140]

Many Christians also preferred to continue to pay extra taxes now rationalized as conscription exemption fee rather than to join the army ranks with little or no opportunity for promotion. Muslims would have liked Christians

---

138. Deringil, Selim, "'There Is No Compulsion in Religion': Conversion and Apostasy in the Late Ottoman Empire," *Comparative Studies in Society and History*, 42, 3 (July 2000): 559.

139. Ibid., pp. 565–568.

140. Osmanagaoglu, *1862 Rum Patrikligi Nizamati*, p. 115.

to bear the burden of the military service but could not accept the possibility of serving under "infidel" officers. The Ottoman reformers also misjudged the often irrational appeal of nationalism. Many of its passionate Greek and Serbian followers wanted no equality with Muslims but union with emerging Serbia and Greece.[141]

Fortunately for the Sublime Porte, the majority of Ottoman Christians were illiterate peasants and as such unable to imagine that kind of modern community.[142] They were initially excited about the reforms. When they rebelled in the Tanzimat period, as under the earlier mob rule of the likes of Pasvanoglu, they did it because they could no longer accept as normal the abuses of local administrators and landlords. For instance, before 1839 the government would sell the right to collect most taxes to the so-called tax farmers. Most premodern empires including Ancient Rome found them preferable to much costlier centralized revenue services. Their right was limited to one year, which tended to increase their greed, making up for their initial investment without much concern for the economic impact of their exactions on the area. No wonder such tax collectors were so hated in the New Testament. They would greatly overvalue the property of people liable to taxation based on the arbitrary unwritten assessment. Then they would squeeze as much as they could from illiterate farmers who would have no record to protest against the unfair rates. The Gulhane Edict replaced tax-farming with a single tax to be collected by a special group of officials.[143]

Amazingly, contrary to the Sultan's decree, this new equivalent of the Internal Revenue Service continued to function alongside the tax farmers. In 1840, in the district of Nish, which is in today's Serbia, local mostly Christian peasants asked the governor for a payment extension because they were faced with overwhelming and confusing tax burdens. He granted it but to encourage them to pay taxes sooner, he had many army units quartered in the villages. The soldiers, all of whom were Muslims, would demand not just food and drink but also women. The governor himself behaved no better and ignored complaints about looting and rape. In April of 1840, several communities revolted with few arms and no chances for success. Yet, the governor

---

141. Davison, Roderic, "Turkish Attitudes Concerning Christian-Muslim Equality in the Nineteenth Century," *American Historical Review*, 59, 4 (July 1954): 853–854.

142. On the importance of literacy for nationalism see Anderson, Benedict, *Imagined Communities: Reflections on the Origins and Spread of Nationalism* (London: Verso, 1991); Gellner, Ernest, *Nations and Nationalism* (Ithaca: Cornell University Press, 1983); Weber, Eugen, *Peasants into Frenchmen: Modernization of Rural France, 1870–1914* (Stanford: Stanford University Press, 1976).

143. Davison, *The Reform in the Ottoman Empire*, p. 40.

called in the notorious Albanian irregulars to help his troops, which led to dozens of burned villages and thousands of refugees fleeing into the autonomous Serbian Principality.[144]

The European powers were not interested in taking advantage of this situation because it could have led to a large-scale uprising with costly international involvement as in Greece. They actually tried to help the Sublime Porte get objective information about what had happened. After exchanging confidential statements to that effect, the French and Russian foreign ministries sent special envoys into Nish, whose reports confirmed the local roots of the insurrection, the main goal of which was to draw attention to the plight of the Christian villagers.[145]

In the decade between 1840 and 1850, the Ottoman authorities sponsored a series of commissions and set up mixed provincial councils of local Muslim and non-Muslim notables to assist the governors. Usually, Muslim notables were drawn from among substantial landowners and non-Muslim members were Christian prelates. The former were usually able to browbeat and overawe the latter. This reform did not decrease peasant discontent, with its unclear tax assessment methods and tax collectors, judges, and police who were apparently able to ignore or bribe the council most of the time. It largely left unregulated another huge source of tension arising from the relationship between mostly Muslim landlords and their often Christian tenants. These problems were not new, but the Tanzimat reforms created higher expectations among the farmers, leading to a sense of "relative deprivation" we discussed earlier. They also appealed to the Serbian and Russian governments but were told to turn to their legitimate ruler. Some communities again organized a rising larger in scale than in 1840 but still easily suppressed within ten days in June 1850.[146]

In contrast to the previous Nish Uprising, the authorities moved beyond suppression into negotiations with the affected communities in the Vidin area. Their delegates went to Istanbul several times to have talks with the central government representatives from 1850 to 1852. For fear of provoking more revolts in the strategic borderland, the Sublime Porte transferred most of the land in the area from abusive Muslim landowners to Christian tenants for compensation in the form of pensions. The peasants received titles to their

---

144. Pinson, Mark, "Ottoman Bulgaria in the First Tanzimat Period: The Revolts in Nish (1840) and Vidin (1850)," *Middle Eastern Studies*, 11 (May 1975): 105–108.

145. Ibid., pp. 111–113.

146. Ibid., pp. 113–119.

plots, albeit often reduced in size, on the condition of paying redemption payments to the Treasury. The taxation was also made somewhat clearer. The case was a victory for Tanzimat because non-Muslims received clear title to land but the amount of pressure involved did not augur well for the general success of the reforms.[147]

Other efforts to improve provincial administration led nowhere. Between the two uprisings, in 1845, the Porte tried to give a boost to flagging Tanzimat reforms and called an ad hoc gathering of delegates elected from among local notables who already served as members of provincial councils. They were supposed to consult the Porte on the most pressing issues. In the spirit of Ottoman equality, each province sent one Muslim and one Christian representative. This government initiative triggered something like the earliest albeit abortive Bulgarian national movement.

Its most charismatic personality was a certain Neofit Bozveli, who was touring Bulgarian towns and villages to encourage craft and merchant guilds to formulate an agenda for their delegates. He clearly walked in the footsteps of Father Paisii, the pioneer of Bulgarian nationalism in the late 1700s. He also began his career as a Hilandar monk but came down from Holy Mount Athos to actually make a difference in the world. Frustrated in his attempt to become a bishop of Turnovo, he turned into a full-time political organizer.[148]

Neofit was trying to reach out to the same social groups that served as the basis of all nationalist movements in late-nineteenth-century Europe. They were uncomfortably positioned between "people of manual toil" and upper- or upper-middle-class superiors. Greek business developed from the late 1700s and after the Kuchuk Kaynarji Treaty of 1774 effectively became the mainstay of Ottoman bourgeoisie, which reduced the economic and political power of Bulgarian traders and guild-masters. Wealthier Jews in Central and Eastern Europe played a similar role for resentful native lower middle classes. As for lay or clerical intelligentsia in the Ottoman Empire and elsewhere, "the social classes which stood or fell by the official use of the written vernacular were the socially modest but educated middle strata, which included those who acquired lower middle class status precisely by virtue of occupying non-manual jobs that required schooling."[149]

---

147. Ibid., p. 129.

148. Mazhdrakova-Chavdarova, Ogniana, "Bulgarskoto natsionalno predstavitelstvo—idei i opiti za suzdavaneto my (40-te–60-te godini na XIX vek)," *Istoricheskii Pregled*, 49, 2 (1993): 11.

149. Hobsbawm, Eric, *Nations and Nationalism since 1780: Programme, Myth, Reality* (Cambridge: Cambridge University Press, 1990), p. 117.

Although most Bulgarian merchants and guild-masters still deferred politically and culturally to their senior Greek partners, some began to chafe under their domination. Instead of sending their children to Greek-language schools, they began to sponsor advanced Bulgarian schools in the 1830s. The connections to Bulgarian immigrant communities in Russia served as an alternative source of educational models and of Slavic pride. From the 1840s, the Russian government also began to provide more and more scholarships for Bulgarian students to study at Russian seminaries and universities. Even Western influence often reached Bulgaria through Russia. Protestant bible societies were allowed to work with the Russian church leaders on the modern Russian translation of the Scriptures. As an outgrowth of that project, American missionaries made contacts with some Greek and Bulgarian clerics to publish the first modern translation of the New Testament into Bulgarian in 1840.[150]

Several Bulgarian delegates traveled through this changing cultural and social landscape to arrive in Istanbul in 1845. They petitioned the Sublime Porte to establish an office of four permanent representatives of Bulgarian lands to lobby for their interests in the imperial capital on the existing model of a few Aegean islands and the vassal Serbian Principality. This new body would help the central government deal with the power abuses of both Muslim governors and Greek bishops in the Balkan areas. Nothing came out of it because there was not enough pressure from below. Most leading Bulgarian notables were culturally, socially, and politically closer to the Ottoman Greek elites or more inclined to echo their Muslim counterparts. Even more importantly, the new ethnic rationale clashed with the still theocratic logic of Ottoman institutions—at that time the Porte was not interested in bypassing the Patriarchate of Constantinople. Bulgarian nationalist activists also failed to win the backing of the Russian embassy for similar reasons.[151]

The degree of Russia's reliance on the Patriarchate is clear from the virtual absence of Russian consuls in most interior Ottoman provinces. For Bosnia-Herzegovina, for example, the closest Russian diplomatic post was on the other side of the border—in Belgrade or Vienna. Thus, local Christians begged the priest of the Russian Embassy in Vienna to help open Russian consulates in Sarajevo and Mostar to check the abuses of both the Ottoman governor and the Greek bishops.

---

150. Clarke, James, *Bible Societies, American Missionaries & the National Revival of Bulgaria* (New York: Arno Press and New York Times, 1971).

151. Mazhdrakova-Chavdarova, "Bulgarskoto," pp. 12–17.

They even asked to forward their request to the Russian Holy Synod so that it could mediate for them and have the Patriarchate of Constantinople remove Bishop Iosif of Mostar. Their dearest wish was to replace him either with the popular local ethnically Serb priest Ioannikii Pamuchina or to reappoint the former ethnically Bulgarian bishop Avksentii Petrovich. If the first two choices were impossible, "then they asked to consecrate some Serb or Bulgarian but by no means a Greek."[152] This case is a good example of the widespread discontent with Greek prelates even outside Bulgarian lands in the early 1800s. It also demonstrates a sense of Slavic solidarity among Serbs, Bulgarians, and local Russian agents.

However, the Bulgarian movement even at this early stage did benefit from the Ottoman reforms. In 1849, they were able to obtain a permission of the Porte and of the Patriarchate to build a church, which would use Slavonic liturgy to serve the needs of the growing Bulgarian immigrant community in Constantinople. That document referred to it as *Bulgar milleti*. It was the first time that the term "Bulgarian nation" was used in official Ottoman language, although this recognition did not extend beyond the walls of that one church. Its priest was given the rank of a titular bishop and the church became an informal national center.[153] The new church, appropriately named after St. Stefan, was itself consecrated in the especially remodeled home of its earthly patron within walking distance of the Patriarchate on the bank of the Golden Horn harbor.[154]

The generous sponsor was none other but the remarkable Stefan Vogoridi (Istefanaki Bey)—one of the few token Christians in the Ottoman reformist officialdom at the time. Even more uncommon was his ethnically Bulgarian background, albeit somewhat obscured by his thoroughly Greek education and Phanariote connections. He started his career in the Foreign Ministry and then as the governor of vassal Moldavia in the 1820s and of the autonomous island of Samos from 1833 to 1852.[155]

He governed Samos through deputies to the growing dissatisfaction of its inhabitants and spent most of the time in the capital as a member of various

152. Priest Mikhail Raevskii to Over-Procurator of the Holy Synod N. A. Protasov, 16/28 October 1850, Pisarev, Iurii, and Ekmechich, Milorad, eds., *Osvoboditelnaia borba narodov Bosnii i Gertsegoviny i Rossiia, 1850–1864* (Moscow: Nauka, 1984), p. 11.

153. Nikov, Putar, *Vuzrazhdenie na bulgarskii narod: Tsurkovno-natsionalno borbi i postizhenia* (Sofia: Nauka i Izkustvo, 1971), pp. 55–56.

154. Mazhdrakova, "Bulgarskoto," pp. 23–24.

155. More on Stefan Vogoridi see Philiou, Christine, *Biography of an Empire: Governing Ottomans in an Age of Revolution* (Berkeley and Los Angeles: University of California Press, 2010).

committees tasked with promoting the Tanzimat. His prominent role in the Porte and in influential Christian circles around the Patriarchate must have nurtured his ambition. In his own time and later in the nineteenth century, it became commonplace to blame Stefan Vogoridi as the principal instigator of the Bulgarian Church Question. Around 1848, he may have nurtured the dream of becoming the Prince of the Bulgars as Milan Obrenovich had done in vassal Serbia.[156] But any hopes for a national Bulgarian representation on the imperial level had to be put on hold by the Crimean War (1853–1856).

Conclusion

Both before and after its fall in 1453, the Second Rome served as a cultural and political magnet for both Kievan Rus and Muscovite Russia. Since the Ottoman conquest of Constantinople in 1453, Moscow's rulers increasingly made implicit and explicit claims on their Byzantine inheritance based on their own growing sense of self-importance of being the sole remaining independent Orthodox power and on the unending flood of Ottoman Christian appeals for assistance. At first expressed on the symbolic level, from the late 1600s, those irredentist claims took on geopolitical significance as Russia was bringing about the "reunification" with Ukraine and with much of the Black Sea coast.

The leadership of the Patriarchate of Constantinople was ethnically Greek or Hellenized in the Eastern Roman tradition. The Islamic theocratic structure further muted ethnic distinctions among Balkan and Middle Eastern Christians by making the religious identity the most relevant one of all. The Age of Enlightenment politicized the concept of ethnicity but this process affected Europe unevenly. The peasant majority would take a century or more than urban upper and middle classes to turn into Frenchmen, Greeks, or Russians. For ideological and political considerations, the Patriarchate of Constantinople actively opposed nationalism. In this context, it made a good deal of sense for Russian diplomats to continue to rely on all Ottoman Christians as their clientele in the Near East. This approach was also in tune with Russia's traditional flattering self-image as powerful sponsors and noble protectors of their downtrodden coreligionists.

In the 1700s, Romanov Russia and Habsburg Austria came close to partitioning the domains of the Sultan, at least in Europe, but the havoc of the Revolutionary and Napoleonic Wars exposed the danger of such self-aggrandizing policy. Instead of helping themselves to parts of the crumbling

---

156. Gedeon, ed., *Engrafa*, p. LXXV.

Ottoman Empire, after 1815, Europe's Great Powers sought to preserve it to avoid having to fight over it. The unplanned emergence and lackluster performance of two new tiny Balkan Christian nation-states also affirmed the policy of the preservation of the status quo in the Near East. Before 1853, Serbia and especially Greece were struggling to survive and seemed to be the sources of regional instability rather than the self-styled beacons of Western civilization. In 1839, the Great Powers also imposed ambitious secularizing and modernizing reforms on the Ottomans to stabilize their domestic situation and to create new opportunities for local Christians to improve their status.

On one hand, the resulting higher expectations led to peasant rebellions around Nish and Vidin in 1840 and 1850 because they created the perception of relative deprivation when local abuses were no longer seen as normal. On the other hand, the concept of equality of all Ottoman subjects encouraged the emergence of a small Bulgarian nationalist movement. Their demands for some sort of institutional representation based on their ethnicity did not make much sense in the existing Ottoman framework that recognized only religious communities and now promised them equal status as part of the Tanzimat. Since the Bulgarian movement in the 1840s was not strong enough to make a difference, Russian policymakers did not have much incentive to switch their traditional support of the Patriarchate to the leaders of one ethnic group with dubious credentials. Culturally, pro-Bulgarian policy would also go against the self-image of Moscow as the Third Rome.

2

Building an Ottoman Civic Nation

SECULARIZATION AND ETHNICIZATION OF CHRISTIAN
MINORITY INSTITUTIONS (1853–1860)

THE LOOMING UNIFICATION and independence of Moldavia and Wallachia "will be a breach of Turkey's territorial integrity. This breach will inevitably open the way for other parts to secede—Serbia, Bulgaria, Bosnia, Montenegro, and Albania etc. etc. At the very least, this act will produce turmoil." What the Ottoman Christian statesman Stefan Vogoridi foresaw in 1855 in a letter to his son-in-law would come to pass within two decades following the Crimean War.[1]

Although the Ottoman Empire was on the winning side, the new round of Westernization brought by that war shook the very foundations of the Islamic polity. While the war was still raging, it accelerated the growth of both civic and, more dangerously, ethnic forms of nationalism. Continued modernization of the Ottoman Empire would encourage a stronger Bulgarian nationalist movement but would also make it possible to develop power-sharing mechanisms to contain ethnonationalism. Russia's post–Crimean War Great Reforms centered on the abolition of serfdom and paved the way for the rise of all sorts of interest groups including Pan-Slavs. Thus, both traditional empires had to reconcile dynastic and religious institutions with new secular and ethnocentric tendencies.

The causes and effects of the Crimean War are still debated in the scholarly and popular literature.[2] Many scholars emphasize traditional Russian

---

1. Gennadius Library (Athens), file 23, Stefan Vogoridi to Constantine Mousouros, 9/21 June 1855, p. 43g.

2. A very helpful recent review is Mara Kozelsky's "Crimean War, 1853–1856," *Kritika*, 13, 4 (Fall 2012): 903–917; a few representative titles include Royle, Trevor, *Crimea: The Great*

expansionism toward the Middle East and the concerns it raised in France and England.[3] Although writing in the Cold War era, some put a larger share of responsibility on the last two powers, which wanted to force a showdown with Russia and for reasons of prestige brushed aside peace initiatives until 1855–1856.[4] The most recent study reminded of Russia's religious motivation for the war and Tsar Nicholas I's personal desire to finally redeem or at least empower Ottoman Christians.[5]

That is how the war was justified to the Russian population at the time but it was the expectation of material benefits, especially personal freedom, rather than the idea of the Crusade that attracted volunteers among the serfs.[6] On the eve of the Crimean War, most segments of the educated society absorbed traditional Russian messianism and religious irredentism toward the Christian East. Even socialists like Alexander Herzen were not immune to it. Herzen can hardly be suspected of being a Russian imperialist. He dedicated his life to overthrowing the Romanovs and other European dynasties to build on the ruins of European monarchies a loose federation where self-governing communes of producers would realize the dream of a society free from class exploitation and government oppression. And yet in 1851 he confidently discerned the contours of the imminent solution of the Eastern Question in the spirit of Catherine the Great's "Greek Project."

> Greek Orthodoxy created a close bond between Russia and Constantinople, strengthened the natural gravitation of Russian Slavs to that city, and prepared with its spiritual conquest the future conquest of the Eastern Empire by the only powerful nation professing Greek Orthodoxy ...

Crimean War, 1854–1856 (New York: Palgrave Macmillan, 2004); Ponting, Clive, *The Truth behind the Myth* (London: Pimlico, 2005); Edgerton, Robert, *Death or Glory: The Legacy of the Crimean War* (Boulder: Westview Press, 1999); Lambert, Andrew, *British Grand Strategy Against Russia, 1853–1856* (Manchester: Manchester University Press, 1990); Conacher, J. B., *The Crimea: 1855–1856: Problems of War and Peace* (New York: St. Martin's, 1988); Palmer, Alan, *The Banner of Battle: The Story of the Crimean War* (New York: St. Martin's, 1987); Temperley, Harold, *England and the Near East: The Crimea* (London, New York, Toronto: Longmans, Green and Co, 1936).

3. Baumgart, Winfried, *The Crimean War, 1853–1856* (London and New York: Arnold and Oxford University Press, 1999).

4. Curtiss, John Shelton, *Russia's Crimean War, 1853–1856* (Durham: Duke University Press, 1979); Rich, Norman, *Why the Crimean War? A Cautionary Tale* (Hanover: University Press of New England, 1985).

5. Figes, Orlando, *Crimea: The Last Crusade* (New York: Metropolitan Books, 2010), p. 9.

6. Moon, David, "Russian Volunteers at the Beginning of the Crimean War," *Slavic Review*, 51, 4 (Winter 1992): 703.

Turkish domination made a positive rather than a negative contribution to the outcome we foresee. Catholic Europe would not have left the Eastern Roman Empire alone in the past four centuries. The Latins lorded it over the Eastern Empire once. They would have exiled the emperors to some place in Asia Minor and would have converted Greece to Catholicism.[7]

The Pan-Orthodox sentiment combined with earlier frustrated irredentist dreams to create a welcoming atmosphere for would-be Russian saviors in the Balkans. The tiny Greek Kingdom with overwhelming popular support prepared to join Russia in the burgeoning conflict and to expand into "unredeemed" Ottoman borderland provinces of Thessaly and Epirus. But England and France quickly nipped that bold Greek initiative in the bud by blockading Athens and even occupying its port of Piraeus. When the Russian army advanced to the Danube, many Bulgarian daredevils joined its ranks. The Greek volunteers formed a special unit fighting the Ottomans and their Western allies around Sebastopol.[8]

Some of those who did not cross the border to join the Russian army asked for money, arms, and munitions. A diverse group of Serb Orthodox clerics, city dwellers, and peasants from the Mostar and Sarajevo districts had the courage to sign that petition addressing Nicholas I "as the only ruler on Earth, the only one anointed by God." As coreligionists and coethnics (*soplemenniki*), they wanted Russian help to avenge for the humiliations they suffered at the hands of the "Turks" who robbed, killed, and raped them with impunity. But the inhuman treatment did not stop at that: "they took over all our lands, we have to work for them and render one half of the produce." The second most hated category of oppressors was the high Greek clergy, who had bought their church offices from the Patriarchate of Constantinople to extort more money from their flock. They were no shepherds but a pack of wolves: "they have no sympathy for us but instead give us up to the Turks to be tortured."[9]

As we saw in chapter 1, the growing Ottoman Christian discontent with the less-than-perfect implementation of the Tanzimat policies was also part

---

7. Herzen, Alexander, *O razvitii revolutsionnykh idei v Rossii* (St. Petersburg: Bussel, 1912 [1851]), p. 30.

8. Todorova, Maria, "The Greek Volunteers in the Crimean War," *Balkan Studies*, 25, 2 (1984): 539–563; Papadopoulos, Stefanos, "O prosanatolismos ton Ellenon pros ten Rosia kata ton Krimaiko polemo (1853–1856)," *Valkanika Symmeikta*, 3 (1989): 71–82.

9. Orthodox representatives of Bosnia-Herzegovina to Nicholas I, 17 December 1854, Pisarev, Iurii. A., and Ekmechich, Milorad, eds., *Osvoboditelnaia borba narodov Bosnii i Gertsegoviny i Rossiia, 1850–1864* (Moscow: Nauka, 1984), pp. 22–24.

of the background of the Crimean War. But the bloodiest European conflict since Napoleon was triggered by the seemingly minor dispute between a few Catholic and Greek Orthodox monks over the control of the Holy Places such as the Church of the Nativity in Bethlehem and the Holy Sepulcher in Jerusalem. That feud lingered since the Crusades, with the monks exchanging blows and occasionally even shots, but it reached a new pitch in the 1840s when two very ambitious and hot-tempered men took over as Latin and Greek Patriarchs of Jerusalem.

Another assertive individual—Louis Napoleon, the nephew of Napoleon—heavily backed the Latin friars in an effort to gain support from devout Catholics in France. He was the president of the short-lived Second Republic from 1849 and was preparing to replace it with his own dictatorship. The magic of his name and the popular discontent with the unabashedly bourgeois regime made it possible for him to launch a successful coup and to emerge as Emperor Napoleon III in 1852. Under French pressure, the Sublime Porte favored the Catholic claims, which Tsar Nicholas I saw as a challenge to the traditional Russian protection of Ottoman Christians.[10]

His special envoy, Prince Menshikov, demanded that the Porte confirm Russia's role as the protector of Sultan's Orthodox subjects. He proposed a treaty that included provisions meant to strengthen the Patriarchate of Constantinople as the firm foundation of Russian influence. The patriarchs would be elected by the synod of the archbishops based strictly on canon law without informal but frequent Ottoman interference. The process was supposed to be similar to the papal conclave. Again like the popes, the Patriarchs would not be deposed but would hold their office for life. Both measures would make the high clergy more independent of the Sublime Porte and of the influential lay circles of the Christian community. Obviously, the official recognition of such rights was more humiliating to Ottoman sovereignty than informal Russian clout that had built over time. Fearful of the growing strength of the Russian bear, France and England moved their naval squadrons to embolden the Sultan to resist. The full-scale war broke out in the summer and fall of 1853 and led to the suspension of the Concert of Europe.[11]

To reduce Russia's popularity among the largest Ottoman minority, England started pressuring the Sublime Porte to jump-start the flagging

10. Broadus, John, "The Church Conflict in Palestine: The Opening of the Holy Places Question in the Period Preceding the Crimean War," *Canadian Journal of History*, 14, 3 (December 1979): 414–416.

11. Stamatopoulos, Demetris, *Metarrythmisi kai Ekkosmikevsi: Pros Mia Anasynthesi tis Istorias tou Oikoumenikou Patriarheiou ton 19o aiona* (Athens: Aleksandreia, 2003), p. 69.

Tanzimat reforms during the Crimean War. Stefan Vogoridi willingly served as the channel of British influence inside both the Ottoman bureaucracy and the Patriarchate of Constantinople. "I can come and ask for full equality between the Christians and the Ottomans but the latter will immediately assume that I am asking for the office of the Grand Vizier and that I am driven by the English policy."[12] Vogoridi's negotiations with the "patriarchs and notables of every subject nation" also brought disappointment. They effectively sabotaged the decree of Sultan Abdul Mejid I to implement conscription among all Ottoman subjects.[13]

France, the second most important Ottoman ally, was playing a very different game behind the frontlines. Inspired by his uncle's experience in Egypt, Napoleon III sought to modernize the Orient. One of his main methods was to teach the locals how to politicize the concept of ethnicity. His Pan-Latin appeals to Romance-speaking Europeans in Italy and the Balkans flattered the sensibilities of the heavily Hellenized Christian Orthodox nobility in the autonomous Ottoman principalities of Moldavia and Wallachia.[14]

They started thinking of themselves as the descendants of the glorious Romans, the cousins and the clients of the most civilized modern Western nation. With this kind of ideological, political, and material support, they began to challenge the dominance of the Ottoman Greek prelates and to demand the creation of unified Romania. The most pressing issue was the control of rich lands willed by pious local princes to the monasteries on Mt. Athos and Greek-dominated patriarchates of Constantinople, Jerusalem, Antioch, and Alexandria. Stefan Vogoridi voiced the sentiment of the Ottoman Christian leadership arguing that those lands in fact belonged to fifteen million Ottoman Christians.[15]

Stefan was very troubled by the prospect of losing the greatest source of revenue because of French-instigated identity politics. On a positive note, he expressed confidence that other sources of funding for churches, schools, and other needs could be found. On the other hand, as a non-Muslim group, "we don't have the right to ask the Sublime Porte to cover those expenses ... the government supports countless mosques, schools, and hospitals but as

---

12. Gennadius Library (Athens), file 23, Stefan Vogoridi to Constantine Mousouros, 24 January/5 February 1854, p. 8/st.

13. Gennadius Library (Athens), file 23, Stefan Vogoridi to Constantine Mousouros, 2 May 1855, p. 36a.

14. Mange, Alyce Edythe, *The Near Eastern Policy of Emperor Napoleon III* (Westport: Greenwood Press, 1975).

15. Gennadius Library (Athens), file 23, Stefan Vogoridi to Constantine Mousouros, 25 July/6 August 1855, p. 54a.

Orthodox Christians we don't have the right to take advantage of them."[16] It is striking that as a key Tanzimat reformer, he could not even conceive of a truly unified Ottoman nation with the same benefits and responsibilities for all of the Sultan's subjects regardless of the creed.

Vogoridis was upset that the Ottoman leadership wrongly suspected the Orthodox Christian population of disloyalty during the Crimean War. They were not pro-Russian, they merely wanted to be treated with justice and fairness.[17] The growing ethnic fragmentation of the Orthodox *millet* was clear in the different reactions to the news of the fall of Sebastopol to the anti-Russian coalition troops in 1855. Stefan Vogoridi shared with his son-in-law that the Moldavians and Wallachians in Constantinople rejoiced "while the Greeks were crying." For some reason, this reaction reminded Stefan of the history of anti-Ottoman attitudes in Moldavia and Wallachia. Without the support lent by local treacherous aristocrats in 1821, the abortive Greek-led uprising there would not have had such a broad mass basis. In addition, in recent decades the Danubian Principalities had been sheltering many revolutionaries who fomented rebellions in Ottoman Bulgaria and elsewhere.[18]

The Crimean War dashed the messianic and irredentist hopes of many Orthodox Christians in Russia and the Balkans. It did not bring about the rebirth of the Byzantine Empire under a Russian prince, the removal of the crescent, and the restoration of the cross on the dome of the Hagia Sophia cathedral, or any other spectacular changes of that sort. There was indeed a lot of fighting in the Crimea but also in the Caucasus, Asia Minor, on the Danube, in the Baltic, the White Sea, and even the Pacific. The now-forgotten global war claimed more lives than the American Civil War—in both conflicts most of the losses were due to diseases such as cholera and dysentery.

Following the law of unintended consequences, the victory in the Crimean War had actually weakened the Ottoman Empire. Western racism and arrogance produced serious cracks within the anti-Russian coalition that could not be papered over by public assurances of friendship and carefully staged photographs (see Figure 2.1).

Although technically an ally of England and France, the Ottoman Empire had in fact become a European protectorate by war's end. It was bankrupted, indebted, and not even allowed to claim a war indemnity or significant territorial concessions from defeated Russia. In exchange for being admitted into

---

16. Ibid., p. 54b.

17. Ibid., 26 September/8 October 1855, pp. 71a–71b.

18. Ibid., 19/25 November 1855, pp. 82a–82b.

FIGURE 2.1 "Ismail Pasha and Mr. Thompson of the Commissariat," photographed by Robert Fenton in 1855. Library of Congress Prints and Photographs Division, Reproduction Number: LC-USZC4-9156.

the Concert of Europe, the Ottoman Empire was pressured to pledge in the peace treaty of Paris of 1856 to implement more sweeping reforms aimed to improve the status of non-Muslim subjects.[19]

Inventing Ottomanism: From a Figment of Western Imagination to a Fixation of the Ottoman Bureaucratic Mindset

Since Russia did not suffer a crushing defeat, its territorial losses were relatively light. Thus, the leaders of Bulgarian volunteers who fought in the Russian army felt that the Russian position in the coming peace negotiations in Paris would be strong enough to relieve the plight of Ottoman Christians.

---

19. Badem, Candan, *The Ottoman Crimean War, 1853–1855* (Leiden-Boston: Brill, 2010), pp. 403–404.

They begged new Tsar Alexander II "not to leave the Bulgarian people at the mercy of the enemies of Orthodoxy."[20] But to restore and enhance its prestige in the Near East, Russia needed to concentrate on overcoming economic backwardness exposed in the struggle with more industrialized France and England. This modernization effort involved enormous transformations such as the emancipation of the serfs, the abolition of social status privileges, the introduction of a citizen army based on universal conscription, elected local self-government, greater freedom of the press and associations.[21]

Russia kept the Crimea but had to give up a narrow strip of the Russo-Ottoman border where it touched the Danube. The most humiliating clause of the 1856 Treaty of Paris was the neutralization of the Black Sea, which meant that both the Ottoman Empire and Russia had to eliminate their coastal fortifications and navies there. Since the Sultan could always bring men-of-war from his Mediterranean ports, southern Russia became much more vulnerable until the abrogation of that clause by the Russian government in 1870. Russia also relinquished its monopoly claim to protect Ottoman Orthodox Christians, and the Concert of Europe as a whole assumed the responsibility for the improvement of their status. Since that issue was the ostensible cause of the Crimean War, Russia was able to publicize this European promise as its own gain in a series of pamphlets and articles in several Balkan languages.[22]

Whereas the Gulhane Edict of 1839 talked about the equality of all Ottoman subjects, the Imperial Reform Edict of 1856 (Hatti Humayun) introduced the important notion of Ottoman patriotism or Ottomanism. This concept went even further away from the Islamic bifurcated state. It was clearly an effort to create an Ottoman nation based on civic territorial secular principles of "loyalty to constitutions or political processes and institutions that bind people together despite their ethnic differences."[23] Ottomanism could be seen as an example of "classical nineteenth century liberal nationalism ... that aimed to *extend* the scale of human social, political and cultural units"[24] (emphasis in

20. The Bulgarian volunteers to Alexander II, 14 February 1856, Mazhdrakova, O., Markova, Z., Tileva, V. et al., eds., *Rusia i bulgarskato natsionalno-osvoboditelno dvizhenie, 1856–1876*, vol. 1, part 1 (Sofia: Bulgarian Academy of Sciences, 1987), pp. 29–30.

21. The literature on this subject is vast. A good introduction is Eklof, Ben, Bushnell, John et al., eds., *Russia's Great Reforms, 1855–1881* (Bloomington: Indiana University Press, 1994).

22. Ibid., E. P. Kovalevskii to A. M. Gorchakov, 26 April 1856, *Rusia i bulgarskato natsionalno-osvoboditelno dvizhenie, 1856–1876*, pp. 40–41.

23. Calhoun, Craig, *Nationalism* (Minneapolis: University of Minnesota Press, 1997), p. 48.

24. Hobsbawm, Eric, "Ethnicity & Nationalism in Europe Today," in Balakrishnan, Gopal, ed., *Mapping the Nation* (London: Verso, 1996), p. 257.

the text) as it was supposed to unite and save the Empire from religious and ethnic separatism.

Easier said than done. The notion of equality with the despised infidels seemed repellent to most common Muslims. Tanzimat's secularizing aspects were rightfully attributed to European influence and legitimately seen to threaten Islamic traditions. On the popular level and in private publications, the Christians were not accepted as Ottomans (*Osmanlis*). More often than not, in the common usage, the "Ottoman nation" was understood to refer to the Muslim majority of the Empire.[25] Although explicitly prohibited since 1856, anti-Christian slurs were widely used. The usual derogatory term for "infidel"—"*gavur*"—still survives in Turkish.

"Now we can't call a *gavur* a *gavur*," it was said sometimes bitterly, sometimes in matter-of-fact explanation that under the new dispensation the plain truth could no longer be spoken openly. Could reforms be acceptable which forbade calling a spade a spade?[26]

However, not all Muslims rejected Ottomanism. The wartime experience and the employment at the Translation Bureau of the Foreign Ministry produced a generation of Westernized Ottoman poets and writers who began to glorify territorial patriotism but also ethnic Turkish nationalism.[27] Sultan Abdul Mejid I signaled his acceptance of Western ways by moving from the fifteenth-century Top Kapi palace into the brand new Dolma Bahche Palace built on European models and loans between 1853 and 1856. While Top Kapi is a complex of several pavilions separated by walls and gardens, the Dolma Bahche is a single multistory building with a giant staircase as illustrated in Figure 2.2. Three more European-style palaces would be built shortly by the same Balyan family of Ottoman Armenian architects—Chiragan and Yildiz on the European side and Beylerbeyi on the Asian shore of the Bosphorus.[28]

The upper levels of Ottoman bureaucracy could also serve as an influential base of support for the reforms. Both because of their higher social status and because of the elements of European education, many of them did not always

---

25. Lewis, Bernard, *The Emergence of Modern Turkey*, 3d ed. (New York and Oxford: Oxford University Press: 2002), p. 336; Davison, "Turkish Attitudes," p. 861.

26. Davison, Roderic, "Turkish Attitudes Concerning Christian-Muslim Equality in the Nineteenth Century," *American Historical Review*, 59, 4 (July 1954): 859.

27. Badem, *The Ottoman Crimean War*, p. 394–398.

28. Boyar, Ebru, and Fleet, Kate, *A Social History of Ottoman Istanbul* (New York: Cambridge University Press, 2010), p. 310.

FIGURE 2.2 Dolmabahche Palace (personal photograph). Built during the Crimean War (1853–1856), the new imperial residence was supposed to prove to Europe how seriously the Sultans took Westernizing Tanzimat reforms.

share a sense of Muslim brotherhood with petty traders, craftsmen, farmers, and herders. Unlike conservative mullahs and jurists, the state reformers did not consider the Tanzimat as the gateway to the flood of alien Western imports threatening to contaminate the spiritual purity of Islam. It was perfectly legitimate to borrow from Europe what they chose to see as the product of the influence of medieval Arabic civilization. As an example of such accommodation, reformist Ottoman intellectuals and bureaucrats found (or pretended to have found) Islamic precursors to many modern Western notions including parliamentarianism in hopes of making them more palatable to themselves and the Muslim population at large.[29]

Turning the tables on Europe allowed them to take advantage of Western colonial ideology. The modernizing logic of state-centered civic Ottomanism envisaged a temporal and geographical division of imperial subjects. Those in backward and restless borderlands of the Balkans, Kurdistan, Iraq, Arabia, or Lebanon were stuck in the past and needed to be civilized by the imperial

29. Berkes, Niyazi, *The Development of Secularism in Turkey* (New York: Routledge, 1998 [1963]), pp. 262–263.

center. This view was a reflection of internalized Western Orientalism. Conscious of their religious distinction from Europe, many Ottoman re-formers strove not to reject but to update Islam in order to join the family of modern nations. This mission of spreading tolerance and modernity to all the corners of the still-vast realm gave Ottoman rule new legitimacy, which was a world away from the traditional ideology of carrying the banner of Islam.[30]

Imbued with that Western-style civilizing mission, the ruling Ottoman elites were reluctant to discover their own ethnic Turkish roots—another factor that made the success of the Ottoman civic nation more likely. The Ottomans knew that in the course of long migrations to and fro their ances-tors came to Asia Minor after defeating a Byzantine army in 1071. But they preserved no memories of kinship to Central Asia—their sense of history was largely dynastic going back to Osman, the founder of the Ottoman dynasty.

The post-Enlightenment obsession with language threatened to change that. European Turcologists, another branch of the flourishing Orientalist scholarship, had discovered the family of Turkic languages and included them together with cognate Finno-Ugric languages into the Altaic linguis-tic family. They had also unearthed and deciphered numerous old texts and inscriptions in Central Asia that testified to the great pre-Islamic history of ancient Turks.[31]

But in the mid-1800s, the news of the newly found kinsmen spanning the territory from the Pacific to Hungary was not received with enthusiasm by the Ottoman elites. When the eminent Hungarian Turcologist Arminius Vambery tried to popularize his views in Istanbul in 1856, the high society of the impe-rial capital resented being lumped together with "the Kyrgyzs and other home-less nomads of Turkistan."[32] Thus, in the mid- to late 1800s, the ruling class embraced and promoted a more or less civic and secular Ottoman identity as opposed to traditionally Muslim or narrowly ethnic Turkish loyalties.

The reforms also found a lot of support among Ottoman Christian elites, where ethnic Greeks or Hellenized non-Greeks predominated. Since the Treaty of Kuchuk Kaynarji of 1774, they began to function as Ottoman bourgeoisie and to fill more civil service posts since the beginning of the Tanzimat in 1839. They could hardly identify with the Great Idea of Greek state irredentism—its success would mean the loss of Ottoman imperial markets and bureaucratic

---

30. Makdisi, Ussama, "Ottoman Orientalism," *American Historical Review*, 107, 3 (June 2002): 780–790.

31. Landau, Jacob, *Pan-Turkism: From Irredentism to Cooperation* (Bloomington: Indiana University Press, 1995), pp. 2, 31.

32. Zarevand, *Turtsia i Panturanizm* (Paris: la Source, 1930), p. 52.

positions. Ottoman patriotism did not involve the rejection of their Greek and Orthodox culture. Far from it, the Greek bankers of Constantinople sponsored private schools and societies for the promotion of Greek letters. They would not hesitate to take advantage of laity-friendly reforms to wrest at least a share of control of the Patriarchate from the hands of the clergy.[33]

The Sublime Porte sought to co-opt influential members of minority elites not just to appease the Great Powers but also to build another pillar of the precarious new order. Stefan Vogoridi represented the Orthodox *millet* in the Supreme Council of Judicial Ordinances established in May 1856. Three other non-Muslim members (all wealthy businessmen) were also appointed to that highest body of central government to represent the Gregorian Armenians, the Armenian Catholics, and the Jews.[34]

Ottomanism, the Reform of the Patriarchate of Constantinople, and Official Russian Reactions

The new logic of individual territorial citizenship implied doing away with the legal membership in religious communities. Aware of the speed bumps that the 1839 Gulhane Decree had to travel through, the Porte was not quite ready to abolish in one stroke all legal implications of one's creed. Instead, it committed itself to gradually creating a system of civil courts as a parallel to sharia and other religious courts. As another step in that direction, in Article 3 of the 1856 Hatti Humayun Reform Edict, the Ottoman government envisioned the reform of non-Muslim *millets* (the Christian Orthodox or *Rum milleti*, the Gregorian Armenian, and the Jewish *millets*) to increase the power of the lay element over clergy in the running of community institutions. The goal was to create a model for a similar transformation of the Islamic religious establishment itself, eventually setting the stage for the complete separation of church and mosque from state. Another objective was to weaken Russian influence on Ottoman Christians, traditionally channeled through high Orthodox clergy as was dramatically demonstrated in the buildup to the Crimean War.[35]

It is no wonder then that it was none other than the British, French, and Austrian ambassadors who suggested the wording of Article 3. On the surface, the empowerment of the laity was justified by the need to fight corruption

---

33. Stamatopoulos, *Metarrythmisi kai Ekkosmikevsi*, pp. 218–219.

34. Davison, *Reform in the Ottoman Empire*, p. 93.

35. Stamatopoulos, *Metarrythmisi*, pp. 70–71.

in the Patriarchate and to put clergy on salary.[36] Russian diplomats indeed had always worked with the Patriarch and key prelates, assuming they truly represented and effectively controlled the Orthodox population of the Sultan. But several developments gradually changed this picture and made Russian agents more supportive of the Ottoman secularization of the *millets* as part of the Tanzimat.

In 1856, the Russian Foreign Ministry resumed diplomatic relations with the Ottoman Empire which had been severed by the Crimean War (1853–1856), drastically expanded its consular network, and instructed the departing Ambassador Butenev to continue to "support the Church and Christian populations" in the face of Islamic oppression and of the encroachments of Western religious proselytizing.[37] This central task was no different from the traditional responsibilities of Russian diplomats in the Christian East. Another visible symbol of continuity was the situation of two monks from the famous Bulgarian Rila monastery. They got permission to come to Russia to collect alms in 1852, stayed there during the Crimean War, and in 1856 were allowed to spend one more year traveling outside St. Petersburg not because they were Slavic cousins but because they were brothers in Christ.[38]

But at the same time, the Russian embassy could not ignore the secularizing thrust of the declared Hatti Humayun, which privileged the lay element. Plus, the increasing number of complaints from Slavic areas about various abuses of ethnically Greek bishops challenged the longstanding Russian assumption about the ability of the Patriarchate in its present form to run the Orthodox *millet* smoothly. Many of those complaints were forwarded by Naiden Gerov, the Bulgarian-born Russian consul in Philippoupolis (Plovdiv), who noted that they truly reflected "the voice of the whole Bulgarian nation looking to co-ethnic Russia and expecting an improvement of their lot from its representative in Constantinople."[39]

The growing Bulgarian national movement approached not just Russian agents but also the Porte. Taking advantage of the promise of reforms, in the

---

36. Osmanagaoglu, *1862 Rum Patrikligi Nizamati*, p. 129.

37. Foreign Ministry's Instruction to Ambassador A. P. Butenev, 14 July 1856, *Rusia i bulgarskato natsionalno-osvoboditelno dvizhenie, 1856–1876*, vol. 1, part 1, Mazhdrakova, O., Markova, Z., Tileva, V. et al., eds. (Sofia: Bulgarian Academy of Sciences, 1987), pp. 52–56.

38. Vinogradov, Secretary at the Holy Synod, 21 June 1856, *Rusia i bulgarskoto natsionalno-osvoboditelno dvizhenie*, pp. 46–47.

39. Ibid., N. Gerov to A. Butenev, 9 July 1856, *Rusia i bulgarskoto natsionalno-osvoboditelno dvizhenie*, p. 46.

spring of 1856, they asked for the same status as the "Greeks"—that of an independent religious community. The detailed petition was prepared and submitted by the Bulgarian delegates, most of whom were resident in the capital but some of whom came from the provinces. All in all, they claimed to speak on behalf of 6,400,000 Bulgarians. Candidly, with no census data and public opinion polls, the claim to represent all those masses of people did not hold ground, but the Bulgarian national movement at this time was clearly developing in major cities at the very least. The Ottoman government left that petition without any official response, forcing the Bulgarians to deal with the Patriarchate directly.[40] That decision made it clear that the Sublime Porte was not yet ready to bypass autonomous minority institutions in the name of greater centralization, although the Bulgarian pleas echoed the pro-laity rhetoric of the post-1856 round of the Tanzimat reforms.

In his turn, Patriarch Cyril VII flatly refused to meet any Bulgarian demands, which alarmed the Russian Foreign Ministry. It tasked two ethnic Bulgarians on its staff to prepare some memos exploring the question of Bulgarian historical rights to have an autocephalous church. Foreign Minister Alexander Gorchakov did not support the independence of a Bulgarian church, but he instructed Ambassador Butenev to convince the Patriarch to defuse the tension by granting Slavonic liturgy and ethnically Bulgarian bishops in predominantly Bulgarian areas. He saw those concessions as the only way to keep the Bulgarians within the Patriarchate given the new opportunities for Ottoman Christian laity.[41]

The Patriarchate responded by trying to impress on its bishops the need for accommodation with ethnic diversity. Archbishop of Sarajevo Dionisii learned the text of Slavonic liturgy by heart to be closer to his flock. It was no small feat for a sixty-five-year-old Greek prelate. He would have been more popular had it not been for his extreme fear of local Muslims and Ottoman authorities. Agathangelos, the younger Bishop of Zvornik, was truly loved by his Herzegovinian parishioners. He mastered the Serbian language and tirelessly fulfilled his pastoral duties. "The Bosnian people are unanimously saying that their land has not seen such a prelate in a long time."[42] Balkan

40. Mazhdrakova-Chavdarova, Ogniana, "Bulgarskoto natsionalno predstavitelstvo—idei i opiti za suzdavaneto my (40-te–60-te godini na XIX vek)," *Istoricheskii Pregled*, 49, 4 (1993): 23–25.

41. E. Kovalevskii to A. Butenev, 18 August 1856, *Rusia i bulgarskoto natsionalno-osvoboditelno dvizhenie*, p. 65.

42. A. F. Gilderding to E. P. Kovalevskii, 16/28 June 1857, *Osvoboditelnaia borba narodov Bosnii i Gertsegoviny i Rossiia, 1850–1864*, pp. 52–53.

and Turkish historiography usually ignores this trend, arguing that the Patriarchate never ceased its efforts to turn the Slavs into the Greeks.[43]

The initial reaction to the post-1856 round of the Bulgarian Church Question would be typical of Russian diplomats later on. The Russian policy line would be to mediate between two sides groping toward an ever-elusive compromise. Indeed, Gorchakov's tone was very mild compared to the viciously anti-Greek language of the Bulgarian memos. By absorbing the Bulgarian Church in the 1760s and by stripping the Bulgarians of their civil rights, the Phanariotes allegedly became willing collaborators of "Turkish" conquerors in the task of obliterating any vestige of independence of defeated Balkan nations. They were tempted by the prospect of greater power and revenue. They also tried to make the false name of *Rum* a reality by turning Bulgarians into Greeks. Only the 1856 Hatti Humayun enabled the Bulgarians to remind everyone of their Slavic identity distinct from *Rum*.[44]

It was the voice of the growing national movement that demanded independent church institutions to develop in the still-theocratic Islamic structure of the Ottoman Empire. Although this statement emphasized peaceful pursuit of its legitimate goals via legal channels, the narrative had a potential to provoke an ethnic conflict. Its main theme is "the fear of extinction," which could justify violence against the Greeks because they supposedly tried to forcibly assimilate the Bulgarians.[45]

Although many Russian consuls had Pan-Slav sympathies, they considered as exaggerated the demands for a separate Bulgarian hierarchy unauthorized by the Ecumenical Patriarchate.[46] In this post-Crimean context, the consuls were instructed to "find the ways to stop the quarrel over national differences (*raznoplemennost*) that arose among our coreligionists." The Russian representatives would do their best to restrain the Bulgarians from demonizing the Greeks as a whole and would also persuade "the Greek pastors of the Church" to grant Slavonic liturgy and Bulgarian-language instruction at parish schools. Mutual concessions would make the Bulgarians immune against "the encroachments of Western missionaries."[47]

---

43. Osmanagaoglu, *1862 Rum Patrikligi Nizamati*, 186.

44. Russian Imperial Foreign Policy Archive (AVPRI), fond 161/3, collection 233, part I, K. Petkovich, "Drevnie prava bolgarskoi tserkvi", pp. 40b–70b.

45. Kaufman, Stuart, *Modern Hatreds: The Symbolic Politics of Ethnic War* (Ithaca: Cornell University Press, 2001), pp. 31–32.

46. N. Mukhin to the Foreign Ministry, 24 September 1856, *Rusia i bulgarskoto natsionalno osvoboditelno dvizhenie*, p. 71.

47. Foreign Ministry to N. D. Stupin, the consul in Adrianople, 26 July 1856, ibid., p. 62.

Thus, in the instructions of the Russian Foreign Ministry, there was an attempt to take into account ethnic distinctions, but religion was still stronger on the cognitive map of Russian elites. Clearly, this Pan-Orthodox policy had the political goal—to preserve Russia's traditional clientele in the area. In the new post-1856 environment, the Russian leadership always invoked the duty of protecting Ottoman Christians rather than the Slavs in the attempts to bring the pressure of the other European Great Powers to bear collectively on the Sultan's government.[48]

But the obsession with the threat of "Rome" went beyond cool political calculations and reflected the religious and dynastic justification of power in Russia proper. More often than not, Russian policy formulations expressed the fear of the danger posed by the Catholic/Protestant Other to the "Orthodox world" rather than by the concern over losing to individual Western powers.

The Russian diplomats in the Christian East worked closely with the representatives of the Russian Church both on the staff of all embassies and consulates and back in St. Petersburg and Moscow. Although both the Foreign Ministry and the Holy Synod were part of the imperial government, their agendas were different because of predictable bureaucratic interbranch strife and the natural differences between lay and clerical perspectives.

The priests in the diplomatic service reported directly to the Holy Synod and received their instructions from it. Thus, Archimandrite Antonin (Kapustin), the priest of the Russian embassy in Athens, wrote about the growing anti-Slavic and anti-Russian feeling in Greece caused by the Bulgarian Church Question already in the late 1850s. For all that, Antonin believed the Greeks "deserve our sympathy more than animosity and punitive measures on our part." Much like the Ottoman government, "all the Greeks" and the Patriarchate of Constantinople perceived the threat to their interests from the rise of national movements in the Ottoman Empire. Antonin predicted that the Bulgarian church would slip from the Patriarchate's control but "this would not put an end to the hostility between two Christian Orthodox nations (*plemena*)" for territory in Thrace and Macedonia.[49]

Despite his pessimism about the final reconciliation of the Greeks and the Slavs, Antonin did his best to promote it in practice. He supported the promotion of the pro-Russian Archimandrite Zacharias Mathas to the post

---

48. Foreign Minister A. M. Gorchakov to P. D. Kiselev, Ambassador in Paris, 19 January 1858, *Rusia i bulgarskoto natsionalno osvoboditelno dvizhenie*, p. 182; A. B. Lobanov-Rostovskii to A. M. Gorchakov, 6 June 1859, ibid., p. 281; A. M. Gorchakov's circular to Russian Embassies in Paris, London, Vienna, and Berlin, 23 April 1860, ibid., pp. 370–371.

49. Russian State Library Manuscript Division (OR RGB), fond 214-60, Antonin to Count Tolstoy, early 1858, pp. 29–290b.

of the Bishop of Santorini. He also backed the reprint of the rare Greek edition of the liturgy in honor of Bulgarian saints. That publication was undertaken by Sophocles Oikonomos, the son of Constantinos Oikonomos, who was the famous pro-Russian leader of Greek conservatives in the early 1800s. Sophocles Oikonomos also added a brief appendix listing all Russian saints along with the preface "likewise written in the spirit of unity, peace, and love, which are supposed to inspire the two co-religionist nations (*naroda*)."[50]

Antonin's counterpart in Constantinople, Archimandrite Peter (Troitskii), worked in the same direction with the Greek prelates of the Ecumenical Patriarchate. While Antonin was more flexible and merely followed the official line of the Russian Holy Synod, Peter adopted almost wholesale the viewpoint of the Patriarchate. The future Patriarch Joachim II (1860–1863) told Peter that "the Bulgarians behave like Jews. The Jew while striking somebody in the chest always shouts at him 'Why are you beating me? How dare you?' etc."[51] This is the first but not the last time when anti-Semitic feelings and images entered the debate on the Bulgarian Church Question.

Whereas Antonin made sweeping generalizations talking about "the Slavs" versus "the Greeks," Peter had a more nuanced understanding of how Bulgarian nationalism mixed with religion. According to his memo, Bulgarian merchants, guild-masters, and landholders, the so-called *chorbadzhii*, both at home and in the diaspora (especially in Odessa and Bucharest) were behind the movement for Bulgarian church independence. Peter denounced them as actually going against the interests of the Church in pursuit of "their nation's separation and achievement of civil rights for it." In Peter's analysis, the reconciliation between Ottoman Bulgarians and Greeks would be possible only if the Bulgarian church hierarchy were made the sole guardian of the Bulgarian people free of its subservience to the rising Bulgarian bourgeoisie.[52]

Archimandrite Peter considered the accusations against the Patriarchate as either exaggerated or slanderous and saw the Bulgarian national movement as a Western subversion organized by French agents during the Crimean War. By replacing "adroit Greeks" with "gullible Bulgarians" as bishops, the West hoped to make it easier to convert Balkan Slavs to Catholicism or Protestantism and thus alienate them from Russia.[53]

---

50. Ibid., 5 May 1860, pp. 79–790b.

51. Petrov, Nikolai, ed., "Vzgliad ochevidtsa na greco-bolgarskuiu raspriu: Pisma A. Petra Troitskogo," Peter to Count Tolstoy, June 1859, *Istoricheskii Vestnik*, 7 (1886): 282.

52. Ibid., p. 284.

53. OR RGB, fond 214-1-29, Peter to Count Tolstoy, 9 March 1857, pp. 210b–22, 8 August 1859, p. 230b.

The most influential nineteenth-century Russian prelate, Metropolitan of Moscow Filaret (1782–1867), read the pro-Patriarchate reports of Archimandrite Peter with a grain of salt. In addition to consulting the Russian government on foreign and domestic church policies, Filaret drafted Alexander II's momentous manifesto on the abolition of serfdom in February 1861—the centerpiece of Russia's Great Reforms. Filaret believed that the "Greek" hierarchy had a long way to go before it would make good on its pronouncements about the support for Slavonic liturgy, Bulgarian-language schools, and appointments of Bulgarians as bishops.[54] But he also saw mostly Western anti-Russian agendas in the process of secularization of the Patriarchate unleashed by the Hatti Humayun. In contrast, the Russian diplomats were more optimistic about new Ottoman reforms and did not condemn them out of hand.

In December of 1857, the Russian Foreign Ministry forwarded to the Holy Synod the decree of the Sublime Porte about how the Hatti Humayun reforms should be applied in the Orthodox *millet*. Its representatives were to be elected to form the Community Assembly (*Ethnosyneleusis* in Greek) to develop the statute or "General Regulations" "in the spirit of modern times, civilization, and Enlightenment" pertaining to the elections of the Patriarch, bishops, budget, and schools. The high clergy would send only seven representatives from among provincial bishops. Lay Christians of Constantinople would prepare a list of twenty names out of which the Porte would pick five "notables" and five guild-masters. Finally, each province (*eyalet*) would send one more delegate designated by propertied notables who had themselves been elected in lower-level territorial units. Given the high property qualifications, most lay delegates came from larger cities and tended to be ethnically Greek.[55]

While these arrangements can hardly be called democratic, they did widen political participation in community affairs previously in the hands of top prelates resident in Constantinople. Ambassador Apollinarii Butenev and the First Dragoman (Interpreter) Emmanuel Argyropoulo supported the reforms. Argyropoulo was himself ethnically Greek and apparently sympathetic to the interests of the Ottoman Greek officials and business community as the main beneficiaries of secularization. The Hatti Humayun would strengthen the

---

54. Metropolitan Filaret about Archimandrite Peters's letters, 5 March–10 September 1859, *Sobranie mnenii i otzyvov Filareta, mitropolita Moskovskogo i Kolomenskogo po delam pravoslavnoi tserkvi na Vostoke* (St. Petersburg: Sinodalnaia tipografia, 1886), pp. 146–156.

55. Matalas, Paraskeuas, *Ethnos kai Orthodoxia: Hoi Peripeteies Mias Scheses: Apo to "Helladiko" sto Voulgariko Schisma* (Herakleio: University of Crete Press, 2002), pp. 164–165.

Church, Mount Athos monasteries, the reputation of the clergy in the eyes of its flock, and Russian influence there.[56]

Metropolitan Filaret, in contrast, saw in them the loss of Patriarchate's autonomy from the Ottoman government. In particular, he opposed the idea of putting the clergy on the government payroll. Existing church fees, dues, and property were a more secure source of income. The talk about abuses was exaggerated, as they seemed to be limited to the Balkan dioceses and uncommon in Asia Minor, where no significant complaints were heard.[57]

Gregory, Metropolitan of Novgorod and St. Petersburg, agreed with Filaret that promoting lay dominance and setting fixed wages for the Orthodox hierarchy would lead to an increase in the taxes levied by the Ottoman government on the Orthodox Christians. Short of cash, bishops would not be able to travel around their dioceses to cultivate Orthodoxy among their flock and keep them from succumbing to Western proselytizing efforts.[58]

In October of 1858, the Community Assembly began its proceedings, which would remain in session until January 1860. The participants were a colorful group of people. Seven prelates wore Ottoman decorations for service to their flocks and the Sultan on long black robes. Depending on the degree of Westernization, some lay members were dressed in European suits. Ottoman bureaucrats among them were adorned with the red fez decreed for all officials since the time of Mahmud II. All Orthodox clergymen were wearing long more or less bushy beards, while the laypersons had moustaches and short beards following the Middle Eastern custom and the European fashion of the day. One would have been hard pressed to find a clean-shaven face among those delegates.

A year earlier, in April of 1857, Grand Vizier Ali Pasha invited Christian Orthodox bishops in the provinces to come to Constantinople to deal with the discontent among Orthodox Christians "created by Patriarchate's oppression." Not surprisingly, the Patriarch and the Synod refused to cooperate in that act of self-flagellation and were able to derail that attempt to pit the local prelates against their superiors in the capital city. Ali Pasha had to send the bishops back.[59] That show of clerical solidarity and esprit de corps must have been another factor that pushed the Sublime Porte to rely on lay notables.

---

56. Russian State Historical Archive (RGIA), 797-27-2-2-426 part 1, 14 December 1857, pp. 2–110b.

57. Ibid., Filaret's memo, 3 April 1858, pp. 18–20.

58. OR RGB, fond 214-1-28, Metropolitan Gregory to Count Tolstoy, 23 April 1858, p. 58.

59. Osmanagaoglu, *1862 Rum Patrikligi Nizamati*, p. 130.

In another report forwarded to the Russian Holy Synod, Butenev explained that only a small corrupt clique was resisting the reforms. Specifically, laity and most clergy, including Patriarch Constantine VII himself, were sick and tired of the oligarchy of the permanent members of the Synod also known as elders (*gerontes*). A few prelates from the dioceses adjacent to Constantinople made all the decisions and controlled all the funds with a total neglect of their responsibilities to their flock.[60]

One of the main reasons the Russian embassy chose to turn down the requests of the elders and to help the reformers was the need to respond to Bulgarian demands. Supporting the implementation of the Hatti Humayun was a way to purge the Patriarchate of its old abuses and preserve its unity. In late 1858, Patriarch Constantine VII gratified Ambassador Butenev by consecrating Hilarion as a titular bishop (not assigned to any diocese) and appointing him as the priest of the Bulgarian St. Stefan's Church in Constantinople. The Patriarch also promised to promote another Bulgarian, Archimandrite Arsenii, to bishop's rank.[61]

Before the Crimean War, Hilarion was Neofit Bozveli's coworker in the task of organizing the Bulgarian national movement. He exuded charisma long remembered by his followers. "His imposing stature and enormous height created an impression of something superhuman, of courage, and audacity evoking awe and reverence in his presence." When he celebrated the Divine Liturgy, "his sweet melodious clear and strong voice commanded attention and elevated the spirit of the worshippers."[62]

While Hilarion's star was rising, five Slav notables (four Bulgarians and one Bosnian out of the total of forty-five delegates) at the Community Assembly cooperated with their Greek counterparts. In January 1859, they proposed to allow participation of lay representatives of the diocese in the selection of the bishop normally appointed by the Patriarchate. This idea was clearly part of the Bulgarian nationalist agenda but it also appeared to promote the interests of all local laity outside the capital city and found support of other delegates, albeit too few to make the motion pass.[63]

Slavonic liturgy spread throughout 1858. In Thrace, many Bulgarian parish priests had to learn it because previously they relied on Greek liturgical texts.

---

60. RGIA, 797-27-2-2-426 part 1, 8 November 1858, pp. 34–430b.

61. RGIA, 797-27-2-2-426 part 1, 16 November 1858, p. 60.

62. Stambolski, Khristo, "Iz spomenite mi za Ilarion Makariopolski (1858–1861)," in Arnaudov, Mikhail, ed., *Ilarion Makariopolski i Bulgarkiiat Cherkoven Vupros* (Sofia: Khudozhnik, 1925), 14.

63. Matalas, *Ethnos kai Orthodoxia*, p. 169.

This trend created a great demand for service books in Old Church Slavonic. Russian consulates ordered them from Russia and made them available in Adrianople and elsewhere. Locally, "all reasonable Greek patriots, notables, and prelates" saw nothing wrong with it and were generally pro-Russian.[64]

This cooperation encouraged Butenev's successor as Russian ambassador, Prince Lobanov-Rostovskii, to write an optimistic report about the progress of Greek-Bulgarian reconciliation. The General Regulations would include provisions meant to improve the position of "non-Greek population of Turkey"—the requirement for the bishop to know the language of the diocese, the right of the local community to nominate a candidate in case of death of an incumbent metropolitan, and their right to complain to the Synod of the Patriarchate about their metropolitan. These measures seemed to have calmed down the Bulgarian activists in Constantinople. From his conversations with the clerical and lay delegates, Lobanov got the impression that they truly wanted to overcome "the misunderstandings that exist between the Greeks and the Slavs."[65]

For several months the Russian diplomats, if not the Holy Synod, supported the Community Assembly as a promising power-sharing arrangement that grew from the Hatti Humayun. Over a year later, the situation did not seem hopeless even after ethnic violence had erupted in Philippoupolis. It is still a major city and is known as Plovdiv in Bulgarian. It was founded by Philip of Macedonia, the father of Alexander the Great. After Slavic migrations/invasions in the Middle Ages, it became part of the Bulgarian Kingdom but in the Ottoman period most cities developed strong Greek communities because extensive Greek trading networks were in a better position to take advantage of the Treaty of Kuchuk Kaynarji, as detailed in chapter 1.

In December of 1859, there was fighting in the church of the Dormition of the Virgin when the Patriarchate allowed the celebration of the Divine Liturgy in Old Church Slavonic parallel to existing services in Koine Greek. Both sacred languages are still in use and are only half-intelligible to native speakers of Bulgarian, Russian, Serbian, and Modern Greek, respectively. The former is based on a mix of South Slavic dialects spoken at the time of SS. Cyril and Methodius in the mid-800s. The latter goes even further back. Koine Greek was a popular form of Ancient Greek that had developed after Alexander's conquests of Asia. Most Apostles and probably Jesus himself knew it as a second language. Needless to say, to a Slavic ear Koine Greek is gibberish.

---

64. N. D. Stupin to A. B. Lobanov-Rostovskii, 8 January 1859, *Rusia i bulgarskoto*, pp. 248–249.

65. RGIA, 797-27-2-2-426 part 1, 7 February 1859, pp. 105–1050b.

So who would be fighting over dead or half-dead languages? Based on the information from the local Russian consul, Ambassador Lobanov-Rostovskii concluded that it was more complicated than simply Greek-Bulgarian clashes. The main culprits were not locals at all but resident Greek citizens. They used violence in churches to put a stop to Bulgarian resurgence because Slavonic chanting and Bulgarian sermons sounded a death knell for the Great Idea of the resurrection of the Greek-dominated Byzantine Empire. This irredentist fever, according to Lobanov, did not affect local Ottoman authorities, including ethnically Greek prelates, who remained supportive of legitimate Bulgarian rights.[66] It stands to reason then that the Russian diplomats did not perceive the incident as the end to cooperation between Ottoman Greeks and Bulgarians.

The significant progress at the Community Assembly to satisfy many Bulgarian demands still fell short of the movement's more ambitious goals voiced before the Crimean War and more forcefully in 1856. In 1860, the Bulgarian nationalist activists were just as far from receiving status as a separate religious community that would serve as a more secure foundation for the still inchoate nationalist project. In January of 1860, shortly before the Assembly finished preparing General Regulations, the Bulgarian delegates stopped all cooperation. They stated six main problems with their continued participation in the Assembly and the Patriarchate.

First, although the Bulgarians allegedly constituted the majority of Ottoman Christians, they were vastly underrepresented at the Assembly because Greek bishops and notables had rigged local elections. Second, the Bulgarians were greatly disadvantaged because their autocephalous archbishoprics of Turnovo and Ohrida had been absorbed into the Patriarchate in the 1760s to the advantage of Greek clergy. Third, Bulgarian clergymen were not promoted to bishop's rank; the predominantly Bulgarian dioceses did not have bishops of the same ethnicity and language. Fourth, Greek prelates excluded the Bulgarian language from churches and schools. Fifth, bishops and metropolitans should be elected by the dioceses. Lastly, those presently in charge of the Orthodox *millet* should be responsible for the enormous debts incurred by the Patriarchate.[67]

Much of this is surprising. Four individuals with acute ethnic consciousness may have felt underrepresented—being only 10% of the total number of delegates (forty-five) may have given them an impression that the deck was stacked against them. On the other hand, we saw some of those demands before and some noticeable positive changes in the period the Assembly

---

66. RGIA, 797-27-2-2-426 part 2, Lobanov to Gorchakov, 16 January 1860, pp. 1–2.

67. Matalas, *Ethnos kai Orthodoxia*, p. 170.

was in session—October 1858 to January 1860. It is also strange that they waited to the very end to demand the breakup of the Patriarchate into several parts. Stephanos Karatheodoris, who was the personal physician of Sultan Abdulmedjid I, a Renaissance man of sorts and one of the chief reformers, gave a speech at the end of the proceedings of the Assembly, where he addressed the Bulgarian protests. Neither the government nor the Patriarchate made ethnic distinctions among the Orthodox clergy. In Karatheodoris' view, the Bulgarian accusations were not justified. There had been abuses when a few elder prelates were in control of the Patriarchate but the Assembly made a serious effort to eliminate them.[68] In effect, he invited the Bulgarian notables to enjoy the fruits of lay victory over domineering prelates.

One of the Bulgarian delegates, Nikola Minchoglu of Turnovo, published an angry rebuttal to Stephanos' response, where he bitterly complained about the Greek nationalist bias of the "Greek Assembly." That was the real reason they refused to consider the Bulgarian demand for ethnically Bulgarian bishops, not because the issue was allegedly beyond the scope of the Assembly or was contrary to canon law. They did not investigate the Bulgarian claims of longstanding anti-Slavic discrimination because the revelations would hurt the Greek cause. How did the Community Assembly tackle its main task of financial reform? They did not even audit the Patriarchate's accounts, and simply accepted the enormous debt at face value. Those actions violated the spirit and the letter of the Imperial Reform Edict.

The Bulgarians saw the Community Assembly as "the anchor of salvation" but found no redress of their grievances. Now there was only one solution—to seek the status of their own Orthodox Christian community from His Majesty Sultan Abdulmejid I. "Only then would the Greeks and the Bulgarians become brotherly nations competing only over who would excel in the loyalty to the government and the canons of the Apostles and the Holy Fathers politically, religiously, and morally."[69] It was a bold divorce announcement but the devil is in the details of what follows from such unilateral statements.

The General Regulations hammered out by the Community Assembly enshrined the new principle of regular lay participation. The main body was now the Permanent Mixed Council of eight lay and four top prelates who were also members of the Synod. The Mixed Council was in charge of schools,

---

68. Karatheodoris, Stephanos, *O Logos epi te apoperatosei ton ergasion tes Ethnosyneleuseos* (Constantinople, 1860).

69. Minchoglu, Nikola, *Metaphrasis ek tou Voulgarikou: Apantisis eis ton Logon tou Kyriou S. Karatheodore* (Constantinople, 1860), 67.

hospitals, and charities, with jurisdiction over family law and economic issues generally (budgets of most Patriarchate institutions, wills, inheritance, dowries, etc.). More representative General Assemblies of elected local notables and high clergy would be periodically called to discuss any changes to the General Regulations or other pressing issues.

The Community Assembly successfully resisted the Ottoman pressure of putting the clergy on government payroll because it would entail more taxes levied on Orthodox Christians. This measure also threatened to lead to government takeover of the church property. Instead, a more efficient management of church property was expected to bring enough income. This change was clearly seen in how the Patriarch was to be elected. The Synod of the highest prelates would still have the final choice but an electoral conference of lay representatives would nominate three metropolitans. Also, the Porte extracted the right to strike down one or two but not all three final candidates off the list.[70]

This new procedure raised some eyebrows in Russia. Andrei Muraviev was an employee of the Russian Holy Synod famous for his theological works and popular travel accounts of his journeys to the Christian East. Stephanos Karatheodoris explained to him that the participation of laity in the election of the Patriarch was necessary because in the Ottoman Empire he combined spiritual and temporal responsibilities as the head of the Orthodox community. There was no contradiction to the canon law since the candidates for Patriarch's office still had to be consecrated by fellow metropolitans and educated in the Patriarchal Theological School, any of four Russian theological academies, or the Theological School in Athens.[71]

The Greek embassy in Constantinople did not oppose the reforms per se but was concerned with the increased involvement of the Sublime Porte through its right to influence the patriarch's elections. Once this right was formalized, it was criticized as an infringement on church independence. The laypersons, who dominated the crucial Permanent Mixed Council, were first and foremost subjects of the Sultan, which could also facilitate Ottoman intervention.[72] The Russian diplomats actively supported the process, hoping against hope that the reformed *millet* would be turning into a working power-sharing structure with common institutions and growing respect for ethnic diversity.

Walking out of the Community Assembly did not mean that the Bulgarian national movement gave up on the Hatti Humayun altogether to achieve its

---

70. Stamatopoulos, *Metarrythmisi*, pp. 105, 107, 121, 125, 144.

71. RGIA, 797-27-2-2-426 part 2, Karatheodoris to Muraviev, 18 February 1860, pp. 790b–82.

72. Stamatopoulos, *Metarrythmisi*, p. 90.

ambitious goals. But other directions of the Ottoman reform were not very encouraging either, because the second Tanzimat period (1856–1878) faced many
of the difficulties of the first one (1839–1856). The Christians often could not
freely practice their religion as promised. The Bulgarians in the Turnovo area
were excited about the prospect of finally using church bells and in the meantime began to signal the beginning of the divine service with the beating of
the wooden board. Local Muslims threatened to attack them if they continued
to do so. Frightened and humiliated, the Christians complained to the governor and pointed to the provisions of the Hatti Humayun, but he only advised them caution because he was unable to guarantee their security. Instead
of a citizen army based on universal conscription, the Ottoman authorities
began to require an exemption tax and to use force to collect it when many
poor Christians could not pay it. Then, the mechanism of relative deprivation
turned on again when about a hundred of them took up arms in the name of
the Sultan and his glorious reforms, unsuccessfully demanding a fair military
draft and separate Bulgarian units with Bulgarians officers and chaplains.[73]

Generally, the Russian diplomats were becoming increasingly pessimistic
about the Hatti Humayun. Amazingly, Grand Vizier Ali Pasha himself told
Lobanov-Rostovskii that the famed Reform Edict was the product of the evil
genius of Lord Redcliffe, the British ambassador. There was "more poetry
than truth" in the document, which was "out of touch with local conditions
and the progress of civilization in our provinces." In addition to the cultural
differences stressed by Ali, Lobanov considered the idea of Christian-Muslim
fusion a chimera because of social divisions. Christian tenants in Bosnia and
Bulgaria hated their mostly Muslim landlords even more than they hated
their stooges among Ottoman officials.[74]

This conversation with Grand Vizier Aali Pasha was not a figment of
Lobanov's imagination. Stefan Vogoridi, the Christian insider in the Sublime
Porte, shared with his son-in-law that "initially excited by the English and
French promises of Turkey's territorial integrity, most pashas began to have
second thoughts and to say that it was and is possible to reach an understanding with the Russians and to avoid all those misfortunes and sacrifices made
by the Porte to fulfill the promises to England and France."[75]

---

73. Bucharest Bulgarian community to the Russian Foreign Ministry, 19 August 1856,
Rusia i bulgarskoto natsionalno-osvoboditelno dvizhenie, pp. 66–68.

74. State Archive of the Russian Federation (GARF), 730-1-629, p. 10b, Lobanov-Rostovskii
to Gorchakov, 9 May 1859.

75. Gennadius Library (Athens), file 23, Stefan Vogoridi to Constantine Mousouros, 3
March 1859, p. 142b.

Bulgarian Nationalism and Russian Pan-Slavism: The Early Debate about Foreign Policy and Cultural Identity

Clearly, the imperfect implementation of the Tanzimat promised no quick fulfillment of Bulgarian aspirations. To bring more pressure to bear on the official Russian policy of reconciliation, Bulgarian nationalist activists tried to mobilize the educated Russian society in presenting themselves as the only truly suffering Orthodox Christians and their agenda as part of the Slavic cause.

The defeat in the Crimean War (1853–1856) led to the Great Reforms in Russia, including the abolition of serfdom, trial by jury, relaxation of censorship, and proliferation of civil society organizations. This is when the obscure ideas of Romantic Russian nationalism also known as Slavophilism began to move from academic ivory towers into a brave new world of mass politics. Pan-Slavism is typically interpreted as a politicized version of Slavophilism.[76] Although commonly used now, "Pan-Slavism" was originally a somewhat pejorative bugaboo term coined by alarmist Western journalists. The Russians tended to prefer the term "Slavophilism" throughout this time period, especially in the positive sense.

The Great Reforms led to a boom in the publishing industry. Editors no longer needed an imprimatur from government censors, who still carefully monitored all publications and could revoke a publishing license after several warnings. The success of Italian and German unification provided another stimulus for the mobilization of an important segment of the Russian educated society behind Pan-Slavism. Given the perceptions of Western Europe as inimical to Russia during and after the Crimean War, increasing numbers of revanchist intellectuals and policymakers saw the way to regaining Russian strength in joining forces with Russia's Slavic brethren in Habsburg and Ottoman domains.[77]

The Bulgarian immigrant community in Russia was instrumental in crystallizing the amorphous Pan-Slav movement in Russia. The Bulgarian-born Russian consul in Philippoupolis, Naiden Gerov, suggested the idea of setting up an organization to send educational materials to Ottoman Bulgarian lands and to provide financial aid to Bulgarian students in Moscow. Such was the modest beginning of the famous Moscow Slavic Benevolent Committee

---

76. Sumner, Benedict, "Russia and Pan-Slavism in the Eighteen Seventies," *Transactions of the Royal Historical Society*, 18 (1935): 26.

77. Petrovich, Michael Boro, *The Emergence of Russian Panslavism, 1856–1870* (Westport: Greenwood Publishers, 1985 [1956]), p. 254.

(later Society) in 1858. Before its closure for sharp criticism of Russian foreign policy in 1878, it spawned similar organizations in St. Petersburg (1868), Kiev (1869), and Odessa (1870).

Contrary to wild rumors in the Western press, their charity commitments were not a cover for some conspiratorial activities—they indeed consumed almost all the meager funds donated by a handful of sympathetic aristocrats, merchants, and officials. Although the Pan-Slavs incessantly discussed various ways to unite Russia and its coethnics abroad, they would become politically significant only during the Eastern Crisis of 1875–1878, when the trickle of donations became a flood they could channel to purchasing arms and sending volunteers to the Balkans.[78]

In the 1850s, Bulgarian nationalist commentators added the Greeks to the traditional Islamic Other as their national enemy.[79] Naturally, it was safer to criticize the latter than the former inside the Ottoman Empire. Radical Bulgarian expatriates castigated both the Turks and the Greeks in the greater security of autonomous Serbia or Romania and smuggled their publications into the realm of the Sultan, bypassing watchful Ottoman censors. The task of demonizing the Greeks for the Russian audience naturally fell on politically active Bulgarian merchants and students resident in Russia.

Khristo Daskalov was a Bulgarian student in Moscow who pioneered the trend toward changing the Russian perception of the Greeks from the main victims of Islamic domination into oppressors of Balkan Slavs. In October 1858, his article in the new Slavophile monthly magazine *Russkaia Beseda* generated a series of clichéd images of powerless Slavs versus predatory Greeks. All Russian Pan-Slav writers would subsequently adopt his imagery and rhetoric, often making explicit references to that article.

Daskalov's main thrust was in focusing traditional Russian sympathies for "the lot of the Christians in the East" on Balkan Slavs and especially on Bulgarians. Thus, the Ottoman Greeks, or Phanariotes, were no "Homeric heroes" or even "saviors of Orthodoxy in the East." In fact, they had been embezzling Russian donations for decades, working together with the Muslim oppressors to exploit the South Slavs.[80] Their alleged corruption, greed,

---

78. Nikitin, Sergei, *Slavianskie komitety v Rossii* (Moscow: Moscow University Press, 1961), pp. 21–31.

79. Todorova, Maria, "Self-Image and Ethnic Stereotypes in Bulgaria," *Modern Greek Studies Yearbook*, 8 (1992):149; Aretov, Nikolay, "Abducted Faith and Bulgarian National Mythology," *Etudes Balkaniques*, 39, 2 (2003): 122.

80. Daskalov, Khristo, "Vozrozhdeniie bolgar ili reaktsiia v Evropeiskoi Turtsii," *Russkaia Beseda*, 10 (1858): 1–2.

self-serving nationalism, and morbid hatred of all things Slavic had led many Balkan Slavs away from the true faith to embrace Western creeds or even Islam.[81] The contrast between cunning and powerful Greeks versus gullible and oppressed Bulgarians would become a recurrent theme in Pan-Slav publications.[82]

The Ecumenical Patriarchate protested about Daskalov's piece in *Russkaia Beseda* and about a similar article by "D." in the popular liberal literary biweekly magazine *Russkii Vestnik*.[83] The last pen name was an alias most probably for Alexander Rachinski, who was a Russian Pan-Slav on the diplomatic service since 1859 (a consul in Ottoman Bulgaria between 1860 and 1861). Deacon Alexander Lascaris, an Ottoman Greek student at the St. Petersburg Theological Academy, delivered the note from the Patriarchate to Count Alexander Tolstoy, the Over-Procurator of the Holy Synod of the Russian Orthodox Church. The Over-Procurator responded by writing an angry letter to the Foreign Minister Gorchakov and the Russian ambassador to Constantinople Butenev where he denounced the articles as "the product of Western propaganda."[84]

In Alexander Tolstoy's opinion, their true aim was not to create sympathy toward the needs of the Bulgarians in Russia. The insults hurled at the Patriarchate in reality aimed "to implant in the Russian people hatred for the coreligionist Greek people and for their church from which our Fatherland has received the light of the Christian faith." Tolstoy foresaw at least one grave domestic consequence of the pro-Bulgarian press campaign—it would embolden and empower the splinter groups of the so-called Old Believers to further criticize the mainstream Russian Orthodox Church. Internationally, the Pan-Slav agitation would lead to "the loss of the trust of the Greek clergy which forms the main Christian Orthodox element in the Turkish Empire."[85]

This ostensibly Pan-Orthodox statement shows awareness of ethnic distinctions[86]—it even refers to the Ecumenical Patriarchate as the church of

---

81. Ibid., pp. 4, 5, 6, 8, 15, 21, 39, 41.

82. Various aspects of South Slav powerlessness are discussed in Vovchenko, Denis, "Gendering Irredentism? Self and Other in Russian Pan-Orthodoxy and Pan-Slavism (1856–1885)," *Ethnic and Racial Studies*, 34, 2 (February 2011): 248–274.

83. "D." [Rachinskii, A. V.], "Turetskie dela," *Russkii Vestnik*, 13, 2 (1858): 245–265.

84. AVPRI, fond 161/3, collection 233, part I, Tolstoy to Gorchakov (cc: Butenev), June 19 1858, pp. 237–238.

85. Ibid., p. 238.

86. On the rise of modern ethnic thinking in late Imperial Russia see Holquist, Peter, "To Count, to Extract, to Exterminate: Population Statistics and Population Politics

the Greek people. However, the document reveals that the religious worldview is still more important in the Russian bureaucratic mindset: "the Greek clergy" is subsumed within "the Christian Orthodox element." The image of the Other is also defined religiously, namely, the Western creeds and the Muslim Turks.

Over-Procurator Tolstoy's reasoning convinced Tsar Alexander II himself, who ordered the Foreign Ministry to convey official Russian apologies to the Patriarchate through the ambassador in Constantinople. To prevent "such senseless and harmful articles," it was necessary to impose pre-publication censorship of the writings concerning not just the doctrine of the Orthodox Church but also its administrative organization.[87] That decision effectively banned the press debate on the Bulgarian Church Question until 1860.

Ironically, in response to official reprimands, Mikhail Katkov used the same anti-Western rationale to justify his decision to publish the anti-Greek article by D. in his *Russkii Vestnik*. He saw it as an attempt to bring the Russian educated society to support the Bulgarian movement for church in-dependence. Having their own church would reduce the attraction the union with the Catholic Church held for them.[88]

In addition to bureaucratic channels, Over-Procurator Alexander Tolstoy felt the need to counterattack anti-Patriarchate articles in the press to explain the "correct" view to the Russian audience. He entrusted Tertii Filippov, his employee and a close friend, the task of vindicating the honor of the Patriarch of Constantinople, who had been attacked by Bulgarian nationalists and Russian Pan-Slavs. At first glance, he was an unlikely man for that job. Whenever his name is mentioned in the existing scholarly literature, it re-ceives a one-sided treatment as one of the early prominent Romantic Russian nationalists, also known as Slavophiles.

Before his career at the Holy Synod, Filippov became quite prominent on the Russian cultural scene, which he entered through popular taverns with live singing in seedy neighborhoods of Moscow. He frequented them in the company of his friends such as the famous playwright Alexander Ostrovskii and well-known publicists of the "back-to-the-people" type. Carousing helped those refined intellectuals fraternize with factory workers and other true

---

in Late Imperial and Soviet Russia," in Suny, Ronald, and Martin, Terry, eds., *A State of Nations: Empire and Nation-Making in the Age of Lenin and Stalin* (Oxford University Press, 2001), pp. 112–113; Jersild, Austin Lee, "Modernity and the Russian Empire: Russian Ethnographers and Caucasian Mountaineers," *Nationalities Papers*, 24, 4 (1996): 641.

87. AVPRI, fond 161/3, collection 233, part I, Tolstoy to Gorchakov (cc: Butenev), June 19 1858, p. 238ob.

88. OR RGB, fond 214-1-58, pp. 1–90b.

Russians. Filippov was an accomplished performer himself, and his singing of folk songs always produced a very emotional effect, bringing some to tears.[89]

Filippov discovered a passion for folklore in the 1830s and 1840s from the lectures and the writings of Mikhail Pogodin and Stepan Shevyrev. The views of those two Moscow University professors about uniqueness and even superiority of Russian culture formed the bedrock of Romantic Russian nationalism. Filippov wrote to Pogodin in the summer of 1852, "I consider you among the people to whom I owe, I dare not say salvation for I am far from it, but at least my return to the life appropriate for a decent man. Whatever happens between us afterwards, I will always be grateful to you."[90] Filippov, along with other like-minded "junior editors," namely, Apollon Grigoriev, Alexander Ostrovskii, and Evgenii Edelson, helped Pogodin's *Moskvitianin* "briefly attain a degree of popular success in the early 1850s." The magazine collapsed on Pogodin's stinginess and petty interference, which naturally alienated his young team.[91]

In the period from 1841 to 1856, *Moskvitianin* was the only Russian journal to systematically promote Pan-Slavism before the Crimean War. Every issue discussed Slavic news thereby bringing "a knowledge of the other Slavs to an apathetic Russian public." It had more influence abroad than at home and had to give way to more vigorous and innovative publications in the more liberal and competitive post–Crimean War era.[92]

After leaving *Moskvitianin*, in 1855 Filippov and Koshelev started *Russkaia Beseda*, "a new Slavophile journal," when the guns of the Crimean War were still thundering.[93] Filippov revealed a lot of his early political views in his intimations about the new publication to Count Alexander Tolstoy on 5 August 1855. The main goal of the project was "to expose Western lies" according to its founders—Koshelev, Khomiakov, and Samarin (all prominent Slavophiles). "Although you in your rather strict judgment find them quite Westernized, nevertheless they sincerely respect and profess (with some liberal interpretation) Orthodoxy, Nationality, and Autocracy."[94]

89. Whittaker, Roger, "The Ostrovski-Grigoriev Circle, Alias the Young Editors of Moskvitianin," *Canadian-American Slavic Studies*, 24, 4 (1990): 387–388.

90. OR RGB, fond "M. P. Pogodin" 231/II-34-64, T. I. Filippov to M. P. Pogodin, p. 8.

91. Thaden, Edward, *Conservative Russian Nationalism in Nineteenth Century Russia* (Seattle: University of Washington Press, 1964), p. 23.

92. Petrovich, *The Emergence of Russian Panslavism*, pp. 106–107.

93. Thaden, *Conservative Nationalism*, p. 35.

94. GARF, fond "T. I. Filippov" 1099-1-1265, T. I. Filippov to A. P. Tolstoy, Rzhev, August 5 1855, p. 10b.

Since the Russian government had long suspected the Slavophiles of being crypto-liberals,[95] it must have been reassuring to Tolstoy that Filippov and his friends embraced all three pillars of the imperial Russian ideology. Ever since its approval in 1833 by Nicholas I, "nationality" has baffled contemporaries and modern scholars alike with its confusing ambiguous meaning of either dynastic patriotism or Romantic nationalism.[96]

Russkaia Beseda was supposed to counteract another new Moscow-based journal, *Russkii Letopisets*, to be edited by Mikhail Katkov. Filippov characterized him as "the Schellingean and the enemy of our patriotic trend (*narodnoie napravlenie*)." Katkov was also the publisher of *Moskovskie Vedomosti* and *Russkii Vestnik*, where some anti-Greek articles would appear in 1858. The founders of the new nationalist journal offered Filippov the job as an editor, which he found "flattering, profitable, morally elevating" and "the kind of activity to my best liking." Filippov hoped his working there would be for the greater good of the society and was asking for Tolstoy's opinion.[97]

Clearly, the common denominator between Tolstoy and Filippov was their opposition to the West understood as a curious combination of old and new threats—Protestant and Catholic encroachments as well as secular materialism. Anti-rational and anti-secular inclinations led both Filippov and Tolstoy to appreciate the political teaching of "sacred history" developed by Father Matfei, a certain mystic from Tver'. The latter apparently brought the two together and served as the link between them. Thus, Filippov used a Biblical quote to explain the Russian predicament in the closing days of the Crimean War, "The recent events leave no shadow of a doubt that we are the New Israel."[98]

As an editor of *Russkaia Beseda*, Filippov received and published a scathing "Letter to the Publisher" where a liberal reader accused him of trying to return Russia to the Dark Ages. *Russkaia Beseda*'s editors and contributors went to the extreme of elevating Russian folk songs high above contemporary Western literature as the moral guide to discussing the issues of women's emancipation, infidelity, and divorce. There could be no excuse for promoting the ridiculous notion that "unenlightened people" are somehow superior to "the civilized society we normally treat as a model."[99]

---

95. Thaden, *Conservative Nationalism*, p. 22.

96. Riasanovsky, Nicholas, "'Nationality' in the State Ideology during the Reign of Nicholas I," *Russian Review*, 19, 1 (January 1960): 41.

97. GARF, fond "T. I. Filippov" 1099-1-1265, T. I. Filippov to A. P. Tolstoy, Rzhev, August 5 1855, pp. 10b–2.

98. GARF, 1099-1-1265, 22 May 1856, p. 16.

99. M. G., "Pis'mo k izdateliu T.I. Filippovu," *Russkaia Beseda*, 4 (1856): 95.

Later that same year, Father Matfei wrote to Filippov that Tolstoy, as the newly appointed Over-Procurator, was offering him a job at the Russian Holy Synod. Filippov seized this opportunity to quit his editorship of *Russkaia Beseda*, which he now considered as a total waste of one year of his life. Because of the general disorder in the journal and personal conflict with Koshelev, he had to make concessions contrary to his conscience.[100] It is interesting that two years later this journal would publish Daskalov's anti-Greek article in 1858.

For Filippov, Slavophilism and Pan-Slavism took a back seat to anti-Westernism in his interpretation of the Russian cultural identity. While working for the Holy Synod, he urged Tolstoy to arrange for two Orthodox Arabs, Abuda and Solomon, to be accepted into the St. Petersburg Theological Academy. This encouragement would attract "more Syrians into our lands," he stated, and he expressed to Tolstoy his certainty that "our rapprochement with the East ranks foremost in your thoughts."[101] He made this statement when Bulgarian nationalist activists were challenging Orthodox unity, demanding the status of a separate religious community for their ethnic group based on the Hatti Humayun.

The publications by "D." and Daskalov gave a flavor of the new Pan-Slav ideology in Russia and Filippov did not like it. Although writing a rebuttal to those articles was an official assignment, Filippov did not compromise his convictions. He sincerely believed that the Bulgarians were treating Orthodoxy lightly to achieve their narrow national goals. With his bona fide Slavophile credentials and publishing experience, Filippov was in a unique position to credibly project public policy and affect public opinion.

His serialized response to "Mr. D." was published in the main Russian daily newspaper and was couched in the spirit of Orthodox unity. He argued that the Russians should take the interests of their religion to heart and be completely impartial to "our ethnic affinity (*plemennoie rodstvo*) with the Bulgarian people or special natural advantages and significance of the Greeks in the history of the Church." But ultimately the message of Filippov (and of the Holy Synod) was not reassuring to the Bulgarians. Filippov took issue with the accusation that the Patriarchate was appointing Greek bishops because of its hidden nationalistic agenda of ultimately Hellenizing the Slavs.[102]

---

100. GARF, 1099-1-1265, 11 November 1856, p. 3.

101. Ibid., 1 November 1856, p. 9.

102. "Otvet G-nu D.", *Moskovskie Vedomosti*, 93 (5 August 1858): 865.

In Filippov's line of argument, the survival of Orthodoxy in the Ottoman Empire depended on the continued leadership of the Greeks, who had almost single-handedly created, maintained, and propagated Orthodox Christianity. He reminded that both the Bulgarians and the Russians had adopted the true faith from the Greeks. Unlike the other Christian Orthodox nations (*plemena*), the Greeks preserved their education "in the four centuries of the Turkish yoke." This unique resilience enabled the Greeks "to continue to repulse the cunning encroachments of Rome to take control of the East under the pretext of achieving unity of the Church." This superiority notwithstanding, the Patriarchate of Constantinople had ten ethnically Bulgarian bishops in both Greek and Bulgarian lands, whom Filippov listed by name and diocese.[103]

In contrast, the Bulgarian nationalists were troublemakers putting forward exaggerated demands, which were dangerous to the common Orthodox cause. Filippov questioned the legitimacy of the medieval Bulgarian Patriarchate of Turnovo (1234–1393) and objected to using history to justify new claims. If followed generally and consistently, that kind of approach would overturn the established order of things and lead to chaos. Filippov rejected the notion of having two independent churches of the same creed within one political unit. He explicitly equated the Ottoman and the Russian empires—neither of them should tolerate such an unstable situation.[104]

However, Filippov shifted on the Ottoman authorities the blame that the Greeks had put an excessive financial burden on the Slavs. Replacing a Greek bishop with a Slav would not relieve the situation since most of the revenues were siphoned by book or by crook from the Christian communities into the pockets of Ottoman officials. Filippov quoted from "a foreign scholar" to prove that "Mr. D." and other enthusiasts of the Ottoman reforms were wrong to support the case for putting the clergy on salary. This novelty would only increase direct taxes levied by the Ottoman government and decrease the amount and quality of Christian community services.[105]

Filippov specifically attacked the myth of "ancient hatreds" and unending conflicts between the Greeks and the Slavs described in anti-Patriarchate articles. He argued that the enmity between the Slavs and the Greeks was of very recent origin and ran along generational lines. "The fathers" were allegedly impervious to "irritating insinuations" and "newly invented hatred." When their overly educated "sons" brought Bishop Chrysanthos to the Ottoman

---

103. Ibid., pp. 865–866.

104. "Otvet G-nu D.," *Moskovskie Vedomosti*, 94 (7 August 1858): 874.

105. "Otvet G-nu D.," *Moskovskie Vedomosti*, 95 (9 August 1858): 885.

court, "the whole population of the diocese of Philippoupolis" testified to his virtues and their respect and love for him. "The citizens of Sophia, Bulgarians as well as Greeks sent a letter of protest to the slanderer" who had defamed the character of their beloved Metropolitan of Sophia in *Tsaregradskii Vestnik*, the main Bulgarian newspaper in Constantinople.[106] Reproduced in full in the supplement, that letter featured signatures of local notables such as merchants and guild-masters.[107]

We should not be under the impression that Filippov attacked nationalism per se. Russia welcomed "the joyful revival of Bulgarian intellectual life." But "the cunning West took advantage of the poor nation's inexperienced barely awakened consciousness to fill it with the poison of hatred for its pastors and brothers." The Catholic propaganda seized on "some problems" (*neustroistvo*) between the laity and the clergy rooted "in the general Turkish order of things." The Pope's silver-tongued agents made the Greeks alone appear culpable in the eyes of the Bulgarians. The Pope's goal was to convert the Bulgarian part of the Orthodox world and separate it from the Greeks, who were "his only fearsome opponents in the East, watchful guardians of Orthodoxy who prevailed over all kinds of heresy."[108]

To thwart the spread of Catholicism and its divide-and-rule tactics was part and parcel of the religious obligations of Russians as good Orthodox Christians, as it was in their geopolitical interest in the Near East. Thus, the Russians should concentrate all efforts on reconciling their brothers in Christ with each other without investigating who was more to blame.[109]

Clearly, Filippov's main goal was to rally the Russians, the Balkan Slavs, and the Greeks to stand united against the threats of Islamic oppression and of papal domination. On one hand, this appeal was highly traditional—the common religious bond largely overshadowed ethnic differences. On the other hand, in the spirit of the Pan-Slav articles he himself attacked, Filippov portrayed the Greeks not so much as suffering Orthodox Christians but more as powerful actors. Their power was not self-serving. It transcended the nationalistic agenda to shield the Slavs (and the Arabs), who were unable by themselves to resist the Pope's "seduction."

Filippov was not the only Russian Slavophile who tried to further bridge the emerging gap between Pan-Orthodox traditions and modern ethnic

---

106. Ibid., p. 886.

107. "Otvet G-nu D.," *Moskovskie Vedomosti*, 97 (16 August 1858): 904.

108. "Otvet G-nu D.," *Moskovskie Vedomosti*, 96 (12 August 1858): 894.

109. Ibid.

consciousness in connection with the Bulgarian Church Question. In December 1858, Vladimir Lamanskii published "A Few Words on Russian Relations with the Greeks" in *Russkaia Beseda*—two months earlier the same journal had featured the article by Daskalov directed against the "Greek" Patriarchate of Constantinople. Just finishing his master's thesis, Lamanskii was a rising star of Slavic studies and one of the main ideologues of political Pan-Slavism. In the 1860s and 1870s, Filippov and Lamanskii participated in the St. Petersburg Slavic Society.[110] In his doctoral dissertation published in 1871, Lamanskii argued that "the Greco-Slavic world was a cultural unit which should be studied as a separate and independent historical entity."[111]

Many of these ideas were previewed in his 1858 article, where Lamanskii called for the systematic study of the relations between the Greeks and the Russians and their mutual influences. For this he believed it necessary to resume the teaching of Classical Greek, to establish chairs of Modern Greek language and history (from 300 AD through the Ottoman period) at the history and philology departments of Russian universities, and "to start intellectual and literary communication with the Greeks." He saw translations and publications about the Greeks in Russia and vice versa as necessary for the advancement of national consciousness in both countries.[112]

The relative neglect of Greek themes was another sign of the isolation of Russian literature from the Russian people with their strong bond with Greek Orthodoxy.[113] The Russian educated public should be ashamed of "its ignorance of its co-religionist brethren who are so attached to us and who have rendered enormous services to us, having enlightened Rus' with Christianity, having given her and all Slavdom the great teachers, Saint Apostles Cyril and Methodius," and many others later.[114] Sustained cultural contacts between the Greeks and the Russians would increase their national self-confidence by liberating them from the dependence on Western Europe. Whereas the prejudiced Westerners did not see the language of "barbarians and semi-savages" worthy of an effort, Russian should become popular among the Greeks.[115]

---

110. Russian State Archive for Literature and Art (RGALI), fond "M. P. Pogodin" 373-1-361, 28 August 1872, p. 130b.

111. Petrovich, *The Emergence of Russian Panslavism*, pp. 63–64.

112. Lamanskii, Vladimir, "Neskolko slov ob otnosheniiakh russkikh k grekam," *Russkaia Beseda*, 12 (1858): 133–136.

113. Ibid., p. 127.

114. Ibid., p. 137.

115. Ibid., p. 128.

Although not alien to the "Romanic and Germanic" Europe, the Greeks and the Slavs were drawn closer together by their shared religion.[116] The study of Byzantine history and literature would contribute to the advancement of Slavic studies and a better understanding of Western culture.[117] Thus, Lamanskii's Greco-Slavic world is more than just a religious community—it is a modern civilization related but not identical to the West.

In the same issue of *Russkaia Beseda*, the Bulgarian Church Question provided an opportunity for another prominent Pan-Slav, Prince Vasilii Cherkasskii, to link these still academic ideas of Greco-Slavic unity to geo-politics. The future governor of Russian-occupied Bulgaria in 1877 called for an active foreign policy in the Ottoman Empire disentangled from any alliances.[118]

Russia needed to act quickly to win the hearts and minds of her coreligion-ists away from the West. Russia's "legitimate task is to liberate the Greco-Slavic world in the East and at the same time to bring mediation and reconciliation between two nations (*narodnosti*) based on the principles that are rational, fair, and just for both sides." For this, the Russians had to consciously rely on "ethnic and religious affinity" and also brush aside any petty selfish concern or any traditional authority standing on the way to that "supreme rational law."[119] In other words, the Greeks and the Slavs should work together but not necessarily through the Patriarchate of Constantinople.

The policy advocated by Prince Cherkasskii was very different from the preservation of the complete authority of the Ecumenical Patriarchate advo-cated by Count Tolstoy, Filippov, and Metropolitans Gregory and Filaret. At the same time, it also differed from the wholesale support of all Bulgarian nation-alist demands at the expense of the Patriarchate as advocated by Alexander Rachinskii ("Mr. D.") and his publisher, Mikhail Katkov. Lamanskii and Cherkasskii blazed the trail for the middle way that would attract an even greater number of Pan-Slavs in the 1870s who would rationalize Orthodoxy as an important part of Slavic cultural traditions instead of seeing it as the body of church doctrine and institutional authority.

Still, the seeds planted by the anti-Patriarchate articles in 1858 pro-duced an anti-Greek trend among the leading Slavophiles. It is clear in *The Message to the Serbs from Moscow* published in 1860. The title is somewhat

---

116. Ibid., p. 135.

117. Ibid., p. 134.

118. Cherkasskii, Vasilii, "Dva slova o Vostochnom voprose," *Russkaia Beseda*, 12 (1858): 65.

119. Ibid., p. 91.

misleading because that hundred-page-long pamphlet was printed not in Moscow but in Leipzig—apparently, it was not cleared by Russian censorship. Its main idea was to warn Serbia of the dangers of Westernization, but European materialism and imperialism were compared to Greek arrogance and expansionism.

> We find the most striking example of spiritual pride not in Rome but in contemporary Greeks ... They consider the faith that their ancestors had served in the past to belong to them alone rather than to all who profess it. They see themselves as the only children of the Church and everyone else as slaves and adoptees. They hate everyone who disagrees with their misplaced pretensions especially the Slavs, they keep us in Turkish bondage to dominate us through the Turks. They hate our language—if they could, they would have driven it out of church and Divine Liturgy in contrast to their own original teachers. The bitterness has reached such a level that the Orthodox Greek is more oppressive to the Slavs than the Mohammedan Turk.[120]

However, the gravest sin of the Greeks was not their ethnic hatred for the Slavs. When the Greeks declared themselves as sworn enemies of the Slavs, they broke Orthodox ranks and let the eternal Western enemy into the fold. They turned from standard-bearers of into traitors to Orthodoxy. Now the Slavs needed to pick up the fallen torch of Orthodoxy and to unify its remaining loyal members. Thus, even those Slavophiles who sided with the Bulgarian nationalists demonstrated not modern ethnic consciousness but traditional Russian messianism.

> The Latin clergy calls itself the Church while dismissing the laypersons and seeing in them merely dumb animals. That is why they don't have the true Church. The Eastern Patriarch and Bishops have recently exposed that Latin lie thereby earning a great everlasting praise from all Orthodox Christians. But many of them do not quite follow their own teaching in reality, restricting the rights of the people. Through their betrayal (*nevernost'*), they give the weapons against themselves to the infidels in Bulgaria.[121]

---

120. Khomiakov, Alexei, Pogodin, Mikhail, Koshelev, Alexander et al., *K Serbam: Poslaniie iz Moskvy* (Leipzig: Franz Wagner, 1860), pp. 10–11.

121. Ibid., p. 98.

Conclusion

The Russian Crusading spirit and commitment to strengthening the position of the Orthodox high clergy became crystal clear in the tragicomic buildup to the Crimean War. The defeat in that global conflict forced Russia to work even closer together with the Concert of Europe. The European Great Powers (Austria, England, France, Prussia, and Russia) now assumed collective responsibility for the improvement of the situation of the Ottoman Christian minority. The Treaty of Paris included the Ottoman Empire into the European state system and guaranteed its territorial integrity on the condition of launching a more ambitious modernization program.

The post-1856 stage of the Tanzimat reforms went even further away from the traditional Islamic bifurcated state. Its aim was to build a civic territorial Ottoman nation with the same rights and laws for all regardless of creed. With this kind of light at the end of the tunnel, the Sublime Porte decided to empower the laypersons over clergy in all non-Muslim communities. After such a test, this model was supposed to be applied in the Islamic institution itself.

Russian diplomats traditionally worked with the Patriarchate, but its legitimacy was undermined by strong allegations of all kinds of abuses. In that chorus of accusations, the growing Bulgarian national movement began to demand a status of a separate religious community. On one hand, this agitation chimed with the Ottoman efforts to empower the laity. On the other hand, the Tanzimat promised equality to all subjects regardless of religion, not ethnicity. Bulgarian nationalists had to deal with the Patriarchate as all other Orthodox Christians under its jurisdiction. The Greek and Slavic delegates met at the Community Assembly from October 1858 to January 1860 to reform the Orthodox community institutions along the Tanzimat lines.

The Russian diplomats actively supported this reform, although the Russian Holy Synod had many second thoughts about it. With Russian backing, the Community Assembly turned into a working power-sharing mechanism and included many accommodations for ethnic diversity into the General Regulations of *Rum milleti*. Although the Bulgarian delegates were in the minority, they cooperated with their Greek colleagues for thirteen months. The Bulgarian nationalist movement could not truly represent all ethnic Bulgarians because most European and Middle Eastern peasants in the late 1800s saw themselves as members not of national but of religious and local communities. Although the Bulgarian activists were not as strong as they claimed, they did have a growing network of supporters in many cities in Bulgarian lands and abroad.

Bulgarian immigrants in Russia helped electrify the new Pan-Slav ideology and organizations. But between 1858 and 1860, their anti-Greek press campaign questioned the traditionally positive image of the Greeks in Russia, but it did not go very far. Between 1858 and 1860, their anti-Greek press campaign was stopped by Russian censorship at the request of the Patriarchate. Even Russian Slavophile intellectuals were not ready to adopt Bulgarian ethnocentrism wholesale. They preferred to update the concept of Orthodox unity by celebrating its ethnic diversity. Thus, the Christian East began to be reinvented as a Greco-Slavic civilization. Clearly, in this period, modern ethnic categories were becoming more important for Russian officials, clerics, and lay commentators than before 1856, but Orthodox Christianity remained the main element of Russian cultural identity and foreign policy in the Near East.

3

The Bulgarian Minority in Search of Ottoman and Orthodox Autonomous Institutions (1860–1870)

IN A CONVERSATION with the Russian consul in Ragusa, Prince Nikolai of the vassal Ottoman Principality of Montenegro "openly said that in his opinion it would be better if our coreligionists in Herzegovina resumed their fight against the Turks, he was planning to supply them with munitions and to encourage their armed bands to scatter across Herzegovina to cause a lot of trouble for the Turks with the goal of finally extracting substantial concessions and improvements." Consul Konstantin Petkovich did his best to dissuade the ruler of rugged Western Balkan highlands from pursuing that reckless policy—"a crime against the essential interests of the people" severely affected by recent crop failures and droughts.

Although the Bulgarian-born Russian consul urged moderation following his instructions from St. Petersburg, he personally did not believe in any positive effects of the Tanzimat by 1863. "The Turks will always be Turks and their attitudes towards the Christians will hardly ever change." He illustrated this dictum with a horrific story of a Christian woman from Zubtsi abducted on her way to fetch some water and gang raped by four Turkish soldiers.[1] The soil of Bosnia-Herzegovina did not produce much food but created a fertile ground for periodic Christian peasant revolts against mostly Muslim landlords and the Ottoman government. Like their

---

1. K. D. Petkovich to N. P. Ignatiev, 31 July/12 August 1863, Pisarev, Iu. A., and Ekmechich, M., eds., *Osvoboditelnaia borba narodov Bosnii i Gertsegoviny i Rossiia, 1850–1864* (Moscow: Nauka, 1984), p. 435.

FIGURE 3.1 "Group of Montenegrins," photographed by Robert Fenton in 1855. Library of Congress Prints and Photographs Division, Reproduction Number: LC-USZC4-9293. The Ottomans never managed to establish effective control of the rugged terrain of Montenegro. Since the 1700s, "the Black Mountain" was a Russian protectorate under nominal suzerainty of the Sultans.

Scottish counterparts, fearsome Montenegrin highlanders were fiercely independent, desperately poor, and always ready to join a cause in the neighboring valleys.[2] Figure 3.1 shows a group of them wearing traditional baggy trousers.

In the 1860s, sectarian tensions often boiled over into violence in the Ottoman Empire and provoked foreign intervention, starting in July 1860 with the massacre of thousands of Maronite and Orthodox Christians in Damascus and elsewhere in Syria. That shocking event galvanized all the members of the Concert of Europe into a joint peacekeeping action. In a rare moment of unanimity, the Great Powers forced the Sublime Porte to accept

---

2. Grandits, Hannes, "Violent Social Disintegration: A Nation-Building Strategy in Late-Ottoman Herzegovina," in Grandits, Hannes, Clayer, Nathalie, and Pichler, Robert, eds., *Conflicting Loyalties in the Balkans: The Great Powers, the Ottoman Empire, and Nation-Building* (London and New York: I. B. Tauris, 2011), pp. 110–111.

temporary occupation of Syria by the French expeditionary corps in 1860–1861 and the broad autonomy of Christian-dominated Lebanon.[3]

The burgeoning Bulgarian church movement would take advantage of those threats to the Ottoman Empire, presenting itself as a moderate alternative and demanding a limited autonomy within the existing administrative framework. Early in 1860, they moved to develop their own church and community institutions outside the Patriarchate. To overcome the opposition of the latter and legitimate its secession, the Bulgarian movement attempted to enlist the support of the Ottoman government and Russian diplomats and publicists as well as of Western representatives and missionaries. After a vigorous but unsuccessful all-or-nothing bid for the status of a separate *millet*, the Bulgarian nationalist leadership would return to the negotiating table.

The Ottoman government, along with the Russian diplomats and clerics, would serve as chief mediators in the tortuous process of developing acceptable power-sharing arrangements. In the process, both the Sublime Porte, Russian officials, and the Patriarchate of Constantinople would twist and turn the already reformed religious institutions to adapt them to the new principle of ethnicity. For their own reasons, for most of this period, Ottoman bureaucrats and Russian representatives worked more or less hand in hand trying to find ways to bring both sides together. But the Sultan's government began to rely on divide-and-rule tactics at the time of separatist conspiracies and rebellions in the late 1860s.

Bulgarian Easter of 1860: Secession from the Patriarchate

When in January of 1860 four Bulgarian deputies walked out of the Community Assembly despite the progress made to accommodate some of their demands, the Bulgarian movement started building its own institutions. On the symbolic level, the St. Stefan's Church in Constantinople was the center of the movement. For day-to-day business, its headquarters moved into the office of Khristo Tapchileshov, one of the richest Bulgarian businessmen in town.[4] Their generous support suggests that many members of the Bulgarian proto-bourgeoisie decided to translate their economic power into

---

3. Panchenkova, Marina, *Politika Frantsii na Blizhnem Vostoke i Siriiskaia ekspeditsiia, 1860–1861* (Moscow: Nauka, 1966), p. 206.

4. Mazhdrakova-Chavdarova, Ogniana, "Bulgarskoto natsionalno predstavitelstvo—idei i opiti za suzdavaneto my (40-te–60-te godini na XIX vek)," *Istoricheskii Pregled*, 49, 4 (1993): 31.

political clout outside the reformed Patriarchate, where more established and better-connected ethnically Greek lay circles had just taken control.

Bulgarian secession from the Patriarchate was finalized on Easter 1860 (3 April) when Hilarion, a titular bishop but essentially just a priest of St. Stefan's Church, at the appropriate moment of the divine service failed to mention the name of his superior, that is, Patriarch of Constantinople Cyril VII. Every time an Orthodox or a Catholic priest celebrates the Divine Liturgy, he (always a man) does not just reaffirm the dogma but also identifies his bishop, archbishop, or patriarch. Although St. Stefan's was considered a Bulgarian church since 1849, it was part of the diocese of Constantinople with the Patriarch himself at its head. His Grace Bishop Hilarion justified his action as a response to the demands of his parish and an attempt to prevent violence on the part of the Bulgarians angered by their continued dependence on the Patriarchate. This explanation did not convince Over-Procurator Count Alexander Tolstoy. He considered Hilarion's action a desecration of the Easter service under mob pressure.[5]

The memoirs of Bulgarian activists make it clear that Hilarion's account was a lie intended to cover his bases if push came to shove. The whole thing had been carefully planned and scripted. To discuss the details, Hilarion invited key lay Bulgarian leaders—Gavril Krustevich, Dimitrii Geshoglu, Nikola Minchoglu, and Khristo and Nikola Tapchileshov. They also secured the approval of two Ottoman officials—Mehmed Ali Pasha and Riza Pasha.[6]

Metropolitan of Moscow Filaret also thought that Hilarion had spoiled the most important Christian celebration but he was more concerned about how to keep the Bulgarians within the Orthodox Church. He proposed what would eventually come to be seen as the most acceptable solution by 1870. Their most justified demands would be satisfied if Bulgarian lands would be administered by a metropolitan with the right to appoint bishops. But this metropolitan should attend local church councils convened by the Patriarchate, should be consecrated by the Ecumenical Patriarch, and should receive from him the Holy Myrrh necessary for many rites.[7]

By rejecting any ecclesiastical authority above him, Hilarion in effect made himself a head of a Bulgarian church. As Russian consuls in Philippoupolis,

---

5. Russian State Historical Archive (RGIA), 797-27-2-2-426 part 2, Tolstoy to Gorchakov, 2 May 1860, pp. 145–1460b.

6. Stambolski, Khristo, "Iz spomenite mi za Ilarion Makariopolski (1858–1861)," in Arnaudov, Mikhail, ed., *Ilarion Makariopolski i Bulgarkiiat Cherkoven Vupros* (Sofia: Khudozhnik, 1925) 13–47.

7. RGIA, 797-27-2-2-426 part 2, Filaret to Tolstoy, 11 May 1860, pp. 152–153.

Adrianople, and Eski Zagora reported, many communities recognized him as such.[8] Given this flurry of petitions and telegrams, Evgenii Novikov, who served as an advisor on the staff of the Russian embassy in Constantinople, felt that Russia was losing the Bulgarians to the West because of the inflexible position of the Russian Holy Synod. He argued in favor of a clearly Pan-Slav pro-Bulgarian policy; otherwise, the Patriarchate would "subject us to its Greek-Byzantine view."[9]

It is interesting that as an ambassador in 1880–1882 Novikov would actually come around to adopting that same view. In 1860, he wrote with a Pan-Slav bias which came naturally to him. Before his diplomatic career, he received a master's degree in Slavic studies. But the Pan-Slav approach did not translate into a real policy. Whenever a local consul seemed too supportive of Bulgarian aspirations at the expense of the unity of the Orthodox Church, the Russian ambassador intervened to bring his subordinate back to the Pan-Orthodox track, which meant urging mutual concessions and moderation in the Bulgarian Church Question.[10]

If Hilarion wanted an Orthodox church rather than a new cult centered on himself, he needed recognition of other Orthodox churches and especially of the Mother Church—the Patriarchate of Constantinople. It took a lot of Russian effort to convince the Patriarch not to adopt a hard line toward Hilarion and his supporters. Metropolitan of Moscow Filaret counseled the Patriarch against turning to the Sublime Porte to punish Hilarion. He suspected the Porte of secretly encouraging Bulgarians to keep the Christians divided especially in the imperial capital. A harsh condemnation might also make Hilarion and Bulgarian nationalists more desperate.[11]

In response to Novikov, Filaret argued against supporting all Bulgarian demands because many of them were not legitimate. Bulgarians had "no *right* [underlined in the original] to seek church independence especially in the form of their own patriarchate." There were not that many Bulgarians and they often lived side by side with the Greeks, especially in the cities, which would make it difficult to find territorial limits of the new church. The city of Constantinople itself would need to be divided between two Orthodox communities, which was unheard of and contrary to canon law. Divided churches

---

8. RGIA, ibid., pp. 223–231.

9. E. P. Novikov to E. P. Kovalevskii, Deputy Foreign Minister, 17 May 1860, *Rusia i bulgarskoto*, vol. 1, part 1, op. cit., p. 389.

10. Consul in Varna A. V. Rachinskii to Ambassador A. B. Lobanov-Rostovskii, 28 May 1860, ibid., p. 401.

11. RGIA, 797-27-2-2-426 part 2, Filaret to Tolstoy, 21 May 1860, pp. 162–163.

would be less able to resist the political pressure of Islam. To make sure the Bulgarians did not turn Catholic or Protestant, Hilarion and the most reasonable Bulgarian leaders needed to ask the Patriarch to forgive them for caving in to popular pressure and to request the establishment of a church with limited autonomy, as outlined in Filaret's earlier letter.[12]

Later in the summer, Hilarion did apologize for his actions before the Holy Synod of the Patriarchate. Filaret realized that its prestige was challenged both by the Bulgarian movement and by the empowerment of the laity. He thought it necessary to have the Porte abandon its new right to strike one or two out of three final candidates at the elections of the Patriarch. If left with one candidate only, the Holy Synod would not obviously have a possibility to choose.[13]

Generally, Hilarion proved to be a difficult person to work with. He came up with a list of fourteen ethnically Bulgarian prelates (archbishops and bishops) but speaking on behalf of all Bulgarians he considered only half of them as "truly national pastors" whereas the rest were Hellenized traitors to their nation.[14] Obviously, they all could serve in Bulgarian areas knowing the language and the culture of their flock. Apparently, they simply did not have much respect for Hilarion and for this reason they were not good enough.

Hilarion's provocation shocked many Greek nationalists. It literally broke the heart of Theocletos Pharmakidis—the architect of the establishment of the Church of Greece in 1833. He recognized in Hilarion's secession the fruit of the seeds of ethnonationalism and uncanonical unilateralism he himself had planted. In the blazing midday heat of the Athenian sun, he rushed to the Ministry of Foreign Affairs to find out more details. After returning home, he became unwell and passed away several days later.[15]

Hilarion's actions raised the specter of an autonomous Bulgarian church and state in the Ottoman provinces that Greek irredentists had been dreaming about. A veteran of the Greek War of Independence, Hikesios Latris published a pamphlet with a strange title: *To the Compatriots in Thrace and Elsewhere Who Call Themselves Bulgarians*. He desperately tried to persuade them that all Balkan Slavs and especially the Bulgarians had inextricably

---

12. Filaret to Tolstoy, 9 June 1860, ibid., pp. 180–1820b.

13. Ibid., Filaret to Acting Over-Procurator Urusov, 22 August 1860, 22 August 1860, pp. 274–2740b.

14. Ibid., Asiatic Department of the Foreign Ministry to Urusov, 2 September 1860, pp. 283–2830b.

15. Papadopoulos, Chrysostomos, *Historia tes Ekklesias tes Hellados*. Vol. 1 (Athens: P. A. Petrakou, 1920), p. 444.

mixed with the Greeks. The Bulgarians did not have a developed literary language. What they spoke at home was "a dialect which was not pure Greek but a shapeless and locally varying blend of ancient and modern Greek, old Slavonic, Latin, and what not." Most Bulgarians knew Greek anyway. They were in fact descended from ancient and modern Greek settlers in the area. Being "of the same race and ethnicity," the Bulgarians should reject the foreign Pan-Slav agents who advocate the destruction of Greek communities and culture under the pretext of ethnic self-defense. Curiously, Latris portrayed Hilarion and other ringleaders of the Bulgarian national movement as the tools of both the Roman Pope and of Russian Pan-Slav societies.[16]

Bizarre as it seems, Latris' logic would justify Greek expansion into Slavic-speaking areas in the nineteenth and early twentieth centuries. Modern ethnonationalism puts a premium on linguistic affinity, thereby giving an advantage to Bulgarian nationalists. But illiterate Christian peasants in Macedonia and Thrace were not eager to sign up for one nationalist cause or another. That is why both Greek and Bulgarian nationalists were determined to turn the village church into the main vehicle of their competing propagandas. When the rhetoric was not persuasive enough, bribes, threats, and violence would come in handy.

We should not assume that the Bulgarian national movement was homogeneous or enjoyed universal support even in the cities, not to speak of the illiterate countryside. The pro-Catholic faction was only its most visible division, while Hilarion's supporters were the most vociferous group because of their bases in Constantinople. The community of Tatar Pazardjik made a deal with the Patriarchate to have a bishop to its liking. The wealthiest landholders and businessmen were often in favor of the Patriarchate because their social equals managed to translate some of their economic power into political influence with the Hatti Humayun. They were usually known as *grecomani*—crazy about all things Greek.[17]

Hilarion could not stay in line and he refused to pay a planned visit to the new Patriarch Joachim II as a sign of his submission to the legitimate authority. Instead he consulted key Bulgarian notables and two bishops who sided with him—Avksentii of Dyrrachium (Albania) and Paisii of Philippoupolis (Plovdiv). After the meeting, he declared that Bulgarians

---

16. Latris, Hikesios, *Pros tous en Thrake kai allahou sympatriotas, tous kalountas eautous Voulgarous* (Athens (probably): 1860), pp. 3–8.

17. Mazhdrakova, "Bulgarskoto natsionalno predstavitelstvo," p. 33.

would not join the Catholic Church but proclaimed himself as the head of the Bulgarian Orthodox Church. He was going to appoint his own bishops to all Bulgarian areas. All appointments by the Patriarch there were declared null and void. The Russian ambassador was relieved that the Catholic danger was not as serious now but thought it necessary for the Patriarch to make drastic concessions before it was too late and nothing short of the coveted prize of complete independence with Western sponsorship would satisfy the Bulgarians.[18]

It is hard to overemphasize the Russian fears of Bulgarians going Catholic to explain this growing sense of urgency to meet the Bulgarian demands. Hilarion presented himself as the only viable alternative to the union with Rome pursued by a smaller part of the nationalist movement as another way to achieve an independent church status. The danger of conversion was one of the strategies a minority movement can use to find outside support for its agenda.

Russian Political and Cultural Response to the Catholic Danger in Bulgaria

The mood of confidence of Filippov and his Pan-Orthodox supporters evaporated after September 1860. The most recent ban on the publications related to the Bulgarian Question was again forgotten. A new outpouring of Pan-Slav articles urged the Russian educated society and the government to force the Patriarchate to grant the Bulgarians "their own" church. That rhetoric again shared the same old leitmotif—the threat (spread by Bulgarians) or the fear (among Russian Pan-Slavs) of the Bulgarians going Catholic. In late 1860, there was a rapidly growing Bulgarian Uniate movement—the *Uniates* were usually allowed to keep Orthodox rites in exchange for recognizing papal supremacy. The Russian foreign policy remained focused on Orthodox unity, but the Russian educated society for the most part was outspoken in favor of the Bulgarian demands. But this unexpected intensity testified to the growing strength not of the ethnic Slavic component of the Russian identity but rather of its traditional Orthodox element. The motivation was to preserve the integrity of the Orthodox flock against the "seduction" by the traditional religious Other.

Thus, Foreign Minister Alexander Gorchakov communicated to Ambassador Lobanov-Rostovskii the alarm felt by the tsar at the news about "the trend among

---

18. Lobanov-Rostovskii to Gorchakov, 29 November 1860, *Rusia i bulgarskoto*, vol. 1, part 1, pp. 494–495.

the Bulgarian masses to abjure the Orthodox faith and convert to Catholicism." The Russian leadership still disapproved of "their exaggerated pretensions and riotous expressions thereof." But in view of the increasing Catholic influence, Lobanov-Rostovskii was given a free hand "within the limits which we neither should nor could overstep" to convince the Bulgarians of the Russian tsar's affection and sympathy of the same kind "that our sovereigns have constantly entertained for our coreligionists under Muslim domination."[19]

Were the Russian diplomats really trying to sit on two chairs? Writing in 1902, Grigorii Trubetskoi called this shift "unconscious replacement of the confessional principle with the national one." For fear of losing the Greeks and the Bulgarians, the Russian diplomats tried to please both sides, which caused both local groups to suspect the sincerity of those maneuvers. In Trubetskoi's line of argument, the Russian diplomats should not have over-reacted to the Uniate threat and should have unwaveringly adhered to the confessional principle with "more firmness in regards to certain unfounded claims of Bulgarian ringleaders (vozhaki)."[20]

The above instruction from Gortchakov to Rostovskii, however, did not mean ignoring the canonical law or working directly through the Ottoman government to establish a Bulgarian national church. Even before the brief Catholic scare of 1860–1861, the main Russian policy line advocated mutual concessions without breaking Orthodox traditions and canons. To prevent the massive Bulgarian defection to Catholicism, the Russian ambassador urged Patriarch Joachim II to guarantee the earlier promises of ethnically Bulgarian hierarchy, Slavonic liturgy, and schooling. But Joachim II later insisted on the prior repentance and submission of the rebellious Bulgarian bishop Hilarion.[21]

In desperation, Lobanov put the blame first on the Patriarchate, then on the Bulgarians, and finally on both. At one point, he concluded that the Bulgarian church movement could not balance for a very long time between "the seductions of one clergy which has good discipline, integrity, gener-ous funds to provide charities and promises all sorts of material assistance and all the benefits of civilization—and the obstinate immobility of a clergy which is ignorant, greedy, blind in their contemptible selfish calculations to

---

19. A. M. Gorchakov to A. B. Lobanov-Rostovskii, 19 November 1860, *Rusia i bulgarskato natsionalno-osvoboditelno dvizhenie, 1856–1876*, vol. 1, part 1, p. 484.

20. Trubetskoi, Grigorii, "Rossia i Vselenskaia Patriarkhia posle Krymskoi voiny, 1856–1860," *Vestnik Evropy*, 6 (1902): 501–502.

21. A. B. Lobanov-Rostovskii to A. M. Gorchakov, 29 November 1860, *Rusia i bulgarskato natsionalno-osvoboditelno dvizhenie, 1856–1876*, vol. 1, part 1, p. 494.

the eternal interests of the Orthodox Church and its noble mission among Eastern Christians."[22]

Far from demonizing the Patriarchate alone, Lobanov also criticized the uncooperative stance of Hilarion with his ambition to become the Bulgarian national Patriarch.[23] Lobanov suspected him of being unscrupulous enough as to be willing to acquire that title from the Pope. Hilarion was not really saying that all roads, including the one of Bulgarian church independence, led to Rome. But he seemed to be exploiting that opportunity and amassing more popular support for his claim to national leadership. In that context, even the Patriarch's concessions would not bring the Bulgarians to the Orthodox fold.[24]

Similarly, the Russian Church leadership praised "the magnanimous and wise tolerance" shown first by Patriarch Cyril VII and then by Joachim II (since October 1860), who refrained from excommunicating the openly insubordinate Bulgarian clergy and laypersons. However, in those six months the patriarchs were not reconciliatory enough but neither were Bulgarians willing to turn to their "legitimate pastor."[25] On balance, the Patriarchate looked a little better in the eyes of Russians.

Still, Prince Lobanov's spirits were sinking as he was losing any hope of stemming the Bulgarian movement for union with the Roman Catholic Church. He perceived it, however, not as a well-calculated loss of influence and clientele to a Western rival. Lobanov worked closely with the French ambassador and was confident that the latter had no part in the Catholic proselytizing effort among the Bulgarians. The earlier pro-Catholic movement on Crete petered out for lack of anticipated political and financial support from France but "the Bulgarian movement, on the contrary, is purely religious and the conflict (*differend*) develops without any relation to the attitude of the French embassy."[26]

In keeping with his "correct line of behavior charted from the very beginning of the dispute," French Ambassador de Lavalette informed Lobanov of having refused financial aid requested by the Catholic clergy to attract more converts.[27]

---

22. A. B. Lobanov-Rostovskii to A. M. Gorchakov, 21 December 1860, ibid., p. 514.

23. A. B. Lobanov-Rostovskii to A. M. Gorchakov, 20 December 1860, ibid., pp. 507–508.

24. A. B. Lobanov-Rostovskii to A. M. Gorchakov, 28 December 1860, ibid., p. 523.

25. Metropolitan Filaret to Alexander Tolstoy, 27 December 1860, *Sobranie mnenii*, p. 171.

26. A. B. Lobanov-Rostovskii to A. M. Gorchakov, 20 December 1860, *Rusia i bulgarskato natsionalno-osvoboditelno dvizhenie, 1856–1876*, pp. 508–509.

27. A. B. Lobanov-Rostovskii to A. M. Gorchakov, 28 December 1860, ibid., p. 528.

Rather than being a political defeat in the Great Power game, the perceived mass conversion of the Bulgarians was seen as a blow to Orthodoxy. This obsession speaks volumes of how strongly religion figured in the consciousness of the Russian elites at this time.

The Greek embassy in Constantinople also seemed to act in the same Pan-Orthodox spirit at the time of the Catholic union scare. From the purely nationalist point of view, Greece and its "Great Idea" would have benefited from keeping the Bulgarians divided into several confessional groups. Instead, Zanos, the Greek ambassador in Constantinople, tried to mediate between Hilarion and Joachim II in November and December of 1860 to make sure that the Uniate trickle would not become a flood.[28]

The reaction to the specter of Bulgarian defection in the Russian educated society was similar to the response in bureaucratic circles. The increased sympathy to Bulgarian nationalist demands was supposed to strengthen Orthodox Christianity rather than Pan-Slavism. If in September of 1860 Filippov and the other Pan-Orthodox felt that they were on the winning side, by December 1860 they perceived themselves completely isolated from the Russian mainstream.

Now Filippov believed publishing his article about the lack of historical justification for the Bulgarian Patriarchate was untimely. Filippov feared "everybody would understand the article as *unconditionally* directed against any change in the relations of the Bulgarian Church to the Ecumenical Patriarch [underlined in the original]." He was afraid of the Russian public's reaction in case of a very likely Uniate success in Bulgaria: "the whole blame will be attributed to the article—why bear such a heavy burden?" The feeling of crisis was sparked by a diplomatic report that "Bulgaria goes Latin (*latinstvo*) unless it is given its own Patriarch."

Although some Bulgarian leaders were willing to settle for a metropolitan (an archbishop), in Russia at this time there was a pervasive sense of the inevitability of Bulgarian separation from the Patriarchate. "This is absolutely correct. We are facing the dilemma: either a separate church administration or Latindom," wrote Filippov to Count Tolstoy.[29] This recognition was miles away from the view Filippov so eloquently argued in 1858—that the "Greek" Patriarchate should continue to shepherd Balkan Slavs without any structural adjustments.

---

28. Matalas, *Ethnos kai Orthodoxia*, p. 185.

29. State Archive of the Russian Federation (GARF), fond "T. I. Filippov" 1099-1-1265, T. I. Filippov to A. P. Tolstoy, undated draft letter to Tolstoy, pp. 92–93.

However, the Russian Church leadership was less impressionable and continued to consider the demand for a patriarchate excessive. In line with Metropolitan Filaret's recommendation, the Russian ambassador in Constantinople sought to limit the Bulgarian demands to an autonomous archbishopric nominally subordinated to the Patriarchate.[30]

Similarly, the mainstream Russian press would not adopt the Bulgarian nationalist agenda wholesale. Even when it supported some of their demands, it would not demonize the Greeks or the Patriarchate. This is especially true of ecclesiastical publications—they often took a dim view of the Bulgarian nationalists and tended to advocate reconciliation on the terms that would uphold the authority of the Patriarch.

Strannik provides a good example of how traditionally conservative church periodicals began to see ethnic divisions in the mass of Ottoman Christians but refused to privilege the Slavs over the Greeks. Even before the Catholic scare of late 1860-early 1861, Roman religious propaganda was described as "sparing no material effort to provide for outward prosperity of all Orthodox Christians seduced into Catholicism." The ensuing spread of Catholic proselytizing threatened "to considerably reduce the number of the Orthodox all over the East" without immediate and effective countermeasures. *Strannik* saw the situation as most dangerous not in Bulgarian lands but on the Greek-populated island of Crete. To illustrate this menace, *Strannik* reprinted an excerpt from *Severnaia Pchela*, a major lay newspaper in St. Petersburg, describing the ongoing conversion of many Cretans hoping to find relief from Islamic persecution.[31]

Amidst this adversity in the Orthodox East, the only hope was the extension of the Russian consular network to Crete. The new Russian consul "who will be able as far as possible to counteract the efforts of the Roman Catholic propaganda against Orthodoxy." Citing extensively from another major lay newspaper, *Sankt-Peterburgskie Vedomosti*, *Strannik* showed that Russian intervention was likewise needed to resist insidious Jesuit propaganda among the Serbs and Czechs.[32]

Overall, the April 1860 article in *Strannik* betrays the signs of the traditional siege mentality and the feeling of fighting a losing battle in the endless struggle between Orthodoxy and Catholicism: "Such is the character and

---

30. Metropolitan Filaret to Alexander Tolstoy, 8–10 December 1860, *Sobranie mnenii i otzyvov Mitropolita Moskovskogo i Kolomenskogo Filareta po dela Pravoslavnoi Tserkvi na Vostoke* (St. Petersburg: Holy Synod Press, 1886), p. 162.

31. *Strannik*, 1 (April 1860): 135–136.

32. Ibid., pp. 137–141.

mode of action of the Roman propaganda, same in the present and in the past! It employs all the means to spread the power of the Roman high priest and almost invariably more or less achieves its goal not only among the oppressed Orthodox Christians of the East but also, to the disgrace of Orthodox Russia, among some of our compatriots who are resident abroad."[33]

Two months later, in June of 1860, *Strannik* discovered "the Bulgarian religious movement, which made a sad impression on us." The first Slavs to embrace Orthodox Christianity, "the Bulgarians kept it in purity and integrity in the course of the millennium despite their political insignificance." *Strannik* detected the growing panic in the Russian press: "Now periodicals and newspapers are circulating the sad news about the Bulgarian religious movement. We hear from here and there that Bulgaria has adopted the *Unia* and the Bulgarians have become Catholics."[34]

But like many Russian prelates, many church publications refused to be pressured by the fear of the Catholic union into supporting the establishment of a completely independent Bulgarian church, *Strannik* went on to explain that the conversion of only a handful of Bulgarians to the *Unia* was the result of the Bulgarian national movement. *Strannik* did not condemn it as evil but pointed to potentially dangerous effects it might have on the Orthodox Church as a whole. After the Hatti Humayun of 1856, "the Bulgarians wanted to have their national spiritual representatives as well and planned political separation from the Patriarchate of Constantinople." The demands for Slavic bishops in majority Slavic areas, Slavonic liturgy, and Bulgarian instruction in schools were "clear evidence of the need of a nation, which is aware of its energies and is searching for ways of channeling them." The article's tone suggested that there was no need for political nationalism for Bulgarians to be good Orthodox and backed the Patriarch, who "did not think that the time was right to satisfy Bulgarian national aspirations (*natsionalnost'*)."[35]

"Irritated" (not a good Christian virtue), the Bulgarians took the novel politicization of religion a step further and began to demand "complete separation from the Patriarchate and their own independent national hierarchy." The discussion of the issue at the Community Assembly of the *Rum milleti* from 1858 to 1860 did not bring reconciliation. In response to Bulgarian demands, the Grand Vizier advised the Bulgarians to submit to the Patriarchate. Here a handful of them showed a total lack of deference to established temporal and

---

33. Ibid., p. 141.

34. *Strannik*, 6 (6 June 1861): 152.

35. Ibid.

religious authorities. "Incited by the Catholics," that group began to advocate joining the *Unia* among many other Bulgarians.[36]

The author of the article described the real threat of "losing" Bulgarians to the Pope, who promised them a separate Uniate Patriarchate. Only faced with this prospect did he explicitly welcome "the strengthening of the movement for the national Bulgarian church." *Strannik* saw it only as the means to combat the unexpected and serious danger of the spread of the *Unia*. That is why it approved of the new Sultan's decree as "the remarkable document." The latter did not impose any restrictions on the authority of the Patriarch, merely advising him to set up a seminary to train Bulgarian clerics, to teach Bulgarian language and literature in Bulgarian schools, to appoint Slavic-speaking bishops to vacant seats in majority Slavic dioceses, and to consider the requests of local communities for specific candidates provided they had necessary qualifications, etc.[37] As shown in chapter 2, most of those accommodations had been included into the General Regulations hammered out by the Community Assembly in 1860.

This obvious and unexpected division of the Orthodox Christian world had to be rationalized and possibly overcome: "United with the Greeks by the bond of common faith and with the Bulgarians by the double bond of faith and blood, let us wish both of them peace, love, and concord."[38] This statement from *Strannik* is remarkably similar to the concept of the Greco-Slavic world expressed by Lamanskii and Cherkasskii in *Russkaia Beseda* in 1858. These ideas are obvious enough to anyone with a decent grasp of history, so it is not clear in this case whether they were borrowed or arrived at independently. Like Filippov and Count Alexander Tolstoy, *Strannik* showed an awareness both of ethnic distinctions and of the comparatively greater importance of religion.

Given a relatively limited impact of the early pro-Bulgarian articles by Khristo Daskalov and others, the Bulgarian community in Russia renewed its efforts to demonize the Greeks and present the Bulgarians as the only truly suffering Ottoman Christians. As in 1858, this agenda was supposed to modernize the Russian cultural identity by orchestrating the transition from traditional Russian religious irredentism to ethnically based Pan-Slav irredentism.

Raiko Zhinzifov, a Bulgarian student in Moscow, became an active contributor in the new Pan-Slav newspaper *Den'*. He himself is a fascinating

---

36. Ibid., p. 153.

37. Ibid., p. 155.

38. Ibid., pp. 156–157.

example of the rapid urban spread of Bulgarian nationalism within one generation. Born in 1839 in Veles (Macedonia), he was named Xenophon, apparently after the famous ancient Athenian historian and adventurer. His father's pro-Greek sympathies also explain why he received education at a Greek secondary school. Only as an assistant teacher in Prilep, he stopped being a Greek wannabe under the influence of another Bulgarian teacher at the same school. When he moved to Russia to continue his education in 1858, the contacts with like-minded Bulgarian immigrants and Russian Pan-Slavs completed his national awakening. He even took the drastic step of changing his first name from Xenophon to Raiko to appear more Slavic.[39]

He published a letter decrying the ignorance of most Russians about all things Slavic. He recounted a personal anecdote of talking to a Russian priest before proceeding to confession: the latter, "seeing a non-Russian face," asked Zhinzifov where he was from. When the Bulgarian said that he was "from Turkey," the priest remarked, "sure, I know—this is where the Turks oppress the Greeks."

Zhinzifov retorted by saying that he was not Greek but a South Slav, a Bulgarian. Pausing, the priest apprehensively asked what his creed was. Having made sure that Zhinzifov was an Orthodox Christian, the priest admitted never having heard about the Bulgarians. In exasperation, Zhinzifov added that he had had a similar experience with Russian merchants and peasants: "I would always have to explain to all of them that it is a mistake to think 'Greek' stands for all Slavs." Zhinzifov insisted that despite their shared faith, the Greeks were just as oppressive to the Bulgarians as the Turks.[40]

In fact, mainstream Russian commentators were learning about the Bulgarians but did not always admire their leaders. Later the same year, *Khristianskoie Chtenie*, an influential church periodical, questioned the integrity and the motivations of the leader of the Bulgarian church movement, Bishop Hilarion. Their demand for ethnically Bulgarian bishops was not quite legitimate because for quite some time there had already been such bishops ordained by the Patriarch of Constantinople. The magazine suggested that Bulgarian bishops aspiring to even greater power fueled the whole Bulgarian Church Question.

Bishop Hilarion exemplified those unhealthy ambitions. The very moment he was consecrated "he began to systematically incite people to

---

39. Smolianinova, Marina, "Raiko Zhinzifov v Rossii," in Grishina, Ritta, ed., *Makedoniia: Problemy istorii i kultury* (Moscow: Institut slavianovedeniia RAN, 1999), pp. 100–104.

40. *Den'*, 3 (28 October 1861): 13–14.

liberate themselves and their church from the control of the Patriarch and the [Permanent Mixed] Council." For this he gained the support of "the patriotic party of the Bulgarian people" with the ultimate goal of "becoming himself the Patriarch of all Bulgaria." It is no wonder that *Khristianskoie Chtenie* upheld the decision of the Local Council of Eastern Orthodox churches to defrock Hilarion and other Bulgarian clerics found in violation of Orthodox canons.[41] Those dubious characters notwithstanding, the article ended up supporting the decree of the Porte urging the Patriarchate to promote Bulgarian language, bishops, etc. Much like *Strannik*, it was horrified at the prospect of losing Bulgarians to Catholics such as the Lazarist missionary Bore: "having a perfect command of Bulgarian, he managed to lead astray 4,000 gullible individuals."[42]

The Uniate movement seemed very attractive to many Bulgarian nationalists at the time, although most of them realized that it would create more divisions because the majority of the Bulgarians would never turn Catholic. Under a special papal dispensation, the former Orthodox Christians could keep all rituals in exchange for recognizing and mentioning the name of an incumbent St. Peter's successor as their spiritual head during the Divine Liturgy. There had already been a precedent of several thousand Arab Orthodox Christians making such a switch in the 1700s. The Ottoman government recognized them as a separate religious group, the Melchites, under their own patriarch.[43]

Similarly, the leadership of a Gregorian Armenian splinter group which had also won the status of an Armenian Catholic *millet* encouraged the Bulgarians to follow in their footsteps. In December of 1860, a couple hundred Bulgarians led by a distinguished elderly abbot, Archimandrite Iosif Sokolski, joined the Catholic Church. In May 1861, Iosif was consecrated Archbishop of all Bulgaria by the Pope himself in Rome. His status was recognized by the Ottoman decree establishing "the Uniate Bulgarian Patriarchate."

But in June 1861, Father Iosif suddenly disappeared and was found in Russia. From Odessa, he denounced the union with the Pope and asked the Patriarch to be readmitted into the Orthodox Church. There were rumors in the Catholic press that he was bribed by the Russian embassy but he may have actually been kidnapped. For years, he lived in Kiev under something

---

41. *Khristiansloie Chtenie*, 11 (1861): 347–349.

42. Ibid., pp. 355–357.

43. Haddad, Robert, *Syrian Christians in a Muslim Society: An Interpretation* (Princeton: Princeton University Press, 1970), pp. 28–29.

like house arrest.[44] The fear of Balkan Slavs turning Catholic or Protestant would never disappear from the minds of Russian diplomats, prelates, and publicists but it would never be as intense and profound as from 1860 to 1861.

From Secession to Negotiations, 1861–1864

During the Catholic scare of early 1861, Patriarch Joachim II used a combination of firmness and flexibility to steer his way toward resuming negotiations with the Bulgarian nationalists. His successors, Sophronius III and Gregory VI, would also have to work with their fellow prelates in the Holy Synod and to go through the new institution of the Permanent Mixed Council and periodic General Assembly sessions. As discussed in chapter 2, this structure enshrined the delicate balance of newly prominent laity and previously dominant high clergy. While Russia consistently urged reconciliation of both parties, the Sublime Porte did not always see its best state interest in it and began to play various factions off against each other.

Although some Russians saw Hilarion as the last bulwark against the Catholic danger, Joachim II had to find another Bulgarian partner to negotiate with. What was wrong with Hilarion? According to Joachim II, the Devil had stolen his mind and he became possessed by demons. " 'Above the stars of God I will set my throne on high.' As Lucifer, the first apostate against God, he moved the angels to terrible and rebellious actions to establish in his own person an independent church authority." He started by refusing to mention the name of the Patriarch and then inspired unbrotherly feelings "among some gullible Bulgarians in the capital and some Bulgarian dioceses."

He used slander to incite them to show no respect or obedience to the Church of Christ and their legitimate hierarchs. He presented himself at the session of the Holy Synod under Cyril VII in the summer of 1860 and promised to submit to church authorities and to stop his uncanonical actions. But he could not come clean of his past actions and behaved in an even more insolent manner. He found an accomplice in Avksentii, formerly the Bishop of Dyrrachium (modern Albania), to conspire together to disturb the peace of the church, to start unauthorized gatherings and factions, to consecrate unknown individuals, and to destroy the unity of the Church. Joachim II and the Holy Synod invited Hilarion several times to give account of his actions but he ignored all those gestures of their

---

44. GARF, 730-1-3472, Muraviev to Ignatiev, 27 May 1869, p. 20.

goodwill. With their patience exhausted, they proceeded to defrock both Bulgarian prelates.[45]

It could have been worse. The Russian Foreign Ministry begged the Patriarchate not to excommunicate Hilarion and his followers. The Russian statesmen were afraid that the extreme disciplinary action would produce an irreparable schism between the Bulgarian nationalists and the Patriarchate. The Russian diplomats encouraged the Russian Holy Synod to advise the Patriarchate to consent to an independent Bulgarian church with its own patriarch. As mentioned above, Metropolitan Filaret had good reasons to oppose this idea.[46]

One would not expect Joachim II to show any flexibility after such a devastating demonization of the Bulgarian nationalist leadership, but he did. Already in the above condemnation, he mentioned "Bulgarian dioceses," which implied the existence of areas with predominantly Bulgarian populations. Less than three weeks later, he made a statement about fifteen concessions confirmed by the Porte and mentioned in the *Strannik* and *Khristianskoie Chtenie* above. The most important one was the pledge to appoint ethnically Bulgarian prelates to "purely Bulgarian dioceses" after they had been nominated by the locals. One or two of those future Bulgarian archbishops would be able to take part in the elections of the Patriarch.

Joachim II did not forget to try to placate the lay instigators of the Bulgarian movement. Some of them who were resident in Constantinople would be elected and appointed to Patriarchate's offices. Clearly, this measure was supposed to make them less insecure of their status. Other concessions concerned the guarantees of Bulgarian cultural development such as the establishment of a theological school to train Bulgarian clergy. Others were granted earlier but were now affirmed—the permission to use Bulgarian as the language of instruction in Bulgarian schools and to celebrate the Divine Liturgy in Old Church Slavonic.[47]

Everything is in the eye of the beholder. Some could see those concessions as too little too late. Some would say they were promising but vague. Where were those "purely Bulgarian dioceses"? By recognizing their existence only theoretically, Joachim II seemed to be encouraging negotiations to strike a bargain on which areas would be included there.

---

45. Act of the Holy Synod, 4 February 1861, Gedeon, Manuel, ed., *Engrafa patriarhika kai synodika peri tou Voulgarikou zetematos, 1852–1873* (Constantinople: Patriarchate Press, 1908), pp. 78–84.

46. Gorchakov to Lobanov-Rostovskii, 24 January 1861, *Rusia i bulgarskoto natsionalno osvoboditelno dvizhenie*, vol. 1, part 2 (Sofia: Bulgarian Academy of Sciences, 1987), p. 31.

47. 23 February 1861, Joachim II, Gedeon, ed., *Engrafa*, pp. 24–27.

For a while, the Bulgarian nationalists ignored Joachim II's gesture until the Patriarchate had the government exile Hilarion with his two closest associates to remote monasteries in March 1861. Without their charismatic but uncooperative leaders, the Bulgarian movement resumed the search for some sort of official recognition. Grand Vizier Mehmed Kibrisli Pasha talked to the Bulgarian leaders, but as before, the Porte wanted them to deal with the Patriarchate. In July of 1861, they came up with eight demands whose goal was not to achieve a status of an independent community but to make Bulgarian notables full partners in the administration of the *Rum milleti*. This relatively moderate stance of the so-called "Eight Points" took a lot of flak from the more radical segments of the Bulgarian nationalist movement.[48]

First of all, the moderates insisted on increased influence on top clergy— participating in the patriarchal elections in accordance with the Bulgarian share in the overall Christian Orthodox population and changing the membership of the Holy Synod to include half Bulgarian prelates. The other six demands aimed at empowering Bulgarian notables through the future Bulgarian Mixed Council to be set up with one clergyman and one lay member in charge of a "community seal," who would be immune to the Patriarch's control and would have direct access to the government. This Council would elect bishops nominated by Bulgarian dioceses but in the mixed areas the bishop was to be elected by the predominant ethnic group. The amount of annual allowance and emoluments of the prelates were required to be specified.[49]

After the Bulgarian secession and the Catholic scare, the Russian embassy was relieved to learn that the Bulgarians were going to recognize the authority of the Patriarch and preserve institutional unity of the Orthodox community. According to Lobanov-Rostovskii, Grand Vizier Ali Pasha was also pleased with the relative moderation of the Bulgarian leaders. But Patriarch Joachim II thought they were still on the extreme side and hell-bent on a de facto separation. He consoled himself saying that they did not truly represent the mass of the Bulgarian people, who were accustomed if not devoted to Orthodoxy and would eventually submit themselves to the legitimate prelates.[50]

The demands were really too far-reaching to be nonnegotiable, as they involved serious revisions of the General Regulations enacted only a year earlier.

---

48. Mazhdrakova, "Bulgarskoto natsionalno predstavitelstvo," pp. 39–40.

49. Gedeon, ed., *Engrafa*, pp. 66–68.

50. Lobanov-Rostovskii to Gorchakov, 25 July 1861, *Rusia i bulgarskoto*, vol. 1, part 2, p. 138.

In June 1861, the Porte forwarded the demands to the Patriarchate, which refused to discuss them as contrary to its existing rights and privileges. Another dead end again conjured up among Russian diplomats the specter of the Bulgarian alliance with the Pope. Lobanov-Rostovskii himself showed to the Patriarch the Russian consular reports from Thessaloniki and Adrianople that discussed renewed efforts of Catholic missionaries to attract Bulgarians with the prospect of an independent church. Joachim II was not to be moved. He reminded the Russian envoy that the Catholic danger had always been around and reiterated his confidence in the devotion of common Bulgarians to the ancestral faith. To him, it was much worse to lose the established status of the Patriarchate than to see the Bulgarians go. The last point sounded shocking to Lobanov but actually made sense.[51]

Metropolitan Filaret of Moscow also believed that the Bulgarians' eight points were extreme and mindless of church canons. For example, the Bulgarian nationalists wanted to participate in the elections of the Patriarch but the latter would not control the Bulgarian clergyman presiding in their Mixed Council and keeping the seal. Their insistence on the autonomy of the Bulgarian Mixed Council in direct communication with the Porte meant that they were not really interested in church unity. Bulgarian political ambitions invited the Ottoman government to use divide-and-rule policies to manipulate the factions of the Orthodox Christian community.

Filaret thought the concessions made by Joachim II in February 1861 were ill-defined but could serve as a better foundation for reconciliation. If "purely Bulgarian dioceses" were specified, the Metropolitan of Turnovo could become the Patriarch's *Exarch* or representative there. Then the Bulgarian idea of nominating bishops by the people could work too as long as the Exarch consecrated them.[52] As before, the Russian diplomats followed his advice, aware of how dangerous it was for "laymen" to traverse the murky waters of church rules and traditions.

Some Greek lay members of the Permanent Mixed Council of the Patriarchate were unhappy with Joachim II. They feared that their significance would be diminished if his forceful reassertion of Patriarchal authority went as far as reversing some of the reforms of 1858–1860. They approached the Bulgarian leaders to make a common front against him and to force him to resign. They could find support among high clergy, some of whom were also tired of Joachim II's domineering personality and alleged corruption.

---

51. Lobanov-Rostovskii to Gorchakov, 8 August 1861, *Rusia i bulgarskoto*, vol. 1, part 2, pp. 144–145.

52. Filaret's memo, 19 August 1861, *Sobranie mnenii*, pp. 228–229.

Rumor had it that the Patriarch had made a fortune selling church offices to the highest bidder. But the Bulgarians did not have enough trust in the Greeks and rejected this cooperation.[53]

After the experience of 1861, the Foreign Ministry concluded that the Bulgarians were too often ready "to sacrifice the faith of their people in pursuit of an independent church." The Bulgarian leaders also allowed the Ottoman government to pit them off against the Greeks. Contrary to its promises, the Patriarchate did not always promote Bulgarian schools and Slavonic liturgy. This sad picture came out of the instructions for Vasilii Kozhevnikov departing for the newly established consulate in Turnovo—the home of Nikola Minchoglu, who published a rebuttal to Stephanos Karatheodoris' response to Bulgarian criticisms in 1860. Still, Kozhevnikov was reminded that Orthodoxy bound Russia to both the Greeks and the Slavs equally. To combat the spread of Western creeds, he was to take along a load of church books sent by the Russian Holy Synod to Constantinople to be sold at half price in Bulgarian lands.[54]

Almost a year later, Kozhevnikov clarified the situation in a way that confirmed the assessment of Patriarch Joachim II. There was no problem with the Bulgarian language and Slavonic liturgy in the medieval Bulgarian capital at the center of today's Bulgaria. The diocese was indeed under the ethnically Greek Metropolitan Gregory but there were almost no other Greeks there. The divine service in Turnovo and elsewhere was celebrated by Bulgarian priests in Old Church Slavonic. The Bulgarian nationalist movement did reach that diocese but had support largely in the cities among younger professionals and lower-level clergy. The more established and propertied citizens tended to back the Patriarchate. According to Kozhevnikov, the countryside was uninvolved because Bulgarian farmers had a different temperament from city dwellers. They put a premium not on politicking but on hard work and patience. In addition to anti-Greek agitation, another example of the restless urban character was an ill-planned abortive uprising in Gabrovo.

General illiteracy also kept Bulgarian nationalism away from most rural areas as its ideas spread through foreign missionary tracts and the Bulgarian newspapers published in Constantinople or by revolutionary émigrés in Romania and Serbia. The Russian consul in Turnovo confirmed what the

---

53. Lobanov-Rostovskii to Gorchakov, 12 September 1861, *Rusia i bulgarskoto*, vol. 1, part 2, p. 148.

54. Foreign Ministry instructions, 30 December 1861, *Rusia i bulgarskoto*, vol. 1, part 2, pp. 184–187.

Patriarchate and the Russian Pan-Orthodox like Filippov had been saying since 1858—Protestant and Catholic missionaries sought to discredit the Orthodox teaching and hierarchy by politicizing a church issue.

According to Kozhevnikov, the financial burden of "Greek" clergy was not excessive. The fees and dues owed to the Metropolitan were less than one seventieth of what the government demanded in taxes and only half of the expected amount was paid over the last several years in the Turnovo diocese. When the Bulgarian nationalist clergy took over all churches in Turnovo except for one, things did not improve for the common man. Those good ethnically Bulgarian pastors fleeced the flock, especially in the country. Bulgarian nationalists squabbled with each other and made confusing statements about their goals.[55]

At this time, the Ottoman government in Istanbul was not yet exploiting the conflict—it made another important move to encourage reconciliation between two sides. It decreed the creation of a ten-member commission without Patriarch's approval to include both lay and clerical representatives to negotiate eight Bulgarian demands. Five Greek members of the Permanent Mixed Council began talks with five Bulgarian representatives. Since April 1862, when the commission began its work, there was more hope for preserving the unity of the Orthodox community. The passions did not run nearly as high as before, even in the nationalist press.

In March 1863, Ali Pasha, serving as the Foreign Minister at the time, introduced two projects for the solution of the Bulgarian Church Question. He proposed to divide all dioceses into three groups to be represented in the Holy Synod by four metropolitans each. The first group would include predominantly Greek dioceses of Thessaly, Epirus, Aegean islands, and Asia Minor. The second group would consist of the majority Slavic dioceses of Bosnia, Herzegovina, and Bulgaria. The third division would incorporate ethnically mixed dioceses of Macedonia, Thrace, and Upper Albania. The Greek members of the commission rejected this plan "under the pretext that the composition of the Holy Synod cannot follow the principle of ethnicity." Those critical words came from Evgenii Novikov, who served as the acting Russian ambassador to Constantinople from 1863 to 1865.

He continued to speak approvingly of Ali Pasha's second plan prepared by his clever aides in anticipation of the objections often made by the Patriarchate. It was based on the new territorial division. Historically, the Greek dioceses tended to be more numerous but smaller than Slavic

---

55. Kozhevnikov to Novikov, 28 November 1862, *Rusia i bulgarskoto*, vol. 1, part 2, pp. 276–280.

ones, sometimes numbering as few as a thousand households. Now all dioceses would be put together into groups of more or less equal size—50,000
persons. Each group would be represented by its prelate. If indeed several
dioceses were joined together, their bishops would sit in the Holy Synod
in turns.

This proposal gained support not just of Bulgarian members but also of
the Greek Metropolitan of Arta Sophronius. This plan did not explicitly promote the principle of ethnicity but seemed to give more power to the high
clergy. For this very reason, the Greek lay leaders opposed it. More surprising
was the opposition of Joachim II but the Russian embassy stressed his personal rivalry with Sophronius to explain it.[56]

Filaret of Moscow could not stay out of this discussion. It broke his heart
to see Orthodox Christians unable to agree without mediation by a Muslim
official. He objected in principle to the argument made by the Patriarchate in
connection with the first plan that the Church could not recognize ethnonational distinctions in its midst. Filaret compared this position to the univer-
salist pretensions of the Roman Catholic church alien to Orthodoxy based on
the communion of several independent local churches.[57]

Almost two years later, the commission did agree on the first demand on the
right of ethnically Bulgarian representatives to be included on a regular basis
into the electoral conference to participate in the elections of the Patriarch.[58]

But even this single gain was annulled at the General Assembly of the *Rum
milleti* that met from February to June 1864. The main issue was something
that sounds familiar across history—the budget crisis. A large portion of the
Patriarchate's revenue was lost after the vassal principalities of Moldavia and
Wallachia unified by 1859 and quickly moved to create a de facto independent
nation-state of Romania by 1861, albeit under nominal Ottoman suzerainty.
The new government of Prince Alexander Cuza gradually nationalized rich
lands that belonged to Ottoman Christian monasteries and the patriarchates
of Constantinople, Jerusalem, Antioch, and Alexandria.

As Consul Kozhevnikov observed in Turnovo, many parishes evaded and
delayed paying church fees and taxes needed to support the clergy and various community institutions. Wherever there developed the Bulgarian nationalist movement, there was even more resistance to meeting those financial

---

56. Novikov to Gorchakov, 4 March 1863, *Rusia i bulgarskoto*, vol. 1, part 2, pp. 324–326.

57. Metropolitan Filaret to Over-Procurator A. P. Akhmatov, 27 March 1863, *Sobranie
mnenii*, p. 272.

58. Matalas, *Ethnos kai Orthodoxia*, pp. 213–214.

obligations. The case of Metropolitan of Varna Joachim (future Patriarch Joachim III) was not unusual. He complained that for six months, no allowance for the Metropolitan was collected and "since my consecration and arrival, I live only on loans and occasional donations." He begged the Patriarchate to secure a government order to the local Ottoman authorities to assist him whenever it was needed. "Without such assistance, nothing works, everything is in vain."[59]

The threats and the blows of Muslim soldiers did not make the Patriarchate any more popular. Apparently in desperation, the Community Assembly still tried a hard line to enforce the General Regulations with the backing of the Sublime Porte.[60] The hand of the government is clear from the language in which the final rejection of eight Bulgarian demands was written. It emphasized their incompatibility not so much with the spirit and canons of the Church as with the Ottoman political structure. While the term "Bulgarians" existed in popular usage, the "Bulgarian nation" had no legal meaning. "Since all citizens of the Ottoman state today constitute one nation, the government of his Majesty the Sultan protects its interests, no other body can make political claims to represent exclusive national interests." In addition to the civic nation, there is a legally recognized Orthodox Christian community, which is often called a religious nation or *millet*.[61]

Given the difficult financial straits of the Patriarchate, it made sense for the Sublime Porte to show the Bulgarians back into the fold to contribute to the economic recovery of the largest Ottoman non-Muslim minority. This greater pressure to enforce fiscal discipline did not work very well. Later the same year, both the Greeks and the Bulgarians did their best to avoid paying a new extraordinary tax enacted to help pay off the debts of the *Rum milleti*, according to Antonin, the priest of the Russian embassy church.[62] Still, he considered the recent pro-laity reforms of the Patriarchate a success and recommended decorating with a Russian medal or order their chief architect, Stephanos Karatheodoris.

The Slavo-maniacs accuse him of not only having done nothing in the Bulgarian interests but also of having actively thwarted their goals

---

59. Metropolitan of Varna Joachim to the Patriarchate, 25 June 1865, Nikov, Petur, ed., *Bulgarskogoto vuzrazhdane vu Varna i Varnensko: Mitropolit Ioakim i negovata korespondentsiia* (Sofia: Pridvorna Pechatnitsa, 1934), p. 226.

60. Stamatopoulos, *Metarrythmisi*, pp. 240–243.

61. 21 February 1864, Gedeon, ed., *Engrafa*, pp. 62–63.

62. RGIA, 797-27-2-2-426 part 6, Antonin to S. N. Urusov, 9 December 1864, p. 128.

when he played such a significant role at the Community Assembly of 1858–1860. But, first, at the Assembly he only said that it was not supposed to solve the issue of a separate Bulgarian nation; second, Russia and its government appreciate not only the services on behalf of this or that Slavic group but also in the interest of the Orthodox Church, which is more important; third, the aim of any wise policy is to win over its influential opponents through kind attention. I know for a fact that Mr. Karatheodoris would be honored to have a Russian decoration.[63]

The implications of the dire financial plight in the Patriarchate provoked a debate in the Russian press on the virtues of the "Greek" leadership of the Ottoman Christian community. Similarly, during his visit to Constantinople in the summer of 1864, Vladimir Lamanskii was alarmed by the pitch of conflict and wrote to convince Ivan Aksakov, the publisher of *Den'*, that most Russian Pan-Slavs "got carried away." They identified too closely with the anti-Patriarchate campaign of Bulgarian nationalists: "The Greeks really do have some rights ... One must protect the Bulgarians against the Greeks where necessary but we, the Russians, should view the Greeks with our own eyes."[64] This middle ground between Pan-Slavism and Pan-Orthodoxy is in the spirit of the concept of the Greco-Slavic world that Lamanskii had been popularizing since 1858.

The Pan-Orthodox activists in Russia promoted not abstract ethnic groups but the specific institution of the Ecumenical Patriarchate. Diplomat Vasilii Nekliudov made even clearer than Filippov the connection between supporting the Patriarchate of Constantinople and the territorial integrity of the Ottoman Empire in the popular monthly *Russkii Vestnik*. Nekhliudov approved of the Russian official stance against the nationalization of the landholdings of Ottoman Orthodox communities in Romania. Without powerful Greek prelates, the Slavs and the Arabs would succumb to the "seduction" of Catholic and Protestant missionaries. To resist Western political and religious influence in the Christian East, Russia needed to strengthen the Greek leadership of the Christian Orthodox churches. In Nekhliudov's view, that policy rather than Pan-Slavism was in line with the traditional Russian policy of

---

63. Antonin to S. N. Urusov, 4 November 1864, Gerd, Lora, ed., *Arkhimandrit Antonin Kapustin: Doneseniia iz Konstantinopolia, 1860–1865* (Moscow: Indrik, 2013), pp. 142–143.

64. Quoted in Nikitin, Sergei, "Natsionalnoie dvizhenie na Balkanakh v osveshenii russkoi periodicheskoi pechati," *Ocherki po istorii iuzhnykh slavian i russko-balkanskikh sviazei, 50-e–70-e gody XIX veka* (Moscow: Nauka, 1970), p. 219.

protecting all Orthodox Christians regardless of ethnic affiliation. Preventing nationalism from destroying the Patriarchate also made sense if Russia was to support egalitarian Tanzimat reforms, to build peaceful relations, and even an alliance with the Ottoman Empire in the post–Crimean War context.[65]

This provocative piece led to the debate with Mikhail Volkov and a certain "D. A-ii" in the Pan-Slav newspaper *Den'*. Volkov argued that Russia's true base of support was not in the self-serving Greek hierarchy but in the masses of Slavic brethren. Increasing the wealth of the prelates would not strengthen the religious devotion of their neglected flock. The Slavs would abandon Orthodoxy unless given a national church.[66] Since the Phanariotes pocketed most of the revenue from the landed property in Romania, nationalizing it would not hurt Ottoman Orthodox Christians and would benefit the Romanian Orthodox. There could also be no long-term accommodation, not to say an alliance with the Ottoman Empire. Russia could not tolerate the persecution of Christians—no internal reforms would stop it as long as the Ottoman Empire remained an Islamic state.[67]

Even when supporting the Bulgarian nationalists, the Russian Pan-Slavs did not adopt their ethnocentric logic in spite of the efforts of the Bulgarian lobby like Raiko Zhinzifov. The Greeks were criticized not because they had become a race hostile to the Slavs but rather because they betrayed the cause of Orthodoxy by hijacking the Ecumenical Patriarchate to serve their nationalist Great Idea.[68]

In 1869, Nikolai Danilevsky produced the most influential Pan-Slav synthesis of religious and ethnic elements of Russian cultural identity. As young men in the 1840s, he and Fyodor Dostoevsky were fellow members of a Fourierist socialist group in St. Petersburg and dreamed of a perfect social order without class exploitation or government oppression. Both were arrested but Danilevsky was quickly released and became a successful fish industry expert, whereas Dostoevsky was sentenced first to death and then to ten years of hard labor and exile in Siberia.[69]

---

65. Nekliudov, Vasilii, "Ob otnoshenii Rossii k Ottomanskoi imperii," *Russkii Vestnik*, 10 (1864): 613–631.

66. Volkov, Mikhail, "Po povodu statii g. Nekliudova," *Den'*, 6 (6 Feb 1865): 134.

67. "D. A-ii," "Po povodu statii "Ob otnoshenii Rossii k Ottomanskoi imperii" g. Nekliudova," *Den'*, 24 (12 June 1865).

68. Popov, Nil, "Raspria mezhdu bolgarami i greakami," *Sovremennaia Letopis*, 28 (1866): 1–4.

69. MacMaster, Robert, *Danilevsky, a Russian Totalitarian Philosopher* (Cambridge, MA: Harvard University Press, 1967), pp. 57–58.

Tired of sorting out schools of fish, Danilevsky turned to classifying people instead. He invented the concept of cultural-historical type to strip post-Enlightenment Western Europe of its pretensions to being the universal civilization. "Romanic-Germanic Europe" was one of many cultural-historical types and was likewise destined to experience its rise and fall. The much more youthful Slavic cultural historical type was only beginning its journey through time to realize its enormous potential within a Russian-led federation. Although its capital would be in Constantinople, Danilevsky foresaw no special role for the Ecumenical Patriarchate. The Greeks would be comfortable as the business elite connecting many parts of the new realm economically.[70]

Although less Greek-friendly than Lamanskii's "Greco-Slavic world," Danilevsky's theory was a more systematic attempt to modernize the existing traditional relationship between Russia and the Christian East. Scientific terminology did not detract from its inherent messianism. Danilevsky clearly saw the future Russian-led Slavic Union as the successor to the Byzantine Empire not just in geographical terms but more importantly in the endless struggle of Orthodox Christianity against Roman Catholicism and Western secularism. He feared that unless brought into a closer union with Russia, the Slavs in general and their intelligentsia in particular were in danger of "losing their Slavic character" via "either religious or political or civilizational seduction" by the West.[71] In 1869, Danilevsky's theory went unnoticed but it would be rediscovered in the 1870s.

The Bulgarian National Movement at the Crossroads: Ottoman Institutionalization versus Orthodox Legitimation

"Ambassador Ignatiev's satanic policy triumphed when he transformed into his minions Sultan Abdulaziz I and Grand Vezier Mahmud Nedim Pasha," in the exasperated words of a modern Greek historian.[72] This infernal reputation intrigued other scholars, who worked hard to explain how Ignatiev had become known as "The Father of Lies" in his time.[73] Indeed, Count Nikolai

---

70. Danilevsky, Nikolai, *Rossia i Evropa* (Moscow: Kniga, 1991 [1869]), pp. 374–375.

71. Danilevsky, *Rossia i Evropa*, pp. 319–320, 358.

72. Letsas, Alexandros, *Ho Aimilianos Grevenon kai to Neotourkikon Komitato* (Thessaloniki: Institute for Balkan Studies, 1964), p. 5.

73. MacKenzie, David, *Count N. P. Ignat'ev: The Father of Lies?* (Boulder: East European Monographs, 2002).

Ignatiev was Russia's most colorful ambassador to Constantinople (from 1865 to 1877). He shared many Pan-Slav ideas and believed in the eventual collapse of the Ottoman Empire into several Christian nation-states. But in the meantime he was content with the prospect of the survival of the Sultan's realm with predominant Russian influence there. In fact, when in Constantinople, that hyperactive and even aggressive diplomat would pursue and largely achieve his goal.[74]

Long before reaching the shores of the Bosphorus, he showed his fearless personality and diplomatic skills in even more exotic places. In 1858, with only fifty men he crossed the wild steppes and deserts of the Central Asian no man's land to arrive at the court of the Emir of Bukhara in modern day Uzbekistan, where he successfully negotiated a trade agreement and the release of kidnapped and enslaved Russian travelers and settlers. In the spring of 1859, he was sent as an extraordinary envoy to China to settle a border dispute. Instead, he obtained significant territorial acquisitions by playing the Qing government off against the representatives of France and England. At that time, those Western powers were fighting another infamous Opium War (1856–1860) and threatened to occupy Beijing in defense of European civilization.[75]

From 1861 to 1865, Ignatiev was in charge of the Asiatic Department of the Russian Foreign Ministry, where he learned of the puzzling ups and downs taking place in the Ottoman Christian community since 1856. As discussed above, Evgenii Novikov accepted if not welcomed Ottoman intervention as the acting ambassador in Constantinople (1863–1865). In contrast, Nikolai Ignatiev wanted the Greek-Bulgarian dispute to stay in the Orthodox family without involving the Sublime Porte in the settlement process, but he would have to compromise on this principle.

In 1865, he managed to have the Porte and Patriarchate return three rebellious Bulgarian prelates who had been defrocked and exiled out of the capital early in 1861. This act created enough goodwill to bring the two sides again to the negotiating table, first under the auspices of the Patriarchate and then with the encouragement of the Porte. The two commissions recycled several power-sharing mechanisms discussed since 1858 and especially between 1861 and 1864—ethnic quotas in the patriarchal electoral conference, in the composition of the Holy Synod, and the election or nomination of the bishops and metropolitans by the dioceses. Although

---

74. MacKenzie, *Count N. P. Ignat'ev: The Father of Lies?*, p. 234.

75. Meininger, Thomas, *Ignatiev and the Establishment of the Bulgarian Exarchate (1864–1872)* (Madison: University of Wisconsin Press, 1970), p. 5.

Patriarch Sophronius III (1863–1866) was quite cooperative, he did not possess enough power to sanction those schemes, as they involved changes in the General Regulations. He convened the general Community Assembly of 1866, which ditched the new projects just like its predecessor had done in 1864.

As before, the Bulgarian demands threatened to tip the balance in the Patriarchate in favor of the laity. This time they also found support among influential families who believed that solving the Bulgarian Church Question was a precondition for the settlement of pressing economic issues. They saw the cooperation of Bulgarian nationalists as key in securing regular monetary contributions from the Bulgarian dioceses desperately needed to pay off the debts of the *Rum milleti* and to provide allowance and emoluments for Patriarchate's bishops.[76]

The Bulgarian church movement was also divided, but because of the lack of established clergy the divisions ran inside lay groups—younger, more radical professionals and older, more moderate, and wealthier business and landed elites. The latter were not too far below top Greek notables and thus were more interested in getting better terms of inclusion into the existing Orthodox community institutions than in breaking away from them completely. Ignatiev identified Bishop Hilarion and Stoian Chomakov as the leaders of the extreme Bulgarian nationalist wing (*ultra-bolgarizm*). They were opposed to any reconciliation with the Patriarchate and argued in favor of establishing some sort of Bulgarian church by the Sultan's decree because they became willing players in the Ottoman "divide-and-rule" game for personal advancement and career growth.[77]

There was a hope that another Patriarch with a broader vision would be able to rise above various interest groups and bring back the much-needed unity. In late 1866, Ignatiev backed Gregory VI, who had already served as the Patriarch from 1835 to 1840. He had such independence and integrity as to make him the most respected living prelate in the Christian East. Probably for the same reasons, the Sublime Porte repeatedly excluded him from the list of candidates for the Patriarch's office, but in early 1867 Ignatiev somehow managed to persuade the Ottoman government not to strike his name off.[78]

---

76. Stamatopoulos, *Metarrythmisi*, p. 263.

77. N. P. Ignatiev to Deputy Foreign Minister Petr Stremoukhov, 26 January 1865, Kiril, Patriarkh Bulgarskii, *Graf N. P. Ignatiev i bulgarskiat tserkoven vupros: Issledvane i dokumenti* (Sofia: Sinodalno izdatelstvo, 1958), pp. 208–209.

78. Meininger, *Ignatiev*, pp. 79–83.

At this crucial time, Tertii Filippov was working within the Slavophile and Pan-Slav circles to improve their attitudes toward the Greeks. Writing to his famous mentor Professor Mikhail Pogodin, he explained the special role of the Greeks as "the nation endowed by the Lord with divine gifts" and "the force of intellect, experienced and ready to act, in the know of all ins and outs in the East." Russia could not afford to spurn them "into the service of our direct enemies." Filippov urged Russian mediation even more than in 1858 since Russia's mission was "to bring reconciliation between the brothers."[79]

On ascending the throne of the bishop of New Rome, Gregory VI worked with Ignatiev to secretly develop a plan that went further than the concessions made in February 1861 under Joachim II. The document proposed to establish an autonomous Bulgarian church under its own metropolitan designated as the Exarch of the Patriarch. He would be elected by the bishops and archbishops of the dioceses to be included into his area and consecrated by the Patriarch. Bulgarian prelates and notables would participate in the Permanent Mixed Council just like their Greek counterparts. This project seems inspired by the earlier suggestions by Filaret of Moscow. According to Ignatiev, Gregory VI said in disbelief, "With my own hands, I have built a bridge to Bulgarian political independence."[80]

The elderly patriarch indeed made clear where "Bulgaria" was—the dioceses included into the plan were located between the Danube and the Balkan range. Ignatiev did his utmost to ensure the acceptance of the long-awaited solution to the Bulgarian Question and was incensed by the new territorial demands made by Bulgarian nationalists. Although the more established individuals among them, led by Bishop Paisii of Philippoupolis, more or less accepted the plan, the poorer and greedier professionals argued that most dioceses south of the Balkan range were also ethnically Bulgarian. Although sympathetic to Pan-Slavism, Ignatiev opposed their threat "to elect the bishops without the participation of the Patriarch" as "leading to a dangerous schism in the Great Church [of Constantinople]."[81]

Like his predecessors, Ignatiev consulted Metropolitan Filaret, who also backed Gregory VI's plan based on the right of the flock to have good pastors

79. RGALI (Russian State Archive for Literature and Arts), fond 373-1-361, Filippov to Pogodin, February 15 1867, p. 140b.

80. N. P. Ignatiev to P. N. Stremoukhov, 28 February 1867, 2 May 1867, Patriarkh Kiril, ed., *Graf Ignatiev*, pp. 239, 241.

81. N. P. Ignatiev to P. N. Stremoukhov, 19 September 1867, Patriarkh Kiril, ed., *Graf Ignatiev*, p. 247.

who would know their language and understand the Divine Liturgy and the teaching of the Church.[82] Filaret believed that the majority of Bulgarian dioceses should be included into the future Bulgarian Exarchate but not at the cost of violating church canons.[83]

The Sublime Porte was also aware of political implications of a Bulgarian national institution with clear territorial boundaries. Gregory VI's plan was being discussed at the time of a major separatist uprising on Crete (1866–1869). Greece was openly helping the rebels sending volunteers and supplies. The reconciliation of Ottoman Greeks and Bulgarians could make it easier to start a general anti-Ottoman revolt on the mainland. This was indeed the goal of the Balkan alliance prepared by the secret agreements that Prince Mikhail Obrenovich of vassal Serbia made with Bulgarian émigré revolutionary groups, Greece (1867), and two other Ottoman vassal states, Montenegro (1866) and Rumania (1868). Fortunately for Sultan Abdulaziz I (r. 1861–1876), the whole conspiracy fell apart when Prince Mikhail was assassinated in 1868.[84]

But before and shortly after that tragic event, the Ottoman Empire seemed on the verge of partial or even complete disintegration—a prelude to the fateful Eastern Crisis of 1875–1878. The Cretan Uprising found much support among both Ottoman Greeks and Bulgarians. Often immune to nationalism, most Macedonian Christian villagers welcomed any anti-Ottoman uprising. According to the local Russian consul in Bitola, the sympathy for the Cretan rebels bridged the gap even between urban pro-Bulgarian and pro-Greek factions (grekomany).[85] In contrast, the "extreme" Bulgarian nationalist group, led by Stoian Chomakov, sent an open letter to the Sultan to condemn the Cretan Uprising. By flaunting their Ottoman patriotism and loyalty, they hoped to win official acceptance of their clearly less dangerous project of an independent Bulgarian religious community. But that glaring breach of Christian solidarity shocked even those who normally supported Chomakov. The Bulgarian activists in Adrianople asked their counterparts in

---

82. Metropolitan Filaret's response to the Foreign Ministry's memo on the Bulgarian Church Question, October 1867, *Sobranie mnenii*, p. 293.

83. Filaret to the Holy Synod, 14 Nov 1867, *Sobranie mnenii*, pp. 296–298.

84. Jelavich, Barbara, *Russia's Balkan Entanglements, 1806–1914* (Cambridge: Cambridge University Press, 1991), p. 153; Stavrianos, Leften, *Balkan Federation: A History of the Movement toward Balkan Unity in Modern Times* (Hamden: Archon Books, 1964), pp. 92–102.

85. N. F. Yakubovskii to N. P. Ignatiev, 23 October 1866, *Rusia i bulgarskoto*, vol. 2, pp. 338–339.

Philippoupolis (Plovdiv) to replace Chomakov with someone more reasonable as their representative in the imperial capital.[86]

Chomakov's coterie was indeed less radical than the Bulgarian nationalist revolutionaries, who were planning to attack the Ottoman installations from their safe havens on the Romanian side of the Danube. Surprisingly, some Russian consuls thought those small bands actually had a chance to spark a general uprising because there were few Ottoman troops left in the interior. In the whole district of Varna, there were only 150 soldiers. Sensing a danger, they began to increase their military preparedness.[87]

The making of the Pan-Orthodox Balkan union between 1866 and 1869 put on hold the growing hostility toward the Greeks among the Russian Pan-Slavs. Their press criticized the Russian government for its neutral stand and even joined liberal publications to encourage donations and demonstrations in support of the Cretan demands for unification with Greece.[88] In Western Europe, the reading public also experienced the revival of Philhellenist enthusiasm not seen since the Greek War of Independence (1821–1830). In 1870, the wildly popular French novelist Jules Verne published *20,000 Leagues Under the Sea*, where among other exploits the mysterious Captain Nemo transported his fabulous treasure to Cretan rebels on the *Nautilus* submarine.

Ambassador Ignatiev was quite sympathetic to Prince Mikhail's plans but the Foreign Ministry in St. Petersburg was much more cautious. Looking at the period from 1856 to 1867, Foreign Minister Gorchakov identified the preservation of the Ottoman Empire as a long-term Russian goal. He reminded Emperor Alexander II that this policy dated back to his uncle Alexander I, who had concluded in the early 1800s that a weak Turkey was the best neighbor to be had in the southwest. At the same time, Russia could not remain indifferent to the aspirations of local Christian populations. Russia was in a special position "to be able to assure their access to political life or to preserve it" but it would be foolish to support every spontaneous ill-conceived anti-Ottoman rising. The last words undoubtedly referred to the Cretan rebels. Since Russia concentrated on domestic reforms, it had no resources to fight for them. It should limit itself to warm moral support.

The 1867 marriage of Princess Olga Romanov to Georgios I, King of Greece, also raised Greek expectations of a firm Russian commitment to the Greek cause generally and of the success of the Cretan Uprising specifically.

---

86. M. I. Zolotarev to N. P. Ignatiev, 11 January 1867, ibid., p. 384.

87. V. I. Niagin to N. P. Ignatiev, 25 April 1867, ibid., p. 439.

88. Senkevich, Inna, *Rossiia i Kritskoie vosstaniie, 1866–1869* (Moscow: Nauka, 1970), pp. 84–90.

To avoid the impression of unilateral intervention, Russia joined the other members of the Concert of Europe in the protests against the violations of Christian rights. Unfortunately, the Ottoman government ignored those collective pronouncements not backed by a credible threat of force. At least, Gorchakov hoped, Russia would not appear responsible for inaction in the eyes of Balkan Christians.[89]

European initiatives were hard to reconcile and impose on the Sublime Porte. The Russian diplomats favored a broad autonomy for Christian-populated areas like Crete and the Balkan provinces. Napoleon III's government insisted on strengthening the power of the Ottoman central government to curb local abuses and to promote national unity.[90] The British cabinet wanted to preserve the status quo or at most to extract from the Porte a promise of moderate reforms to pacify Europe's public opinion. Ignatiev did not think any imposed reforms would improve the situation of Ottoman Christians because they would remain a dead letter. The best way to help Russia's coreligionists would be to make sure that Ottoman judges and officials were paid on time and in full. Then they would not be forced to extort money from the common people, driving them to rise in doomed rebellions.[91]

In addition to corruption, government taxes had also dramatically increased following the post-1856 Tanzimat reforms. Before the Crimean War, the city of Varna paid 40,000 piastres in taxes a year; a decade later, that amount reached 300,000. The tax on non-Muslims (*harach*) was not merely renamed into more politically correct "conscription exemption tax" (*bedel*) but was also raised from 30 to 45 and 60 piastres per male adult.[92]

Not all Christians chafed under the often-decried Muslim yoke. Well-connected and wealthy individuals took advantage of the Tanzimat reforms and began to play a greater political role in provincial councils or in the capital. Established families of Greek or Hellenized bankers and bureaucrats became even more prominent both through the Permanent Mixed Council of the *Rum milleti* and in the civil service. New churches were built without any bureaucratic red tape in and outside the capital city.

---

89. Gorchakov to Alexander II, 23 December 1867, Zueva, N. V., Shatokhina, E. M., eds., "Iz istorii balkanskoi politiki Rossii, 1856–1867 (otnoshenie russkoi diplomatii k bolgarskomu natsionalno-osvoboditelnomu dvizheniu)," in *Balkanskie narody i evropeiskie pravitelstva, konets XVIII-nachalo XX veka: Dokumenty i issledovania* (Moscow: Nauka, 1982), pp. 163–166.

90. Senkevich, *Rossiia i Kritskoie Vosstaniie*, p. 133.

91. N. P. Ignatiev to A. M. Gorchakov, 21 March 1867, *Rusia i bulgarskoto*, vol. 2, pp. 408–409.

92. N. G. Daskalov to N. P. Ignatiev, 2 December 1866, ibid., p. 355.

FIGURE 3.2 Panaghia Elpida Orthodox Church, Kumkapi, Istanbul (personal photograph). A much older church was rebuilt in the 1850s in the mixed Byzantine and rococo style.

Their changing appearance also reflected greater Christian confidence. For centuries, they looked no different than surrounding residences. The fancier ones were tucked behind high walls away from the sensitive Muslim eye. After 1856, new churches began to openly display crosses and even to ring bells in bigger cities. For example, in just one neighborhood of Constantinople, Kumkapi, there were two Orthodox churches constructed in the 1850s in the mixed neo-Byzantine and European rococo style—Haghia Kyriake and Panaghia Elpida (see Figure 3.2).[93]

Ottoman Greek elites did not necessarily welcome the fusion of all Ottoman subjects but something like a federation. They supported the establishment of territorial autonomy in Christian-majority areas but not as wide as in only nominally vassal Serbia or Romania. They advocated a stronger role for central government, which would appoint Christian governors. This arrangement worked on the island of Samos and would soon be adopted for Crete in 1869. Dionysios, the Archbishop of Crete, condemned the uprising

93. Massavetas, Alexandros, *Going Back to Constantinople Istanbul: A City of Absences* (Athens: Athens News, 2007), p. 47.

and joined the special committee that consisted of Grand Vizier Ali Pasha and three Ottoman Greek officials—Adasidi Efendi, Karateodori Efendi (the son of Stephanos Karatheodoris), and Savas Efendi. Together they worked out a plan that included an offer of amnesty to the repentant rebels and a new administrative structure for Crete, but the rebels rejected the deal hoping in vain for some outside relief.[94]

In this connection, it is intriguing to examine the correspondence of several such loyal servants of the Sultan. In a letter to Ioannis Photiadis, the Ottoman ambassador in Greece, Constantinos Mousouros, the Sultan's long-term representative in London, lamented "the prolonged tragic scene" of the destruction of his ancestral Crete in the flames of the uprising and of its bloody suppression. He denounced "chimerical and fantastic dreams" of expansionist Greek nationalism in general and the adventurous policy of "Mad George," the incumbent Greek Prime Minister Deligeorgis. The first part in that composite last name includes the Turkish word for "mad." Like Gorchakov above, Mousouros was critical of the Concert of Europe and contrasted its hypocritical humanitarian declarations with "paternal forbearance" of the Porte toward the Cretan rebels.[95] From his post in Athens, Photiadis confirmed that "deranged hotheads" took charge of Greek politics: "everyone went mad and I believe I am literally in a mental asylum."[96]

Like his friend in London, Photiades was generally pro-British but in the case of Crete, he also became disenchanted by the failure of the Western powers to act on their 1856 pledge of preserving the peace and integrity of the Ottoman Empire.[97] Influential Ottoman Greek families often appreciated the conduct of Russian foreign policy, which tended to be supportive of the Patriarchate of Constantinople and respectful of traditional Ottoman Greek rights "in the East."[98]

Constantinos Mousouros' brother Pavlos was the son-in-law of Stefan Vogoridi and a regular member of several commissions dealing with the Bulgarian Church Question. Most Bulgarian nationalist leaders were a step or two below those established Greek families in terms of wealth and status. But they likewise saw opportunities for advancement through legal Ottoman channels, not in dangerous insurrections.

---

94. Senkevich, *Kritskoie Vosstaniie*, p. 99.

95. Gennadeios Library Archive, Constantine Mousouros Collection, file 11, C. Mousouros to I. Fotiadis, 14 August 1866, p. 349a.

96. Ibid., file 11, I. Fotiadis to C. Mousouros, 16 November 1866, p. 352a.

97. Ibid., file 12, I. Fotiadis to C. Mousouros 14 March 1868, p. 19b.

98. Ibid., file 11, I. Mousouros to C. Mousouros 18 May 1866, p. 246a.

Although in the past the Ottoman authorities often acted as bona fide mediators between two sides, at that challenging time, they decided to divide their Orthodox subjects and rule them. This was not difficult to do, as there were factions on both sides. In the summer of 1868, the Grand Vizier despite the protests of the Patriarchate set up a Bulgarian commission to rework Gregory VI's plan. By October he presented two new projects based on the less reconciliatory agendas of the younger and more ambitious Bulgarian nationalists.[99]

Both plans envisioned the extension of a future Bulgarian church wherever ethnic Bulgarians predominated under its own archbishop and a synod with the seat in the imperial capital. The first one envisioned a single structure of the Patriarchate with bishops elected by the dioceses. The second one proposed a parallel Bulgarian hierarchy. Ignatiev took a particular issue with the idea of establishing the seat of the future Bulgarian church in Constantinople. This solution would perpetuate the division and the competition for scarce resources, and "would naturally push them [Bulgarians] to seek material support for the functioning of the national church in the union with Rome."[100] Ignatiev perceived the threat of Catholic and Protestant proselytizing not just as a competition between Russian and Western powers but also in traditional messianic terms of danger to Orthodoxy.[101]

Gregory VI refused to have anything to do with the Ottoman-sponsored projects. He called the General Assembly, which also rejected them later in 1868. Some Greek notables of Constantinople were ready to turn to Western diplomats to pressure the Porte to back down. But Greek Ambassador Kallerges discouraged them from doing that because he counted on Ignatiev's efforts.[102]

Gregory VI put forward the idea of calling a new Ecumenical Council of all Orthodox churches in connection with the government-sponsored plans. It was a truly extraordinary proposal of how to solve the Bulgarian Church Question. Ecumenical Councils do not happen very often. The last one convened in 787AD. In 1868 and 1869, in his letters to the Russian Holy Synod, Gregory VI explained why the situation required such a desperate step. Since the spirit of the Church is indestructible, Satan started using nationalism to destroy its body. The Bulgarian movement was part of the devilish plot because in the modern age "careless of heavenly things, many had given

---

99. Khevrolina, Victoriia, *Rossiiskii diplomat graf Nikolai Pavlovich Ignatiev* (Moscow: Russian Academy of Sciences, 2004), pp. 170–171.

100. N. P. Ignatiev to P. N. Stremoukhov, 11 June 1868, Patriarkh Kiril, ed., *Graf Ignatiev*, p. 259.

101. N. P. Ignatiev to A. M. Gorchakov, 4 June 1868, ibid., p. 258.

102. Matalas, *Ethnos kai Orthodoxia*, p. 237.

themselves to the worldly things." With their minds closed to any reconciliatory gestures of the Patriarchate, the Bulgarian leaders insisted on essentially
political demands—pastors having the same ethnicity as the flock. In the
mixed communities, there would be a situation that would violate fundamental principles of church organization such as the ban on the existence of two
bishops of the same creed in one diocese.[103]

In 1868, Ignatiev backed and even helped conceive the idea of a new
Ecumenical Council at the suggestion of Neophytos, Metropolitan of Derkon,
as early as 1866. It seemed to be a very Orthodox way to inspire and legitimate
a canonical solution. The Russian and Serbian churches rejected the call,
anticipating the opposition of the Sultan and considering the matter wholly
within the local jurisdiction.[104]

But some important Russian clerics supported the idea of the Ecumenical
Council. One of them was Archimandrite Leonid—the priest at the church
of the Russian embassy in Constantinople (1865–1869). Although a Pan-Slav
sympathizer, he believed the Council to be the only way to stop the disillusioned Bulgarians from going Catholic en masse and to extricate the Bulgarian
Question from its political complications, namely, the influence of expansionist Greek nationalism and the allure of the promises of the Ottoman government to satisfy Bulgarian aspirations. In addition to solving the Bulgarian
Question, the Ecumenical Council would also remedy many problems in the
Russian Church, for example, that of the Old Believers.[105]

Archimandrite Antonin (Kapustin), Leonid's predecessor in Constantinople
and the head of the Russian Ecclesiastical Mission in Jerusalem in 1869, also
supported the idea of the Ecumenical Council for similar reasons. Antonin was
more optimistic than Leonid about the continued ability of the Patriarchate of
Constantinople to act as a supranational Pan-Orthodox body. He welcomed the
call of Patriarch Gregory VI to summon the Ecumenical Council as the sign
of at least an aspiration on his behalf toward independence from the pervasive influence of Greek nationalism on the Orthodox churches in the Ottoman
Empire. Like Leonid, Antonin believed that the Ecumenical Council would
expose Greek nationalist-minded prelates and allow for an unprejudiced adjudication of the Bulgarian Question.[106]

---

103. Russian translation of Gregory VI's letter to the Russian Holy Synod, *Khristianskoie
Chtenie*, 3 (1871): 420–421.

104. Teplov, Vasilii, *Greko-bolgarskii tserkovnyi vopros po neizdannym istochnikam* (St.
Petersburg: V.S. Balashev, 1889), p. 66.

105. RGALI, 373-1-206, Archimandrite Leonid to M. P. Pogodin, 12 March 1869, pp. 3–40b.

106. GARF, f. 730-1-2294, Antonin to Ignatiev, 5 January 1869, p. 107.

With the Cretan Uprising and the Balkan Alliance petering out, the Porte was no longer in such a hurry to push through those projects and called a small committee composed of ethnically Greek and Bulgarian government employees in January 1869. They began working in the spring and managed to get some reluctant behind-the-scenes feedback from Gregory VI. Despite questionable motives of the Porte, Greek and Russian diplomats still hoped for an acceptable compromise to come out of its last initiative.

The new Greek ambassador, Alexandros Rangavis, arrived in April 1869 and, thanks to his family connections, quickly became well received in Greek lay circles in the Ottoman capital. He began working closely with his old friend Alexandros Karatheodoris, a member of the commission dealing with two government projects. He also had a lot of influence as a son of Stephanos Karatheodoris, one of the principal movers of the reforms of 1858. After a strictly Lenten dinner in the spring of 1869, Rangavis and Ignatiev looked into each other's eyes and confirmed their Orthodox credentials. This trust helped them to cooperate to moderate both sides. Even stern Gregory VI softened his opposition at the urgings of two diplomats, but the Patriarchate did not officially endorse the work of the commission.[107]

By December of 1869, to judge from Russian reports, the Bulgarian Church Question neared a peaceful resolution. There seemed to be no major disagreements except for seemingly minor issues of geography and the degree of subordination of the Exarch to the Patriarch.[108] By early 1870, the discussions and map drawings of the Ottoman-sponsored committee would be the basis for the government *firman* or decree establishing the Bulgarian church.

Conclusion

The Bulgarian secession from the Patriarchate of Constantinople of 1860 led to the creation of new self-styled institutions of the Bulgarian nationalist movement. Its main economic and social base was among Bulgarian businessmen and craft guilds in the imperial capital and in provincial cities. It benefited from small- and large-scale sectarian conflicts that plagued the Ottoman Empire throughout the 1860s. The Sublime Porte had to be more receptive to the demands of the Bulgarian church movement to avoid creating another potential hot spot. A smaller part of the movement looked for support in Roman Catholic missions also in Constantinople. It is a great example of

---

107. Matalas, *Ethnos kai Orthodoxia*, pp. 245–247.

108. GARF, 730-1-3472, Andrei Muraviev to Nikolai Ignatiev, 11 December 1869, p. 320b.

how active minority movements can play locally involved outside forces off against each other to gain more leverage.

Bulgarian pro-Catholic agitation played on Russian traditional political and cultural rivalry with the West in the Christian East. During the Bulgarian Uniate scare of 1860–1861, both Russian diplomats and publicists backed more Bulgarian demands but never accepted all of them. Pro-Bulgarian articles helped fuel the interest in Pan-Slavism that had been growing in the Russian educated society after the defeat in the Crimean War. But their efforts to demonize the Greeks were resisted by the advocates of supraethnic ideas of Pan-Orthodoxy and the Greek-Slavic world. The modern prophet of Pan-Slavism, Nikolai Danilevsky, also envisioned an important place for the Greeks in a Slavic Federation—the political structure of the newly invented Slavic civilization that would succeed the Byzantine Empire by uniting all Slavs as well as all Orthodox Christians against the West.

Since the Sublime Porte and the Russian government refused to sanction independent Bulgarian institutions, the movement had to obtain a legal status in negotiations with the Patriarchate. In 1867, Gregory VI offered an acceptable arrangement that contained nationalism in the framework of *Rum milleti*, under nominal supervision of the Patriarch, and within clear territorial boundaries. But because of various security threats in the late 1860s, the Porte did not consistently promote reconciliation and unity in the Orthodox Christian community. Although the Sultan's government was sponsoring more extreme Bulgarian demands in 1868 and 1869, Greek and Russian diplomats still managed to get both sides to discuss them as a starting point of a compromise.

4

Reconciling Rival Ottoman Orthodox Churches (1870–1875)

"THE OPIUM-POISONED TURKISH brain" had finally conceived the solution of the Bulgarian Church Question but it was too little, too late. The Bulgarian people remained indifferent since they realized that "the Greek clergy will be replaced by another hierarchy hungry for the same privileges." The masses were already preparing to fight for a constitutional monarchy, a republic, and eventually a communist society. Writing from the safety of autonomous Romania, Khristo Botev condemned "silver-tongued sermonizing robbers, stupefying seminaries, depraved young clergymen, open lies" in a national revolutionary émigré newspaper.[1] An admirer of the Paris Commune, he helped organize armed bands that crossed the Danube to spark a popular uprising not just against Ottoman domination but also against feudalism and capitalism.

Given this radical alternative, the Bulgarian church movement appeared hopelessly moderate but also more practical. In February of 1870, the Ottoman government established the Bulgarian Exarchate by government decree without the consent of the Patriarchate as required by church regulations in such situations. Russian diplomats, clerics, and commentators continued to put forward various power-sharing institutional arrangements and compromises to prevent the breakup of the unity of all Orthodox Christians and stop the growing ethnic conflict in the mixed Greek-Bulgarian communities. The Russian effort was made more difficult by the increasingly uncooperative stance of the Greek and Ottoman governments. Extremist factions

---

1. Botev, Khristo, "Reshen li tserkovnyi vopros?" in *Izbrannoie* (Moscow: Khudozhestvennaia literatura, 1976), p. 112. Originally published in *Duma na bulgarskite emigranti*, 4 (1871).

in the Patriarchate and the Bulgarian church movement derailed significant progress made to modify the Ottoman decree to mutual satisfaction mostly on the issue of territorial jurisdiction of the Bulgarian Exarchate.

As a result, in September of 1872, the Local Council of Ottoman Christian churches proclaimed schismatic Bulgarian church leaders and their followers for introducing the heresy of *phyletismos*, or ethnically based Christian organization. Specifically, that term meant rejection of the only legitimate territorial principle and seeking to have jurisdiction over all ethnic Bulgarians regardless of residence. To lift the schism, Russian diplomats continued to mediate between rival churches and used their leverage with the Ottoman and Greek governments to pressure both sides to agree on a territorial and hierarchical compromise. The Schism provoked a great controversy in Russia and the Greek lands, which showed the continued importance of religion in the age of nationalism.

Political Responses to the Establishment of the Bulgarian Exarchate and the Schism (1870–1875)

Since the late 1860s, the Ottoman government under Ali Pasha rarely played the role of an honest broker. On 17 February 1870, the Porte issued the *firman* in the name of Sultan Abdulaziz that established the Bulgarian Exarchate hierarchically subordinated to the Ecumenical Patriarchate and territorially limited to northern and central Bulgarian lands (see Map 4.1). The Ottoman statesmen clearly wanted to drive a wedge between two Christian communities by making Constantinople the seat of the Exarch and of his Synod. Even more controversially, Article X allowed the Exarchate to extend its authority from the modest number of assigned dioceses to all areas where at least two-thirds of the Orthodox Christian population desired to join it as determined in a referendum. In spite of the name and clear ethnic appeal of the Bulgarian Exarchate, the *firman* for its establishment was theoretically consistent with the theocratic structure of the Ottoman Empire. For Ottoman legal purposes, the Bulgarian Exarchate was a religious community that could potentially include any Orthodox Christians regardless of linguistic or ethnic background.[2]

Ignatiev opposed the Ottoman-sponsored projects of 1868 because they made Constantinople the seat of the future Bulgarian church. Article X was likewise designed to perpetuate tension between the Bulgarian Exarchate and

---

2. Konortas, Paraskevas, *Othomanikes theoriseis gia to Oikoumeniko Patriarheio, 170s-arhes 20ou aiona* (Athens: Alexandreia, 1998), p. 307.

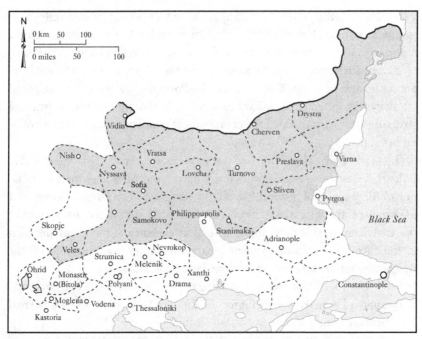

MAP 4.1 The Sultan's decree defined the borders of the Bulgarian Exarchate in February of 1870 (gray-shaded dioceses).

the Patriarchate. So Ignatiev had to put on a brave face reporting on the event to the Foreign Ministry in St. Petersburg.

Although he would prefer a direct agreement between two parties, the *firman* was in fact "a happy finale of five years of our efforts." The intervention of the temporal authorities had cut the political part of the Gordian knot on the basis of the work of the last committee. It could only serve as a starting point for solving the religious question. The Bulgarian wishes were fulfilled and the Patriarch's responsibility "in regard to the Greeks" was also reduced by that accomplished fact.[3] Ignatiev had encouraged the Porte to enact by decree the last project of the mixed committee which had benefited from Gregory VI's feedback but he had not expected the inclusion of Article X.

Ignatiev reported his conversation with his friend, Greek Ambassador Alexander Rangavis, pointing out that the Bulgarians would not have accepted the *firman* without Article X because there were fewer Bulgarian dioceses than they had demanded. Rangavis agreed to view the *firman* not as

3. Russian Imperial Foreign Policy Archive (AVPRI), f. 161/3-233-part 3, Ignatiev to the Foreign Ministry, 3 March 1870, pp. 1342–13430b.

a lost Greek battle in the zero-sum game, which would benefit only their common enemies. It was not the end of the world but the beginning of an era destined to unite Ottoman Christians. Ignatiev himself was not satisfied—he sounded irritated in his comment about the negative implications of the *firman* for the Ottoman Empire. Now the Porte recognized the principle of ethnicity that it had tried so hard to avoid up to that moment in its internal structure and acknowledged the expression of popular aspirations as a political principle.[4]

In May of 1870, Ignatiev was even more annoyed: "This inextricable Bulgarian Question seems destined to frustrate our most legitimate expectations." All prospect of resumption of talks was gone when Gregory VI refused to recognize "the Bulgarian nation" and the hastily improvised institutions of the Exarchate. Ignatiev saw this as the clear evidence of the Greek decision to "produce an explosion, a violent separation" rather than to recognize the Bulgarian church based on the *firman* because it would lead sooner or later to Slavic control of Macedonia and Thrace. The refusal of the Patriarch was also supposed to make it difficult for the Russian Holy Synod to have normal canonical relations with the Bulgarian church.[5]

Rejecting the new *firman*, Gregory VI continued to call for an Ecumenical Council as the only legitimate solution to the Bulgarian Question. Since the Porte and the Russian Holy Synod disapproved of the idea, each for their own reasons, the elderly patriarch repeatedly tendered his resignation to wash his hands of the whole affair. As an alternative, some other prelates proposed to convene a local council of autocephalous Ottoman Orthodox churches, which included the Patriarchates of Constantinople, Jerusalem, of Alexandria, and of Antioch, and the Archbishopric of Cyprus. Prophetically, Ignatiev worried that this gathering would end up separating the Greeks and the Slavs instead of bringing them together.[6]

The more moderate wing of the Bulgarian church movement was prepared to limit the territorial extent of the Bulgarian Exarchate through negotiations with the Patriarchate. The most popular early Bulgarian nationalist historian denounced those "elders" for their fear of the schism and their lack of faith in the Bulgarian people. Gavrilo Krustevich, Todor Burmov, Marko Balabanov, and Archbishop Grigorii of Rushchuk were influenced by the Russian embassy "that aimed above all to preserve the unity of the Orthodox

---

4. Ibid., Ignatiev to the Foreign Ministry, 10 March 1870, pp. 1346–1347.

5. Ibid., Ignatiev to the Foreign Ministry, 26 May 1870, pp. 1394–1395.

6. Ibid., Ignatiev to the Foreign Ministry, 26 August 1870, p. 1405.

world." Their plan to turn the Exarchate into "a vassal institution in control of a mutilated Bulgaria" was derailed by true Bulgarian patriots such as Stoian Chomakov, Petko Slaveikov, Dragan Tsankov, Todor Ikonomov, and Archbishop Panaret of Philippoupolis.[7]

Although the leadership of the official Russian Church did not support the idea of the Ecumenical Council, it strongly encouraged direct talks between the two parties to the dispute instead. Since these negotiations were not successful, the Russian Church leaders recognized the issue of the *firman* establishing the Bulgarian Exarchate as justified by the gridlock. At the same time, they did not consider it sufficient to set up a legitimate Orthodox church and urged the Bulgarian leaders to receive the consent of the Patriarchate.

The Russian Holy Synod understood that the Patriarchate of Constantinople needed the Ecumenical Council to oppose the interference of the Ottoman government into ecclesiastical affairs. However, the Russian Church leadership feared the Council would expose the disagreement between the Slavic and Greek churches over the Bulgarian Question. According to the public statement of the Over-Procurator of the Russian Holy Synod, the Bulgarian Church did not pursue a total break with the Patriarchate, and their differences were not important enough to merit the convening of the Ecumenical Council. Furthermore, the Ottoman government was unlikely to accept the decisions of the Ecumenical Council if they contradicted the *firman* it had issued.[8] With his last major initiative rejected, Patriarch Gregory VI tendered his resignation in June of 1871.

Ignatiev's Greek counterpart, Alexander Rangavis, was also concerned about the growing tension between the Greeks and the Slavs. He instructed the Greek consul in Thessaloniki to urge "our priests," i.e., those of the Patriarchate, to be good spiritual shepherds to their congregations instead of engaging in a political fight against the Bulgarians. Rangavis also believed in a healthy competition in the field of education. Instead of suppressing Bulgarian schools, the schools of the Patriarchate should become more competitive through better funding, more advanced curriculum, and superior teachers and management. Through fair play, both nations could live in peace and harmony instead of becoming enemies.[9]

7. Radev, Simeon, *Stroitelite na suvremenna Bulgariia*. Vol. 1 (Sofia: P. Glushkov, 1911), p. IX.

8. *Izvlechenia iz vsepoddaneishego otcheta Ober-Prokurora Sviateishego Sinoda Grafa D. A. Tolstogo po vedomstvu pravoslavnogo ispovedania za 1870 god* (St. Petersburg: Russian Holy Synod Publications, 1871), pp. 211–213.

9. AYE (Greek Foreign Ministry Archive), f. 1870-76.1, Rangavis to Vatikiotis, 5 May 1870, no. 1344.

While Ali Pasha served as Grand Vizier, most Bulgarian leaders were too confident of Ottoman backing to be interested in making a deal with the Patriarchate. The Porte began to play a role of a more honest broker, when Ali died in August of 1871 and Mahmud Nedim Pasha took over. The new prime minister often sought and followed Ignatiev's advice out of respect for his wisdom and, possibly, hard cash. He was considered so pro-Russian that on the streets of the imperial capital he was popularly known as Nedimoff, and the Russian ambassador was referred to as "Ignatiev Sultan."[10]

The *firman*'s apparent goal of further fragmenting Christians along ethnic lines was partially achieved already in 1870. It did accelerate and accentuate the emerging divisions and disputes over community resources. Two such sad examples were reported by Archbishop Joachim of Varna (future Patriarch Joachim III). In the town of Kavarna, thirty Bulgarians requested and received the Sultan's permission to build a new Bulgarian church. Those heads of household first had moved into traditionally Greek Kavarna as shepherds and then had married into local Greek families. When they joined the Bulgarian church movement, they refused to pay a fee to the Archbishop in Varna but still used the services of the local priest. Now with two rival churches, how would those families live a good Christian life? All of those Bulgarian activists lived in the homes of their Greek wives and Greek fathers-in-law. Ridiculous as it seemed, two different priests would come to them separately for baptism, confessions, catechism, and holy water rites. "Here the Bulgarian Question had long taken off its church garments to put on ethnic dress in all its glory and splendor."

In the neighboring village of Savla, the process of ethnic polarization had gone much further. Around 1850, the Greek and the Bulgarian members of the local Orthodox community pulled their resources to build a church "bravely overcoming the dangerous resistance of some Ottoman neighbors." Christian solidarity continued as they jointly administered the church and celebrated the Divine Liturgy in both Greek and Slavonic. For a decade, the Greeks raised no objection to the Bulgarian priest and chanter. Occasionally, someone would chant in Greek in the left choir of the church.

Even when the Bulgarians rejected Archbishop Joachim's authority, the Greeks obeyed the priest sent by the local Bulgarian abbot and "his gang," although some continued to recognize the Archbishop in Varna. "This seemed too much to the Bulgarians because they swore to destroy any Greek trace in the church." They banned all Greek books and, on pain of death, any Greek chanting. To make fun of the Greek notables, they removed their chairs and allowed Bulgarian shepherds to stand there during the Divine Liturgy. After

---

10. Davison, *Reform in the Ottoman Empire*, p. 283.

unsuccessful appeals to the Ottoman authorities, the Greeks demanded a refund of their share of the money spent on church construction and of the value of the land on which the church had been built because it was a gift from a Greek donor. They needed those funds to build a separate chapel and a school.[11]

Against that depressing background of breaking up Greco-Slavic communities, there was an important event in 1871 that reminded both the Russians and the Greeks of close religious ties between the two parts of the Orthodox world. I am referring to the transfer of the relics of Ecumenical Patriarch Gregory V, who was executed in April of 1821 during the Greek War of Independence. As described in chapter 1, Gregory V had publically condemned the Greek rebels, but based on some incriminating evidence, Sultan Mahmud II still sentenced him to be hanged on Easter Sunday from the gate of the Patriarchate. Having mutilated his body, the mob of fanatics dragged it through the streets and dumped it into the Golden Horn harbor, where it was picked up by a Greek merchantman bound for the Russian port of Odessa.

Placed in a special reliquary in the courtyard of the Holy Trinity Church, Gregory V's relics not only had become an object of veneration of the Greek immigrant community in the Black Sea provinces but also attracted pilgrims from all over Russia. Since 1838, Greece celebrated the anniversary of the Greek War of Independence, also known as "the Revolution of 1821." But the official celebrations did not invoke the memory of Gregory V before 1870. By the fiftieth anniversary, he suddenly rose to prominence as a symbol of identification of Greekness with Orthodox Christianity and as an expression of irredentism—reburying the remains of Gregory V in Athens would literally embody the unity of Greek citizens with hopelessly oppressed "unredeemed" ethnically Greek subjects of the Sultan. As seen in Figure 4.1, the "national martyrdom" of Gregory became an enduring myth of Greek nationalism.

Surprisingly, the Ottoman government also had designs on Gregory V. Executed as a traitor in 1821, he would be interred in Constantinople with honors to demonstrate how much the Tanzimat reforms transformed the Ottoman Empire. Faced with two conflicting claims on the deceased patriarch, Tsar Alexander II granted the Greek request because it had been submitted earlier. Plus, it was a family issue—he did not want to upset a dear family member—his Danish-born nephew, George I, King of Greece, who also was married to his niece Olga.[12]

---

11. Archbishop Joachim of Varna to the Patriarchate, 5 November 1870, Petur Nikov, ed., *Bulgarskoto Vuzrazhdane*, pp. 386–388.

12. Exertzoglou, Haris, "Politikes teletourgies ste neotere Ellada: E metakomise ton oston tou Grigoriou E' kai e pentekontaeterida tes Ellenikes Epanastases," *Mnemon*, 23 (2001): 157–171.

ΝΕΟΣ ΑΡΙΣΤΟΦΑΝΗΣ   N 61

Ο ΠΑΤΡΙΑΡΧΗΣ ΓΡΗΓΟΡΙΟΣ Ε΄.

ΚΡΕΜΑΣΘΕΙΣ ΕΝ ΚΩΝΣΤΑΝΤΙΝΟΥΠΟΛΕΙ ΤΗΝ 10 ΑΠΡΙΛΙΟΥ 1821 ΗΜΕΡΑΝ ΤΟΥ ΠΑΣΧΑ

ΣΥΡΕΤΑΙ ΕΙΣ ΤΑΣ ΟΔΟΥΣ ΥΠΟ ΤΩΝ ΕΒΡΑΙΩΝ ΚΑΙ ΤΟΥΡΚΩΝ ΚΑΙ ΡΙΠΤΕΤΑΙ ΕΙΣ ΤΗΝ ΘΑΛΑΣΣΑΝ

FIGURE 4.1 Since 1871, Gregory V has been officially described as a national martyr of the Greek War of Independence. "Patriarch Gregory V, hanged in Constantinople on Easter Sunday, 10 April 1821, dragged through the streets and thrown into the sea by the Jews and the Turks" in *Neos Aristophanes*, 12 (21 March 1887).

Some Russians were saddened by the news of the transfer of Gregory V's relics from Odessa to Athens to be enshrined in the main Greek church, the Metropolitan Cathedral in Athens. A retired Holy Synod official and a famous Christian writer, Andrei Muraviev, actually opposed the removal of Gregory V's relics from Russia. In a letter to his friend Ambassador Nikolai Ignatiev, he argued that the relics of Gregory V had become such a popular and important object of veneration in Odessa and Russia at large that their "abduction" would be a great loss to Russian Orthodox culture.[13]

The timing of the transfer in the spring 1871 at least helped to somewhat dampen ethnic flames fanned during the critical point in the Bulgarian Church Question. Thus, in his report of the Holy Synod's activities in 1871, Over-Procurator Dmitrii Tolstoy considered the reburial of Gregory V to be a great opportunity to placate Greek national sensibilities and to remind everyone of Russia's traditional role as protector of Orthodox Christianity. Tolstoy endorsed the Greek national myth of Gregory V as "the stalwart fighter and martyr for the independence of the Greek people." He also stressed "the memories of the hard days of slavery and oppression, heroic struggle for independence, many victims of the struggle, and finally of the freedom won and consolidated with the magnanimous support of coreligionist Russia."[14]

This occasion brought many high society Greek and Russian dignitaries to Odessa and Athens followed by a veritable outpouring of Pan-Orthodox pronouncements in both Greek and Russian publications across the whole political spectrum. The Russian press, painfully aware of the often anti-Slav tone of the mainstream Greek press, carefully noted and welcomed the change.[15]

These pronouncements made an impression of an upward turn in Greek-Slavic relations against the background of tension produced by the Sultan's *firman* establishing the Bulgarian Exarchate. On 25April 1871 in Athens, Archbishop of Syros and Tenos Alexander Lycourgos recounted the history of the beginning of the Greek uprising against the Ottomans in 1821 and of Gregory V's role there. He expressed Greek gratitude to "the most humane Russian Emperor," "pious Russian people," "pious and most powerful Russia," and "the fraternal feelings of noble and philhellene Russians."[16] A year later, he would be actively promoting the break with the Bulgarian Exarchate but without openly demonizing Russia.

But some like the First Secretary of the Greek Synod Averkios Lambiris would live through a change of heart. On 10 April 1871 in Odessa, he was

---

13. State Archive of the Russian Federation (GARF), f 730-1-3472, A. N. Muraviev to N. P. Ignatiev, Kiev 10 May 1871, p. 890b.

14. *Izvlechenia iz vsepoddaneishego otcheta Ober-Prokurora Sviateishego Sinoda Grafa D. A. Tolstogo po vedomstvu pravoslavnogo ispovedania za 1871 god* (St. Petersburg: Russian Holy Synod Publications, 1872), pp. 184–186.

15. Hieromonk Nikolai, "Perenesenie ostankov Sviateishego Patriarkha Konstatinopolskogo Grigoria V iz Odessy v Afiny," *Khristianskoie Chtenie*, 5 (1871): 905–935.

16. Lykourgos, Alexandros, *Logos paneigyrikos eis tin 50etereda tou yper anexartisias Ellinon kai ten ex Odessou eis Athinas anakomiden tou leipsanou tou aoidimou Patriarhou Gregoriou V* (Ermoupolis, 1871), pp. 25–26.

heaping praise on "the pious Russian Emperor and his Orthodox people" on behalf of "the eternally grateful Hellenic people."[17] In September of 1872, in Athens, he publicly welcomed the Bulgarian Schism and lambasted Russia's alleged sponsorship of Pan-Slav conspiracies. His speech caused a diplomatic scandal and his eventual removal from the high position in the Greek Archbishopric in November of the same year.[18]

Another hopeful sign came in the summer of 1871 with the reshuffling of the Greek cabinet, now led by Alexandros Koumoundouros, who wanted to benefit himself and his country by means of Russian patronage and cooperation with the moderate and radical Bulgarian movements, Serbia, and Romania. Although Greece was now expected to more consistently back Russian mediation, nobody was under the illusion that Koumoundouros would not work hard to keep as many mixed dioceses as possible outside the Bulgarian Exarchate to save them for the future triumph of the Great Idea of Greek irredentism.[19]

With Mahmud Nedim Pasha as Grand Vizier and Koumoundouros as prime minister, the Russian embassy in Constantinople was in a great position to influence the elections of new patriarch in August-September 1871. Neophytos, Metropolitan of Derkon, could be a good bet. He was the éminence grise under Gregory VI, widely believed to have authored the 1867 project of an autonomous Bulgarian church under an exarch and the idea of calling an Ecumenical Council. But for his election campaign, Neophytos decided to play the Greek nationalist card and to surf the wave of the growing fear of Pan-Slavism. He turned to the Greek nationalist newspaper *Neologos* of Constantinople to publish an article criticizing the Russian publications that described the 1870 *firman* as a basis for the final solution of the Bulgarian Church Question.[20]

So the Russian choice fell on the eighty-two-year-old Anthimus VI, who had already served as Patriarch in 1845–1848 and 1853–1855. To ensure Russian support, he discussed with Ignatiev his views on the Bulgarian Question and even promised not to make any decision about it without first consulting the Russian embassy. Ignatiev pushed the Bulgarian movement to the negotiation table, threatening to withdraw any Russian support and to leave them at the mercy of the Ottoman government. To raise the prestige

---

17. *Khristianskoie Chtenie*, 7 (1871): 139–143.

18. AVPRI, f. 161/3-233-part 3, Sabourow to Westmann, 10 November 1872, p. 19690b.

19. AVPRI, f. 161/3-233-part 3, Stremoukhov to Saburov, 28 July 1871, pp. 1543–15440b.

20. Ibid., Coumany to Stremoukhov, 3 August 1871, pp. 15480b–1549.

of the Patriarchate, Ignatiev made sure that the first reception of Anthimus VI by the Sultan in the Dolma Bahche Palace and his inauguration in the Patriarchate were full of ceremonial splendor.[21]

The Russian Church leaders interpreted as their victory the replacement of Gregory VI by Anthimos VI at the helm of the Patriarchate in 1871. They saw him as determined to solve the Bulgarian Question as a local problem without agitating for an Ecumenical Council. The change of leadership made the Russian Holy Synod hopeful for a turn to reconciliation in 1871 and 1872.[22]

As the new Patriarch, Anthimos VI did not fail Ignatiev. He came to see the Bulgarian leaders and was friendly with them. He actually embraced as brothers in Christ the defrocked bishops including the notorious trouble-maker Hilarion. Anthimos made negotiations more focused by including into the process only high clergy and Ottoman Christian officials, thereby excluding many lay notables. He sent out from the capital those prelates who were known for their opposition to peace talks. For instance, Neophytos had to travel to his nearby diocese in Derkon.[23]

The Sublime Porte under Nedim Pasha not only stopped the divide-and-rule game but was also prepared to change Article X of the 1870 *firman* if both sides agreed to that. Many Ottoman ministers realized that the *firman* would encourage other nationalist movements.[24] But the peace process was running into serious roadblocks. Many influential Ottoman Greek and Bulgarian layper-sons resented being sidelined and feared a possibility of laity's marginalization in the Ottoman Orthodox community. In addition, younger foreign-educated Bulgarians did not want to see the Bulgarian Church Question resolved by either the Porte or the Patriarchate. They argued that constant tension would mobilize more people into the movement.[25]

By late November of 1871, Anthimus VI and the Bulgarian negotiators reached an agreement. The *firman* would be modified to eliminate Article X and to move the Bulgarian Exarch's residence and his Synod from Constantinople to Turnovo, the capital of medieval Bulgaria. In exchange, the Patriarchate

21. Ibid., Ignatiev to Stremoukhov, 14 September 1871, pp. 1555–1555ob.

22. *Izvlechenia iz vsepoddaneishego otcheta Ober-Prokurora Sviateishego Sinoda Grafa D. A. Tolstogo po vedomstvu pravoslavnogo ispovedania za 1871 god* (St. Petersburg: Russian Holy Synod Publications, 1872), pp. 181–183.

23. AVPRI, f. 161/3-233-part 3, Coumany to Stremoukhov, 5 October 1871, pp. 1566–1566ob.

24. Ibid., Ignatiev to Stremoukhov, 26 October 1871, p. 1576ob.

25. Ibid., Ignatiev to Stremoukhov, 2 November 1871, p. 1580.

added most northern and western Macedonian dioceses with Ohrid and Skopje. Anthimus explained to the Greek ambassador, Rhazis, that pragmatism was one of his main motivations in those territorial concessions. Many of those communities where the Bulgarian nationalist movement was strong had long stopped recognizing the Patriarchate's bishops and paying any dues and fees. The Patriarch was overall pleased with the progress of the talks because "pressed on all sides the Bulgarians were more open to compromises." He appreciated Ignatiev's "stern language" with extremist Bulgarians such as Stoian Chomakov.[26]

The stance of the new Patriarch and like-minded prelates found support in the Ottoman government and in a segment of the Ottoman Greek laity community affiliated with the members of the Ottoman bureaucracy. Moderate Greek nationalist newspapers of Constantinople supported the project of Anthimos VI because clear church boundaries were in Greek interests—they would prevent confrontation and promote cooperation among Christians.[27]

Those articles actually reflected the view of the Greek government at the time. It looked to natural geographical and ethnographic boundaries between the Bulgarian Exarchate and the Patriarchate in Ottoman Balkan provinces. The Greek Foreign Ministry assumed that in case of Ottoman collapse they would serve as the basis for state borders between Bulgaria and Greece and would help avoid future conflicts. But the territorial quid pro quos that the Bulgarians and Anthimus VI had to make were not always to the liking of the Greek policymakers. Instead of following rivers and mountain ranges, proposed church borderlines cut across some existing dioceses and left quite a few curves and bulges on the map.[28]

Anatolikos Aster helped reduce anti-Slav feelings in the Ottoman Greek community by attacking the common enemy. It accused *Courier d'Orient*, the newspaper affiliated with the French embassy and Catholic proselytizing missions in the Ottoman Empire, of inciting the Bulgarians against negotiating with the Ecumenical Patriarchate.[29] At the same time, *Anatolikos Aster* highlighted cases of continued support of Orthodox churches in the Ottoman Empire by Russian charities.[30]

---

26. AYE, f. 1872-76.1b, 20 December 1871, Rhazis to Zaimis, no. 3892.

27. *Anatolikos Aster*, 924 (27 November 1871); *Konstantinoupolis*, 1153 (15 December 1871); 1154 (17 December 1871).

28. AYE, f. 1871-76.1, Zaimis to Rhazis, 20 December 1871, no. 186.

29. *Anatolikos Aster*, 925 (30 November 1871).

30. Ibid., 938 (15 December 1871).

Ignatiev also had information about Catholic intrigues but more dangerous were the attempts of some members of the Ottoman cabinet to unseat
Mahmud Nedim Pasha by encouraging less moderate Bulgarian leaders such
as Stoian Chomakov and Archbishop Panaret of Philipoupolis to demand
more from the negotiators.[31] Apparently, the Grand Vizier was so committed to the success of the talks that their failure would go a long way toward
discrediting him.

More extreme Ottoman Greek nationalist newspapers attacked the project
of Anthimus VI not as anti-Greek but as anti-Orthodox because it invited the
intervention of the temporal authorities and introduced the uncanonical principle of ethnicity. Outwardly, they did not fear assimilation of local Greeks
into Slavic culture but opposed "the church of Bulgarians rather than of
Bulgaria." They advocated an Ecumenical Council as the only legitimate solution of the Bulgarian Church Question.[32] Good as it may sound, the idea of
the council was the highly publicized alternative to more comfortable behind-
the-scenes bipartisan negotiations and as such it meant conflict.

It was the sidelined veterans of the Bulgarian nationalist movement
who derailed the agreement. Many of them like Dr. Stoian Chomakov of
Philippoupolis made a career representing the Bulgarian nation from as early
as 1858. For them, the agreement meant returning to unenlightened back-
woods, losing comfortable lifestyles in the cosmopolitan capital and "lucra-
tive jobs of the so called Bulgarian delegates entertained at the expense of
the poor population who had been expecting the settlement of the Greek-
Bulgarian dispute for ten years." According to Ignatiev, the Bulgarian leaders
were not men of integrity devoted to their homeland and Orthodoxy. They
lacked sufficient theological training and "even religious convictions."[33]

All of these devastating characteristics applied to three Bulgarian prelates,
including defrocked bishop Hilarion and former metropolitans Hilarion of
Lovcha and Panaret of Philippoupolis. Although pardoned by Anthimus VI,
they followed those lay leaders, who believed that the movement and their
own importance would grow more in a state of conflict with the Patriarchate.

Around midnight on 5 January 1872, leading the crowd of Bulgarian
laymen, they came to the private residence of Anthimus VI and woke up the
octogenarian patriarch to demand his permission to officiate at the Feast of
Theophany. When in somebody else's diocese, Orthodox clerics need to ask

---

31. AVPRI, f. 161/3-233-part 3, Ignatiev to Stremoukhov, 7 December 1871, pp. 16000b–1601.

32. *Neologos* 898 (16 December 1871), 900 (18 December 1871); *Typos*, 262 (16 December 1871).

33. AVPRI, f. 161/3-233-part 3, Ignatiev to Stremoukhov, 11 January 1872, pp. 16080b–1609.

local church authorities before celebrating the Divine Liturgy. The whole thing was intended to make the patriarch angry. It worked. He was understandably upset and not in any way disposed to talk to them. The conspirators proceeded to the Bulgarian church of St. Stefan for the culmination of their "coup," as most commentators called this event at the time.

And a coup it was. Things changed completely and a real parting of the ways set in. Anthimus VI made a turn of 180 degrees. He had his Holy Synod try the perpetrators of the coup, naturally in absentia. Two of them were defrocked, and Hilarion, who had already been defrocked in 1862, was excommunicated. Now the Patriarch joined his erstwhile opponents to push for a church council, local if not ecumenical, to cut the Gordian knot of the Bulgarian Question by expelling its main instigators from the Church into a dark Satan's realm.[34]

Ignatiev thought those repressions were too harsh and inspired by Greek nationalism among the members of the Holy Synod of the Patriarchate. But Ignatiev himself was very critical of the extreme faction of younger Bulgarian nationalists that undermined overnight what he himself had been preparing for a long time. Russian consuls in Balkan provinces were instructed on how to convey to the local Bulgarians the Russian view of what had happened on the Feast of Theophany in Constantinople.

"If the bishops themselves were to trample down church canons on which all their authority and spiritual significance are based, it would no longer be a church hierarchy in the Christian sense of the word and would become a mere playground and a human institution." If Bulgarians wanted to found their church only on a government decree and illegitimate actions of a few adventurers, they would find no support in any other Orthodox church. Instead, they should stop the intrigues of self-interested individuals who served as "a blind tool of Western religious propaganda, of enemies of Slavdom and Orthodoxy."[35]

The Russian Church also condemned the illegitimate officiating on 6 January 1872 by three Bulgarian prelates. But it counseled against the Patriarch's applying excessively strict and "irrevocable" punishment to them. In 1872, it repeated its judgment of 12 March 1871 about the Bulgarian Exarchate. Established only by the decree of the Islamic authorities, the Exarchate had no legitimacy without the consent of the Patriarch according to canon law.[36]

---

34. Ibid., Ignatiev to Stremoukhov, 15 January 1872, p. 16100b.

35. Ibid., Ignatiev's circular note, 18 January 1872, pp. 1631–1632.

36. Ibid., Tolstoy to Prince Gorchakov, 8 March 1872, p. 16950b.

To the modern reader, all those intense reactions to a simple night serv-ice seem extreme. Clearly, Anthimus VI was offended on a personal level by the ingratitude of three wayward Bulgarian prelates, but it also was a public offense to him as the leader of *Rum milleti*. There must have been another motivation for his opting for the break with the Bulgarian Exarchate. He must have felt pressure from Greek lay notables whom he tried to keep out of his negotiations with the Bulgarians in the fall of 1871. His rival, Metropolitan Neophytos of Derkon, turned to those same groups in his bid for the office of the Patriarch. The Bulgarian insult questioned the value of Anthimus VI's policy of reconciliation and justified a turn in the opposite direction.[37]

The newspapers *Neologos* and *Typos* provided a sounding board for this group of Ottoman Greek laity centered on the guilds in the capital and, more importantly, on the patronage networks of major Greek Ottoman bankers such as Ioannis Psyharis and Georgios Zarifis.[38] The anti-Slavic stance of those lay members of the Orthodox community was not just a product of Greek nationalist passions. Rather, it was a weapon in their competition with high clergy for leadership of the Ottoman Orthodox community. Many of its lay members feared further erosion of their influence if they went along with the monopoly decision-making by the prelates in "spiritual" matters such as the Bulgarian Question.[39]

The defection of Anthimus VI to their camp shocked Ambassador Ignatiev. He wondered how "an accident" and "a slight paralysis" had turned the eighty-two-year-old shrewd prelate into "a gullible child" manipulated by skilled plot-ters. In Ignatiev's analysis, the extreme Greek nationalist faction had joined pro-Western Greeks. "What they want is not equality with the Slavs but us or *somebody else* to help them oppress and subjugate the Bulgarian Slavs to eventually prepare the restoration of the Byzantine Empire [underlined in the original]." Those Greeks realized that "they could no longer fool us" and that "we would not sacrifice our co-ethnics in the name of fake Orthodoxy" "for the sake of beautiful Phanariote eyes."

Encouraged by British and Austrian agents, the extreme Greek national-ists saw Greece as a far stronger Western bulwark against feared Slavic expan-sion than declining Turkey. If Russia openly sided with the Bulgarians after the excommunication of their leaders, then "we would be falsely accused of

---

37. Matalas, *Ethnos kai Orthodoxia*, pp. 272–273.

38. Stamatopoulos, Dimitris, *Metarrythmisi kai Ekkosmikevsi* (Athens: Aleksandreia, 2003), pp. 314, 329.

39. Ibid., p. 327.

Pan-Slavism." In a private letter to the Deputy Foreign Minister, Ignatiev confessed that between 1864 and 1872 he was able to avoid the dilemma of having to choose between Orthodoxy and Slavdom.[40]

By siding with the economically dominant segments of the Ottoman Greek community, Anthimus VI abandoned the other faction of the laity connected to the Ottoman Greek bureaucrats, who were naturally the strongest supporters and main beneficiaries of the Tanzimat. Their patronage networks were the so-called moderates in the Bulgarian Church Question led by Stavrakis Aristarkhis, Patriarchate's Spokesman in the Sublime Porte (*Megas Logothetes*), and Alexander Karatheodoris Pasha, Deputy Foreign Minister. The latter inherited his pro-Russian stance from his father, Stephanos Karatheodoris, who was friends with Andrei Muraviev.[41]

Both of those Greek Ottoman officials took part in the last round of negotiations in the fall of 1871 and in most other committees that had been tasked with hammering out compromise solutions to the Bulgarian Question since 1862. In the aftermath of the Bulgarian Theophany coup, Alexander Karatheodoris offered his views at the crucial session of the General Assembly (*genike synelevsis*) of the lay and clerical representatives of the Ottoman Orthodox community on 30 January 1872. The main goal of the General Assembly was to reach a consensus on how to react to the recent developments. He defended the intervention of the Porte, saying that Patriarch Gregory VI's 1867 project and the 1870 *firman* of the Bulgarian Exarchate had grown from the proposals of Greek-Bulgarian lay committees.[42]

Karatheodoris preferred direct negotiations between the two parties to an Ecumenical Council, which was likely to polarize the issue further if the parties involved had not reached a compromise on their own. Upset and personally discouraged as Karatheodoris was by the provocative actions of three Bulgarian prelates, he proposed "to forget about the sad coup" and to continue working on a compromise solution free from Greek nationalist agitation by "those who are always vociferous about their feelings about the Church and the Nation."[43]

The alternative to reconciliation based on careful territorial delimitation of the Bulgarian Exarchate from the Patriarchate would be unending conflict.

---

40. AVPRI, f. 161/3-233-part 3, Ignatiev to Stremoukhov, 19 February 1872, pp. 1677–1679ob.

41. Stamatopoulos, *Metarrythmisi kai Ekkosmikevsi*, p. 314.

42. Karatheodoris, Alexandros, *O Logos* (Speech made on January 30 1872 at the session of the General Assembly of the Christian Orthodox community) (Constantinople, 1872), p. 11.

43. Ibid., pp. 12–14.

To Karatheodoris, the schism would be tantamount to "a declaration of the religious war against the [Bulgarian] people (*laos*)" and would introduce "racial distinction" into the Church. Its unorthodox novelty aside, the latter would be a source of unending trouble as it would lead to the existence of two Orthodox churches in one area for ethnic Greeks and ethnic Bulgarians, respectively.[44]

Ioannis Mousouros, the governor of Samos, went even further than Karatheodoris in the letter to his brother Constantine Mousouros, the long-time Ottoman ambassador in London. He denounced Patriarch Anthimos VI as "prediluvian" and the only one to blame for the heightening of conflict. He should have granted the Bulgarian prelates their request to officiate on 6 January 1872. Even after the illegal Theophany liturgy, Anthimos VI should have forgiven them as a Christian instead of condemning them. Repressions only pushed toward a schism, which no other Orthodox nation (Russia, Serbia, and Romania) would recognize. Ioannis Mousouros pinned his hopes on the newly elected Bulgarian Exarch Anfim I. He also believed the talks between the Patriarchate and the Exarchate could resume based on the *firman* and the not too different project developed by Patriarch Gregory VI.[45]

Much of the Greek press indeed interpreted the "coup" as the betrayal by Bulgarians of the joint commitment to solve the Bulgarian Question based on the principles of moderation, goodwill, and decency.[46] But after initial shock and indignation, the moderate Greek press began to discern signs of moderation in the Bulgarian movement. Now the hopes of reaching a negotiated settlement and clear delimitation of the Bulgarian Exarchate were focused on Anfim, the ethnically Bulgarian Metropolitan of Vidin, and his supporters.

Anfim stayed in his remote diocese on the Danube and was not compromised by the actions of rebellious Bulgarian bishops living in Constantinople. He was educated in Russia and supported by the Russian embassy. At the same time, he was well connected to many Greek prelates because for a while he taught at the Patriarchal Seminary on the island of Halki. All these credentials made Anfim appear as an acceptable candidate for the position of the Bulgarian Exarch, vacant since the establishment of the Exarchate in February 1870.[47]

---

44. Karatheodoris, Alexandros, *O Logos*, p. 10.

45. Gennadeios Library Archive, Constantine Mousouros Collection, file 12, I. Mousouros to C. Mousouros 22 February 1872, pp. 252b, 252g.

46. *Anatolikos Aster*, 945 (8 January 1872), 947 (15 January 1872), 950 (26 January 1872), 951 (29 January 1872), 954 (9 February 1872).

47. Ibid., 957 (19 February 1872).

After the Russian-sponsored election of the first Bulgarian Exarch Anfim I, the Russian Holy Synod and the Foreign Ministry co-sponsored the unofficial peacemaking mission of Archpriest (*Protoierei*) Bazarov, the confessor of the Duchess of Wuertemberg, née Romanova. He went to the Christian East disguised as a common traveler but would return as a disillusioned Slavophile on the pattern of many educated Russian intellectuals like Tertii Filippov himself. Initially, well-connected Bazarov was sympathetic to the Bulgarian demands. As he got to know the situation better, he came to support the Patriarchate.

Writing from St. Petersburg to the Foreign Ministry before his departure for Constantinople, Bazarov suspected that the Patriarchate's insistence on the purely canonical basis of the Bulgarian Church Question was the product of their allegiance to expansionist Greek nationalism and the consequent fear of the Slavs. However, Bazarov firmly believed that the Exarchate needed to be recognized by the Patriarch for the good of the Bulgarians themselves. To have this solid foundation of their church, the Bulgarians needed "to make a concession to the just demands of the Patriarch" and to conclude "a friendly agreement" on the number of the dioceses to be included into the Exarchate.[48]

During his reconciliatory tour, on 16 May 1872, Bazarov wrote to the Foreign Ministry that the Metropolitan of Athens promised him to give a prior notification to the Russian Church of all his actions in the Bulgarian Question, especially, sending his representative to the Local Council in Constantinople. Bazarov was received by Greek King George I himself and they agreed that the spirit of moderation and reconciliation would prevail in the Bulgarian Question if Russia and Greece put pressure on the Bulgarians and the Patriarchate, respectively.[49]

In Constantinople, Bazarov had a meeting with Exarch Anfim and other Bulgarian Exarchist prelates. They said that they were horrified at their defrocking and excommunication but blamed the escalation of the problem on Greek intransigence. To justify many instances of illegitimate officiation and ordination they had performed, they alleged the already familiar danger of losing masses of the Bulgarian people to the lurking agents of the Pope. "In a fit of patriotic enthusiasm," the Bulgarian church leaders "passionately" talked of taking Constantinople from the Greek hands. Bazarov suddenly felt as if he were "in the club of revolutionaries determined to use every means to achieve the national (*narodnoi*) goal."

---

48. AVPRI, f. 161/3-233-part 3, Archpriest Bazarov to the Foreign Ministry, 12 March 1872, p. 1697ob–1699.

49. Ibid., 16 May 1872, p. 1793ob.

Furthermore, Bazarov made it clear to the Bulgarian leaders that the Russian Church would recognize the Patriarchate to be on the right side in the dispute. The Russian Church would support the independent status of the Bulgarian Exarchate only if it was obtained with the consent of the Patriarchate. When more complaints against the Greeks ensued, Bazarov bid farewell to "these personalities pathetic in every respect."

In contrast, Bazarov found in the Patriarchate "composure and confidence in their authority (*vlasti*)" but also the alarming tendency to blame the disturbances and acts of disobedience not just on a few leaders but on the Bulgarian people as a whole. Summing up his report, Bazarov urged a more active intervention of the Russian Church both to support the canonical demands of the Patriarch and to show some concern for the Bulgarian Church as well.

This well-intended conclusion had been the leitmotif of the Russian foreign and ecclesiastical policy from the beginning of the Bulgarian Question. To make it more practical, Bazarov recommended introducing the office of a special envoy (*apokrisarii*) of the Russian Church in Constantinople to establish better liaison with the Patriarchate. Alexander II and the Foreign Ministry were opposed to the idea of an independent ecclesiastic policy. In his marginal notes the Tsar wrote, "I have my doubts about that and they are shared by Ignatiev."[50]

There was no return to the bilateral peace talks after Anfim I celebrated the Divine Liturgy as the head of an autonomous church on 11 May 1872—the day of SS. Cyril and Methodius, the Enlighteners of the Slavs. Many contemporaries at the time and today's scholars likewise believe that given the Bulgarian refusal, the insistence of the Patriarchate after 6 January 1872 on either an ecumenical or a local council tended to play into the hands of lay notables and extreme Greek nationalists. In this view, those groups hoped to secure their leadership in the reformed Orthodox community and to subsequently assimilate all non-Greek Orthodox under the jurisdiction of the Patriarchate.[51]

The agitation among Ottoman Greeks for a council as the ostensibly Orthodox canonical solution began to receive support from Greece when the turmoil of its parliamentary politics had brought Deligeorgis again to the post of prime minister. Since 1871, when Koumoundouros and Voulgaris were in charge, Ignatiev worked closely with Rangavis and Rhazis in the Greek embassy in Constantinople. Under "Mad George," Kallergis replaced Rhazis as the acting ambassador in Constantinople in June 1872 and started working together with England and the Porte against Russia and the menace of Pan-Slavism.

---

50. Ibid., 19 May 1872, pp. 18190b–1822.

51. Konortas, *Othomanikes theoriseis*, p. 307.

Turning the Slavs from brothers in Christ to alien heretics made sense for this new Greek policy. Although his reports use a somewhat ambiguous language, it is clear that Kallergis consistently brushed aside any attempts to return to bilateral peace talks. He personally knew many prelates who arrived at Constantinople in preparation for the Local Council and tried to win them over to adopting a firm stand "to save the Church through noble actions." Kallergis "heard with regret" about the opposition to the expected Schism formed around Cyril, the influential Patriarch of Jerusalem, which also included the Patriarch of Antioch and the Archbishop of Cyprus. Kallergis arranged for the dispatch of the well-connected Bishop of Syros and Tenos Lycourgos with a secret task of overcoming any resistance among Ottoman Greek prelates to the schism between Hellenism and Pan-Slavism.[52]

To make things worse, Ignatiev's protégé Mahmud Nedim Pasha was replaced by the much less pro-Russian Midhat Pasha as Grand Vizier in July 1872. After the ineffective mission of Archpriest Bazarov, Ambassador Ignatiev urged a more active intervention of the Russian Church as a mediator in the Greek-Bulgarian dispute. But the Russian Holy Synod considered the situation as too politicized and preferred not to interfere with "the conflict of Greek and Bulgarian nationalities (natsionalnosti)." The Synod allowed Ambassador Ignatiev to summon to Constantinople Archimandrite Antonin, the head of the Russian Ecclesiastical Mission in Jerusalem, but refused to grant him the status of a representative of the Russian Church. Antonin was famous for his intimate knowledge of the Greek language and culture acquired over twenty years of service in the Christian East.[53]

Even Antonin's experience and resources of the embassy were not enough to reverse the trend set in motion by the alliance of Anthimus VI, lay notables, and Mad George. Despite the opposition from King George I, Deligeorgis endorsed Kallergis' choice of Archbishop Lycourgos to be sent on a secret mission to Constantinople to help thwart negotiations and bring about a definitive break with the Bulgarian Exarchate. The parting of the ways with Orthodox Slavs was supposed to turn Greece from the allegedly Pan-Slav Russia to hopefully Philhellenist England. Lycourgos was famous for agitating for a union of the Eastern Orthodox and the Anglicans.[54]

---

52. AYE, f. 1872-76.1b, 20 June 1872, no. 272.

53. Ibid., An Excerpt from the Proceedings of the Holy Synod, 18 August 1872, p. 18850b–1886.

54. More about it in Bees, Nikos, "O Alexandros Lycourgos kai e kata tou panslavismou drasis aftou," Byzantinisch-Neugriechische Jahrbuecher, 8 (1929/1930): 253.

These efforts of the Greek government and of segments of the Ottoman Greek community led to the Local Council of Ottoman Orthodox Churches, which met in August and September 1872. It declared schismatic the Bulgarian church leaders and their communicants for "insolently organizing an illegal ethnic-based gathering" and for following the heresy of *phyletismos*. This word literally means "racism" and was specifically defined as "ethnic distinctions, hatreds, passions, and divisions in the Church of Christ as contrary to the teaching of the Gospel and of sacred canons of our blessed fathers."[55]

The Schism formalized ethnic divorce under way in many Balkan cities, as we saw in the Varna area. But most Greek and Slavic villagers were blissfully ignorant of how ethnonationalism was wreaking havoc on the Patriarchate of Constantinople. Like their cousins elsewhere in Europe, they had no problem with ethnic diversity and remained loyal primarily to their region and religion. The tradition of interethnic coexistence is vividly illustrated in Figure 4.2 from the photo album of Ottoman folk costumes published in 1873 by Osman Hamdi Bey. Widely regarded as the first modern Ottoman painter and museum curator, he clearly intended to dazzle the world with an astonishing ethnographic variety of the still-vast Sultan's domains.

In response to the Schism, the official report by Over-Procurator Tolstoy painted a self-righteous picture of the relations between the Russian Church and Orthodox Churches of "the East." The deadlock in the Bulgarian Question meant "a diminution of the Apostolic spirit among some of our Eastern coreligionists." Throughout the crisis, the Russian Church remained "the protector of the highest interests of Orthodoxy." The overall message of the report was to put the blame for the Schism on the influence of extreme Greek nationalism on the Patriarchate. The Russian Church claimed the traditional messianic Pan-Orthodox rather than Pan-Slavic role in "the East."[56] While assuming a hands-off approach to the Bulgarian Question, the Russian Church leadership in a highly patronizing tone reaffirmed its commitment to providing material assistance to "Eastern" churches and to "furthering the spread of Orthodox enlightenment among them" regardless of nationality.[57]

In the official Russian version of the buildup to the Schism, the Over-Procurator of the Russian Holy Synod criticized both the uncanonical officiation by three recalcitrant Bulgarian prelates during the feast of Epiphany on

---

55. Gedeon, ed., *Engrafa*, pp. 427–428.

56. *Izvlechenia iz vsepoddaneishego otcheta Ober-Prokurora Sviateishego Sinoda Grafa D. A. Tolstogo po vedomstvu pravoslavnogo ispovedania za 1872 god* (St. Petersburg: Russian Holy Synod Publications, 1873), pp. 214–215.

57. Ibid., p. 222.

FIGURE 4.2 "Studio portrait of models wearing traditional clothing from the province of Adrianople (Edirne), Ottoman Empire: (1) Greek peasant of Manastir, (2) Greek peasant woman of Manastir; and (3) Bulgarian woman of Scutari." Library of Congress Prints and Photographs Division, Reproduction Number: LC-USZC4-11824. Photographed by Pascal Sebah, originally published in Osman Hamdy Bey and Marie de Launay, *Les Costumes populaires de la Turquie en 1873* (Constantinople: Levant Times and Shipping Gazette Press, 1873).

6 January 1872 and the Patriarchate's Synod, which excommunicated them. According to the Over-Procurator, in both actions the Bulgarian and Greek prelates were influenced by their respective lay groups. However, the proclamation of the Schism was the wrong response to the crisis dictated by extreme Greek nationalists. The Russian Holy Synod joined Cyril, the Patriarch of Jerusalem, in opposing the Schism and urging moderation and reconciliation instead. Since this stance of the Russian Church was well-known, its leaders decided to leave unanswered the messages of both Patriarch Anthimos V and Bulgarian Exarch Anfim I about the Schism as motivated by "nationalistic passions." At the same time, the Russian Church did not recognize the Bulgarian Exarchate since it had been established by a government decree without the Patriarchate's consent.[58]

In that crisis, ethnocentric Bulgarian and Greek factions were not the only ones motivated by nationalism. The Serbian government was not moved by the considerations of Slavic brotherhood or Orthodox unity. It was prepared to support the Patriarchate politically and financially in exchange for appointing an ethnically Serb bishop to Kosovo. The Serbs usually referred to that predominantly Albanian province as "Old Serbia." Mikhail, Metropolitan of Belgrade, shared this news with the Russian ambassador in Vienna, Evgenii Novikov.[59]

Russia's Orthodox zeal reflected in its domestic policies as well. To consolidate its control of the Caucasus, the Russian leadership sought to roll back the advance of Islam by encouraging conversion to Orthodox Christianity. That project was presented as a restoration of historical justice and pre-Islamic native culture. The Adygei and other Caucasian tribes had adopted Christianity as part of Byzantine influence. Disseminated via incomprehensible Greek, the seeds of Orthodoxy failed to strike deep enough roots to resist the arrival of Islam. The nineteenth-century Russian observers were confident that they would promote Orthodoxy better than the Byzantine Greeks by relying on the translated Scriptures and native education.[60]

Orthodox Greeks and Slavs could still assist in that task under Russian direction. With that in mind, the Russian government organized a population exchange pressuring the irredeemably Islamic Caucasian tribes to emigrate to the Sultan's realm while encouraging Ottoman Christians to relocate to the Black Sea area throughout the 1800s.[61]

---

58. Ibid., pp. 215–221.

59. AVPRI, f. 161/3-233-part 3, Novikov to the Foreign Ministry, 18 December 1872, p. 2110.

60. Jersild, Austin, *Orientalism and Empire: North Caucasus Mountain Peoples and the Georgian Frontier, 1845–1917* (Montreal and Kingston: McGill-Queen's University Press, 2002), p. 48.

61. Ibid., p. 138.

The task of raising the Apostolic spirit among Russia's coreligionists fell again on Ambassador Ignatiev. His favorite method was to exert financial pressure to extinguish "the anti-Slav flame smoldering inside every Greek." He secured the sequestration of the income of Russian properties of the Patriarchate of Jerusalem to punish its Holy Synod for deposing Patriarch Cyril and supporting the Bulgarian Schism. Ignatiev and Russian consuls also encouraged Arab laity and clergy in Jerusalem and Damascus to protest against the Schism and to demand more rights from their ethnically Greek leadership.[62]

Since Archbishop Lycourgos visited Mount Athos as part of his anti-Slav and pro-Schism tour, Ignatiev proposed to cut the flow of funds to two most influential monasteries (Vatopedi and Kseropotami). He expected them to nip in the bud any anti-Slav agitation in the Precinct of the Mother of God and to bring the Patriarchate to its senses. Finally, Ignatiev suggested that any Greek clerics should not be given permission to collect alms in Russia "so that Pan-Slav money would not stick in their throat."[63]

Ten days later Ignatiev recommended the sequestering of the income of all Ottoman patriarchates and Athonite monasteries in Russian Bessarabia and Transcaucasia. But the Foreign Ministry and the Tsar considered that action "inconvenient and hard to implement."[64] In 1873, the punishment of just one Patriarchate of Jerusalem was no longer enough. The Ottoman patriarchates and monasteries would receive two-fifths of their Russian income. The rest would cover administrative expenses and fund Bessarabia's economy and schools. Any remaining sums would be deposited into a special fund that the Russian government would use to aid Ottoman Christian churches on a case-by-case basis.[65]

In addition to the external pressure, Ignatiev was working with various Ottoman Greek factions to remove Anthimus VI, who was strongly associated with the Schism. By late 1873, the allegations of corruption cost Anthimus VI the support of the Sublime Porte, of most high clergy, and of rich laity. He preferred resignation to deposition. Metropolitan Neophytos of Derkon and former Patriarch Joachim II began to compete for the hearts, minds, and purses of key prelates and leading laypersons of Constantinople.

---

62. Vovchenko, Denis, "Creating Arab Nationalism? Russia and Greece in Ottoman Syria and Palestine (1840–1909)," *Middle Eastern Studies*, 6, 49 (2013): 906.

63. AVPRI, f. 161/3-233-part 3, Ignatiev to Stremoukhov, 30 November 1872, pp. 2053ob–2055ob.

64. Ibid., Ignatiev to the Foreign Ministry, 11 December 1872, p. 2070.

65. Gerd, Lora, *Konstantinopolskii Patriarkhat i Rossiia, 1901–1914* (Moscow: Indrik, 2014), p. 114.

Russian support may have tipped the balance in favor of Joachim II. During his first tenure as Patriarch from 1860 to 1863, he granted the first modest concessions to the principle of ethnicity in the Bulgarian Church Question. In his conversation with Ignatiev, he was sorry for not having been more generous at the time and made an election promise to move the Bulgarian Church Question forward.[66]

Bulgarian nationalists again took the initiative. Building on the experience with the pro-Catholic movement in 1860–1861, they began to play games with Catholic missions as "a tactical move to exert pressure on the Russian embassy, the Exarch, and the Sublime Porte." The message was that unless allowed to join the Exarchate, many Bulgarian communities in Macedonia would switch to the still-minuscule Bulgarian Uniate *millet* to secure their language rights and effective Western consular protection from local administrative abuses. Joachim II proposed to set up a Greek-Bulgarian commission to supervise plebiscites—according to Article X of the *firman*, two-thirds of local Orthodox Christians needed to drop their ballots for either the Patriarchate or the Exarchate. Their progress was stopped by the 1875 Uprising in Bosnia-Herzegovina, which, the Sultan feared could spill over into other Balkan provinces.[67]

In anticipation of that crisis, Alexandros Rangavis tirelessly urged King George I and successive Greek prime ministers to stop fomenting scandalous inter-Christian squabbles and to reach a reconciliation with the Bulgarian movement. The benefits would be enormous—Greece's tarnished reputation in Europe would improve, Greece would be in the position to lead the struggle of Balkan Christians for liberation from Ottoman domination; and Russia would support Greece in the division of the spoils of the doomed Ottoman Empire. In effect, in his new post of Greek Ambassador in Berlin (1874–1886), he promoted what he had advocated as Ignatiev's friend and Greek envoy in Contantinople in 1870.[68]

Ignatiev could not make more decisive steps toward lifting the Schism given the changing balance of forces in the Porte and Greece. Ignatiev's holy task was made easier in August and October of 1875 when his friend Mahmud Nedim Pasha and pro-Russian Alexander Koumoundouros were back in

---

66. AVPRI, f. 161/3-233-part 4, Ignatiev to Gorchakov, 26 November 1873, pp. 2342–2344ob.

67. Markova, Zina, "Russia and the Bulgarian-Greek Church Question in the Seventies of the 19th Century," *Etudes Historiques*, 11 (1983): 177–180.

68. Rangavis to King George I, 2 October 1874, 2 April 1875, Soulogiannis, Th, and Botoroupoolou, Iphig., eds., *Alexandrou Rizou Rangavi Heirographos Kodix ar. 35* (Athens: Academy of Athens, 1997), pp. 81–82, 90–91.

charge of the Ottoman and the Greek governments, respectively. Thus, in 1875 Ignatiev managed to bring the Patriarchate and the Exarchate again to the negotiation table and early in 1876 the committee of two Greeks and two Bulgarians presided by Foreign Minister Rashid Pasha began its work.

By February 1876, they had a draft agreement where church organization accommodated the principle of ethnicity even more than before. The Exarchate would include fewer dioceses than in the 1871 plan sponsored by Anthimus VI. The Bulgarians agreed to cede Veles, Ohrid, and Skopje in exchange for gaining Philippoupolis and the compact, ethnically Greek cities of Varna, Anchialos, Messembria, and Sozopol on the Black Sea coast, which were invariably placed under the Patriarchate's jurisdiction in earlier projects.

Both sides were prepared to promise extensive cultural rights to allay each other's fear of extinction through assimilation. Local communities would elect bishops of their cultural background who would be approved and consecrated by the archbishop of that diocese. Well ahead of its time, the agreement granted the right to have assistant bishops (*khorepiskopos*) for ethnic minorities in each mixed diocese.

Those clear church boundaries meant revising the *firman* to eliminate Article X and to move the Exarch's residence outside the imperial capital. The Exarch would now be elected from among and by the prelates in the Bulgarian Exarchate. He himself would mention the name of the Patriarch at the liturgy, but the Exarchate's priests and bishops would mention his name only. The Bulgarian Exarchate's internal autonomy was strengthened by the right to deal with the Ottoman authorities directly without the Patriarchate's mediation. Most importantly, the Bulgarian Exarch himself would apply to the Sultan for *berat*—the term refers to any license to practice a trade, in this case a church office.[69]

Joachim II was satisfied with this nominal and almost purely spiritual control of the Exarchate, but he was not happy about seeing Philippoupolis go to the Exarchate and offered to swap it for some areas in northern Macedonia. In a confidential conversation with Greek Ambassador Kountouriotis, Joachim II said that if all Macedonia was going to stay under direct jurisdiction of the Patriarchate it would take a lot of effort to Hellenize its many Slavic-speaking parts.[70]

This statement does not necessarily mean that the Patriarch served the cause of the Great Idea. It is likelier that he was using the Greek irredentist

---

69. AYE, Embassy in Constantinople Collection, 1874-76, supplement to the report of 26 February 1876, no. 715.

70. Ibid., Kountouriotis to Konstostavlos, 17 February 1876, no. 597.

terms to better make his case and to encourage Greece to contribute more to the maintenance of the Patriarchate's schools and churches. The desperate financial crisis of the Patriarchate was the constant background of all other developments. The Sublime Porte provided no material support. On Easter Sunday of 1876, the Patriarchate had to cancel traditional giving out of alms to needy Christians. Ottoman Greek businessmen complained about bad markets. The Greek government began to subsidize the Patriarchate with annual grants of 10,000 French francs, which obviously served as a source of leverage.[71]

Joachim II also categorically refused to consider church boundaries as future national borders. He raised specific objections against subdividing dioceses along ethnic lines and especially against bishops elected by local communities. Those concessions adopted by the mixed commission went against "the dignity of the patriarch's throne" and church canons.[72] So the Greek-Bulgarian committee had to return to the negotiating table.

The continuing resistance of Herzegovinian and Bosnian Christian rebels were reminiscent called attention to the traditional religious divisions of the Islamic bifurcated state and could conceivably inspire the Greeks and the Bulgarians to overcome their ethnic differences. In 1876, Alexander Nelidov served as an advisor at the embassy in Constantinople and an interim chargé d'affaires in Ignatiev's absence. Nelidov intimated to Tertii Filippov his hopes for an agreement between the Bulgarian Exarchate and the Patriarchate as a result of the growing persecution of Balkan Christians by Ottoman authorities.[73]

Some Ottoman officials, such as former Grand Vizier Midhat Pasha, plotted to have Joachim II deposed to stop the reconciliation process and to keep Christians divided. According to the Greek envoy, only three or four Ottoman Greek journalists supported this line of widening the gap between Greeks and Slavs "because of their anti-Russian passion." Kountouriotis urged his government to persevere in its efforts to find a peaceful solution to the Bulgarian Church Question because it would serve as the basis of future cooperation between Balkan nations. Specifically, it would help if the Greek press exposed those anti-Slav designs as dangerous to Hellenism and leading to its isolation.[74] Being left out was an understandable concern at the time when the Herzegovinian and Bosnian rebels continued to defy the Sultan and were expected to spark a general Christian uprising.

---

71. Ibid., Kountouriotis to Konstostavlos, 17 March 1876, no. 1025.

72. Ibid., Kountouriotis to Konstostavlos, 12 March 1876, no. 833.

73. GARF, f. 1099-1-2252, Nelidov to Filippov, 22 March 1876, p. 2.

74. Ibid., 12 May 1872, Kountouriotis to Konstostavlos, no. 1874.

In May of 1876, the Sublime Porte and the Russian Foreign Ministry were "seriously considering" the modified project of reconciliation.[75] This relatively smooth process was disrupted by showers of bullets and floods of blood. The ongoing drama of the Eastern Crisis reached a climax and challenged the very survival of the Sultan's empire in the Balkans.

Cultural Responses to the Establishment of the Bulgarian Exarchate and the Schism

"I told you that Constantinople should be yours ... It is painful to see how the Yids and their German cousins along with savage Hungarians are slandering both you and us while oppressing our brothers. We should tell them, 'Halt! We are not giving in any further!'"[76] In May of 1872, Metropolitan Mikhail of Belgrade shared this mix of hope and despair with one of the leaders of Moscow-based Pan-Slavs—Professor Nil Popov. Only renewed Russian expansion into the Ottoman Empire could improve the lot of Slavic people in the Balkans.

After the short and disastrous war with Prussia in 1866, the Habsburgs had to reinvent themselves as the Dual Monarchy also known as Austria-Hungary. In this new federated structure, the Germans and the Hungarians would be treating various Slavic groups as second-class subjects. That is why many of them pinned their hopes on Mother Russia and sent their delegates to the Slavic Congress in Moscow in 1867.[77]

Even more ominous was Prussia's defeat of France and the emergence of unified Germany in 1870–1871. The drastic change in the balance of power set the stage for German domination of Europe but also allowed Russia to reclaim the right to have a navy and fortifications in the Black Sea. The demilitarization of the Black Sea was the most humiliating clause of the Treaty of Paris concluded after the Crimean War (1853–1856). German success not only inspired fear but also served as a model for a future Slavic federation often discussed in the Russian and South Slav press of this period.[78]

---

75. AVPRI, f. 161/3-233-part 4, Foreign Ministry to Ignatiev, 28 May 1876, p. 2446.

76. Russian State Library Manuscript Division (OR RGB), f. 239-13-45, Metropolitan Mikhail to Popov, 13 May 1872, p. 19.

77. Petrovich, Michael, *The Emergence of Russian Panslavism, 1856–1870* (Westport: Greenwood Publishers, 1985. First published: New York: Columbia University Press, 1956), p. 254.

78. Nikitin, S. A., "Balkanskiie sobytiia v russkoi periodicheskoi pechati kanuna Vostochnogo Krizisa," *Ocherki po istorii iuzhnykh slavian i russko-balkanskikh sviazei v 50–70-e gody XIX veka* (Moscow: Nauka, 1970), pp. 285–293.

In this menacing geopolitical context, many Russian commentators welcomed the establishment of the Bulgarian Exarchate as a symbolic victory for the Slavic cause. But this backing was not unconditional. From 1870 to 1875, the discussions of the Bulgarian Church Question revealed that, as earlier, only Bulgarian activists consistently put nationalism over religion. Russian Pan-Slavs supported them typically because they saw the Greeks in the Patriarchate of Constantinople as failing in their original Orthodox mission. The Pan-Orthodox publicists like Filippov no longer had strong government support at this time. But they were able to spread their views on the Russian role in the Christian East and on proper church-state relations in the educated society and even among Pan-Slavs themselves. In 1875, they also managed to reach a new level of intellectual synthesis and sophistication by producing a modern alternative to Western civilization.

The Bulgarian lobby in Russia argued that the *firman* had resolved the Bulgarian Question. Since the Archbishopric of Ohrid had been allegedly abolished solely by the Sultan's decree in the late 1700s, it could be reinstated in the form of the Exarchate by another decree of the Ottoman government without the consent of the Ecumenical Patriarchate.[79]

A typical example of the attitude of Russian Pan-Slavs was in the 1871 book by the eminent authority in church history Evgenii Golubinskii. He explained the Bulgarian church movement as a legitimate reaction to the suppression of Bulgarian nationality by the "Greek Phanariotes" of the Patriarchate of Constantinople. Golubinskii treated national liturgy and church hierarchy as the necessary trappings of nationhood.[80]

He justified the ethnically based church by interpreting the New Testament principle "Neither Jew, nor Greek" as sanctioning equality among Christian nations. However, unlike extreme Bulgarian nationalists, Golubinskii believed that the autonomous church status conceded by Patriarch Gregory VI before the *firman* of 1870 had secured the basis from which the Bulgarian nation could develop. Golubinskii insisted that in the interests of Orthodox unity the Bulgarians needed to agree to the compromise solution offered by the Patriarch even though it limited their territorial aspirations. Even after the issue of the *firman*, the recognition of the Bulgarian Exarchate by the Patriarch was necessary.[81]

---

79. Zhinzifov, Raiko, "Greko-bolgarskii tserkovnyi vopros," *Pravoslavnoie Obozrenie*, 7 (1870): 212–223.

80. Golubinskii, Elpidifor, *Kratkii ocherk istorii pravoslavnykh tserkvei bolgarskoi, serbskoi, i rumynskoi ili moldo-valashskoi* (Moscow: Moscow University Press, 1871), pp. 176–181.

81. Ibid., pp. 190–192.

The Greek newspapers were very sensitive to the Russian reactions to the decree establishing the Bulgarian Exarchate. *Anatolikos Aster*, the newspaper affiliated with the Patriarchate of Constantinople at the time, protested the discussion of the Bulgarian Question as basically solved even in official Russian newspapers. It referred to the pronouncements of the "elderly Metropolitan of Derkon" and to other Greek newspapers such as *Neologos* and *Kleio*, implicitly suggesting that all the factions of the educated Greek society in the Ottoman Empire and beyond were unanimous in their protest—be they either of pro-Russian, or moderate or extreme Greek nationalist leanings.[82]

The generally moderately nationalist *Kleio* published in Austrian Trieste went a step further and opened its pages to articles decrying Russian involvement in the Bulgarian Question. It published translations of German newspaper articles treating the Bulgarian church movement as the spearhead of Russian-sponsored expansionist Pan-Slavism.[83] These perceptions were "confirmed" in the translations of anti-Greek Pan-Slav articles from the German and Russian press.[84] At the same time, *Kleio* highlighted an article from the official newspaper of the Russian government ridiculing the very idea of Pan-Slavism and the fantasies of its influence on Russian foreign policy.[85]

However, even more balanced articles in *Kleio* put the blame for the escalation of the Bulgarian Question on the perceived shift in Russian foreign policy from Pan-Orthodoxy to Pan-Slavism after the Crimean War (1853–1856). Even when local roots of the Bulgarian nationalist discontent were acknowledged, the abuses by Greek prelates of the Patriarchate were explained away on the corrupt Ottoman system. Obliged to buy their offices from the government, the high clergy allegedly had no choice but to increase taxation of their flock to satisfy insatiable Ottoman officials.

At the same time, the Ecumenical Patriarchate did not pursue Hellenization of its Slavic flock. It followed from those articles that local administrative and financial abuses were not sufficient causes of the Bulgarian Church Question. Consequently, Russian-sponsored "Pan-Slavism" was the main driving force inciting Bulgarian nationalist passions against the Greeks generally and the

---

82. *Anatolikos Aster*, 900 (16 April 1871).

83. *Kleio*, 571 (27 May 1872); 578 (15 July 1872).

84. Ibid., 563 (1 April 1872) by Kanitz from *Allgemeine Zeitung*; ibid., 29 May 1872 from *Birzhevyie Vedomosti* of St. Petersburg.

85. *Kleio*, 550 (1 January 1872).

Ecumenical Patriarchate specifically. The same turn away from Pan-Orthodoxy to Pan-Slavism supposedly explained the refusal of the Russian Holy Synod to support the Ecumenical Patriarchate's call for an Ecumenical Council.[86]

A One Man Show? Tertii Filippov's Second Entry into the Bulgarian Church Question Debate

Although Filippov left the Holy Synod to join the staff of the office of the Comptroller General in 1864, he remained active in Pan-Slav groups and publications. In the fall of 1869, while working on his article in support of Patriarch Gregory VI, he delivered an enthusiastic speech at a special session of the St. Petersburg Slavic Society to welcome the visiting Metropolitan of Serbia Mikhail. The prelate was educated in Russia, known as a "Pan-Slav," with many connections in the intellectual, ecclesiastical, and diplomatic circles. In his speech, Filippov called for renaming the German-sounding "St. Petersburg" into a more Slavic sounding "Petrograd." He also prayed that "God might grant that Russia and those of her faith and blood might one day present a peaceful united front strong enough to resist the violations of Slavonic rights in every quarter."[87]

In the immediate aftermath of the issue of the *firman* of 1870, Filippov published an article in the influential journal of the Ministry of Education, where he continued to unabashedly assert the intellectual and spiritual superiority of the Greeks over the other Orthodox Christians in the Ottoman Empire. But at the same time, Filippov accorded more legitimacy to Bulgarian national aspirations. To be sure, in his opinion, the flames of the Bulgarian Question were still fanned by outside forces, "joint efforts of the common enemies of the Orthodox East—Muslims, Catholics, and Protestants." However, the Bulgarian national movement was rooted in the "rebirth of the Bulgarian nation," which, in contrast to what Filippov argued in his 1858 article, could not have been accommodated within the existing framework of the Ecumenical Patriarchate and its ethnically Greek leadership.[88] The problem was with the methods they chose to achieve their national goals.[89]

---

86. *Kleio*, 570 (20 May 1872); 573 (10 June 1872).

87. Fadner, Frank, *Seventy Years of Pan-Slavism in Russia: Karazin to Danilevskii, 1800–1870* (Georgetown: Georgetown University Press, 1982), p. 253.

88. Filippov, Tertii, "Vselenskii Patriarch Grigorii VI i greko-bolgarskaia raspria," *Zhurnal Ministerstva Narodnogo Prosveshenia*, 2 (February 1870): 245–247.

89. Ibid., p. 254.

Another departure from his views of 1858 was his willingness to allot the blame to both parties. To be sure, the main culprits were the young Bulgarians educated in the West and Western missionary schools in the Ottoman Empire, but these culprits were also influenced by "Polish and Hungarian émigrés" who had found political refuge in the Ottoman Empire after the failure of the 1848 revolutions. Bulgarian intelligentsia's lack of appreciation of religion combined with the divide-and-rule tactics of the Ottoman government to bring the Bulgarian Question to the impasse. In addition to these usual suspects, Filippov deplored the hard line of Patriarch Joachim II, whose tenure (1860–1863) "represented the saddest period in the history of the Greek-Bulgarian conflict."[90]

His more or less balanced treatment of the issue was consistent with his appeal to the Russian reading public and the government to be less biased against the Greeks and to play a mediating role instead of taking sides. Both the Slavs and the Greeks were connected to Russia through the work of SS. Cyril and Methodius. Politically, both nations were equally important to Russian influence in "Eastern affairs" as well. "More educated and experienced in statecraft, the Greeks are the most advanced element of the Orthodox East" whereas Bulgarians were not fully mature but numerically superior and quickly developing. Russia could not afford to alienate either one.[91] With the impending collapse of the Ottoman Empire, "the union of all Orthodox nations of Turkey is critical to the success of their common cause."[92]

Gregory VI gave full approval to Filippov's article dedicated to that patriarch in the first place. Gregory VI sent a request to Filippov for copies of his article through Professor Ianyshev, the President of the St. Petersburg Theological Academy. Filippov eagerly obliged and again confirmed his role as a supporter of Patriarch's policy of Orthodox unity and reconciliation, "which was rejected to the chagrin of many children of the Russian Church."[93]

In 1870, Filippov put a new emphasis on the idea of church independence from the state touched on in his earlier correspondence with Count Tolstoy. In the popular literary monthly magazine *Russkii Vestnik*, Filippov characterized the issue of the Sultan's *firman* as an example of state intervention into an area that should always be beyond the reach not only of non-Christian authorities but of Orthodox rulers as well. The real solution of the Bulgarian

---

90. Ibid., pp. 255–257.

91. Ibid., p. 251.

92. Ibid., p. 245.

93. GARF, f.1099-1-733, T. I. Filippov to Gregory VI, 3 September 1870, p. 1.

Question would be to convene an Ecumenical Council as urged by Patriarch Gregory VI.[94]

Filippov's sophisticated defense of that idea was ahead of similar attempts in the Greek world. A year later in 1871, Metropolitan Neophytos of Derkon sponsored the publication of a pamphlet making a case for the Ecumenical Council as the only appropriate solution of the Bulgarian Question. Using the pen name of M. H. G.,[95] its author, Georgios Plethonidis, took issue with the Bulgarian nationalist argument that there was no need for an Ecumenical Council since it was not the question of the Orthodox dogma but merely of administrative adjustments. Plethonidis denounced the Bulgarian case as dictated by "badly-intentioned nationalism" and argued that the decree of the Sultan had not solved the Bulgarian Question. The Sublime Porte interfered with strictly ecclesiastical affairs and substituted "race" for clear territorial delimitation as the only legitimate basis for church organization.[96]

Filippov's support of the Patriarchate of Constantinople was directly linked to the idea of restoring the same institution in Russia to increase church independence of state control. In a letter to then-retired Count Alexander Tolstoy, Filippov decried further encroachment of the imperial government on church prerogatives in Russia. This issue came to the fore when the bishops were stripped of the last vestiges of judicial authority. To remedy the situation, Filippov thought it necessary to restore both the regular meetings of local bishops' councils and the Patriarchate of Moscow, which "had been destroyed at the same time by the ambition of the genius tyrant." Filippov argued for the abolition of the Holy Synod designed by Peter the Great with the express purpose of "enslaving the Church."[97] Had Filippov openly published those antigovernment views, it would have cost him his job at the very least.

The Ecumenical Council would bring together not only "Greek" churches but also those of Russia, Serbia, and Romania, who were sympathetic to the Bulgarians. Since non-Greek churches objected to it, deep down they felt they were on the wrong side. In pursuit of their personal ambitions and emboldened by the self-interested Ottoman government, the Bulgarian nationalist

---

94. Filippov, Tertii, "Reshenie greko-bolgarskogo voprosa," *Russkii Vestnik*, 87, 6 (June 1870): 679–680, 686.

95. The author's name is revealed in Stamatopoulos, *Metarrythmisi kai ekkosmikefsi*, p. 482.

96. M. H. G., *E Diefkrinisis tou Voulgarikou zitimatos* (Constantinople: K. Plethonidis Publications, 1871), p. 27.

97. GARF, f.1099-1-1265, T. I. Filippov to A. P. Tolstoy, 4 January 1872, p. 150.

leaders misled the "poor Bulgarian people."[98] The Bulgarian prelates who gathered together in Constantinople to set up the Exarchate were in defiance of basic church discipline and regulations and already in an open schism with the Patriarchate.[99] Following Filippov's lead, the Russian supporters of Pan-Orthodox unity would consistently advocate an Ecumenical Council to solve the Bulgarian Question and to bring about the reform within the Russian Church.

In addition to monthly magazines, Filippov became active as a contributor and an editor in *Grazhdanin*—a new monarchist newspaper published by the well-connected Prince Vladimir Meshcherskii between 1872 and 1914. Its influence in anti-liberal circles quickly grew—Fyodor Dostoevsky himself served as the main editor in 1872–1874. Using that platform, Filippov crossed swords with Nikita Giliarov, a Slavophile theologian and the publisher of the daily Moscow-based newspaper *Sovremennyie Izvestiia* ("News Today"). Right after the Bulgarian Schism passed in September 1872, Filippov defended Gregory VI's call for the Ecumenical Council after the rejection of his conflict resolution project of 1867. The alternative Ottoman-backed projects of 1868 went against the fundamental regulations of the Orthodox Church that ban parallel ecclesiastical authority in the same diocese.[100]

To justify the condemnation of the uncanonical Bulgarian Exarchate, Filippov used a rather bold analogy originally suggested in the Greek press.[101] The Russian Church would have likewise condemned a similar movement for the restoration of the Georgian Orthodox Church, which had been independent until Georgia's incorporation into Russia in the early 1800s.[102] The Pan-Orthodox activists in Russia would henceforth be linking the Bulgarian Question to the challenge of ethnic diversity within the Russian Church and Empire.

To explain the decision of the 1872 Council of Constantinople, Filippov defined *ethnophyletism* as the sacrifice of the interests of the Church in favor of those of the nation (*narodnost'*) by one of the members of the supranational

---

98. Filippov, Tertii, "Vselenskii Patriarch Grigorii VI i greko-bolgarskaia raspria," *Zhurnal Ministerstva Narodnogo Prosveshenia*, 3 (March 1871): 41.

99. Ibid., p. 51.

100. Filippov, Tertii, "Opredelenie Kostantinopolskogo sobora po voprosu o bolgarskom ekzarkhate," *Grazhdanin*, 23 (9 October 1872): 161–164; 24 (10 October 1872): 194–197.

101. For example in Anonymous, *Les Slavianophiles en Orient* (Leipzig: Brockhaus, 1872?), p. 14.

102. Filippov, Tertii, "Opredelenie Kostantinopolskogo sobora po voprosu o bolgarskom ekzarkhate," *Grazhdanin*, 26 (30 October 1872): 252–253.

Orthodox Christian community. Furthermore, Filippov accused the Bulgarians of "shamelessly" accepting their church from the Sultan. He stressed again that this act violated the idea of church independence of the state and went against canon law.

Filippov referred to famous Pan-Orthodox figures such as the poet and theologian Ioannes Tantalides and former Patriarch Gregory VI present at the 1872 Council to prove that the latter could not be ignored as allegedly composed of Greek nationalists. Back in 1865, to nominate Tantalides for a Russian decoration, the priest of the Russian embassy in Constantinople reminded of his 1850 two-volume monograph titled "Exposing the Papacy" (*Papistika Elenha*) and of two poems composed in honor of the official visits to the Ottoman Empire of Grand Prince Konstantin, the brother of Alexander II and the father of Olga, Queen of Greece. During the Crimean War, Tantalides was very friendly to captured Russian officers imprisoned on the Princes' Islands.[103] In what would become an article of faith for his Pan-Orthodox followers, Filippov argued in favor of convening a bigger truly Ecumenical Council to include Russia, Serbia, and Rumania. It would overwrite the verdict of the 1872 Council and thus remedy the Bulgarian Schism.[104]

Metropolitan Mikhail of Belgrade criticized "the Greeks" for inciting nationalist fervor and not giving the Bulgarians a hearing at the Council of Constantinople. But like Filippov he advocated calling a greater council with the participation of independent churches from outside the Ottoman Empire to lift the Schism. At the insistence of the Serbian government, Mikhail delayed sending letters to that effect to the Bulgarian Exarchate and the Patriarchate of Constantinople.[105]

Similarly, the Foreign Ministry in St. Petersburg brushed aside almost identical prescriptions of the Russian prelates and considered inexpedient their canon-based recommendations. A new council would incite more passions and question the existence of the Bulgarian church, which was an accomplished fact. A penitential letter from Bulgarian prelates would diminish the importance of their new hard-won status. It should be sufficient for them to produce a formal acknowledgement of the primacy of

103. Antonin to Over-Procurator A. P. Akhmatov, 15 February 1865, Gerd, Lora, ed., *Arkhimandrit Antonin Kapustin: Doneseniia iz Konstantinopolia, 1860–1865* (Moscow: Indrik, 2013), p. 164.

104. Filippov, Tertii, "Opredelenie Kostantinopolskogo sobora po voprosu o bolgarskom ekzarkhate," *Grazhdanin*, 27 (6 November 1872): 289–294.

105. AVPRI, f. 161/3-233-part 3, Tseretelev to the Foreign Ministry, 11 December 1872, pp. 2074–2074ob.

the Patriarch, a renunciation of phyletism, and a request for recognition by other Orthodox churches.[106]

Politics aside, in a private letter to his mentor Pogodin, Filippov identified the Ecumenical Council as the cure-all for all Russia's church problems and the key to "bringing us back to the true church life, of which we were deprived for a long time, to restoring to us the salutary principle of council (*sovet*), to resurrecting in us the otherwise completely frozen sense of our ecumenical union with co-religionist nations (*narod*)." The awakening of the Church from "its lethargy" is the only hope for "a future of Russia and the Slavic world."

He envisaged this union of the Russians, the Slavs, and the Greeks as a world apart. In Filippov's mind, the Church was "our only salvation and the only claim to fame before the rest of the humanity. We will have to borrow everything else from others but we could share with more advanced nations the light of the truth preserved by the Church. Even if this does not happen, for ourselves it is the source of life, renewal, and enlightenment."[107]

The Greek press appreciated Filippov's stance in defense of the authority of the Patriarchate of Constantinople, of the Local Council of August–September 1872, and the idea of the Ecumenical Council to lift the Schism and finally solve the Bulgarian Question. The influential Greek diaspora newspaper *Kleio* praised *Grazhdanin* of St. Petersburg, its editor Professor Gradovskii, and its publisher Prince Meshcherskii for having given a platform to Filippov's views.[108] This gesture of goodwill toward Russia may have been funded by the Russian embassy in Athens to create "a diversion in the Bulgarian affair." More moderate articles in *Hemera* and *Kleio* were supposed to rebut the more extreme views of Ottoman Greek publications.[109]

According to *Kleio*, most other Russian publications were rather blindly supportive of Pan-Slav and Bulgarian interests as they saw them. Even when some of them gave credit to Filippov's expertise in canon law such as *Akademicheskaia Gazeta*, they themselves stressed financial and political motives that drove the Patriarchate and broadly the Greek world to the Schism from Slavdom. *Kleio* took note of a reconciliatory article in *Akademicheskaia Gazeta*, which denounced a Slavophobe clique but not the Greek people as a

---

106. AVPRI, f. 161/3-233-part 4, Stremoukhov to Tolstoy, pp. 2235–2235ob.

107. Russian State Archive for Literature and Art (RGALI), 373-1-361, T. I. Filippov to M. P. Pogodin, 25 August 1870, p. 300b–310b.

108. *Kleio*, 595 (11 November 1872).

109. AVPRI, 161/3-233-part 3, P. A. Sabourov to P. N. Stremoukhov, 8 November 1872, p. 1964.

whole. Owing so much to the Greeks historically, Russia could not side exclusively with the Slavs against them.[110]

Although Filippov believed he was representing the true interests of Russia and "the Slavic world," he often felt alienated from the rest of the Russian educated society on this issue at the time.[111] In fact, many ecclesiastics, intellectuals, and officials were either able to come to similar conclusions with or without direct Filippov's influence. Filippov's impact became immediately felt in 1870–1872 and steadily grew ever since.

Thus, in their comments on the Bulgarian Schism, the editors in the authoritative church periodical *Pravoslavnoie Obozrenie* could not ignore Filippov's position on the issue. They praised the neutrality of the Russian Church in staying out of the supposedly Greek-nationalist-dominated Council of Constantinople of 1872. That prudent act on the part of the Russian church leaders made it possible to consider the excommunication of the Bulgarian prelates a non-binding decision. Even those of "our disguised and undisguised, conscious and unconscious Greco-philes who are now reproaching the Russian Church for not participating directly in that affair" would not really like to see the Bulgarian schism universally recognized.[112]

Filippov's opponents criticized him not as a maverick but as a representative of the "Grecophile trend" who relied on moralizing tone and emotional appeal "to reduce Russian ethnic sympathy for Bulgarians." But their Russian supporters were not too different from Filippov. They could not accept the Sultan's decree as the solution of the Bulgarian Church Question and tried to integrate Bulgarian ethnocentric demands with the Orthodox tradition. In their words, anyone without Filippov's pro-Greek bias could support the Bulgarian desire for an independent church based on canon law and church history. Although the Bulgarian Church Question alone did not merit the convening of an Ecumenical Council, other pressing problems of Orthodox Christianity certainly called for it.[113]

In its own effort to contain nationalism within the Russian Empire, the Russian Ministry of Internal Affairs opposed Pan-Slav agitation and periodically closed their publications. They criticized many government steps generally and sowed the seeds of rebellion in Polish-populated areas specifically.

---

110. *Kleio*, 600 (16 December 1872).

111. RGALI, 373-1-361, T. I. Filippov to M. P. Pogodin, 18 March 1872, pp. 380b–39.

112. *Pravoslavnoie Obozrenie*, "Po povodu otlucheniia sostoiavshegosia v Konstantinopole protiv Bolgarskoi Tserkvi," 12 (1872): 493–494.

113. Tesovskii, P. [Shiraiev, Grigorii], "Greko-bolgarskii tserkovnyi vopros," *Zaria*, 6 (1871): 94–105.

The censorship office in Warsaw ordered the editor of the local Russian-language newspaper *Varshavskii Dnevnik* to stop publishing "articles sympathetic to the Slavs of Austria and Turkey."

In the censor's opinion, promoting separatist aspirations of Balkan Slavs was particularly "inappropriate" in the official newspaper in the Vistula province "where our Government strives for the reconciliation and unification of the Poles with the predominant population of the Empire."[114] The timing of the order (28 August 1871) coincided with the heightening of the Bulgarian Church Question before the patriarch's elections extensively covered in the Russian press. Clearly, the Internal Ministry was not particularly open toward the changes in the status quo of the Bulgarians in the Ottoman Empire and implicitly backed the continued authority of the Ecumenical Patriarch over all Ottoman Christians.

Although not directly engaged in the post-1870 debate on the Bulgarian Church Question, Professor Vladimir Lamanskii continued to develop his earlier ideas of the unity and interdependence of the Greco-Slavic world in his 1871 book *Concerning the Historical Study of the Greco-Slavic World in Europe.*[115] Although not discussing the role of Filippov or the Patriarchate of Constantinople, the most authoritative Russian Slavicist was still building new supranational bridges between the Greeks and the Slavs. Lamanskii's views would eventually attract many followers among professional Slavic studies scholars. One of them, Anton Budilovich, started his involvement in journalism as a Filippov's protégé. Far from being a stranger in the Slavophile print media, Filippov recommended him to the editor of the Slavophile magazine *Beseda.*[116] That same year Budilovich published a large article there popularizing Danilevsky's concept of a Russia-centered Slavic federation.[117]

In addition to engaging in a lively press polemic with the pro-Bulgarian lobby, Filippov remained an active member of the St. Petersburg Slavic Society, where he made a public speech commemorating Alexander Gilferding, a diplomat, a Slavic and famous scholar of Slavic studies. Filippov used that occasion to stress that the early Slavophiles first of all were fervent Orthodox

---

114. GARF, f. 730 (N. P. Ignatiev)-1-648, Warsaw Censor to the Editor of *Varshavskii Dnevnik*, 28 August 1871, p. 1.

115. Vladimir Lamanskii's book *Ob istoricheskom izuchenii Greko-Slavianskogo mira v Evrope* (St. Petersburg, 1871) is the elaboration of his "Neskolko slov ob otnoshenii russkikh k grekam," *Russkaia Beseda*, 12 (1858): 103–140.

116. RGALI, f. 636-1-506, T. I. Filippov to S. A. Iuriev, 19 April 1871, p. 19.

117. Nikitin, Sergei, "Balkanskiie sobytiia v russkoi periodicheskoi pechati kanuna Vostochnogo Krizisa," pp. 285–286.

Christians, then Russian nationalists, and, finally, supporters of their Slavic brethren in Austria and Turkey.[118]

Filippov's appeals did not fall on deaf ears. He gained his most articulate follower in Fedor Kurganov—a professor at the Kazan Theological Academy and one of the leading Russian experts on church law and history. In 1872, in his published dissertation on the Church of the Kingdom of Greece, he criticized its establishment without the consent of the Patriarchate between 1833 and 1852.[119]

In 1873, he serialized a detailed study of the Bulgarian Church Question in the organ of the Kazan Theological Academy. He believed that the Bulgarian leaders deliberately pushed the Patriarchate to the Schism by refusing to renegotiate the Sultan's *firman* and by committing numerous defiant acts of church insubordination. At the same time, the Exarchate's leaders hypocritically presented themselves as victims of the Patriarch's intransigence. In Kurganov's view, most Russian church and lay publications including *Khristianskoie Chtenie* and *Moskovskie Vedomosti* took at face value "the tendentious lie" of the Bulgarian Exarch's circular letters.[120]

Kurganov openly sided with Filippov—the Schism was legitimate and binding even for the Russian Church. Kurganov went into detail exposing "the racial bias" (*plemennoie pristrastie*) of the Russian press reactions to the Schism. He specifically took issue with the typically Pan-Slav assertions of the liberal newspaper *Golos* that the Slavs allegedly kept their faith in a much more intact and pure form and usually expelled Greek priests from their lands. In contrast, Kurganov supported the condemnation of the Bulgarian church movement as an example of the new heresy of phyletism or "racism" not permissible in the Church. In his mind, this act meant that "among the Greeks there is not only a higher percentage but generally a higher number of people renouncing national interests and rising to the [supranational] idea itself, to its relationship to the teaching of the Church on dogma and canons."[121]

However, many in the Ottoman Greek community did not share Kurganov's optimism about the unshakeable Greek commitment to Orthodoxy. There

---

118. Filippov, Tertii, "V pamiat A. F. Gilferdinga" (first delivered as a speech at the session of the St. Petersburg Slavic Committee, 14 February 1873) in *Slavianofilstvo: Pro et contra: Tvorchestvo i deiatelnost slavianofilov v otsenke russkikh myslitelei i issledovatelei* (St. Petersburg: Russian Christian Academy for Humanities Publications, 2006), pp. 393–394.

119. Kurganov, Fedor, *Ustroistvo upravleniia v Tserkvi Korolevstva Grecheskogo* (Kazan: Kazan Theological Academy Press, 1872).

120. Kurganov, Fedor, "Istoricheskii ocherk greco-bolgarskoi raspri," *Pravoslavnyi Sobesednik*, 11 (1873): 360–361.

121. Ibid., pp. 378–386.

were rumors that Archbishop of Varna and future patriarch Joachim was opposing Greek national and church interests in the Bulgarian Church Question. When former Patriarch Joachim II questioned Joachim's archdeacon passing through Constantinople, Joachim decided to explain himself to his old benefactor. He indeed disapproved of the Patriarchate's inconsistent policy in the Bulgarian Question and especially of the Bulgarian Schism. Contrary to the assurances of the Greek press, proclaiming Bulgarian leaders schismatic would not deter more Ottoman Slavic-speaking communities from supporting them. In fact, they would become more determined enemies of "poor subjugated Greeks" (atyhes doulos Ellenismos) who had "no sincere friend or protector." He implied that the irredentist Greek kingdom posed as their homeland but had its own agendas.[122]

Those disagreements were not limited to private correspondence. As part of that heated debate, the future renowned official archivist and chronicler of the Patriarchate made his debut as a young journalist. In an anonymous pamphlet, Manuel Gedeon (1851–1943) argued that the Greeks were just as guilty of phyletism as the Bulgarians and increasingly lost track of the supranational Christian path. It broke his heart when many Greek commentators rejoiced in the Schism as liberating Greek Orthodoxy from the Slavs.

Even the Patriarchate, in discussions of the Bulgarian Church Question, was eventually prepared to draw new ecclesiastical boundaries cutting across existing dioceses in order to avoid including pockets of the Greek population in the Bulgarian Exarchate. Gedeon considered the Bulgarian national church movement as a legitimate response to the abuses of Greek prelates in the Balkan provinces and even compared it to the Reformation. In contrast to the Patriarchate's official line, Gedeon put less blame on the Catholic missionaries who spread nationalist ideas to further divide the Bulgarian flock from their Greek shepherds. The Bulgarian activists were often disrespectful of church authority but did not deserve such an extreme condemnation.[123]

This Ottoman Greek criticism of the Schism mirrored Russian Pan-Slav reactions to that event while Filippov's views reflected the Patriarchate's stance. In another parallel development, as more Greeks began to doubt the sincerity or even the expediency of the Schism, Filippov's interpretation of

---

122. Archbishop Joachim to Joachim II, 16 October 1872, Peter Nikov, ed., Bulgarskogoto vuzrazhdane vu Varna i Varnensko: Mitropolit Ioakim i negovata korespondentsiia (Sofia: Pridvorna Pechatnitsa, 1934), pp. 432–436.

123. Anonymous [Gedeon, Manuel], Mia selis tes istorias tes synhronou Ekklesias: Skepseis enos Orthdoxou (Athens: Evangelistria, 1874), pp. 7–13.

what constituted true Orthodoxy made inroads into the Pan-Slav camp. Let us take Andrei Muraviev as an example.

He was the most popular nineteenth-century Russian lay author writing on spiritual topics. Especially famous were his travelogues based on several pilgrimages to "the Christian East" where he had made a lot of contacts with Greek and Slavic prelates. As a former Holy Synod official and a personal friend of Ambassador Ignatiev, Muraviev was in a good position to supply advice and information to him on many issues of church politics. Muraviev's prestige was strengthened by his long-time friendship with the towering figure of the nineteenth-century Russian Church, Metropolitan Filaret of Moscow, whose 440 letters to himself Muraviev was able to publish.[124]

Much like Archpriest Bazarov or Metropolitan Mikhail of Belgrade, Muraviev was initially sympathetic to the Bulgarians and suspicious of the influence of Greek nationalism in the Ecumenical Patriarchate. When the dispute over the division of the dioceses between the future Bulgarian Exarchate and the Patriarchate reached its height, Muraviev wanted Ignatiev to make sure Ohrid stayed in Bulgarian hands. As part of the medieval Serbian Patriarchate, Ohrid had to return to the Slavs, or else the Greeks would dig up and dump the bodies of the deceased Serbian patriarchs in a fit of uncontrollable hatred for all things Slavic. But Muraviev did not see the Bulgarian Question as a purely ethnic conflict. Like all Russian Pan-Slavs, he feared that if the demands of the Bulgarians were not met, they could go Catholic or Protestant.[125]

When the Sublime Porte established the Bulgarian Exarchate in February 1870, Muraviev "rejoiced in the success of the Bulgarian cause." His joy was reduced to sadness, though, by the negative impression that the Orthodox Christians made on the world when they failed to sort out their family feud without the intervention of the Ottoman authorities: "Only one thing is regrettable in the Greco-Bulgarian affair, that the problem of church organization is resolved by the Sultan's *firman* rather than by the Greek hierarchy on its own; that is the reason the Westerners are finding fault with us."[126] Sympathetic as he was to "the Slavic cause," the religious Western Other and the interests of the Orthodox world as a whole figured more prominently in his mind.

Like most Russian Pan-Slavs, Muraviev believed that the *firman* could serve as a basis for a modified canonical solution. As the hope for reconciliation of the parties evaporated, Muraviev became increasingly disturbed by

---

124. Muraviev, Andrei, ed., *Pisma Filareta, Metropolita Moskovskogo k A. N. Muravievu (1832–1867)* (Kiev: I. Ia. Davidenko, 1869).

125. GARF, f.730-1-3472, Muraviev to Ignatiev, 11 December 1869, pp. 33–330b.

126. Ibid., 18 March 1870, pp. 41–42.

the intransigent demands of the Bulgarian leaders. Muraviev was shocked by the Bulgarian readiness to accept the jarring Turkish-style title of the Exarch "*bash mitropolit*" and their insistence on Constantinople as the seat of the Exarch and his Synod in the very heart of the Ecumenical Patriarch's own jurisdiction. He almost begged Ignatiev to pull his strings within the Ottoman government to remove from Constantinople the notorious Bulgarian troublemaker Stoian Chomakov along with his Greek counterpart Eustathios Cleovoulos. Not to forget the home front, Muraviev also asked Ignatiev to have the Russian Internal Ministry restrain the Russian Pan-Slav Professor Nil Popov from lashing out in the press in support of the Bulgarians.[127]

In these efforts to moderate the extremists on all sides, Muraviev found Filippov's articles very helpful. On several occasions Muraviev advised Ignatiev on how to use Filippov's arguments to undermine the historical and canonical validity of the Bulgarian claims to more and more ecclesiastical territory and power.[128] To encourage Filippov, Muraviev suggested that Ignatiev obtain a letter of acknowledgement for Filippov from the Ecumenical Patriarch.[129] Clearly, Filippov's voice was not that of one crying in the wilderness, as many scholars argued.[130]

Convinced by Filippov's publications, Muraviev abandoned his earlier emotional support for assigning Ohrid to the Bulgarian Exarchate. In a remarkable Pan-Orthodox gesture, he placed great expectations on Gregory VI and the Ecumenical Council and was deeply disappointed when the Russian Holy Synod rejected that noble idea. Andrei Muraviev urged Ignatiev to convey to his superiors the bad impression that "absurd" response had made in the Patriarchate of Constantinople.[131]

With the Ecumenical Council no longer in the offing, Muraviev began to promote the idea of another local council of the Ottoman Orthodox churches as the last chance to solve the Bulgarian Question. Muraviev agreed with Mikhail, Metropolitan of Serbia, that even if he wished "the Ecumenical Patriarch could not turn the *firman* into a church canon."[132] Muraviev informed Ignatiev that he

---

127. Ibid., 14 June 1870, p. 50.

128. Ibid., 23 May 1870, p. 430b.

129. Ibid., 10 July 1870, p. 53.

130. Markova, Zina, *Bulgarskata ekzarkhia, 1870–1879* (Sofia: Bulgarian Academy of Sciences, 1989), p.254; Nikitin, Sergei, *Slavianskie komitety v Rossii v 1858–1876* (Moscow: Moscow State University Press, 1960), p. 124.

131. GARF, f.730-1-3472, Muraviev to Ignatiev, 10 May 1871, p. 890b.

132. Ibid., 28 May 1870, pp. 46–47.

had instructed Metropolitan Mikhail as a prospective delegate to that local council "to mind not only the Slavic interests but the Pan-Orthodox ones as well." For this, Muraviev urged Mikhail to pacify the Bulgarians through his agents.[133]

In his attempt to reconcile the two sides, he exchanged letters with Bulgarian Exarch Anfim I and Patriarchs Gregory VI and Anthimos VI that were later published in one of the major Russian church periodicals. Although occasionally pro-Bulgarian in tone, Muraviev encouraged both sides to moderation and exposed the reading public in Russia to a wide range of views on the Bulgarian Question.[134]

Filippov's correspondence with Pogodin is another example of his continued insider status in the Slavophile circles. In contrast to Filippov, Pogodin did not accept the Bulgarian Schism passed by the Local Council of September 1872. Denying the legitimacy of the Bulgarian Exarchate, "the Greeks" were motivated by the "unspiritual" pursuit of material gain and the Great Idea of Greek irredentism. That is why they excommunicated and persecuted Pogodin's friend, the reconciliatory Patriarch of Jerusalem Cyril. Still, to Pogodin not all Greek people or clergy were hostile to the Slavs. The source of polarization and conflict was in "a certain party favored by the Turks" that launched a defamation campaign against what they perceived as sinister Russian designs on the "East." After a recent personal visit there, Pogodin became convinced that "all Christian churches in the East and all monasteries on Mount Athos pin their hopes solely on Russia."[135]

Filippov clearly disagreed with this messianic view and advocated a lower profile for Russia in "the East," its reliance on and support of the continued authority of the Ecumenical Patriarchate instead. But this serious difference over the Bulgarian Question and the proper role for Russia did not preclude friendship and communication between Filippov and Pogodin or other Pan-Slavs. In fact, in 1875 Pogodin proved open-minded enough to sponsor the publication of the landmark Pan-Orthodox book *Byzantinism and Slavdom* by Konstantin Leontiev.[136]

Leontiev is the most famous of the disillusioned Russian Slavophiles. Like many Pan-Slav intellectuals, he started as a moderately known novelist and a

133. Ibid., 10 July 1870, pp 520b–53.

134. Muraviev, Andrei, "Perepiska s vostochnymi ierarkhami po greco-bolgarskomu delu," *Trudy Kievskoi Dukhovnoi Akademii*, 1 (1873): 105–148.

135. Letter dated 16 May 1873 in Mikhail Pogodin, *Neizdannyie pisma* (Moscow, 1878), pp. 114–115.

136. Leontiev, Konstantin, *Moia literaturnaia sudba: Vospominania* (Moscow: Russkaia kniga, 2002), p. 59.

literary critic. Unlike most of them, he had direct contacts with the South Slavs as a consul in Crete, Adrianople, Tulcha, Yanina, and Thessaloniki from 1863 to 1873. Ambassador Ignatiev was his supervisor most of that time. First-hand observations of the unsavory characters of the Greek-Bulgarian drama spoiled his appetite for Pan-Slavism and gradually inspired him to crusade against nationalism and to invent a modern supraethnic anti-liberal alternative to it.

In Leontiev's own admission, his conversion from earlier Pan-Slavism to Pan-Orthodoxy came as a result of Filippov's articles "full of firmness and clarity" published in 1870–1872. Without much knowledge of church canons, Leontiev moved in the same direction following *"instincts* and *demonstration effect (po nagliadnost)"* "first and foremost disgusted at the way those liberal Bulgarian *boors (khamie)* were putting on airs in regard to the Church in which I *personally believe and historically venerate* [underlined in the original]." Out of their solidarity on the Bulgarian Question, Filippov and Leontiev grew to become very close lifetime friends.[137]

In *Byzantinism and Slavdom*, Leontiev adopted Danilevsky's methodology[138] but questioned his conclusions about the possibility and desirability of the Slavic cultural-historical type. Although more sympathetic to Ottoman Greeks than to their cousins in the independent Kingdom of Greece, Leontiev suspected both middle-class Greeks and Slavs of being infected by Western liberalism, of which nationalism was a by-product. If Danilevsky's Slavic federation came into being, that same disease would destroy Russia. Having absorbed the messianic spirit of the idea of the Third Rome, both Leontiev and Danilevsky envisioned Russia's conquest of the Ottoman Empire, but they disagreed about the form of the brave new world to come out of it. "Byzantine cultural-historical type" would be a much healthier alternative to Western civilization because it would preserve and develop the Russian dynastic monarchy side by side with the strengthened Ecumenical Patriarchate based on adapted Byzantine traditions. In contrast, "Pan-Slavism" was an empty dream—there were no shared Slavic culture or institutions. Even worse, if adopted by Russia, it would be a Trojan horse bringing with it bourgeois democracy, consumerism, and secularism.[139]

---

137. RGALI, f. 2980-1-1023, Leontiev to Filippov, Moscow, 8 January 1876, p. 2.

138. K. N. Leontiev to I. I. Fudel, 6 July 1888, Leontiev, Konstantin, Soloviev D., ed., *Izbrannyie Pisma (1854–1891)* (St. Petersburg: Pushkinskii Fond, 1993), p. 380.

139. Leontiev, Konstantin, "Vizantizm i Slavianstvo," in *Vostok, Rossia, Slavianstvo: Filosofskaia i politicheskaia publitsistika, dukhovnaia proza (1872–1891)* (Moscow: Respublika, 1996), p. 116. Originally published in *Chteniia v Imperatorskom Obshestve istorii i drevnostei rossiiskikh pri Moskovskom Universitete*, 3 (1875). Published as a separate issue in 1876.

The leaders of the Bulgarian church movement in particular brought the Russians to the dangerous Rubicon by forcing them to choose between their ethnicity and the Byzantine traditions of autocracy and Orthodoxy. That is why Leontiev was much more sympathetic to Ottoman Turks than to other Balkan ethnicities or Westerners. During his ten-year stay in the Ottoman Empire, Leontiev noticed that in addition to Russian obedience to authorities "the Turks respect the ecclesiastical character of our Empire seeing much affinity with the religious character of their own nation." If the Sultan's government had to flee from Constantinople, "the Turks would be always looking to Russians as protectors from the inevitable oppression and abuse inflicted on them by their former slaves, the Greeks and the South Slavs, who are generally rather cruel and rude."[140]

Leontiev's Byzantine civilization was an intellectual framework to underpin the arguments Filippov, Count Alexander Tolstoy, and other Pan-Orthodox activists had put forward earlier. Specifically, Leontiev's formula provided a kind of logical coherence to the persistent Russian fears that without the administrative and/or spiritual leadership of the Ecumenical Patriarchate the Orthodox Slavs (and the Arabs) would be unable to resist Western temptations of both religious propaganda and ungodly secularism. These views struck most Russian Pan-Slavs as paradoxical and eccentric. Leontiev was still invited to their social soirées as "a very gifted person but a terrible Byzantinist."[141]

Conclusion

By the late 1860s, the Bulgarian nationalist movement had become a significant player in Ottoman domestic and Balkan regional politics. The Ottoman government gave the green light to its more ambitious demands in order to keep the Christians divided in the aftermath of the abortive Cretan Uprising (1866–1869). Russian diplomats managed to bring the two sides together only when they convinced the Sublime Porte about the negative implications of encouraging nationalist agitation and establishing ethnically based institutions. While it was essential for the Grand Vizier to play a role of an honest broker, it also helped if the government of Greece as the most involved regional power used its influence in the Patriarchate to promote cooperation among Balkan Christians. For its part, since the late 1860s, the Patriarchate was flexible enough to adjust church canons and structure to the principle

---

140. Ibid., p. 106.

141. OR RGB, f. 239-4-5, I. S. Aksakov to N. A. Popov, 10 October 1874, p. 50.

of ethnicity. The Bulgarian nationalist movement proved the least reliable partner because its factions did not always act in common and derailed the agreement reached in late 1871. In the spring of 1876, the negotiations were put on hold by the escalation of violence in the Balkans triggered by the 1875 uprising in Bosnia-Herzegovina.

The Greek and Russian press actively discussed the buildup to the Schism of 1872 and its aftermath. Some denounced the idea of the church council and the heresy of phyletism as self-serving tools of Greek nationalism. Russian Pan-Slavs expressed this criticism most consistently but they did not draw the conclusion that Orthodoxy was dead. The Greeks dropped its banner but the Orthodox Slavs picked it up and carried it forward. Religion was even more alive with Russian Pan-Orthodox commentators who connected the reform of the Russian Church to the calls for an Ecumenical Council. They remained an integral part of the Russian Slavophile circles and assimilated Danilevsky's theory of cultural-historical types to invent Byzantinism as a vision of a cultural and political union of Russia with the Christian East.

The debate around the Bulgarian Church Question implicitly posed the question of whether Russia was a modern ethnocentric nation-state and a nucleus of a future Pan-Slav union or a multinational empire with dynastic and religious foundations. Russian diplomats and church dignitaries answered that question in their efforts to return the Bulgarian movement into the institutional framework of the Patriarchate based on mutual concessions. The reactions to the issue of the 1870 *firman* and the 1872 Schism demonstrated how seriously the Russian and Greek educated societies took Orthodoxy, whether they accepted the decision of the Local Council of 1872 or criticized it as the product of Greek irredentism and Slavophobia.

As in the previous period, Russian state and nonstate actors relied on official diplomatic and church channels, although the press, and personal contacts within the Patriarchate and the Bulgarian movement, were also important. Although highly motivated and ready to use substantial political and economic resources, the Russian representatives were not able to completely control the situation. The experience of those years suggests that determined, well-organized minority groups such as the lay-dominated Patriarchate of Constantinople or the Bulgarian church movement can find ways to play the host state and outside powers off against each other.

5

Making Peace in Times
of War (1875–1885)

"DOES ANY SOUTH Slav heart fail to beat faster at the news of this revolution?" "Is there any doubt that the death of Turkey has come?" Khristo Botev urged radical Bulgarian émigrés in Rumania in July of 1875, "We must rise and put an end to our terrible inhuman suffering; we must make the tyrant pay for it; we must help Herzegovina and ourselves; we must show the diplomats that we are not a herd but a people capable of life and development."[1] Although the Slavic rebels in the name of the Cross, the Nation, or a socialist utopia had been mostly defeated in 1876, their actions triggered a chain of events leading to a drastic redrawing of the Balkan map and massive refugee movements.

The successful talks between the Patriarchate and the Exarchate were interrupted by one of the worst crises in Ottoman history produced by internal revolts, divisions in the elites, warlike Balkan neighbors, and interference of the Great Powers. It was a perfect storm. The Sublime Porte's response ranged from military action to negotiations and one last round of the Tanzimat reforms.

Russian involvement in the so-called Eastern Crisis of 1875–1878 is usually characterized as the triumph of the modern ethnically based ideology of Pan-Slavism.[2] The Russian military occupation of Bulgaria during and after the Russo-Turkish War of 1877–1878 did give the former Ottoman province

---

1. Botev, Khristo, "Revolutsia narodna, nezabavna, otchaianna," *Zname*, 23 (27 July 1875).

2. A typical example of this view is in Astrid Tuminez, *Russian Nationalism since 1856: Ideology and the Making of Foreign Policy* (Lanham: Rowman & Littlefield, 2000), pp. 57–100.

most of the trappings of a modern Western-style nation-state. But analyzing Russian attitudes and policies in the Bulgarian Church Question at that time complicates this straightforward modernization story.

The Russian policymakers generally did not promote modern ethnonational identities and institutions at the expense of their premodern religious counterparts because Orthodox Christianity remained more important both culturally and politically for Russian elites themselves. In this period of Russian military occupation and domination of Ottoman Bulgarian lands, not only diplomats and clerics but also army commanders, encouraged power-sharing arrangements to reconcile the Patriarchate of Constantinople and the Bulgarian Exarchate.

Thus, unlike earlier periods, this time the Russian government was able to impose its policy on rival churches by force during its occupation of Ottoman Bulgaria. This direct local control usually led to ethnic peace and restoration of the authority of the Patriarchate. However, occasionally Bulgarian nationalists were able to manipulate Russian representatives to their advantage by threatening to defect from Orthodoxy. Russian efforts to contain the expansion of the newly created Bulgarian Principality led to a break between two countries and the crisis of Russian Pan-Slavism.

The Year of Three Sultans, Two Uprisings, and Two Wars

1873 was the year of the calm before the storm. The Sublime Porte faced no serious separatist challenges. The Cretan Uprising had been crushed. The Greeks and the Bulgarians were quarrelling among themselves and jockeying for attention of the Ottoman government. All this seemed to have given the Ottoman civic territorial nation another lease on life. Published by Osman Hamdi Bey in 1873, the ambitious photo album illustrated that mood by celebrating Ottoman diversity and papering over the differences of many religious and ethnic groups. The photographs typically include a careful mix of Muslim and Christian models wearing regional folk costumes. But instead of creating the image of national harmony, they often reveal tensions, especially when only Muslims conspicuously bear weapons, as in Figure 5.1.

In July of 1875, Christian brigands attacked a trade caravan in Herzegovina, killing five Muslim merchants and taking off with fifty loads of coffee, sugar, and rice. That raid provoked Ottoman reprisals and ignited the explosive mix created by tense relations between Muslim landlords, tax farmers, and

FIGURE 5.1 "Studio portrait of models wearing traditional clothing from the province of Adrianople (Edirne), Ottoman Empire: (1) Muslim inhabitant of Adrianople, (2) Muslim horseman of Adrianople (Edirne), (3) Christian artisan of Adrianople (Edirne)." Library of Congress Prints and Photographs Division, Reproduction Number: LC-USZC4-11826. Photographed by Pascal Sebah, originally published in Osman Hamdy Bey and Marie de Launay, *Les Costumes populaires de la Turquie en 1873* (Constantinople: Levant Times and Shipping Gazette Press, 1873).

Christian sharecroppers. Many became refugees and vengeful insurgents who found support in the autonomous Montenegro.[3]

While the rebellion in Western Balkan borderlands was developing, the Sublime Porte defaulted on the payments to its European creditors in October of 1875. The bankruptcy highlighted political failures. The inability of the Sultan's government to quickly suppress the 1875 uprising in Bosnia-Herzegovina emboldened small groups of Bulgarian revolutionary nationalists who had nothing to do with the loyalist Bulgarian church movement. In the previous ten years or so, the conspirators could not build a stronghold inside Bulgaria and limited themselves to short raids from Rumania across the Danube. All of them were miserable failures. With this kind of record, it is not surprising that the mass of Bulgarian farmers did not support the so-called April Uprising of 1876.[4]

Herzegovinian and Bosnian peasant rebels were a much greater nuisance that pinned most available Ottoman regular army units. The insurrection in Bulgaria had to be crushed by notoriously ill-disciplined Muslim irregulars or *bashibazouks*, who included many dispossessed Circassian emigrants from the Russian Caucasus. They destroyed most organized revolutionary bands including the one led by Khristo Botev. In their revenge for the Muslim civilians killed by Christian rebels, they got carried away and massacred whole towns and villages. About 15,000 were murdered, countless more raped and turned into refugees. The whole area in southwestern Bulgaria was sealed off so the news did not make headlines until the beginning of June 1876.[5]

At the same time, there was a lot to report about in the imperial capital itself. On May 30, a group of Ottoman bureaucrats including the former Grand Vizier Midhat Pasha deposed Sultan Abdulaziz I and installed his nephew Murad as the new caliph. Within a month, Abdulaziz committed a suspicious suicide while under house arrest in the Chiragan Palace. In August, the same conspirators deposed Murad V on the pretext of his deteriorating

---

3. Grandits, Hannes, "Violent Social Disintegration: A Nation-Building Strategy in Late-Ottoman Herzegovina," in Grandits, Hannes, Clayer, Nathalie, and Pichler, Robert, eds., *Conflicting Loyalties in the Balkans: The Great Powers, the Ottoman Empire, and Nation-Building* (London and New York: I. B. Tauris, 2011), pp. 117–119.

4. Nikitin, Sergei, "Revolutsionnaia borba v Bolgariii v 1875–1876 i Aprelskoie Vosstanie," in *Ocherki po istorii iuzhnykh slavian i russko-balkanskikh sviazei v 50–70-e gody XIX veka* (Moscow: Nauka, 1970), pp. 90–103.

5. Jelavich, Barbara, *History of the Balkans: Eighteenth and Nineteenth Centuries* (Cambridge: Cambridge University Press, 1983), pp. 348–355.

mental illness and placed on the throne his brother, who would rule until 1909 as Abdulhamid II.[6]

As the Sultans were being shuffled as a stack of cards, Russian and American diplomats led an investigative mission into the area of the April Uprising. Sensational photos featuring heaps of skulls and other graphic details accompanied lurid accounts of all sorts of violence done to help-less local Christian subjects by their cruel Muslim masters. The reports about "the Bulgarian atrocities" called for a pan-European Crusade against the Ottomans. The coverage of those events was important as a landmark in the development of mass circulation press in Russia and elsewhere in Europe.[7]

The Sultan's vassal states of Montenegro and Serbia took advantage of the now-favorable European public opinion even in the traditionally pro-Ottoman England to attack the Ottoman Empire on June 30. The Ottoman troops proved more than a match for them and by late October threatened to take Belgrade. On October 31, in a determined effort to save Serbia, the Russian Tsar Alexander II sent an ultimatum to the Sultan demanding a two-month ceasefire within forty-eight hours for Serbia, Montenegro, and the rebels in Bosnia-Herzegovina. Abdulhamid II complied and allowed an extraordinary session of the Concert of Europe to take place in his capital. [8]

By mid-December 1876, the ambassadors of the Great Powers in Constantinople met to develop and impose reforms meant to improve the lot of Ottoman Christians and prevent future rebellions. The reforms would turn the Sultan's realm into a federation with significant territorial autonomy for Bosnia-Herzegovina and especially for Bulgarian lands. They would be divided into two provinces north and south of the Balkan range under gov-ernors approved by the Great Powers. But back in London, Prime Minister Disraeli made it clear to the Ottoman Ambassador Konstantin Mousouros that England would not join the other Great Powers if they tried to coerce the Porte into adopting the program of reforms.[9]

This high-level discussion of new different administrative boundaries in the Ottoman Balkans put aside the issue of the delimitation of the Bulgarian

---

6. Davison, Roderic, *The Reform in the Ottoman Empire, 1856–1876* (Princeton: Princeton University Press, 1963), pp. 336–353.

7. McReynolds, Louise, *The News under Russia's Old Regime: The Development of Mass Circulation Press* (Princeton: Princeton University Press, 1991), p. 81.

8. Kovic, Milos, *Disraeli and the Eastern Question* (New York: Oxford University Press, 2011), p. 166.

9. Ibid., pp. 178–181.

Exarchate. The Greek activists in Philippoupolis actively protested the inclusion of their area into the Bulgarian majority province. On behalf of all ambassadors of the Great Powers, Ignatiev assured their representative Antonios Psycharis that the main principle of the reform project was greater autonomy of local communities (*autonomie cantonale*). Psycharis recognized Russia's traditional commitment to improving the lot of all Ottoman Christians but newspapers made it appear that the Great Powers were mostly concerned with Slavic populations.[10]

English Ambassador Elliott also explained to Psycharis that the Sublime Porte was going to extend the same degree of autonomy to all Christian communities. The negotiations focused on the Slavic areas because they were the scene of so much turmoil and bloodshed. Still, Elliott asked where Ottoman Greek loyalties would be in case of a Russo-Turkish war and was apparently glad to hear that the Greeks would side with the Sultan against the Balkan Slavs and Russia.[11] Clearly, many seeds of ethnic hatred bore fruit on the tree of Christian brotherhood over two decades of the Bulgarian Church Question.

Aware of the divisions among the Great Powers, Midhat Pasha, newly reappointed as Grand Vizier, rejected the European reform program on 23 December 1876. In the name of Sultan Abdulhamid II, he declared to the European ambassadors that the Ottoman Empire was now a constitutional monarchy. The Constitution would guarantee the same rights to all Ottoman citizens and would make improvements only for Christians unnecessary. The ambassadors and many other observers thought it was merely a delaying tactic. But it could be seen as the culmination of the effort to overcome the divisive legacy of the Islamic "bifurcated state" and to build a civic territorial Ottoman nation. For only fourteen months from December 1876 to January 1878, the vision of liberal reformers seemed to be coming true as both Muslim and Christian deputies elected on a property franchise met in the first Ottoman parliament.

Although there was a lot of cooperation and joint opposition to the increasingly autocratic Abdulhamid II, the deputies could not overcome their sectarian loyalties. Non-Muslim members argued against the critical bill of eliminating minority quota representation in provincial administrative councils and elections to the Chamber. Their logic was very revealing: "if the law reads that 'deputies will be elected from among Ottomans,' there is

10. Greek Foreign Ministry Archive (AYE), "Embassy in Constantinople" collection, 1874–1876, Psycharis to Kountouriotes, 26 November 1876.

11. Ibid., Psycharis and Sarakiotes to Kountouriotes, 20 December 1876.

no doubt that the people will think only of Islam and elect only Muslims."[12] Indeed, despite government rhetoric, "Ottoman" meant "Muslim" rather than any subject of the Sultan.

Russian Reactions to the Beginning of the Eastern Crisis (1875–1876)

At the end of Leo Tolstoy's *Anna Karenina*, after his lover's suicide Count Vronskii is leaving for Serbia to join over two thousand Russian volunteers fighting there under General Chernaiev. At that time, tens of thousands of Russians of all walks of life showed their support not so much for fellow Slavs but more typically for "suffering Christian Orthodox coreligionists."[13] Thus, the president of the Gorokhovets county board raised eighty rubles "after the announcements issued by the Slavic Committee for the benefit of the Slavic population of the East who are shedding their blood for Christian faith, freedom, and the liberation of the Eastern Church from Turkish abuses."[14] A group of Muscovites presented an icon to General Chernaiev as the banner "to lead the Christians oppressed by cruel Mohammedans who drove our Slavic brothers to the limit."[15]

Indeed, the Moscow Slavic Benevolent Committee rose from obscurity to national prominence during the Eastern Crisis of 1875–1878. From 1856 to 1875, its leaders Ivan Aksakov and Nil Popov had been struggling to raise funds, mostly among Moscow merchants to provide scholarships for South Slav students and to send church paraphernalia to the poor Balkan areas.[16] Publishing reports about atrocities and "scenes of famine" in major Russian newspapers helped revive the slow flow of donations: "the subscription goes well. The provinces are moving like ice on the Volga."[17] As a result, the Moscow Slavic Committee became a significant political force. Aksakov was soon able to send two thousand rubles to Odessa to help organize a unit of three thousand

---

12. Devereux, Robert, *The First Ottoman Constitutional Period* (Baltimore: The Johns Hopkins University Press, 1963), p. 221.

13. State Archive of the Russian Federation (GARF), f. 1750 (Moscow Slavic Benevolent Society), files 80–96, 106, 230, 233, 287, 238, 259–312, 387, 399, 400, 411–421.

14. GARF, f. 1750-1-282, President of the Gorokhovets county board to the Slavic Committee, 12 August 1876, p. 55.

15. GARF, f. 1750-1-78, 24 June 1876, p. 8.

16. Russian State Library Manuscript Division (OR RGB), f. 239-4-5, I. S. Aksakov to N. A. Popov, 26 January 1872, p. 27.

17. Ibid., f. 239-4-6, I. S. Aksakov to N. A. Popov, fall 1875, pp. 15, 34.

Bulgarian and Russian volunteers preparing to capture the city of Vidin on the Ottoman bank of the Danube and to use it as "a cell of future Bulgaria."[18]

However, not all Russians were burning with Pan-Slav or Pan-Orthodox fervor. Some considered "the Slavic struggle for survival" as a revolt against their legitimate monarch similar to the Polish Uprising of 1863 against Russian domination. A village priest asked the Moscow Slavic Committee to devote a special article to clarify for his parishioners the difference between those events.[19]

Even with passions running high, Slavophile commentators were not uniformly hostile to the Greeks for sitting on the fences, biding their time, and thereby betraying the Christian Orthodox cause. In 1876, Ivan Troitskii, a professor of the St. Petersburg Theological Academy, launched a series of articles in one of the main ecclesiastical magazines, *Tserkovnyi Vestnik*, where he explained the inability of the Kingdom of Greece to join the war against the Ottoman Empire on strategic grounds. He went even further, proclaiming the unity of the Greeks and the Slavs as part of the Greco-Slavic cultural type, thereby promoting the earlier ideas of Professor Lamanskii.[20]

Tertii Filippov, the main Russian Pan-Orthodox commentator, let Troitskii know that Greek periodicals such as *Kleio* of Trieste appreciated his conciliatory gestures.[21] Filippov invited him to his home, where Konstantin Pobedonostsev was also expected. Then a member of the State Council (the supreme advisory body to the Tsar), Pobedonostsev took a positive view of Troitskii's ideas and even discussed them with the Greek ambassador.[22] Later in the Eastern Crisis, Filippov's famous disciple[23] Konstantin Leontiev

---

18. Ibid., f. 239-4-7, I. S. Aksakov to N. A. Popov, spring-summer 1876, pp. 1, 38.

19. GARF, f. 1750-1-283, Mikhail Kurochkin to the Moscow Slavic Committee, 17 August 1876, p. 360b.

20. "Raziasnenie polozhenia zaniatogo grekami svobodnoi Ellady v borbe slavian s turkami," in *Tserkovnyi Vestnik*, 35 (4 September 1876): 4–6; "K voprosu ob edinomyslii mezhdu grekami i slavianami," ibid., 4 (16 October 1876): 1–2; "Sblizhenie mezhdu grekami i bolgarami," ibid., 41 (16 October 1876): 14; "Religioznaia storona vostochnogo voprosa," ibid., 44 (6 November 1876): 1–4; "Rossia, Gretsia i Zapadnaia Evropa vo vremia Krymskoi voiny," ibid., 45 (13 November 1876): 1–4; "Istoria kak orudie k vozbuzhdeniu plemennoi vrazhdy mezhdu grekami i russkimi," ibid., 46 (20 November 1876): 1–3; "Odno iz vernykh sredstv k nravstvennomu edineniu grekov s nami i s slavianami," ibid., 47 (27 November 1876): 1–3.

21. Russian State Public Library, Manuscript Division, 790-1-716, T. I. Filippov to I. E. Troitskii, 4 December 1876, p. 1.

22. Ibid., 12 December 1876, p. 2.

23. Russian State Archive for Literature and Art (RGALI), f. 2980, op.1, d. 1023, K. N. Leontiev to T. I. Filippov, Moscow, 8 January 1876, p. 2.

FIGURE 5.2 "Eastern Nations Moving to Independence" (c. 1877–1878). Courtesy of the National Historical Museum (Athens, Greece). Poster catalog number 4949/133.

explained that nationalist Greek elites continued to see Pan-Slavism as a threat especially because of perceived Russian support for the uncanonical Bulgarian Exarchate. Russia needed to reassure coreligionist Greeks by resolutely intervening in the solution of the Greek-Bulgarian Church Question in the interests of the Ecumenical Patriarchate of Constantinople.[24]

Still, there were Greek voices in favor of joining the other Balkan Christian struggle against the Ottomans. A contemporary poster seen in Figure 5.2 reminds the viewers of the legacy of the 1821 Greek War of Independence and features a Christian banner held by a priest with the "Liberty or Death" slogan in Greek and less prominently in Bulgarian and Romanian. Liberty is represented as a beautiful Christian queen welcoming women and children in Balkan folk costumes. The flags in the lower left corner make it clear that they symbolize Thrace, Thessaly, Macedonia, and Bulgaria. Death is portrayed as an Orientalized old man surrounded only by dogs. In the poem

---

24. Leontiev, Konstantin, "Vragi li my s grekami?" in *Vostok, Rossia, Slavianstvo: Filosofskaia i politicheskaia publitsistika, dukhovnaia proza (1872–1891)* (Moscow: Respublika, 1996), p. 158. Originally published in *Russkii Mir* 1878, no. 9.

below, Liberty calls on her children to join forces against the common enemy in the same three languages. The poster title is only in Greek and Romanian.

The Russo-Turkish War and the Russian Occupation of Ottoman Bulgaria, 1877–1878

When the Ottoman leadership rejected the reform project developed by European ambassadors in Constantinople to grant greater autonomy to Balkan Christian provinces, the Russian government was humiliated as the main sponsor of that initiative. Tsar Alexander II decided to strengthen his country's Great Power status and local influence by pressing those demands through military force. Metropolitan Mikhail of Belgrade welcomed the outbreak of the Russo-Turkish War in March 1877. He saw the Russian intervention as the only chance to stop the growing conflict among South Slavs, who failed to unite even in the face of Ottoman repressions. Mikhail asked his Russian Pan-Slav friend Professor Nil Popov to use his influence to stop continued Bulgarian encroachments on Serbian patrimony in Kosovo. "May the Lord grant Russia victory and then it will depend not on the Serbs and Bulgarians but on Russian justice and conscience."[25] Still, Serbia and Montenegro soon rejoined the war on the side of Russia and its ally Rumania.

The Crusading spirit is strongly emphasized in the imperial manifesto where Tsar Alexander II explained to the Bulgarians the reasons for the declaration of war on the Ottoman Empire. First of all, he stressed the continuity of the traditional Russian policy of the protection of Orthodox Christians. In 1877, Russia continued "to treat with equal benevolence and love all the numerous members of the extensive Christian family on the Balkan Peninsula." In this spirit, the Russian army was supposed to safeguard the guarantees of political development of the long-suffering Bulgarian nation. The Emperor also called on "the Christians of Bulgaria" to forget "old domestic quarrels," to strictly observe "the legitimate rights of each nation," and to make a common effort to help the Russians to liberate them from "Muslim oppression."[26]

To implement those broad guidelines, Prince Vasilii Cherkasskii led the initial stage of Russian civilian administration of liberated Bulgarian areas from the summer of 1877 to the spring of 1878. He was quite critical of the Greeks for failing to promote the Orthodox cause in the East rather than for being

---

25. OR RGB, f. 239-13-48, Metropolitan Mikhail to Nil Popov, 14 May 1877, p. 330b–34.

26. Alexander II, 19 June 1877, *Rusiia i vuzstanoviavaneto na bulgarskata durzhavnost (1878–1885)* (Sofia: State Archives Agency, 2008), pp. 34–35.

ethnic enemies of Slavdom. In his report to War Minister Dmitrii Miliutin, Cherkasskii argued that Bulgaria was "our brainchild . . . destined to develop in the close alliance with us." The Greeks were the opposite of Bulgarians as "they had long lost faith in anything and are exploiting religion."[27] However, this arrogant sense of religious mission did not actually mean wholehearted support for Bulgarian nationalist leadership. Cherkasskii was notoriously abrupt and strict with Bulgarians because "he saw among their intelligentsia the desire for self-seeking politicking under the protection of Russian bayonets."[28]

As a result of this soberness about both parties, Cherkasskii himself instructed district commanders in their main duty—to keep order by preventing and stopping any possible religious conflicts.[29] Although he had in mind mostly Christian-Muslim relations, Cherkasskii clearly drew on his earlier public statements about the Greek-Bulgarian Question in the Slavophile journal *Russkaia Beseda* in 1858, as discussed in chapter 2.[30]

When Cherkasskii was in charge of the Civilian Administration of occupied Ottoman Bulgaria, many regional commanders indeed attempted to promote reconciliation between Bulgarian and Greek communities. This was appreciated by the local Greek consuls, who were far from sympathetic to the Russians or to the Slavs generally following the pro-Western line of the Greek government at the time.[31]

Thus, the Greek consul in Tulcha (on the Danube), P. Pyrgos, praised the conduct of Ivan Belotserkovich, Governor General of that area. Belotserkovich had the Russian chaplains celebrate the Divine Service in the open air on the day of Russian entry into Tulcha. Belotserkovich invited both the Patriarchist and the Exarchist bishops to attend the event. Since only the Russian priests were involved in the liturgy, there was no violation of the canons and neither side received preferential treatment. In effect, the Patriarchate's prelate had a higher status because the Russian priests recognized his supreme authority in the area.[32]

---

27. V. Cherkasskii to D. Miliutin, undated in Ovsianyi, N., ed., *Russkoie upravlenie v Bolgarii v 1877, 1878, 1879 godakh.* Vol. 1 (St. Petersburg: Military History Commission of the General Staff, 1906), p. 174.

28. Ibid., p. 145.

29. Russian State Military History Archive (RGVIA) 846-16-32367, pp. 120b–13.

30. Cherkasskii, Vasilii, "Dva slova o Vostochnom voprose," *Russkaia Beseda*, 12 (1858): 65, 91.

31. Kofos, Evangelos, *Greece and the Eastern Crisis, 1875–1878* (Thessaloniki: Institute for Balkan Studies, 1975), pp. 98–99.

32. AYE, AAK1, E5, no. 275, 17 June 1877.

Two days later, Pyrgos reported the gloomy prospects of the wholesale attack on the privileges of Greek citizens and of the Patriarchate by the newly elected administrative council dominated by Bulgarian nationalists.[33] In September, these fears were put to rest when Belotserkovich dissolved the council, harshly criticizing the Bulgarian majority for discriminating against non-Bulgarians and voting economic measures in violation of the existing treaties and local laws respected by Russia.[34]

This action was preceded by the growing alienation between the Bulgarians and the Russians, made visible at the celebration of the anniversary of the coronation of Tsar Alexander II. The liturgy took place in the Patriarchate's church, whence the Governor General with his staff followed "our" bishop with Greek, Russian, and Romanian priests to the square on the river bank, where Russian troops and Bulgarian priests without celebratory garments had been waiting. In Pyrgos' analysis, the Russians reacted against perceived Bulgarian arrogance in the face of "rivers of blood and treasure" sacrificed for "the undeserving treacherous rude and uncouth nation."[35]

According to the Greek consul, local Bulgarians were outraged at Belotserkovich for having equated their status with that of the Patriarchate's supporters in the membership of the administrative council. They even sent a certain Doctor Yankulov to the Russian headquarters with the official complaint. Pyrgos added approvingly that the Governor General did not remain passive but had many of them arrested and imprisoned. Most Bulgarians were released but three of them were court-martialed. In response, the Bulgarian activists boycotted the elections to the administrative council, thereby forcing Belotserkovich to appoint four members ex officio.[36]

On 11 November 1877, Pyrgos again praised Belotserkovich for protecting the interests of the Patriarchist community even at the cost of alienating the local Bulgarian Exarchist community. The church of St. Nicholas was closed for some time before the Russian occupation because many local "Moldavians" had switched from the Patriarchate to the Bulgarian Exarchate. The remaining supporters of the Patriarchate had to use the old church building. To deal with the problem, Belotserkovich set up a mixed committee presided by the local commander, Lieutenant-Colonel Kastyrko, but it failed to resolve the situation. During his visit to Tulcha, Archbishop Niceforas, Patriarchist locum tenens for

---

33. Ibid., no. 277, 19 June 1877.

34. AYE, AAK, E4, no. 440, 25 September 1877.

35. Ibid., no. 386, 28 August 1877.

36. AYE, AAK1, E5, no. 453, 2 October 1877.

the diocese of Drystra, launched a "coup." Ignoring the order of the Russian authorities to surrender the keys to the St. Nicholas church and to refrain from officiating there, he opened the church, consecrated it, and moved icons and other liturgical ware from the old church. Impressed by Niceforas' forcefulness (*epimoni*), the Russian authorities accepted the accomplished fact. To crown it all, Niceforas proceeded to have the old church building demolished to the foundation in just one day. The Bulgarian community "breathes anger" at Belotserkovich, suspecting some kind of previous agreement with Niceforas.[37]

In the meantime, after a long siege of Plevna lasting most of the fall of 1877, the Russian army forced Osman Pasha's garrison to surrender. To capitalize on that victory, the Russians broke through remaining Ottoman defenses along the Balkan range and in difficult winter conditions crossed into the Southern Bulgarian plains in January 1878. Listening to silver-tongued poster sellers, even illiterate Russian peasants were able to learn about how the dashing General Mikhail Skobelev rushed into the thick of battle on his white steed (see Figure 5.3).

In February 1878, the Russian victors were dictating the conditions of the armistice to the Ottoman government in San Stefano, a suburb of Constantinople today known as Yeshilkoy. Ignatiev, who followed the army headquarters, extracted the Sultan's consent to the creation of a large autonomous Bulgaria stretching from the slightly enlarged Serbia to the Black Sea coast and from the Danube to the Aegean albeit excluding Thessaloniki.

That monster was not the intended product of the Constantinople project of December 1876, which envisioned two separate Bulgarian provinces. But the Treaty of San Stefano was supposed to be preliminary and was probably expected to be revised. Widely seen as a Russian satellite, the specter of a huge Bulgaria raised protests among the other Great Powers and in Greece. A few months later, in June-July 1878, the Congress of Berlin stripped the vassal Bulgarian Principality of its southern part, which became known as the autonomous province of Eastern Rumelia. All Macedonia and Thrace returned under the Sultan's direct control but Thessaly was assigned to Greece. Although nominally an Ottoman province, Bosnia-Herzegovina was occupied by Austria-Hungary on the pretext of implementing modern reforms (see Map 5.1). In the words of one prominent Balkan historian, "this treaty is outstanding for the fact that it managed to leave every one of the Balkan nationalities thoroughly dissatisfied."[38]

---

37. AYE, 76.1, 1877, no. 541, 11 November 1877.

38. Stavrianos, Leften, *The Balkan Federation: A History of the Movement toward Balkan Unity in Modern Times* (Hamden: Archon, 1964), p. 114.

FIGURE 5.3 "Another Brilliant Victory of Lieutenant General M. D. Skobelev at Sheynovo" (1878). Courtesy of the National Historical Museum (Athens, Greece). Poster catalog number 12215.

Some Bosnian Orthodox notables petitioned Alexander II as "glorious Tsar-Liberator" to help them avoid Austrian annexation. Instead, they very much desired unification with Serbia based on their shared language and traditions. In the early 1800s, Serbia "was able to organize itself without any foreign occupation." If it was impossible to prevent, then foreign control should be brief and include the participation of several powers.[39] Alas, under German and British pressure all Great Power representatives at the Congress of Berlin agreed to indefinite Austrian occupation of Bosnia-Herzegovina and unofficially recognized it as tantamount to permanent annexation.[40] This is the beginning of the long road to the outbreak of the First World War.

During the peace negotiations, many Serb publicists and politicians feared that Russia was going to make Bulgaria the cornerstone of its Balkan influence. When this growing hostility among South Slavs was discussed in

39. Bosnian Orthodox notables to Alexander II, 1–2 March 1878, Nikiforov, K. V., et al., eds., *Rossiia i vosstaniie v Bosnii i Herzegovine, 1875–1878* (Moscow: Indrik, 2008), p. 394.

40. P. A. Shuvalov to the Foreign Ministry, 23 June 1878, ibid., p. 416.

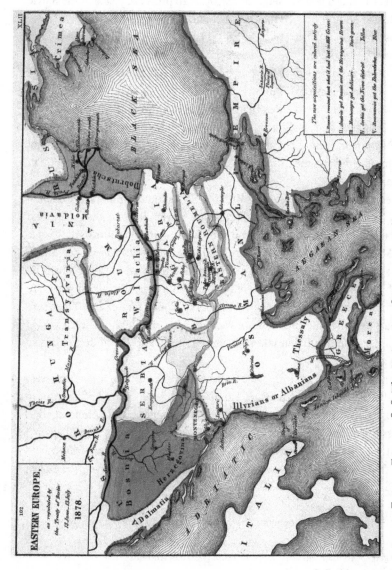

MAP 5.1 Eastern Europe, 1878. The University of Texas Map Collection.

http://www.lib.utexas.edu/maps/historical/eastern_europe1878.jpg

Originally published in 1884 in "An Historical Atlas" by Robert H. Labberton, E. Elaxton and Co., the map details the boundaries redrawn at the Congress of Berlin.

the Russian liberal press, Metropolitan Mikhail tried to explain the situation to his well-connected Russian friend. Common Serbs and Bulgarians treated each other as brothers and lived in peace but "Turkish policy, on one hand, and Papist propaganda, on the other, diverted Bulgarian intelligentsia from the right path and sowed the seeds of discord." To preserve peace in the Slavic family, Russia should help Serbia reach "its natural borders—the Isker river in the east and the Struma river in the northwest."[41] That demand was not likely to revive brotherly love between the Serbs and Bulgarians. If implemented, those borders would have made even the Bulgarian capital part of Serbia, since Sofia is west of the Isker River.

It appeared to the Serb elites that Mother Russia was turning away from them to Bulgaria and assigning the Western Balkans with Serbia to the Austrian sphere of influence.[42] But Bulgaria's value as a strategic backyard of Constantinople did not mean that Russia would make all Bulgarian nationalist dreams come true.

Between San Stefano and Berlin, the Russian diplomats received a flood of petitions from prominent Bulgarian clerics like Russian-educated Archimandrite Mefodii Kusev[43] and Bulgarians in the Russian service such as Marin Drinov, the former University of Kharkov Professor of Slavic Studies and acting Education Secretary in the Russian civilian administration.[44] The Bulgarian activists lobbied the Russian officials to pressure the Sublime Porte to extend the jurisdiction of the Exarchate. They predictably argued that the inclusion of most of Macedonia and Thrace would prevent otherwise inevitable Islamization, Hellenization, and defections to Catholicism there.

Under Leo XIII (1878–1903), the Papacy did indeed have a keen interest in the Balkans and the Middle East. Paradoxically, a new round of aggressive missionizing was justified as part of "the plan to oppose and defend against the incessant political-religious attacks by Russian-Orthodox Pan-Slavism." Apparently, offense was Vatican's best defense. To neutralize "Muscovite agents," Catholic missionaries were supposed to take advantage of the laws

---

41. OR RGB, f. 239-13-48, Metropolitan Mikhail to Nil Popov, 17 January 1878, pp. 37–38.

42. Jelavich, Charles, *Tsarist Russia and Balkan Nationalism: Russian Influence in the Internal Affairs of Bulgaria and Serbia, 1870–1886* (Berkeley and Los Angeles: University of California Press 1958), p. 5.

43. M. Kusev to N. P. Ignatiev, 12 February 1878, *Osvobozhdenie Bolgarii ot turetskogo iga*, vol. 2 (Moscow: Nauka, 1964), pp. 515–516.

44. M. Drinov to A. B. Lobanov-Rostovskii (Ambassador to Constantinople), 6 August 1878, ibid., pp. 190–191.

protecting religious freedom and to spread in Orthodox majority countries such as Serbia, Montenegro, Bulgaria, and Romania.[45]

Taking advantage of Papal ambitions, Bulgarian nationalist activists created a pro-Catholic agitation to put pressure on Imperial High Commissioner Dondukov-Korsakov to allow the newly elected Exarch Iosif to move from Philippoupolis to Constantinople. Archbishop of Philippoupolis Panaret sent Abbot Mefodii Kusev to Constantinople to mobilize Bulgarian residents to write a petition to the Exarch. If their spiritual leader did not come back, Ottoman Bulgarians would switch to Catholicism to find Austrian protection against savage repressions in Macedonia and elsewhere. Jean Pietri, the pro-Bulgarian editor of the Constantinople-based French language newspaper *Courrier d'Orient*, mediated between them and the Papal legate Burnoni. The Pontiff agreed in writing to the substantial autonomy of the Bulgarian Uniate Church, and Austrian Ambassador Sitchi promised to appoint consuls to all Macedonian cities to better protect Bulgarian interests before Ottoman authorities and to demand autonomy for that province. Mefodii Kusev made sure to leak all the details to the Russian embassy in Constantinople and "the trick with the Union worked."[46]

In early October 1878, Dondukov-Korsakov felt that he had to let Exarch Iosif move to Constantinople "to negotiate with the Porte and the Ecumenical Patriarch which dioceses were to be included into the Exarchate and also to come to an agreement with a few clerics who recently started talking about the need to embrace the *Unia* given the state of anarchy in Macedonia and Catholic propaganda of Austrian missionaries."[47] Thus, even when the Russian occupation authorities supported the Bulgarian Exarchate, they did it not in the name of Pan-Slavism or modern Bulgarian nationalism but rather with the goal of strengthening Orthodoxy and traditional Russian political interests in the area.

Violence in Macedonia could not be blamed solely on Ottoman authorities and embittered Muslim refugees. In addition to plotting clever intrigues, at least some Bulgarian prelates actively helped organize the Kresna-Razlog Uprising in southeastern Macedonia to derail the decisions of the Berlin Congress in late 1878 and early 1879. Archbishop Nathaniel of Ohrid was

---

45. Del Zanna, Giorgio, *Roma e l'Oriente: Leone XIII e l'Impero Ottomano (1878–1903)* (Milan: Guerini e Associati, 2003), p. 87.

46. Radev, Simeon, *Stroitelite na Sovremenna Bulgariia*, vol 1 (Sofia: Bulgarski Pisatel, 1990 [1910–1911]), pp. 115–118.

47. RGVIA, 430-1-59, A. M. Dondukov-Korsakov to D. A. Miliutin, 16 October 1878, p. 1940b.

coordinating the distribution of money, rifles, and ammunition sent from adjacent Bulgarian areas.[48] In a special letter, Nathaniel openly encouraged the nascent Bulgarian Parliament to restore national unity as enshrined in the San Stefano treaty and to liberate "from the heavy burden of the Turkish yoke" the Bulgarians in Macedonia.[49]

It is not surprising then that the Ottoman government was suspicious of the Bulgarian Exarchate and was seriously considering revoking the *firman* of 1870. In the aftermath of the Russo-Turkish War, no Exarchist prelates were allowed to return to their Macedonian dioceses, i.e., Veles, Kiustendil, Samokov, Ohrid, Skopje, Debar, and the districts of Prilep and Nevrokop. In the late 1870s and early 1880s, the Porte clearly favored the Patriarchate of Constantinople.[50]

Despite Bulgarian pressure, as before the Russo-Turkish War, Russian policymakers continued to promote reconciliation between the Bulgarian Exarchate and the Patriarchate. With the approval of Emperor Alexander II, Nikolai Girs, the acting Foreign Minister at the time, sent Dondukov-Korsakov the instructions to discourage Bulgarians from using Article 62 of the Berlin Treaty concerning religious freedom to extend the jurisdiction of the Exarchate into Macedonia.

Dondukov-Korsakov needed to persuade them that this kind of agitation was sure to lead to more conflict with the Patriarchate and further undermine the already precarious standing of the Exarchate. Instead of pursuing dubious independence, the Exarchate should achieve a solid canonical status through reconciliation with the Ecumenical Patriarchate. Dondukov was to make every effort to avoid creating an impression in Constantinople that Russia was somehow behind the aggressive moves of the Bulgarian church leaders. To halt the spread of Catholic proselytizing in Macedonia, the embassy in Constantinople would not rely on the Exarchate but rather would send a secretary of its Consulate General to examine and deal with the issue on the spot.[51]

---

48. Stefan Stambolov to Metropolitan Nathaniel, 20 February 1879, Bozhinov, Voin, and Panaiotov, Liubomir, eds., *Macedonia: Documents and Materials* (Sofia: Bulgarian Academy of Sciences, 1978), pp. 382–383.

49. Metropolitan Nathaniel to the Bulgarian Constituent Assembly, 14 March 1879, ibid., p. 384.

50. Aarbakke, Vemund, *Ethnic Rivalry and the Quest for Macedonia, 1870–1913* (Boulder: East European Monographs. Distributed by Columbia University Press, New York, 2003), pp. 64–66.

51. N. K. Girs to A. M. Dondukov-Korsakov, 28 October 1878, *Osvobozhdenie Bolgarii*, vol. 3, pp. 291–292.

Despite the Pan-Slav pro-Bulgarian bias of individual commanders, the Russian top brass consistently deferred to the Patriarchate as the supreme canonical authority. A good example was the situation in Adrianople. On 29 October 1878, Archbishop Dionysios asked the local Russian governor, Major General Molostvov, to prevent further disruptions of church order such as the one that took place when a Bulgarian teacher interrupted the liturgy. Soon Dionysios had reasons to complain about Molostvov himself.

The latter sided with the Bulgarian Exarchists in their dispute with the Greek community over the rights in regard to the Holy Trinity church. He found out that the Bulgarians had pooled resources with the Greeks to build that church eleven years earlier on the condition that the liturgy would be celebrated both in Greek and Old Church Slavonic, but in 1875 Greek became the sole language used in the church. According to Molostvov, the Bulgarian teacher who interrupted the service merely expressed the desire of the whole community to hear the sermon and liturgy in the language they could understand.

Molostvov sent the case for further consideration at the district court in accordance with local laws. Since the church was built in the Bulgarian neighborhood mostly with Bulgarian money, the court decided to resume officiation in both languages. But Dionysios refused to share the keys to the church. At the request of the Bulgarian deputation, Molostvov wrote to the Greek Archbishop explaining that the question of church possession was under secular rather than ecclesiastical jurisdiction and suggested that he open the church. Dionysios refused to comply because he did not receive any instructions from the Patriarchate to that effect and could not permit any joint divine service with the Bulgarian schismatics. Molostvov sent the chief of police with another letter threatening to submit the issue for consideration to the central Russian authorities and to seal the church, making it unavailable for either community in the meantime.[52]

In response to Molostvov's report, his superior, Lieutenant-General Stolypin, Governor General of Eastern Rumelia and the District of Adrianople, expressed his "extreme displeasure" at how Molostvov had handled the matter. He emphasized the strategic importance of promoting Christian unity especially in the area soon to be returned to the Ottoman Empire. Stolypin ruled out any notion of the Russian intervention. Instead, the representatives of both Bulgarian and Greek communities should work out a mutually acceptable agreement.

---

52. RGVIA, 846-16-32983, 27 December 1878, pp. 48–49.

The question of co-officiation in that church, as a purely canonical problem, should not have concerned the Russian administration at all. If the
Patriarchate gave such permission, the Russian army command would
not stand in the way. In the meantime, Molostvov needed to limit himself
to the purely police duties of preventing any clashes between Greeks and
Bulgarians over the church. Furthermore, Molostvov was to communicate to
the Bulgarian bishop Sinesios Stolypin's point of view, his wish, and if necessary his demand to bring the matter to a peaceful conclusion "to avoid intra-
Christian conflict so harmful at precisely the moment when they need to
join ranks." An even harsher reprimand was to be delivered to the Bulgarian
teacher styling himself as a "lay preacher" for the highly inappropriate violation of church peace and order.[53] Clearly, in the mind of Stolypin, both political and cultural considerations were important—traditional Russian support
for the Patriarchate and genuine identification with besieged Orthodoxy.

But the Patriarchate of Constantinople failed to read or trust this general
policy of reconciliation pursued at the high levels of Russian power structures. New Patriarch Joachim III (1878–1884) and the Ottoman Greek elites
at the time perceived Russia as fully supportive of political Pan-Slavism and
encouraging of the rebellious Bulgarian Exarchate. The Patriarchate stopped
short of taking "appropriate steps", i.e., up to declaring the Russian Church
itself schismatic because some Russian army chaplains in Bulgaria participated in the liturgy and partook of the Holy Communion along with the
priests of the Bulgarian Exarchate. The response of the Russian Holy Synod
matched the aggressive and hostile tone of the Patriarch. For the first time
since the Schism of 1872, the Russian Church broke silence over the Bulgarian
Exarchate and condemned the Schism.[54]

However, this response remained a draft albeit approved by Emperor
Alexander II. The Russian church leadership and the government entrusted
the ambassador to Constantinople, Prince Lobanov-Rostovskii, with choosing
the moment of handing the response. In the meantime, he was supposed to
demonstrate to the Patriarch Joachim III the spirit of reconciliation and the
moment never actually came.[55]

The situation seemed less bleak to the Patriarchate in the spring of
1879, when the Constitution of autonomous Bulgaria was adopted by the
Constituent Assembly organized by the transitional Russian administration

---

53. RGVIA, 846-16-32983, 6 January 1879, pp. 44–45ob.

54. Russian Imperial Foreign Policy Archive (AVPRI), f. 161/3, collection 233 (1850–1884),
part IV, 3 March 1879, pp. 2466–2469.

55. Ibid., 13 March 1879, p. 2472.

in Turnovo, the capital of the medieval Bulgarian Kingdom. Joachim III was glad to learn about the protection of minority rights enshrined in that surprisingly liberal document. In the areas where a majority spoke Turkish or Greek, those languages would have the official status in courts and other government institutions. "The Ottomans, the Greeks, the Armenians, and the Jews would be exempt from conscription for five years." Joachim III welcomed the reconciliation feelers put out by the Bulgarian Exarchate but instructed Metropolitan Cyril of Varna to insist on a canonical basis of any future plan.[56]

The neverending financial crisis of the Patriarchate was another strong motivation to cooperate with the Russian government. Joachim III asked Ambassador Lobanov-Rostovskii to facilitate the approval by Metropolitan Isidore of St. Petersburg of an entry visa for Bishop Iakovos. He had been waiting for it for some time in Romania to be able to come to "the divinely-protected state of Orthodox Russia" and to collect donations of pious Christians there. Those funds would help cover the needs of the Theological School on the island of Halki—the Patriarchate's main clergy-training institution.[57]

The Patriarchate also asked and received funding from the Greek governments for its schools. This meant gradual, reluctant acceptance of Greek nationalist influence on the curriculum. Ottoman Greek bankers and urban middle classes strengthened that nationalist trend as they sponsored private literary clubs (*syllogoi*). The earliest institution of this kind, the Greek Literary Association of Constantinople, was established in 1861 in response to the first serious crisis of the Bulgarian Church Question. The presidents of the Greek Literary Association of Constantinople encouraged the creation of similar organizations in the provinces to Hellenize non-Greek Christians as a way to civilize the "East." The Patriarchate initially opposed those lay-controlled nationalist educational initiatives as "insulting and revolutionary" but eventually sanctioned them in hopes of stopping defections to the Bulgarian Exarchate.[58]

Having tricked the Russians into letting him move to Constantinople in 1878, Exarch Iosif did not make combating Catholic encroachments his number one goal. He requested funds from autonomous Bulgaria and Eastern Rumelia to expand the Exarchate's education system in Macedonia.

---

56. Joachim III to Cyril of Varna, 18 April 1879, the Archive of the Ecumenical Patriarchate, A51, p. 132, Number 1944.

57. Joachim III to Lobanov-Rostovskii, sometime in 1879, the Archive of the Ecumenical Patriarchate, A51, p. 258, Number 6046.

58. Kamouzis, Dimitris, "Elites and the Formation of National Identity: The Case of the Greek Orthodox Millet (Mid-Nineteenth Century to 1922)," in Fortna, Benjamin et al., eds., *State Nationalisms in the Ottoman Empire, Greece, and Turkey: Orthodox and Muslims, 1830–1945* (London and New York: Routledge, 2013), pp. 20–24.

Since the Sublime Porte ignored the provisions of its own 1870 *firman* and the promise of reforms enshrined in the Berlin Treaty, "the only means at our disposal is to rely on schools and teachers in order to undermine Hellenism among Macedonians and to defend their sense of nationality from Greek-Serbian pressure and Protestant deception."[59]

The following year, the Exarch expressed more confidence in his report to the Bulgarian Foreign Ministry about the expenditure of the previous year and the proposed three-year budget. He was concerned about the Schism and considered it to be the main reason for the decline of popular piety among Ottoman Christians. His solution was to install Exarchate's archbishops in "the Macedonian dioceses populated exclusively by the Bulgarians" and to promote instruction in their mother tongue, which would easily win them away from the Greek schools. In that case, the Greek politicians and Ottoman Greek nationalist laypersons would have to acknowledge the demise of their irredentist plans to Hellenize Macedonia and the futility of the Schism. Without their pressure, the Patriarchate would easily lift the Schism and recognize the Exarchate within its ethnic borders.

Exarch Iosif mentioned the ethnically Greek and Romanian-speaking Vlach brigands who attacked Bulgarian activists in collaboration with the Greek nationalists and hostile Ottoman authorities. At that point, they were not a critical problem. One dark cloud on the horizon was Austrian-supported Serb propaganda in Northern Macedonia, where "the Bulgarians have close relations with neighboring Serbia and lean towards Serbianism because their dialect is mixed with Serbian language forms."[60]

The Ottoman authorities did not always take the side of the Patriarchate in the 1880s. In the archbishopric of Kastoria, the followers of the Exarchate successfully petitioned the district governor (*kaymakam*) to stop the minority of their fellow "Greco-maniac" villagers from excluding the pro-Bulgarian majority from the parish board and the church in the village of Krupisha.[61] But northeast of Kastoria, due to "the unbridled fanaticism of Hasan Pasha and the Archbishop of Seres," the Bulgarian notables were arrested and subjected to inhumane treatment in the prison. Russian

---

59. Iosif to G. Gruev, 29 October 1881, Arnaudov, Mikhail, ed., *Kum istoriiata na Bulgarskata Ekzarkhiia: Dokumenti ot 1881 do 1890 godina* (Sofia: Sofia University Press, 1944), p. 27.

60. Exarch Iosif to the Bulgarian Foreign Minister, 25 December 1882, Georgiev, Velichko, and Trifonov, Staiko, eds., *Ekzarkh Bulgarski Iosif I. Pisma i Dokladi* (Sofia: Klub '90, 1994), pp. 23–24, 33.

61. N. Sprostranov to the Bulgarian Foreign Ministry, 4 March 1885, *Kum istoriiata na Bulgarskata Ekzarkhiia: Dokumenti ot 1881 do 1890 godina*, p. 83.

Ambassador Nelidov brought that case to the attention of the Sublime Porte but to no avail.[62]

Still, Bulgarian agents and activists did not lose faith in Ottoman institutions. The Bulgarian Principality officially disavowed any ties with the armed bands that crossed into Ottoman territory to incite insurrections—they allegedly consisted of Macedonian immigrants and individual Bulgarian citizens who did not represent the government in Sofia.[63] When the "Greco-maniacs" began to send petitions to the Porte protesting against sending the Exarchate's prelates to their Macedonian cities, Exarch Iosif and the Bulgarian consul in Thessaloniki instructed pro-Bulgarian communities to demand the return of Exarchate's archbishops that had been appointed to their dioceses before the Russo-Turkish War of 1877–1878. They also urged the Porte to implement Article X of the 1870 *firman* by holding a referendum (*istilam*) where the two-thirds majority would determine which dioceses should be assigned to the Bulgarian Exarchate.[64]

Although the Porte hesitated in that issue, it requested letters of gratitude from all Ottoman communities to the Sultan's local and central government. It was not a one-time event but a ritual periodically enacted for both domestic and international consumption. Notorious for his anti-Bulgarian conduct, the Governor of Thessaloniki Hassan Pasha was embarrassed when too few such letters were coming from his province. He asked the Russian General Consul Iakobson to encourage his Bulgarian counterpart to stage that show of Ottoman patriotism and loyalty. Although the Bulgarian diplomat was not enthusiastic, he chose to cooperate because "one can't deny the absolute necessity of developing the friendliest possible relations between the Bulgarian people and the Sultan's government in order to realize our national ideals."[65]

Abdulhamid II's Revised Edition of the Tanzimat: Building the Sacred Body of the Ottoman Nation after the Eastern Crisis of 1875–1878

The Sultan lost most Christian-majority lands after the Congress of Berlin concluded the Eastern Crisis. England occupied Cyprus although most Aegean islands were still in the Ottoman Empire. The newly created Bulgarian Principality and Eastern Rumelia were autonomous parts of the

---

62. N. Sprostranov to the Bulgarian Foreign Ministry, 10 April 1885, ibid., p. 89.

63. Bulgarian Foreign Minister I. Tsanov to Exarch Iosif, 4 March 1885, ibid., p. 85.

64. N. Sprostranov to the Bulgarian Foreign Minister, 10 April 1885, ibid., p. 90.

65. N. Sprostranov to the Bulgarian Foreign Ministry, 20 December 1885, ibid., p. 94.

Ottoman Empire but were effectively on their own under strong Russian influence. Austria-Hungary was allowed to occupy Bosnia-Herzegovina under the fig leaf of introducing administrative reforms. Greece received Thessaly by 1881. In the Balkans, only Albania, Epirus, Macedonia, and Thrace were under direct Ottoman control.

Tens of thousands of Muslim refugees escaped from the theater of war, Christian rule, and retributions. Years of fighting and turmoil did not help the Ottoman economy improve. In fact, the Ottoman Empire entered into a semi-colonial relationship with the advanced Western countries. In 1881, the Great Powers, led by England and France, imposed the Ottoman Public Debt Administration that effectively took control of the country's finances.[66]

In the final weeks of the Russo-Turkish war, in January 1878, Sultan Abdulhamid II suspended the Parliament and Constitution after only fourteen months of operation. Ottomanism had to be revamped to suit new demographics. Although the Muslims predominated in the Empire, they were composed of roughly equal shares of Turks and Arabs with smaller contingents of Kurds and Albanians. All ethnic distinctions were now supposed to be overshadowed by the umbrella of Muslim brotherhood. The sultan stressed his traditional role of the caliph, successor to Muhammad as the head of the universal Islamic community. This buttressed Sultan's legitimacy both at home and abroad. Dozens of delegations from all over the Islamic world would come to ask him for help in overthrowing or repelling European and Chinese invaders.[67]

In spite of its conservative and traditional flavor, the so-called Pan-Islamism did not signal reneging on the commitments to reformism and modernization. Unable to lead a worldwide jihad against imperialism, Abdulhamid II projected an international image of a spiritual caliphate. This would not really help the colonized to shake the infidel intruders off the Islamic lands but would conveniently increase Ottoman diplomatic leverage necessary to forestall further European inroads into the Sultan's realm. The main thrust of Pan-Islamism was actually domestic—to garner support of common Muslims and conservative elite, especially *ulema* or Islamic jurists in control of sharia courts. This is hardly similar to what Chatterjee describes as peculiarly anti-colonial nationalist division of the world into Western material and native spiritual domains.[68]

---

66. Lewis, Bernard, *The Emergence of Modern Turkey* (New York: Oxford University Press, 2002), p. 159.

67. Fadeeva, Irma, *Ofitsialnyie doktriny v ideologii i politike Osmanskoi imperii: Osmanism, panislamizm* (Moscow: Nauka, 1985), pp. 135–136.

68. Chatterjee, Partha, "Whose Imagined Community?," *Mapping the Nation*, p. 217.

The government did its best propaganda efforts to eliminate that potential dichotomy. The borrowings of the achievements of European economy, science, and technology continued to be justified as the original products of the Arab Islamic civilization. After 1878, there was no need to discover Islamic prototypes for Western liberal institutions since the Sultan suspended the Constitution of 1876. He portrayed himself as the traditional absolute ruler openly opposed to any novel notions such as nationalism in its civic or ethnic garb. After the disturbing secular rhetoric of the earlier reformers, it was reassuring for traditional-minded Muslims to hear familiar language. Whereas the previous two sultans Abdulmecid I and Abdulaziz I were popularly referred to as *gaur* or infidels for their support of Westernizing bureaucrats, Abdulhamid II publicized his piety to create a credible image of the righteous caliph.

All this Islamic rhetoric did not involve closing civil courts or undoing positive changes in the Christian legal status achieved under the Tanzimat but it encouraged Christians to supplement their individual rights as Ottoman subjects with external guarantees of their communal rights. So they turned both to new regional powers like Greece or Bulgaria and to the Great Powers whenever the Porte tried to strip the Patriarchate and the Exarchate of their autonomy. These protégé games remind of new identity politics by Muslim minorities in the European Union today.[69]

Ottoman Christians appealed to universalistic principles of Christian solidarity to assert their particularistic local claims and identities. Ironically, the Tanzimat reforms strengthened separatist tendencies among borderland Christian Slav populations by transferring administrative power from conservative prelates to laity-dominated councils. Many among middle-class professionals were increasingly tempted by the irredentist propaganda away from the Church and the Sultan to the secular religion of nationalism and career prospects in swelling bureaucracies of neighboring nation-states of Greece, Serbia, and Bulgaria.[70]

But the illiterate peasant majority was not infatuated with the new Western fashions. They focused their loyalties on their place of birth, religion and any stable government. Against this background of passive acceptance, Christian upper classes actively supported the Ottoman Empire. During the earlier Tanzimat period and under Abdulhamid II, many of them were increasingly included into the Ottoman bureaucracy. Thus, Alexander Karatheodori Pasha who as a deputy foreign minister had

---

69. Soysal, Yasemin, "Citizenship & Identity: Living in Diasporas in Post-War Europe?" *Ethnic & Racial Studies*, 23, 1 (Jan 2000): 6–7.

70. Devereux, *The First Ottoman Constitutional Period*, p. 224.

opposed the Schism in 1872 became the first Christian foreign minister in December 1878. Rich Greeks and Armenians were in fact the backbone of Ottoman bourgeoisie and their fortunes were tied with the imperial market. There was no border region with a predominantly Greek (except possibly for Epirus) or Armenian population.

Furthermore, ambitious liberals and left-outs of all creeds could and did unite against the post-1878 autocratic regime of Abdulhamid II. The policy of banning subversive publications often backfired by advertising the forbidden fruit readily available in the Pera neighborhood of Istanbul. Protected by European embassies, foreign-owned postal services there operated outside Ottoman control and supplied any popular literature. One could read and discuss it in Pera shops and clubs typically run by non-Muslims.[71]

The sense of vulnerability and resentment vis-à-vis the Great Powers bred Muslim distrust of Ottoman Christians perceived as their puppets. This pervasive xenophobia sometimes made ethnicity more important. Since later in the nineteenth century, the conservative Islamic discourse began to single out the Turks as the mainstay of the true religion. Salutary simplicity of ancestral culture was stressed to criticize those aping the Westerners and thus betraying their "Turkishness." This defensive posture sometimes acquired aggressive overtones as "Turkishness" became embedded in the occasional irredentist and expansionist rhetoric among the elites who were outside government circles and often in comfortable European exile. They saw the mission of Ottoman Turks not only in saving their own state but also in liberating "outside Turks"—Turkic-speaking Muslim brethren in Central Asia that had fallen victim to the Russian juggernaut in the 1860s.[72]

Under the guise of Abdulhamid II's Pan-Islamism, there continued to develop an essentially modern secular state. It valued membership in the Ottoman Empire over that in the universal Islamic community. Non-Ottoman Muslims were perceived not as brothers but as foreigners. They were forbidden to own land in the empire, including that in the Holy Sites of Islam in Arabia. The state also promoted a subtle rationalization of the legal system by substituting the uniform sharia of the Hanefi rite for the patchwork of other juridical rites current in diverse Islamic communities of the empire.[73]

---

71. Boyar, Ebru, and Fleet, Kate, *A Social History of Ottoman Istanbul* (New York: Cambridge University Press, 2010), p. 321.

72. Kushner, David, *The Rise of Turkish Nationalism, 1876–1908* (London, Frank Cass: 1977), pp. 87–96.

73. Deringil, Selim, *The Well-Protected Domains: Ideology & the Legitimation of Power in the Ottoman Empire, 1876–1909* (London and New York: I. B. Tauris, 1998), pp. 51–60.

The imperial center continued its Tanzimat discourse of the civilizing mission aimed not at replacing but rather at co-opting and acculturating local elites into the modernizing project. For this purpose the Tribal School was established, where the scions of Arab and Kurdish nomadic chieftains could adopt and then spread a modern Ottoman value system. The intent is similar to Anthony Smith's model of an aristocratic culture gradually adopted by disparate populations as the cultural core of a nation in the making.[74]

State and private schools in non-Turkish areas continued to be run in local languages but promoting the same package of Western and native themes. Islam was subtly reinterpreted as a material civilization capable of change and not as an immutable spiritual doctrine. The main task of the expanding education system was to build an emperor cult as the focus of loyalty for the people. This was made easier by the imposition of strict censorship that helped silence any opposition after 1878, especially in the cosmopolitan imperial capital.[75]

Although not suprareligious as before 1878, the "official nationality" project was still supraethnic. In the Ottoman context, the Habermasian ideals of civic allegiance to liberal texts and institutions proved to be lacking a necessary emotional attraction. In keeping with Hobsbawm's model of protonationalism, the image of the caliph was to be "an integrative 'icon' in the new 'religio-ethnic identification.'"[76] The emerging communitarian Ottoman nation could be understood as the "sacred body" while for Abdulhamid II's modernizing coterie the true God was indeed developmentalism and modernization.[77]

Haunted by the memories of the 1876 palace coups, Abdulhamid II stayed away from the Dolmabahche and Chiragan palaces. But he did not return to the old Top Kapi palace, which served as the residence of the Sultans until 1856. Instead, he moved to the wooded hill overlooking the Bosphorus, where he had an Italian architect build a residence in the Swiss chalet style. He hired European artists as court painters and enjoyed photography immensely. He willed his large collection to the Library of Congress (it is now digitized and available online). We would expect such a traditionalist Ottoman sultan to be sitting on a divan (a couch-like throne). Despite the rhetoric of Pan-Islamism and publicized Islamic piety, Abdulhamid II often appeared in a Western-style military uniform using a European-style chair as a throne as in Figure 5.4.

---

74. Ibid., p. 66.

75. Ibid., p. 106.

76. Ibid., p. 46.

77. Manzo, Kathryn, *Creating Boundaries: The Politics of Race & Nation* (Boulder and London: Lynne Rienner Publishers, 1996), pp. 44, 53.

FIGURE 5.4 "Abdulhamit II, Sultan of the Turks, 1842–1918" (c. 1890). Library of Congress Prints and Photographs Division, Reproduction Number: LC-USZ62-77295.

The True Heirs of Classical Slavophilism: Pan-Orthodoxy versus Pan-Slavism

The Russo-Turkish War of 1877–1878 and its aftermath brought to the Pan-Orthodox circles renewed confidence in the success of their cause. They continued to feel as a minority in the Russian educated society. But their calls for strengthening the Patriarchate of Constantinople within the Ottoman Empire and establishing a supraethnic Russian-Balkan Orthodox union were heard more than before among Russian intellectuals, in the Russian church leadership, and in the government.

At this time, Pan-Orthodox commentators often claimed to have inherited the intellectual mantle of classical Slavophilism as they projected their own vision of the anti-Western anti-liberal supranational civilization. Konstantin Leontiev first made that bid when he was trying to publish and popularize his above-mentioned landmark *Byzantinism and Slavdom* in 1874–1875. His views on the primacy of the Church over "Slavic race," autocracy over the individual, and nobility over legal equality met with the support of some high-ranking government officials[78] and eventually of Alexander II.[79]

Leontiev believed that contemporary senior Pan-Slavs such as Prince Vasilii Cherkasskii and especially Ivan Aksakov departed from the original Slavophile views on the central role of Orthodox Christianity in the Slavic way of life. He saw this deviation most clearly in their take on the Bulgarian Church Question. This discovery led Leontiev to discern "a chasm that often exists between a teacher and a disciple who went further along the same road."[80]

In 1878, in the influential anti-liberal *Grazhdanin* newspaper, Leontiev argued that the general Slavic rather than the narrowly Balkan Slavic interests made it necessary to support the Patriarchate of Constantinople against the Bulgarian church movement. Although both the Bulgarians and the Greeks pursued cliquish nationalistic agendas with the Schism of 1872, the age-old Ecumenical Patriarchate along with the Russian autocracy was the institutional bedrock of the future "Eastern-Orthodox alliance."[81]

Ironically, the Pan-Orthodox trend benefited from the Congress of Berlin of 1878, which had greatly limited Russian and Bulgarian gains from the Russo-Turkish War of 1877–1878. The most active Pan-Slav committee—the Moscow Slavic Benevolent Society—was closed because of its open criticism of Russian foreign policy as "the betrayal of the cause of Slavdom to please Europe" at the Congress of Berlin.[82]

Another major example of this trend away from Pan-Slavism was the permission by the Interior Ministry to Nikolai Durnovo in 1879 to publish the openly Pan-Orthodox newspaper *Vostok*, which means "East" or "Orient." One of the major Slavophile newspapers, *Sovremennyie Izvestia* published by Nikita Giliarov-Platonov, supported this initiative of Durnovo, who was its former employee from 1876 to 1879. It welcomed the agenda of *Vostok* because the new publication aimed at bringing Russia back to its traditional role of the protector

78. Leontiev, Konstantin, *Moia literaturnaia sudba: Vospominania* (Moscow: Russkaia kniga, 2002), p. 64.

79. Nelson, Dale, *Kosntantin Leontiev and the Orthodox East* (unpublished Ph.D. dissertation, University of Minnesota, 1975), p. 317.

80. Leontiev, *Moia literaturnaia sudba*, pp. 72–73.

81. Leontiev, "Khram i Tserkov," in *Vostok, Rossia, Slavianstvo: Filosofskaia i politicheskaia publitsistika, dukhovnaia proza (1872–1891)* (Moscow: Respublika, 1996), pp. 164–166. Originally published in the *Grazhdanin* newspaper, 10–12 (1878).

82. Thaden, *Conservative Nationalism in 19th Century Russia*, p. 139.

of all Orthodox Christians—the principle supposedly broken in the Bulgarian Church Question.[83]

Similar to Tertii Filippov in his journalistic background and interests, Nikolai Durnovo was one the founders of the Moscow Slavic Society in the 1850s. As its active member, he was instrumental in establishing in 1872 in Moscow the town church (*podvorie, metochion*) of the Metropolitanate of Serbia.[84] He was also very active in raising money and organizing Russian volunteers during the anti-Ottoman uprisings of 1875–1876 in Bosnia-Herzegovina and the Serbian-Montenegrin-Turkish War of 1876.[85] Although Ivan Aksakov tried to bring him back to Pan-Slavism, Durnovo adopted Filippov's Pan-Orthodox views on the Bulgarian Church Question as early as 1878.[86]

His Pan-Slav background was clear in the editorial program in the first issue of *Vostok* on 2 May 1879. His statement was itself modeled on the famous programmatic article of 15 October 1861 by Ivan Aksakov, who was the editor of the first Russian Pan-Slav newspaper *Den'* and of many similar subsequent publications. Nikolai Durnovo shifted the emphasis from the Slavs to the Christian Orthodox "Greco-Slavic world" as the main ally of Russia in Europe.

In 1861, Aksakov took pride in the freedom of powerful Russians against the background of the Slavs oppressed by "Germans or Turks." In contrast, Durnovo emphasized that Russia had been consistently protecting and promoting reconciliation among coreligionist nations of the Greco-Slavic world. Russia had never fought for the Slavs "among whom there are worshippers of the false prophet Mohammad," To make matters worse, pro-Western Catholic Croats and Poles were themselves oppressing Orthodox Serbs and Ukrainians, respectively. Aksakov's appeal to the Russians to use their mighty empire to save powerless Slavs turned into Durnovo's triumphant vision of powerful Russia liberating helpless and hapless Orthodox Christians. Central to that dream was the anticipated collapse of Austria-Hungary and Turkey as "moribund and crumbling empires built on alien nationalities (*narodnosti*)."[87]

Rejecting that kind of religiously and ethnically heterogeneous supranational structures, Durnovo, Leontiev, and Filippov promoted their vision of an ethnically diverse but religiously homogeneous supranational entity. When established, it would be open specifically to Greeks, Serbs, Bulgarians, and Rumanians while

---

83. *Sovremennyie Izvestia*, 98 (11 April 1879).

84. OR RGB, f. 239-8-32, Nikolai Durnovo to Nil Popov, sometime in 1872, p. 2.

85. N. N. Durnovo to N. A. Popov, 11 January 1876, ibid., p. 39.

86. Manuscript Division of the State Historical Museum (OPI GIM), f. 177-1-10, I. S. Aksakov to N. D. Durnovo, 13 January 1878, p. 160b.

87. *Vostok*, 1 (2 May 1879): 1–2.

non-Slavic and non-Orthodox minorities were not adequately discussed.[88] To foster ties between them, Russia needed to turn from the Pan-Slavism of the Russo-Turkish War of 1877–1878 to its traditional Pan-Orthodox policy in the Near East. Durnovo saw the main source of Orthodox divisions in the Bulgarian Church Question, which separated the Bulgarians from the Greeks, Serbs, Rumanians, and Russians. While not demonizing common Bulgarian people, Durnovo like Filippov and Leontiev blamed the Schism on the Westernized Bulgarian intelligentsia that had put their narrow national interests above Orthodoxy.[89]

Durnovo's "Greco-Slavic world" was evidently inspired by Vladimir Lamanskii's "Greco-Slavic world" as well as by Leontiev's "Byzantinism" and "Eastern Orthodox Alliance." But Durnovo went further in allying himself with similar projects in the Greek world. He was a member of "The Hellenismos Society," which advanced the Great Idea of Greek irredentis, and of Leonidas Voulgares' "Eastern Confederation," which advocated the creation of a Balkan Union through a magazine with the same title in French "La Confederation Orientale."[90] Durnovo consistently promoted the idea of the Russian-led Eastern or Balkan confederation of Christian Orthodox nations.[91] *Vostok*'s Athens-based correspondent and self-described "Philhellene" Ivan Petrov also promoted the idea of the Balkan Union to resist Austrian expansion toward the Aegean.[92] This idea resonated with many Russian diplomats who resented the Austrian occupation of Bosnia-Herzegovina and would eventually cobble together the Balkan Alliance of 1912.

Although always under one thousand copies in circulation, *Vostok* truly became the missing link, the meeting place, and the sounding board of the Pan-Orthodox circles both in Russia and in the Christian East from 1879 to 1886. Although critical of "nonsense" in *Vostok*, many Pan-Slavs were sympathetic to it because "we are still unable to start any Slavic periodical after the war."[93] According to Durnovo, over sixty Orthodox prelates were among his subscribers and at least three Russian Metropolitans sent letters of approval to *Vostok* in 1880.[94] Durnovo sought to popularize the writings of Filippov

---

88. Ibid., p. 2.

89. Ibid., p. 10.

90. OPI GIM, f. 177-1-31, N. Kazazis to N. N. Durnovo, 1899–1907, pp. 16–320b, editors of *La Confederation Orientale* to N. N. Durnovo, 1888, pp. 39–400b.

91. *Vostok*, 30 (24 January 1880): 25; *Vostok*, 40 (6 April 1880): 105.

92. *Vostok*, 118 (22 June 1881): 351.

93. OR RGB, f. 239-12-2, P. A. Kulakovskii to N. A. Popov, 11 June 1879, pp. 10–11.

94. *Vostok*, 53 (27 July 1880): 218.

and Leontiev throughout the period.[95] He asked Filippov to invite Leontiev to contribute to *Vostok*, which he did, describing the newspaper as "very sympathetic" to their common cause.[96]

In his three articles in *Vostok* titled "The Letters of a Hermit," Leontiev further elaborated on the main ideas put forward in his 1875 *Byzantinism and Slavdom* and developed his relation to classical Slavophilism. In "Bulgaromania" (*bolgarobesie*), he conceptualized the Bulgarian Question within the context of the struggle between conservatism and liberalism across Europe at the time. In his framework, the Ottoman Greeks generally and the hierarchy of the Ecumenical Patriarchate specifically represented the conservative principle, whereas the Bulgarian church movement and its Russian Pan-Slav supporters promoted rational secular liberalism.[97]

These trends within the Bulgarian Church Question had dire consequences for Russia because "never before in the history of Russia and Slavdom has the principle of ethnic (*plemennoi*) Slavism had to conflict with Orthodox canons and traditions." Divorced from religion, nationalism tended to promote the ideas of universal liberty and equality of the French Revolution of 1789. The resulting Westernization promoted cultural blandness and social homogenization. According to Leontiev, "cultural Slavophilism was supposed to blossom from the unshakeable ancient roots of Orthodoxy" into a separate anti-Western civilization in the teachings of classical Slavophiles of 1840s such as Alexei Khomiakov and Ivan Kireevskii. Leontiev argued that the contemporary "liberal Pan-Slavism is death first of all for Russia" whereas his own "Orthodox Pan-Slavism is salvation." The latter would be in conformity with classical Slavophilism because "the policy of the Orthodox spirit must be chosen over the policy of the Slavic flesh and the agitation of the Bulgarian meat." To ensure the primacy of Orthodoxy over nationalism in the Christian East, it was necessary to preserve the theocratic institutions of the Ottoman Empire for the foreseeable future.[98]

In other issues of *Vostok*, Durnovo also supported Leontiev's pro-Ottoman line. For example, he denounced the Bulgarian Exarchate as a tool of Bulgarian irredentism in Macedonia. For this reason, he urged the Sublime Porte to give no credence to unfounded claims of alleged popular demands for Bulgarian

---

95. Ibid.

96. Tertii Filippov to Konstantin Leontiev, 8 March 1879 published in "Brat ot brata pomogaem . . ." Fetisenko, O. L., ed., *Nestor*, 1 (2000): 169.

97. "Pisma otshelnika: Bolgarobesie I," *Vostok*, 7 (10 June 1879): 99–101.

98. Leontiev, Konstantin, "Pisma otshelnika: Bolgarobesie II," *Vostok*, 8 (17 June 1879):114–115.

Exarchist prelates in Skopje, Shtip, and Bitol. Durnovo published a letter from Philippoupolis in Eastern Rumelia—the province of the Ottoman Empire that received autonomy in 1878. The Greek minority in the province suffered increasing persecution by the Bulgarian majority. The unchecked ethnic tension made the Greeks nostalgic for the times of direct Ottoman rule, when both ethnic groups had the same rights as Orthodox Christians.[99]

This advocacy of supranational institutions of the Church and multiconfessional empire gave a clearer expression to the thoughts previewed in Leontiev's *Byzantinism and Slavdom* of 1875, especially with the statement that "the principle of autocracy and the principle of Patriarchal authority are so closely connected as to be virtually the same."[100]

Consequently, Pan-Slavs' mistake was to consider the South Slavs and specifically the Bulgarians as the repository of the "ancient Slavic spirit" and "pristine fresh Christianity." These classical Slavophile ideals were incompatible with the Bulgarian movement's "ethnic (*plemennoi*) Machiavellianism destroying the Church." The original Christian Orthodox values were more likely to be found among Ottoman Greeks, who had been able to preserve them from Byzantium through the Ottoman domination.[101]

Leontiev indirectly promoted the same idea in his 1879 obituary of the prominent monastic figure Father Kliment Sederholm. Leontiev emphasized how Sederholm was a spiritual disciple of Ivan Kireevskii and Alexis Khomiakov, Tertii Filippov and Count Alexander Tolstoy. The influence of classical Slavophiles led German Protestant Sederholm to Orthodoxy and explained his support for the venerated Patriarch Gregory VI and the Ecumenical Patriarchate against the Bulgarian church movement.[102]

As the editor of the *Varshavskii Dnevnik* newspaper in 1880, Leontiev continued to argue that the Pan-Orthodox "party" was the only group of the educated Russian society to uphold the classical Slavophile ideals. Leontiev concluded that the central vision of the founding fathers of Slavophilism was "the period, original in ideas and forms, of a *multicolored* Slavdom within the greater unity of Orthodoxy [emphasis in the original]." He contrasted this "cultural Slavophilism" with "political Pan-Slavism." "The strange hallucination

99. P. S.-s., "Iz Filippopolia," *Vostok*, 34 (19 February 1880): 82, 83.

100. Leontiev, Konstantin, "Pisma otshelnika: Bolgarobesie II," *Vostok*, 8 (17 June 1879): 114–115.

101. Leontiev, Konstantin, "Pismo otshelnika. Pismo vtoroe. O porokakh fanariotov i o russkom neznanii," *Vostok*, 12 (15 July 1879): 180–183.

102. Leontiev, "Otets Kliment Sederholm, ieromonakh Optinoi Pustyni," in *Vostok, Rossia, Slavianstvo*, pp. 176–180. Originally published in *Russkii Vestnik*, 11–12 (1879).

of ethnic nationalism" often forced the Russians "to follow unwillingly with our mighty foot along the path trodden by a small but strong hoof of South Slavs."

The "purely ethnic principle" led to the loss of traditional complex society based on the social and cultural role of clergy, nobility, and monarchy. "Cosmopolitan, i.e., anti-national democratization" of Europe created bland uniform bourgeois culture and a very simple social division between haves and have-nots. The way to realize the classical Slavophile ideals was in preserving supranational structures such as the Church and multiethnic empires.[103] Thus, although Pan-Orthodox writers like Leontiev dreamed of a brave new Eastern Union of Russia and the Christian East, for the foreseeable future they saw Ottoman and Austrian empires as the best defense against the disruptive forces of nationalism.

Vostok welcomed the decision of the Russian Church to avoid celebrating liturgy and taking communion with Bulgarian clerics on their visits to Russia. Durnovo reprimanded the liberal daily *Novoe Vremia* newspaper for misinforming its readers that the Russian Holy Synod had allegedly sent the harsh response to the Patriarchate about the issue of Russian army priests in Bulgaria in 1879.[104]

Nikolai Durnovo became even more enthusiastic when Count Dmitrii Tolstoy resigned from his position as the Over-Procurator of the Russian Holy Synod (1866–1880). *Vostok* joined *Sovremennyie Izvestia* to harshly criticize the results of Tolstoy's tenure. The Pan-Orthodox publicists blamed the Schism of 1872 almost exclusively on the inactivity and procrastination of the leadership of the Russian Holy Synod at the time.

Specifically, Count Tolstoy's gravest sin was to refuse to send Russian representatives to the projected Ecumenical Council summoned by Patriarch Gregory VI in 1871. Furthermore, Durnovo alleged that in 1872 Tolstoy single-handedly had put on hold the incomes of the Patriarchate of Jerusalem and foreign monasteries in order to pressure the Greek nationalists at the helm of Ottoman Christian churches into lifting the Schism. As a result, "thousands of Christians fell from Orthodoxy and the Mother Church ran into great hardships."[105]

Domestically, Durnovo lashed out against Tolstoy for introducing Old Church Slavonic liturgy everywhere and thereby suppressing the rights of Moldavian

103. Leontiev, Konstantin, "Panslavism" in "Peredovye statii 'Varshavskogo Dnevnika' 1880 goda," in *Vostok, Rossia, Slavianstvo*, pp. 234–235.

104. *Vostok*, 1 (2 May 1879): 5.

105. *Vostok*, 53 (27 July 1880): 218.

and Georgian Orthodox Christians in Russia while allegedly lending support to the Bulgarians demands for church independence. In terms of tolerance to ethnic diversity, unswerving adherence to the true Orthodox tradition, and especially firmness in the face of the Papacy's encroachments, *Vostok, Bereg,* and *Varshavskii Dnevnik* agreed with *Neologos* of Constantinople: "Orthodoxy in Russia needs help from the Eastern Churches."[106]

Taking his cue from *Anatolikos Aster* of Constantinople, Durnovo informed his readers that the question of the restoration of the Moscow Patriarchate might be discussed when "Eastern Patriarchs" would come to Moscow for the occasion of the sanctification of the new Moscow Cathedral of Christ the Savior. The idea of inviting the Patriarchs was raised at the session of the St. Petersburg Society for the Advancement of Spiritual Enlightenment (*Obshchestvo Liubitelei Dukhovnogo Prosveshcheniia*).[107]

When the same issue was raised by another Greek newspaper—*Neologos* of Constantinople—Durnovo argued enthusiastically in favor of the restoration of the Patriarchate, as Filippov had done in the 1860s and 1870s. This reform would elevate the Russian Church and liberate it from what he saw as subjugation to government officials. In Durnovo's view, the future Russian Patriarch would run the Church together with the Synod of about seven hierarchs plus a representative of the Georgian Church, which would regain its autocephalous status.

This structure would be patterned on the organization of "the Eastern Patriarchates," which managed to preserve Orthodoxy "despite many centuries of the heavy Turkish yoke." Durnovo believed that the autocephalous churches of every Orthodox country needed to be raised to the status of the Patriarchate. In the future Russian-led Balkan Union, those Patriarchs would congregate in Constantinople or in other capitals of the confederation to discuss church affairs of the whole Christian Orthodox world.[108]

Pan-Orthodox agitation in *Vostok* echoed the trend among many Russian bishops in favor of the restoration of the Russian Patriarchate and against government interference in church matters.[109] Durnovo found an early ally in the person of Archbishop Mitrofan of Don (*Zadonskii*). The latter wrote in support of Russia's relations with the Ecumenical Patriarchate and especially of

---

106. *Vostok*, 43 (5 May 1880): 131–134.

107. *Vostok*, 34 (19 February 1880): 86.

108. *Vostok*, 40 (6 April 1880): 105–106.

109. Basil, John, *Church and State in Late Imperial Russia: Critics of the Synodal System of Church Government* (Minneapolis: Minnesota Mediterranean and Eastern European Monographs, 2005), pp. 7–33.

bishops' authority, which was threatened by rebellious Bulgarians. Archbishop Mitrofan linked the Schism to the issue of the projected church reform in Russia:

> In practice, the slightest weakening of the Christ-given power of bishops may cause religious scandal and hesitation among Orthodox people, undermine bishops' moral, religious and any beneficial influence on the flock, clergy, and laity, provide the heterodox Christians, the heretics, and the Old Believers with a pretext to criticize and mock the dignity of bishops and the Orthodox Church in general and its inability to defend its rights. The growing distance between the Russian Church and the original Christian Church, represented by the Greek Churches today, may move the Russian Church closer to the Presbyterian Church, weaken spiritual authority generally and chip away at the dignity, weight, and significance of the Orthodox Church in the eyes of the whole world.[110]

Durnovo perceived a wave of change rising in the Russian Church in connection with the departure of Tolstoy from the Holy Synod. *Vostok* highlighted the proposal of the *Rossiia* newspaper to convene councils of local bishops "to give a proper direction to the church life in general." As for interchurch relations, Durnovo welcomed increased attention to the plight of the impoverished Patriarchates of Jerusalem and Antioch, whose income from their property in Russia had been sequestered. He referred specifically to the report of Vasilii Khitrovo at the session of the St. Petersburg Society of the Admirers of Spiritual Enlightenment.[111]

In the early 1880s, Durnovo took issue with Moscow-based but Syrian-born Professor Georgii Murkos. He was voicing the resentment of many Syrian Arab Orthodox nationalists against their Greek prelates at the Patriarchates of Jerusalem and Antioch. Murkos provocatively argued that the situation of Arab Orthodox suffering the abuses and Hellenization at the hands of the "corrupt" Greek clergy was identical to the situation of Bulgarian Slavs "struggling to shake off the Phanariot yoke" of the Patriarchate of Constantinople.[112]

Durnovo did his best to undermine the credibility of Murkos as allegedly secretly working for Catholic propaganda. Without the Greek church

---

110. *Vostok*, 10 (1 July 1879): 157.

111. Ibid., 44 (9 May 1880): 142.

112. Murkos, Georgii, *O mnenii pravoslavnykh arabov o greko-bolgarskom tserkovnom voprose* (Moscow: Pravoslavnoie Obozrenie, 1880).

leadership, the Arabs, like the Slavs, would be unable to resist the "seduction" of the Jesuits. Plus, Greek bishops were not alien to their Arabic-speaking flock who were Greek by blood themselves. Durnovo borrowed this Greek irredentist argument as part of Greek-Russian exchange of ideas.[113] Still, in the early 1880s, Durnovo did not see the leadership of the Russian Church and Pan-Slavs conspiring with Murkos as he would in the 1890s.

Tertii Filippov also published in the 1880s. From the Holy Synod he moved up in the world to take the position of Comptroller General (1889–1899). But he continued to enjoy an unrivaled reputation of the preeminent expert in canon law. This fame was increasingly causing envy on the part of the new Over-Procurator of the Holy Synod, Konstantin Pobedonostsev himself.[114] In 1881, Alexander II himself entrusted Filippov with the sensitive task of finding legal arguments to enable the Tsar to crown his morganatic spouse as Empress of Russia. After Alexander II's assassination by anarchists in 1881, Filippov became one of the leading "reactionary" statesmen bent on reversing earlier liberal trends.[115]

In addition to contributing to *Grazhdanin*, in 1882, Filippov put together his writings since the 1860s including his Pan-Slav speech welcoming Metropolitan of Serbia Mikhail in 1869. The main thrust of the book was to advocate an Ecumenical Council of all Orthodox churches to lift two schisms—over the Bulgarian and Old Belief Questions.[116] Filippov's book was acclaimed in the official periodical of the Patriarchate of Constantinople in several issues in the summer and fall of 1882. One of its contributors, Constantinos Vafeidis, wrote an extensive review that also included a positive overview of the history of the Russian Church and of its relations with the Patriarchate.[117] Even ten years later, Filippov's book continued to be "a loud voice in defense of traditional institutions and of the unity of Christ's flock" threatened by the "alien principle of ethnicity (*phyletismos*)." As such, the book "brought relief" to the Patriarchate going through difficult times.[118]

---

113. *Vostok*, 60 (24 September 1880), p.276; *Vostok*, 70 (6 December 1880), p. 354.

114. Meshcherskii, Vladimir, *Vospominania* (Moscow: Zakharov, 2001), p. 635.

115. Zaionchkovskii, Petr, *Krizis Samoderzhaviia na rubezhe 1870-kh–1880-kh godov* (Moscow: Moscow State University Press, 1964), pp. 233, 428.

116. Filippov, Tertii, *Sovremennye Tserkovnyie Voprosy* (St. Petersburg: Obshchestvennaia Pol'za, 1882).

117. *Ekklesiastiki Aletheia*, 30 June 1882, 7 July 1882, 21 July 1882, 5 August 1882, 18 August 1882, 1 September 1882, 8 September 1882, 6 October 1882.

118. Patriarch Neophytos VIII to Filippov, 23 November 1892, The Archive of the Patriarchate of Constantinople, A62, pp. 513–515, Number 6650.

In 1894, during his personal visit to Constantinople, Filippov suggested that the Patriarchate see to the translation of the second part of his book dealing with the issue of Russian Old Belief sectarians.[119]

But the major Moscow-based ecclesiastical journal *Pravoslavnoie Obozrenie* took issue with Filippov's diagnosis of the problems of the Orthodox world as well as with his solutions. Durnovo denounced "its editor and candle-trader" Preobrazhenskii as "the notorious ringleader (*vozhak*) of Moscow's liberal priests together with the famous editor of *Tserkovno-Obshestvennyi Vestnik* M-r Popovitskii, the laughable Arab theologian M-r Murkos and Protestant theologian Belliustin from Kaliazin who are attacking supposedly only the Ecumenical Patriarchate but in actuality the Orthodox Church itself which in their mind is long overdue to be reformed into a Protestant church with married prelates at its head."[120]

Vostok disagreed that Filippov was an isolated lay amateur. According to Durnovo, in 1871–1872, only Metropolitan of Lithuania (later of Moscow) Makarii supported the Over-Procurator of the Holy Synod Dmitrii Tolstoy in his opposition to Patriarch Gregory VI's call of the Ecumenical Council over the Bulgarian Question. The majority opinion of the Russian prelates such as Metropolitans of Moscow Innokentii, Arsenii of Kiev, and Filofei of Tver (later of Kiev) was in favor of the Ecumenical Council. Filippov's ideas found supporters in Professor Kurganov, Konstantin Leontiev, and Nikita Giliarov-Platonov, the editor of *Sovremennyie Izvestia*, who "as the former Theological Academy Professor could not help condemning uncanonical Bulgarian acts." Durnovo also referred Filippov's critics to the official minutes of the Council of Constantinople of 1872, Greek, and Serbian newspapers such as *Neologos, Aion, Thrake, Istok,* and *Sion*.[121]

Overall, even the mainstream Russian press had become less sympathetic to Pan-Slavism. According to Durnovo, most Russian publications stopped publishing stories of persecution of defenseless Bulgarians by the Patriarchate. This change came after the revelations of the oppression of the Greek and Rumanian minorities in the Bulgarian Principality and the anti-Serbian policies in the Ottoman dioceses under the purview of the Bulgarian Exarchate such as Nish, Pirot, Skopje, Debar, Ohrid, etc.[122]

As before, the Pan-Orthodox camp attracted converts from Pan-Slavism. One notable acquisition was Professor Apollon Maikov. He published

---

119. The Patriarchate to the Archbishop of Smyrna, 26 March 1894, ibid., A65, p. 93, Number 1624.

120. *Vostok*, 201 (10 October 1882): 394.

121. *Vostok*, 208 (November 1882): 448–450.

122. *Vostok*, 166 (11 February 1882): 73.

scholarly works on Serbian language and culture, held the honorary rank of court chamberlain, and regularly contributed to the foreign policy section of the most important Russian "thick" journal, *Russkaia Mysl*. In his view, Russia would fulfill its messianic role in the "Christian East by upholding the institutions of the "Eastern Patriarchates" unable to defend themselves against Catholic and Protestant religious propaganda.

To avoid further cracks in the unity of the Orthodox Church, Russia had to be an active and impartial mediator among its coreligionists. As a counterbalance to Western religious missions and the excessively Westernized governments of Bulgaria, Greece, and Serbia, Russia needed to empower the Orthodox churches by securing autocephalous status for them. But church independence should be achieved legitimately. The 1872 Council of Constantinople rightly condemned the methods employed by the Bulgarian Exarchate as "impassioned and clumsy."[123]

Equality among autocephalous churches would ensure reconciliation and cooperation of the Orthodox nations vis-à-vis "the educated, resourceful and rich Jesuits" who "oppress, seduce, and forcefully divert them into a different faith." The resulting "spiritual union" would prevent the Orthodox churches from "straying aside as happened with the Serbian Church or from offending each other as is happening in the Bulgarian Church whose representative, the Exarch, recently voiced in his Synod impassioned and unbecoming accusations against the Greek Church."[124]

Thus, Maikov reiterated the traditional perception of unredeemed coreligionists as powerless to resist the age-old Catholic or Protestant crusade. Unless brought into some kind of union with Russia, they were doomed to succumb to the seduction of the West. In the influential *Russkaia Mysl*, Maikov disseminated the Pan-Orthodox agenda set by Leontiev and Durnovo of containing ethnonationalism within some sort of Russian-led federation of Orthodox countries. Generally, all of Pan-Orthodox commentators felt that after 1880 the Russian government and church authorities were getting on the right track regarding the relationship to the Christian East.

The Russian Domination of Autonomous Bulgaria and Eastern Rumelia, 1878–1885

Even after the official end of the Russian military occupation in 1879, Russian advisers continued to direct the development of Bulgarian and Eastern

---

123. Maikov, Apollon, "Pravoslavie na Vostoke," *Russkaia Mysl'*, 3 (1884): 146.

124. Ibid., pp. 150–151.

Rumelian administration, especially in the military.[125] Many of them supported the Bulgarian Church and totally ignored the Schism of 1872 not so
much in the name of modern Pan-Slavism but because they saw it as clear
evidence of the Greek betrayal of Orthodoxy in favor of their narrow nationalist agendas.

For example, the Russian military attaché in Philippoupolis, Colonel Ekk,
opposed efforts to lift the Schism. Russia would alienate the Bulgarians if it
continued its pressure to limit the jurisdiction of the Bulgarian Exarchate to
the Bulgarian Principality and Eastern Rumelia. In his letter to the General
Chief of Staff, Ekk warned that their kinsmen in Macedonia would prefer the
"abandonment of their faith" and the adoption of Catholicism from very active
Austrian-sponsored missionaries to "the final subjugation to the Phanar," i.e.,
the seat of the Patriarchate of Constantinople.[126]

This great danger was impressed on Ekk by Bulgarian politicians in
Eastern Rumelia such as the Popular Party leader Ivan Geshov and Exarch
Iosif himself. The spiritual father of all Bulgarians admitted to Ekk the un-
satisfactory condition of his clergy that did not enjoy respect of the common
people. This situation would improve not with the reconciliation with the
Patriarchate but with the new generation of priests to be trained by Russian
clerics according to Russian standards. Iosif asked Ekk to request the Russian
Holy Synod to establish a theological seminary alongside the Russian church
built in Shipka to commemorate one of the most dramatic battles of the last
Russo-Turkish war. The Exarch believed it necessary for the Russian priests
there to train enough clergymen and then "the Bulgarian people would treat
all Orthodox rites with their original piety."[127]

This sentiment was echoed in the letters to the Holy Synod and the St.
Petersburg Slavic Benevolent Society sent by Nikolai Ponomarev, who served
as a priest at the Russian consulate's church in Sofia in 1879–1880. He was
convinced that without Russian direction the Bulgarian Church would not be
able to develop normally and purge itself of Protestant and Catholic "tumors"
that developed under "Turkish and Phanariote oppression."

The Bulgarian prelates were concerned only with their personal business
and politicking. Parish priests were almost illiterate. As a result, "gullible
Bulgarians" turned to Catholics and Protestants: "one has to wonder how on

---

125. Black, Cyril, *The Establishment of Constitutional Government in Bulgaria*
(Princeton: Princeton University Press, 1943), pp. 142–148; Jelavich, Charles, *Tsarist
Russia & Balkan Nationalism: Russian Influence in the Internal Affairs of Bulgaria & Serbia,
1879–1886* (Berkeley and Los Angeles: University of California Press, 1958), pp. 31–161.

126. RGVIA, f. 401-4/928-1881, Ekk to Obruchev, 28 September 1881, p. 1290b.

127. Ibid., pp. 1330b–134.

earth Orthodoxy survived at all on the Balkan Peninsula." Ponomarev apparently thought nothing of the Schism, as he personally taught all Sofia priests to officiate in the Russian style from June 1879 to October 1880 often in the presence of the Imperial High Commissioner Prince Dondukov-Korsakov. In Ponomarev's view, there should be Russian priests at all consulates and vice-consulates in Bulgaria to help renew the Bulgarian church.

With the same goal in mind, the Imperial High Commissioner set up two seminaries in the Turnovo and Samokov areas. But they were not quite up to the task because of inadequate staffing. According to Ponomarev, the Samokov seminary should be transferred to Kyustendil right across the administrative border in Ottoman Macedonia to benefit local priests there. The latter were just as ill-trained as in Bulgaria proper and were consequently powerless "to fight cunning Greeks who managed to take control of most churches and schools that used to belong to Bulgarians."

The main reform of the seminary education Ponomarev envisioned was "to run the two theological schools in exactly the same way as the Sofia military school, namely, with the Russian teaching staff and instruction in the Russian language." The most capable students should be able to continue their education in the Russian theological academies.[128]

But Ponomarev's pro-Bulgarian views did not find support in the new leadership of the Russian Church—Over-Procurator of the Holy Synod Konstantin Pobedonostsev (1880–1905). He attempted to decisively solve the Bulgarian Church Question. His predecessor, Count Dmitrii Tolstoy, and the majority opinion of the Pan-Slav-leaning Russian educated society blamed the Schism on Greek nationalist hardliners who allegedly took over the Patriarchate of Constantinople. But Pobedonostsev put the burden of responsibility squarely on the Bulgarian Exarchate and made friends with Filippov and other Russian supporters of the Patriarchate.[129]

He condemned the policy of the Bulgarian prelates aimed at establishing a Bulgarian "ethnic" hierarchy parallel to the existing network of the Patriarchate. He explained to the like-minded ambassador in Constantinople, "the regulation of the Ecumenical Councils banning the existence of two coreligionist bishops in the same city was not supposed to help maintain outward administrative order only but had a much deeper meaning touching on the dogma of church unity."[130]

---

128. GARF, f. 1099-1-790 (Copies of Ponomarev's letters, 1880), pp. 1–2.

129. Filippov to Pobedonostsev, 4 May 1881, *K. P. Pobedonostsev i ego korrespondenty*. Vol. 1 (Minsk: Harvest, 2003), p. 167.

130. AVPRI, f. 161/3-233-part 4, Pobedonostsev to Novikov, undated, pp. 2510–25120b.

The recipient of this letter was none other than Evgenii Novikov, who worked in the Russian embassy in Constantinople under Butenev and Lobanov-Rostovskii from 1856 to 1860 and as the chargé d'affaires from 1862–1864. Before his diplomatic career, he got a master's degree in Slavic studies and when in Constantinople he initially sympathized with Bulgarian nationalists. After his assignments in Athens and Vienna, he returned to Constantinople a changed man and promoted Pan-Orthodox views and policies there from 1879 to 1882.

As a pressure tactic, Over-Procurator Pobedonostsev refused to help the Bulgarian Church assert a greater role vis-à-vis the government of the autonomous Bulgarian Principality unless there was some progress in the Greek-Bulgarian reconciliation. He took issue with the fact that the statute of the Bulgarian Church had been drawn up solely by the Bulgarian government and, more fundamentally, that "the Bulgarian Church does not have canonical communion (*obshchenia*) with the Patriarchate of Constantinople." Pobedonostsev wrote to the acting Foreign Minister Nikolai Girs that Russian representatives had to make it clear to the Bulgarian Exarch that he needed to restore "the union and communion with the Ecumenical Patriarch."

The normalization of the canonical standing would give the Bulgarian Exarchate "that firm moral foundation" needed to resist the attack of the government on the church prerogatives in newly autonomous Bulgaria. Pobedonostsev saw the moment for reconciliation particularly appropriate because of the initiatives of Patriarch Joachim III (1878–1884) and Russian Ambassador Evgenii Novikov in that direction. The Bulgarian Exarchate was clearly on the wrong side and needed to follow their suggestions. Specifically, all members of the Holy Synod of the Russian Church unanimously believed that the uncanonical stay of the Bulgarian Exarch in the city under the undisputable jurisdiction of the Patriarch was a major irritant. The Exarch's move out of Constantinople would be the first step to reconciliation.[131]

The Exarch had no desire to move out of the Ottoman capital because it would greatly reduce his clout. His ambition was the main source of his disagreements with the Bulgarian government, which demanded greater accountability for the vast funds transferred to the Exarchate. He was angry at the attempts to turn the Exarchate into a passive tool of the Bulgarian Foreign Ministry. He refused to employ Bulgarian financial officers and to even provide a detailed account of expenditures. The Exarch had a point there—such documents, if revealed, could indeed have compromised his standing in the eyes of the Sublime Porte as a traitor to the Sultan. The Bulgarian bureaucrats

---

131. Ibid., Pobedonostsev to the Foreign Minister, 9 December 1880, pp. 25170b–25180b.

backed off when the Exarch threatened to shut down the Exarchate's schools. There was little room for financial transparency in the grand Bulgarian nationalist scheme of things.[132]

Vostok emphasized the negative role of Lukianov, Dondukov-Korsakov's successor as Russian Imperial Commissioner in Bulgaria. Although "totally incompetent in church matters," he coauthored with Stoilov, the leader of the Bulgarian Liberals, the uncanonical statute of the Bulgarian Church. Instead of church canons, it was ostensibly based on Article 62 of the Treaty of Berlin permitting freedom of worship and religious cults in autonomous Bulgaria and the rest of the Ottoman Empire.[133]

The Church in the Bulgarian Principality was proclaimed part of the jurisdiction of the Exarch seated in Constantinople. This statute clearly aimed at expanding Bulgarian influence through the Exarchate into Ottoman provinces of Thrace and Macedonia but met with the opposition of the more conservative and moderate Minister of Foreign and Ecclesiastical Affairs, Marko Balabanov. He insisted that if the Bulgarian Church functioned according to that statute, it could easily descend into chaos because the Exarch, dependent solely on the Sultan's *firman*, would be free to violate canons with impunity.

Balabanov was the spokesman of the most important metropolitans in autonomous Bulgaria—Kliment of Turnovo, Grigorii of Cherven, and Meletii of Sofia. It was clearly an example of the bureaucratic interbranch strife. Those prelates did not want the Exarch in the far-away Ottoman capital to tell them what to do on their own turf. However, the statute admirably suited the agenda of state-sponsored irredentism and went through the *Subranie* or Parliament of the Bulgarian Principality with the support of the Liberals like alleged "Papist" Tsankov and "atheist" Slaveikov, Karavelov, Chomakov, and Molov. Those lost souls fell for the trick masterminded by "Turkish" and "Jesuit" puppeteers to keep the Patriarchate and the Exarchate forever divided.[134]

The anti-Exarch stance of many prelates in Bulgaria proper dovetailed nicely with the effort of Patriarch Joachim III to lift the Schism. The requirements of the church canons would be met if the area of the Bulgarian Exarchate were confined to the political boundaries of the Bulgarian Principality.[135] The ensuing negotiations involving Exarch Iosif, the Bulgarian prelates, the

---

132. Exarch Iosif to the Bulgarian Foreign Ministry, 29 September 1884, Georgiev, Velichko, and Trifonov, Staiko, eds., *Exarkh Bulgarski Iosif I. Pisma i Dokladi*, p. 159.

133. *Vostok*, 19 (31 October 1879): 287–288.

134. Ibid.

135. *Vostok*, 20 (7 November 1879): 303.

German-born Bulgarian Prince Alexander Battenberg and Patriarch Joachim III collapsed in November 1879 on the disagreement over the territorial extension of the Exarchate into Ottoman provinces.[136]

Given the pro-Patriarchate stance of Pobedonostsev in the 1880s, the Pan-Orthodox intellectuals considered him one of their own supporters. Tertii Filippov, then Comptroller General, engaged Pobedonostsev in the specific cases of providing financial aid to the Patriarchate of Constantinople. In 1881, he asked the Over-Procurator to "unleash" former Ambassador Ignatiev (then Interior Minister) on Nikolai Bunge, the Minister of Finance, to secure a subsidy of 25,000 rubles. Filippov was sure that "Ignatiev would be pleased to at least partially atone for his grave sin against the Patriarchate and the whole Church." Filippov was hopeful that disbursing the subsidy would pave the way toward lifting the Bulgarian Schism. In addition to such specific policy decisions, Pobedonostsev habitually visited with Filippov, Leontiev, and Golitsyn (then publisher and co-editor together with Leontiev of *Varshavskii Dnevnik*) at Filippov's residence in St. Petersburg.[137]

Ambassador Novikov helped modify the terms of a new round of negotiations that sought to limit the authority of the Bulgarian Exarchate to autonomous Bulgaria and Eastern Rumelia, leaving Ottoman Macedonia and Thrace in the exclusive control of the Patriarchate. The latter, in its turn, needed to recognize "the national element in the church and schools." This compromise would lift the Schism and remove mutual hostility of rival church leaders.[138]

This formula was not simply a theoretical construct but was suggested in his discussions with Patriarch Joachim III and positive changes on the ground. Thus, Novikov learned from Kartsev, the Russian consul in Adrianople, that the Patriarchist archbishop Neophytos successfully promoted reintegration of Bulgarian and Greek communities by endorsing a locally preferred language of the liturgy and of school instruction. Neophytos had earlier been decorated with a medal by Russian occupation authorities when serving as the Archbishop of Philippoupolis in Eastern Rumelia.

In contrast, local Exarchist bishop Sinesii appeared as an extreme Bulgarian nationalist determined to preserve the independence of the Bulgarian church by appealing to Western support even at the price of "seceding from Orthodoxy" and alienating Russia. Kartsev asked Novikov to have Sinesii removed using his influence with the Sublime Porte or Bulgarian Exarch Iosif.

---

136. *Vostok*, 23 (29 November 1879): 350.

137. Filippov to Pobedonostsev, 4 May 1881, *K. P. Pobedonostsev i ego korrespondenty*. Vol. 1 (Minsk: Harvest, 2003), p. 167.

138. AVPRI, f. 151-482-3555/1, Novikov to Girs, 21 October 1881, p. 10.

Neophytos' local policy pointed to a more general and mutually acceptable model of reconciliation where a Greek archbishop and a Bulgarian bishop appointed by the Patriarch would represent their respective groups. In terms of spiritual hierarchy, the Greek prelate would be superior to his Bulgarian counterpart but the latter would have a free hand administratively.[139]

At that time, the Patriarchate's freedom of action was limited by its increasing dependence on subsidies from Greece. Joachim III begged Ambassador Kountouriotes to have the remainder of the annual 150,000 drachmas sent to the Patriarchate and even attached a budget to justify the expenses.[140] Despite that, Joachim III did not become a pawn of Greek foreign policy and managed to maneuver between the Porte, Greek, and Russian ambassadors. Joachim III refused to remove the ethnically Bulgarian Archbishop of Melenik whom Greek consular reports denounced as a Pan-Slav sympathizer, because "his pastoral activities give no evidence of this."[141] The Greek consuls in Ottoman Macedonia did not like the fact that Joachim III acted as the Patriarch of all Orthodox Christians, not just of ethnic Greeks. The Greek government had to accept his relatively independent stance because if they targeted only ethnic Greeks in their expansionist plans, their ambitions would be limited to the narrow Aegean coastline.[142]

The new Russian ambassador in Constantinople, Alexander Nelidov (1883–1897), attempted to contain Greek nationalism outside the Patriarchate and repeatedly counseled Patriarch Joachim III against accepting "the protection which Greece seeks to assume in his respect."[143] Alexander Nelidov confided in Filippov his personal views on the need to promote a more reconciliatory and Pan-Orthodox policy as the only way to disarm Greek hostility in the "Christian East" in 1880s. He opposed the policy of his subordinate V. F. Kozhevnikov, the Russian Consul in Jerusalem, who took the side of Arab Orthodox laity in their Bulgarian-style efforts to overthrow Greek hierarchy of the Patriarchate of Jerusalem. Probably to Filippov's thunderous applause, Nelidov argued that "in this for us there should be neither Scythian,

---

139. Ibid., f. 180-517/2-3242, Kartsev to Novikov, 20 January 1881, pp. 1490b–150.

140. Joachim III to Kountouriotes, 18 November 1880, Kardaras, Chrestos, ed., *He antiparathese: Ioakeim III-Charilaos Trikoupes: Apo ten anekdote allelographia tou Oikoumenikou Patriarche, 1878–1884* (Athens: Trohalia, 1998), pp. 99–100.

141. Joachim III to Kountouriotes, 16 June 1883, ibid., p. 193.

142. Paparrhegopoulos to Trikoupis, 20 May 1882, pp. 123–125; Joachim III to Kountouriotes, 16 June 1883, ibid., p. 193.

143. AVPRI, f. 151-482 (1880–1884)-3555/1, A. I. Nelidov to N. K. Girs, 1 December 1883, pp. 3–5.

nor Hellene, and we should by no means imitate some crazy Athenian politicians to reduce the interests of the Orthodox Church to the level of some
ethnic (*plemennoi*) rivalry between us and the Greeks whom we ourselves
have brought to national (*narodnoi*) life."[144]

The Russian Foreign Ministry was optimistic that after the explosion of
Russophobia in the 1870s "practically in all segments of the Greek society
over our moderate and impartial policy," the Ottoman Greeks were no longer
willing "to risk Russia's old friendship." Although the Russian policymakers
in St. Petersburg perceived the Patriarchate of Constantinople as the historical bedrock of Greek national interests, "we cannot refuse it our assistance
without undermining the significance of Russia as an Orthodox power and
without betraying our history."

Were Russia to oppose Greek national interests, it would strengthen the
pro-Western and anti-Russian ideology of "the extreme Greek nationalist
party" for the masses of the Greek people. As confirmed by Nelidov himself,
unlike their elites, they "preserve as sacred the feeling of gratitude towards
Russia" because "popular masses believe the concrete proof of the benevolence of the Imperial Government rather than the modern theories preached
by the ringleaders of Hellenism."[145]

With that in mind, in 1884, Nelidov helped defeat Ottoman attempts to incorporate the Patriarchate's courts into the Interior Ministry. If successful, that
measure would have greatly diminished the prestige of Patriarchate's prelates—
they would be subject to arrest and prosecution by regular Ottoman police and
courts. It would also deprive the Patriarchate of significant income coming
from the fees for adjudicating the cases pertaining to family law and inheritance.[146] In a desperate effort to reassert the Patriarchate's traditional autonomy,
Joachim III even sponsored the publication of the poster featuring Mehmet II
granting generous privileges to then-Patriarch Gennadios Scholarios following
the 1453 conquest of Constantinople (see Figure 5.5). To reach every possible
audience, the poster's legend is in French, Greek, and Ottoman Turkish.[147]

---

144. GARF, f. 1099-1-2252, A. I. Nelidov to T. I. Filippov, 29 December 1883, p. 50b.

145. Ibid., N. K. Girs to A. I. Nelidov, 19 December 1883, pp. 7–9.

146. Vovchenko, Denis, "Triumph of Orthodoxy in the Age of Nationalism: The
Ecumenical Patriarchate, the Sublime Porte, Russia, and Greece (1856–1890)," *Modern
Greek Studies Yearbook*, 28/29 (2012/2013): 261.

147. Joachim III asked the ethnically Greek Ottoman ambassador in London to reproduce
a book engraving as a poster on 25 June 1880, Joachim III to Konstantine Mousouros,
Kardaras, Chrestos, ed., *He antiparathese Ioakeim III-Charilaos Trikoupes: Apo ten anecdote
allelographia tou Oikoumenikou Patriarche, 1878–1884*, pp. 97–98.

FIGURE 5.5 "Mehmed II, the Conqueror of Constantinople, Officially Granting Church Privileges to Patriarch Gennadios in 1453" (c. 1880). Courtesy of the National Historical Museum (Athens, Greece). Poster catalog number 4948/130.

Fearful of antagonizing the "Greeks," Nelidov attempted to dissuade the Exarchate from demanding of the Ottoman government the issue of licenses (*berat*) for Bulgarian archbishops in Macedonia. At the same time, in a major effort at centralization the Sublime Porte launched an assault on Patriarchate's residual legal jurisdiction over its flock. Nelidov argued that Bulgarian policies made it easy for the Ottoman ministers to divide and manipulate Ottoman Christians. Unconvinced, Bulgarian Exarch Iosif turned to the British ambassador for leverage in dealing with the Ottoman government.[148]

Clearly, the fear of "losing" the Bulgarians to Russia's rivals increased as the uncertain situation continued into 1885, and Nelidov did what his Pan-Orthodox friend Filippov would have disapproved of. He urged Ottoman Foreign Minister Said Pasha to act on his promise of sending Bulgarian archbishops to Ohrid and Skopje. When Said Pasha referred to the opposition of the Patriarchate, Nelidov noted that "without touching on the canonical side of the problem" the Porte could invoke its *firman* of 1870 in accordance with

---

148. GARF, f. 1099-1-2252, a memo on the state of church affairs at the Patriarchate of Constantinople, 1884–1885, p. 320b.

which Bulgarian bishops were authorized to serve in the same localities even before the Russo-Turkish War of 1877–1878.[149]

Nelidov took the matter to the Sultan himself and sought to convince him that sending the Bulgarian bishops to those predominantly Slavic areas was the only way to deliver them from Catholic and Protestant propaganda because local populations would not recognize the prelates appointed by the Patriarchate.[150]

Nelidov was more willing than Novikov to consider ethnographic data and popular aspirations to strengthen Orthodoxy as he saw it. He did not see a danger of provoking an ethnic conflict in Ohrid and Skopje if the Ottoman government authorized the dispatch of Bulgarian Exarchist archbishops there. In those purely Slavic lands of northern Macedonia, even though there were Patriarchist metropolitans, there would be no ethnic conflict if the Exarchate were allowed to take root in that area. According to Nelidov, the locals generally supported the Bulgarian Exarchate's prelates, in whom they supposedly had found better community leaders and representatives in their dealings with local Ottoman authorities. Nelidov explained to Joachim IV his fear that Macedonian Slavs might switch to Catholicism to find Austrian protection if the Exarchist archbishops were not reappointed.[151]

In this instance, as Ignatiev had done in 1870 with the *firman* establishing the Bulgarian Exarchate, the Russian foreign policymakers again broke the principle of avoiding the intervention of the Ottoman government into the affairs of the Orthodox Church. But as earlier they were motivated not by the new sense of ethnic affinity with the Slavs but by Great Power rivalry and the age-old obsession with the religious Western Other.

Patriarch Joachim IV as the successor to Joachim III (1884–1887) continued to promote the solution developed under his predecessor as the only possible plan that could be reconciled with the canons of the Orthodox Church. Ecclesiastical autonomy could only follow political autonomy. Based on this principle, the Patriarchate was prepared to recognize the Bulgarian Church within the limits of autonomous Bulgaria and Eastern Rumelia. Joachim IV also agreed to appoint ethnically Bulgarian bishops in Ottoman Macedonia, to facilitate the use of Old Church Slavonic in the liturgy and of Bulgarian in community schools.[152]

---

149. Ibid., A. I. Nelidov to N. K. Girs, 7/19 February 1885, pp. 115ob–116.

150. Ibid., A. I. Nelidov to N. K. Girs, 12/24 February 1885, pp. 122ob–123.

151. AVPRI, f. 151-482-3555/2, Nelidov to Girs, 7 March 1885, p. 134.

152. AVPRI, f. 151-482-3555/2, Nelidov to Girs, 23 May 1885, pp. 141ob–142ob.

Following the orders from St. Petersburg, Nelidov tried to persuade Bulgarian Exarch Iosif to stop relying on the Ottoman government to extend the authority of the Bulgarian church in Macedonia. Echoing the reasoning of Foreign Minister Girs and Over-Procurator Pobedonostsev, Nelidov argued that its very existence would be uncertain if the Ottoman policy were to become pro-Greek. Since the 1870 decree of the Sultan remained the only foundation of the Bulgarian Exarchate, the latter was open to Catholic and Protestant influences, which could eventually divide the Bulgarian nation along sectarian lines. On the other hand, obtaining recognition of the Patriarchate would give the Exarchate a solid canonical basis in autonomous Bulgaria and Eastern Rumelia. With concessions from the Patriarchate, Bulgarians in Macedonia did not need to fear losing their ethnic identity either. But Exarch Iosif was convinced that this compromise would be unacceptable to Bulgarian prelates and nationalist activists.[153]

These expressions of Bulgarian independent policy annoyed not just the Russian diplomats but also the Russians, who occupied all key posts in liberated Bulgaria after the Russo-Turkish War of 1877–1878 until 1885. The Russian "advisers" would not allow Bulgarians to rise to positions of leadership, most notably in the military, because they firmly believed that on their own the Bulgarians were unable to run their military forces or to play any other leading role in the administration.[154] Only the Russian officers in charge of Bulgarian forces were supposedly able to maintain order in the autonomous Bulgarian-populated Ottoman province of Eastern Rumelia. The Russian military attaché in the province's capital of Philippoupolis (now Plovdiv), Colonel Ekk, objected to the removal of any Russian officers from the province's military forces. He believed that "the [Bulgarian] soldiers themselves love our officers more than their own officers. They see in them experienced caring leaders who both teach and spare them."[155] Ekk supported the view that the Bulgarians would always need Russian leadership in all areas of life.[156]

Having to play by the rules of the game of the European Concert and the Treaty of Berlin, the Russian government discouraged further Bulgarian expansion into other Balkan areas of the Ottoman Empire. This understandably bred discontent and resentment. By refusing to be led, the Bulgarians

---

153. AVPRI, f. 151-482-3555/2, Nelidov to Girs, 23 May 1885, pp. 145–146.

154. RGVIA, f. 401-4/928, 2 August 1881, p. 78ob.

155. Ibid., 24 August 1881, p. 86ob.

156. Ibid., 15 September 1881, p. 104.

were not playing the role assigned to them by the decades-long Pan-Slav propaganda and Russia's strategic interests in the area. This in turn made the Russians repeatedly accuse the Bulgarians of "ingratitude" and finally "abandon" them when the Bulgarian Principality embarked on independent foreign policy and annexed Eastern Rumelia in 1885.[157]

That action was a clear violation of the Treaty of Berlin. Its consequences included a danger of Bulgaria's conflict with the Ottoman Empire and the actual war in 1886 between Bulgaria and Austrian-backed Serbia that objected to Bulgarian expansion without territorial compensation for itself. The unfolding chaos deeply shocked Tsar Alexander III. A veteran of the recent Russo-Turkish War himself, he decided to sever relations with Bulgaria and recalled all Russian advisers.

The next goal of state-sponsored Bulgarian nationalist agitation was to use the Bulgarian church Exarchate to extend its influence in the remaining Ottoman Balkan provinces. This aggressive policy led to identical responses by Greece and Serbia, which tried to influence the Patriarchate of Constantinople to promote their own irredentist agendas.[158] The resulting rivalry in Ottoman Thrace and Macedonia greatly complicated the ongoing Russian efforts to lift the Schism and achieve a power-sharing institutional compromise between the Patriarchate and the Bulgarian Exarchate.

Conclusion

This chapter has attempted to explain the combination of traditional ideals and power considerations behind the Russian attitudes and policies in the buildup to the Russo-Turkish War as well as during the military occupation and domination of Bulgaria in 1877–1885. Although that war was justified as a latter-day Crusade, as during the Cretan Uprising, the Russian government's goal was not to erase the Sultan's realm off the map but to turn it into a federal structure with significant autonomy for predominantly Christian provinces. The Russian treatment of the "schismatic" Bulgarian clergy and the disputes over church property suggest that the Russian goal was not to create a homogenous Slavic Bulgarian nation but to defend embattled Orthodoxy.

Echoing Pan-Slav commentators, some lower-level Russian government agents on the ground saw the support for the Bulgarian Exarchate as the best means to achieve that messianic goal. But senior army commanders and

---

157. Jelavich, *Tsarist Russia and Balkan Nationalism*, p. 256.

158. Dialla, Ada, *He Rosia apenanti sta Valkania: Ideologia kai politike sto deutero miso tou 19ou aiona* (Athens: Alexandreia, 2009), pp. 301–306.

diplomats remained committed to reconciling rival churches through an institutional compromise that would also take into account the growing importance of ethnicity. It was to be based on limiting the Exarchate's authority to newly autonomous Bulgaria and Eastern Rumelia. But the Patriarchate would appoint Bulgarian bishops to the predominantly ethnic Bulgarian areas of the remaining Ottoman Balkan provinces. This arrangement would restore the unity of Ottoman Christians under a single spiritual leadership with significant cultural and administrative autonomy of constituent ethnic groups.

With the end of effective Russian military occupation in 1878, those goals were more difficult to accomplish. In the post-1878 period, the new leadership of the Russian Church under Pobedonostsev made common cause with the Pan-Orthodox commentators and cooperated more actively with the Foreign Ministry. Russian policymakers supported the solution suggested by the Patriarchate but did not break with the Bulgarian church movement. In addition to mediation between two parties, Russian officials pressured the Ottoman government, the newly established Bulgarian Principality, and the Bulgarian Exarchate to move toward a compromise. As in the previous periods, Russian influence was limited by the Bulgarian ability to appeal to or threaten to seek patronage of other Great Powers. During the next stage, the Russian diplomats would try among other steps to defuse this danger by closely cooperating with Austria-Hungary to internationalize the management of the growing conflict among Ottoman Christians.

6

Coping with State-Sponsored
Balkan Irredentism (1885–1914)

"THE BULGARIANS HAVE not shed a drop of their blood for their freedom and would still be Turkish *reaya* if the Russians, the Serbs, and Rumanians had not spilled their blood for them. What are those Bulgarians doing now? They are spreading their bloody propaganda against the Serbs, killing and burning priests and teachers only because they say that they are not Bulgarians but Serbs. And in this situation you are promoting an alliance with Bulgaria! Strange!"[1] This angry reply of a Serbian commentator to a Russian general and a leading Pan-Slav organizer showed how vicious the struggle for the hearts and minds of Orthodox peasants in Ottoman Macedonia had become by 1900.

The incorporation of Eastern Rumelia in 1885 and the victory over Serbia the following year had greatly strengthened the brand new Bulgarian nation-state. Its next goal was to use the Bulgarian Exarchate to extend its influence in the remaining Ottoman Balkan provinces through schools, charities, and churches. But the Exarchist school teachers and even prelates would often get involved in armed nationalist bands. This expansion would make Greek and Serbian nationalist activists respond in kind. Their governments tried to influence the Patriarchate of Constantinople to promote their own irredentist agendas and invested into their own networks of education, trade, and violence. The ensuing rivalry in Ottoman Thrace and Macedonia clearly demonstrated the lack of Slavic brotherhood and strengthened Pan-Orthodox criticism of ethnonationalism. By their intense even frenetic

---

1. Dragutin Ilich to Artemii Cherep-Spiridovich, 20 December 1901, Drakul, Simon, ed., *Makedonia mezu avtonomiata i delezot: Sbornik ruska diplomatska dokumentatsiia* (Kumanovo: Prosveta, 1995), pp. 301–302.

meddling, Bulgaria, Greece, Serbia, and eventually Romania greatly complicated the ongoing Russian efforts to lift the Schism of 1872 and achieve a power-sharing institutional compromise between the Patriarchate and the Bulgarian Exarchate.

The Russian containment policy now had to include putting more pressure on Balkan nation-states to cooperate in reconciling all the parties involved. When the prospects of this potential Balkan federation looked particularly bleak, Russian policymakers would seek the support of the other Great Powers to reduce their regional competition and impose stabilizing reforms on the Sublime Porte. But the international commitment to peace was gradually evaporating as the deadly jigsaw puzzle of interlocking alliances was coming together to produce the Great War. The Young Turk Revolution also changed the status quo when it introduced parliamentary politics and greatly accelerated centralization efforts. As a result, the Ottoman government quickly lost its proven ability to play off the Christian groups against each other. Unwittingly, the Young Turks helped bring together traditionally divided non-Turkish minorities and even hopelessly fractious Balkan nation-states on its doorstep. The Balkan Wars started in 1912 as a Crusade ending five hundred years of Ottoman presence in Europe, but in 1913 they degenerated into an ethnic war of all against all.

The Internationalization of the Containment of Violent Irredentism (1885–1908)

After the war with Serbia and break with Russia in 1885–1886, the Bulgarian Principality was isolated from the international community and even from its own church. Its young prince, Alexander Battenberg, had to step down under Russian pressure in 1886 after the annexation of Eastern Rumelia. The widowed Bulgarian government was in the hands of the former nationalist revolutionary Stefan Stambolov. After several rejections, in 1887 he found another foreign aristocrat willing to become a constitutional monarch of Bulgaria in spite of the disapproval and even anger of the House of Romanov. Austrian-born Ferdinand of Saxe-Coburg-Gotha was endowed at birth with blood ties to most European dynasties and with political talents that would later earn him a very telling nickname: "the Fox."

He was well placed to lead Bulgaria "back" into Europe. But while Alexander III was on the throne, indignant Russia stood in the way of Ferdinand's international recognition. Even Abdulhamid II ignored his vassal. To add insult to injury, from 1887 to 1888, key metropolitans in Bulgaria proper also defied Ferdinand by not mentioning him as their ruler during the liturgy. Led by

Kliment of Turnovo, they eulogized Mother Russia and publicly denounced Ferdinand as an illegitimate foreigner and a Catholic infiltrator. Stambolov unleashed police on them but only the intervention of Exarch Iosif from Constantinople ended the impasse.[2]

Stambolov's ruthlessness soon earned him the sobriquet of "the Balkan Bismarck." In fact, he was even less tolerant than his German counterpart of the political opposition. The best-known Bulgarian novel, *Bay Ganyo* by Aleko Konstantinov, vividly captures the atmosphere of corruption and police brutality generously applied to rig elections. A pro-government candidate called police to the polling station, "They killed me, officer, they wanted to kill me. When I shouted 'Long live the Prince!', they attacked me with knives." Using whips and sabers, the gendarmes removed opposition leaders and the member of Stambolov's party was able to run unopposed. The Bulgarians on the receiving end of those blows remembered the savage Ottoman reprisals in the aftermath of the April Uprising of 1876.[3]

Why did the Exarch eventually choose to side with unsavory Stambolov and his dubious Catholic prince? He risked incurring Russian displeasure but he lost hope of ever winning consistent Russian support for the Exarchate in the aftermath of Bulgarian unilateral annexation of Eastern Rumelia in 1885–1886. Tellingly, he perceived Russian Pan-Orthodox backing of the Patriarchate in purely ethnic terms: "the Russian Embassy in Constantinople will always oppose sending Bulgarian prelates to Macedonia and will be siding with the Greeks." The Sultan would be trapped between Bulgarian ambitions, Russian pro-Greek policy, and Austrian support for Serbia. To tip the balance, Exarch Iosif urged the Bulgarian statesmen to make a strong statement protesting discrimination and persecution of ethnic Bulgarians in Ottoman provinces.[4]

Stambolov managed to raise the popularity of his government by scoring a foreign policy success. As in Greece, irredentism was indeed a great idea that helped distract attention from domestic problems. The *berats* for Exarchist metropolitans of Ohrid, Skopje, and Veles had been pending since 1885 in spite of the Russian ambassador's intervention before the Porte. In 1890, Stambolov finally secured their issue with Austrian and German backing, which shows how small regional states can manipulate the Great Powers

---

2. Perry, Duncan, *Stefan Stambolov and the Emergence of Modern Bulgaria, 1870–1895* (Durham: Duke University Press, 1993), pp. 150–151.

3. Konstantinov, Aleko, *Bay Ganyo*, trans. N. Simakova (Moscow: Pravda, 1988), p. 117.

4. Exarch Iosif to Kliment of Turnovo, 26 July 1886, Georgiev, Velichko, and Trifonov, Staiko, eds., *Ekzarkh Bulgarski Iosif I. Pisma i Dokladi* (Sofia: Klub '90, 1994), p. 168.

to their advantage.[5] In the end, however, the Sublime Porte handed out only two *berats* (for Ohrid and Skopje).[6]

The issue of the Bulgarian *berats* went hand in hand with the renewed Ottoman centralization drive aimed at stripping the Patriarchate of its remaining jurisdiction over family law, canon law, clerical privileges, and parish schools. Throughout the 1880s, Greece and Russia worked together to derail Abdulhamid II's project of fully incorporating *Rum milleti* into the civic Ottoman nation. By 1890, under pressure from all sides, the Sultan gave up and restored the status quo.[7]

In the meantime, Bulgarian Prime Minister Stambolov continued to pursue a pro-Ottoman policy of reducing Russian influence and discouraging insurrections in Thrace and Macedonia. In addition to two long-disputed and -delayed appointments, the Exarchate secured at least the benevolent neutrality of the Porte to promote new Bulgarian-language schools and Old Church Slavonic liturgy across Macedonia and Thrace. In the late 1880s, around 150 communities switched from the Patriarchate to the Bulgarian Exarchate as far south as in the Thessaloniki area.[8]

Despite that, in 1891, the Patriarchate hesitated to promote Slavic liturgy among "Bulgarian-speaking Orthodox" in the ethnically mixed areas of Southern Macedonia. Local archbishops did not have a clear sense of established policies and procedures in that important cultural issue.[9] While they waited, Bulgarian activists seized local churches and schools, sometimes assaulting the Patriarchate's teachers, as in the village of Nevolia in the diocese of Moglena. In such cases, local Ottoman authorities stayed aloof and the Patriarchate had to petition the Interior Ministry in the capital to order its subordinates to restore order.[10] In contrast, in northern Macedonia, the

---

5. Hering, Gunnar, "Der Konflikt des Oekumenischen Patriarchats und des Bulgarischen Exarchats mit der Pforte, 1890," in *Nostos: Gesammelte Schrifte zur suedeuropaeischen Geschichte* (Frankfurt am Mein: Peter Lang, 1995), pp. 315–316.

6. Gerd, Lora, "Rossiia i greko-bolgarskii tserkovnyi vopros v 80–90-e gody XIX veka," *Konstantinopol i Peterburg: Tserkovnaia politika Rossii na Pravoslavnom Vostoke (1878–1898)* (Moscow: Indrik, 2006), p. 273.

7. Vovchenko, Denis, "Triumph of Orthodoxy in the Age of Nationalism: The Ecumenical Patriarchate, the Sublime Porte, Russia, and Greece (1856–1890)," *Modern Greek Studies Yearbook*, 28/29 (2012/2013): 255–266.

8. Poulton, Hugh, *Who Are the Macedonians?* (Bloomington: Indiana University Press, 1995), p. 51.

9. The Patriarchate to the Archbishop of Thessaloniki, 28 March 1891, The Archive of the Ecumenical Patriarchate, A 61, pp. 120–121, Number 1434.

10. The Patriarchate to the Archbishop of Moglena, 31 January 1892, ibid., A 62, pp. 25–26, Number 361.

Patriarchate favored Slavic-language education. In 1892, the Patriarchate took pride in having secured the issue of the Sublime Porte's orders to reopen a Slavic school in Kosovo.[11]

With the wind in his sails, Exarch Iosif rejected a peace overture from Patriarch Neophytos VIII in 1893. His terms were quite generous—the Patriarchate would not only recognize the Exarchate within the borders of Bulgaria but would also allow it to appoint bishops to the dioceses in Ottoman Macedonia and Thrace with Exarchist majorities. Exarch Iosif declined the offer, because in many areas most ethnic "Bulgarians" were not yet patriotic or even conscious of their national belonging.[12] Iosif's intransigence nipped in the bud several other initiatives sponsored by both the Patriarchate and the Russian embassy in Constantinople.[13]

Having sown the wind, the Exarch began to reap storm in 1894. In a panic-stricken letter to the Bulgarian Foreign Minister, he feared the loss of 35,000 "Bulgarian" households to the Serbs who had taken over the educational system of the Archbishopric of Skopje. Patriarchate's Archbishop Maximos appointed an ethnically Serb suffragan with several assistants. The Serbs enjoyed the support of the Greek and Russian consuls to infiltrate other northern Macedonian dioceses where they installed Serb teachers through the Patriarchate. To counteract Serbian efforts, the Exarch requested the Bulgarian government to provide additional funds and to pressure the Sublime Porte "to stop favoring the foreign propaganda aimed at dividing and stealing our coethnic and coreligionist Bulgarian population in Skopje or elsewhere."[14]

In addition to the new challenge of Bulgarian irredentism, the Patriarchate, Serbia, and Russia never lost sight of the old enemy. As a "brotherly" gesture, the Serb Church published the Serb translation of the Patriarchate's "anti-Papal" encyclical in response to the Catholic pamphlet entitled "Filioque and Orthodoxy."[15] An act of God also brought together the Greeks and the Slavs. When the earthquake destroyed the Theological School on the island of Halki, the Patriarchate asked Ambassadors Alexander Nelidov and Vladan

---

11. The Patriarchate to the Archbishop of Skopje, 4 March 1892, ibid., A 62, p. 65, Number 109.

12. Gerd, "Rossiia i greko-bolgarskii tserkovnyi vopros v 80–90-e gody XIX veka," p. 282.

13. Ibid., pp. 294–297.

14. Exarch Iosif to the Bulgarian Foreign Minister, 27 October 1894, Georgiev, Velichko, Trifonov, Staiko, eds., Ekzarkh Bulgarski Iosif I. Pisma i Dokladi, pp. 171–172.

15. The Patriarchate to Archbishop Mikhail of Serbia, 16 May 1896, The Archive of the Ecumenical Patriarchate, A65, p. 185, Number 2758.

Georgievich to encourage the flow of donations from Russia and Serbia to rebuild the Patriarchate's main clergy-training institution.[16]

The Patriarchate, however, maintained a distance from the Serbs in northern Macedonia—the Divine Liturgy in the Skopje cathedral would continue to be celebrated in both Greek and Slavonic (from the right and left galleries, respectively) in the name of peace and unity among the Orthodox Christians.[17] When the archbishop of Rashko-Prizren Dionysios began to use Serbian in his correspondence, he was sharply reminded that Greek was the official language in all dioceses under Patriarchate's jurisdiction. Writing in Greek had never been a problem for Dionysios in the past, not least because of his education at the Halki Theological School.[18]

As another blow to the Bulgarian Exarchate, the Patriarchate discouraged the main Macedonian monastery (of St. John the Baptist in Serres) from sending their holy relics to "schismatic villages." At the same time, the abbot should allow any pilgrims to the shrine to venerate the remains of famous saints.[19] It is not hard to see the logic of that decision. If excluded from the age-old local cult, the supporters of the Exarchate would perhaps understand the horror of separation from the Mother Church.

The school rivalry in particular led to a generation of urban Christian Macedonians uprooted from the traditionally mixed local Ottoman milieu and raised with their minds set not on Istanbul but on Sofia, Athens, and Belgrade. Ethnocentric education explained numerous brawls between students who would later be attracted to the Romantic notion of fighting for a nationalist cause.[20]

Violence became more systematic and even systemic with the formation of the Internal Macedonian Revolutionary Organization (IMRO) in 1893. The leaders of this conspiratorial group were mostly impoverished schoolteachers employed by the Exarchate who had lost faith in its ability to satisfy their worldly ambitions and to significantly improve the situation

---

16. The Patriarchate to Ambassadors Nelidov and Georgievich, 19 July 1894, ibid., A 65, pp. 214–215, Number 3741.

17. The Patriarchate to the Archbishop of Skopje, 13 April 1896, ibid., A67, p. 128, Number 1857.

18. The Patriarchate to the Archbishop of Rashko-Prizren, 1 May 1897, ibid., A69, p. 102, Number 1671.

19. The Patriarchate to the Abbot of the St. John the Baptist Monastery in Serres, 11 November 1894, ibid., A 65, p. 336, Number 5272.

20. Lory, Bernard, "Schools for the Destruction of Society: School Propaganda in Bitola, 1860–1912," *Conflicting Loyalties in the Balkans: The Great Powers, the Ottoman Empire, and Nation-Building* (London and New York: I. B. Tauris, 2011), pp. 57–62.

of common Macedonian Christians. Communal autonomy within the Exarchate could give the South Slav peasants cultural rights and more control over the amount of church dues and fees than the Patriarchate. But they were still exploited by mostly Muslim landlords, tax farmers, and abusive Ottoman officials. Despite the pent-up social discontent, most peasants were understandably afraid or unwilling to join a Bulgarian nationalist uprising or a Christian rebellion. The IMRO activists typically used or threatened to use force to secure their cooperation or monetary contributions for the cause.[21]

The goal of the IMRO was to more or less replicate the situation of the Eastern Crisis of 1875–1878—to gain territorial autonomy for Macedonia by sparking a revolt, provoking Ottoman reprisals, making headlines to sway European public opinion, and inviting Great Power intervention. The choice of autonomy over annexation to Bulgaria was supposed to attract all discontented elements including Patriarchist Slavs, Greeks, and Muslims. The slogan of "Macedonia for Macedonians!" was also expected to prevent partition of the province by rival Balkan stats.[22]

The Cretan Uprising of 1896–1897 showed that the Eastern Crisis scenario was still realistic. Figure 6.1 captures the public mood in Greece at the time. Interestingly, it does not include any references to Orthodox Christianity. The slain Ottoman soldier with the Islamic crescent was defeated apparently not by the forces of the Cross but by pagan Greek gods. In the distance, Zeus' thunderbolt scattered the fleeing Ottoman troops. Hermes is flying a banner, which reads "Long Live the Union of Crete with Greece!" Goddess Athena in full armor is sad because she cannot intervene. Crete is represented as a lady with broken chains wearing a classical tunic in the midst of picturesque classical ruins covered with the names of famous ancient Greeks like Homer and of contemporary rebel heroes on a separate stele.

Unlike the uprising of 1866–1869, the 1897 rebellion on Crete led to the Greco-Turkish War, where the Sick Man of Europe unexpectedly thrashed the Greek army on the mainland and occupied Thessaly ceded to Greece following the Treaty of Berlin. Greece's defeat caused the intervention of the Great Powers—Abdulhamid II had to evacuate Thessaly and increase Cretan autonomy (see Map 6.1).

---

21. Perry, Duncan, *Politics of Terror: The Macedonian Liberation Movements, 1893–1903* (Durham: Duke University Press, 1988), pp. 146–148, 190; Poulton, *Who Are the Macedonians?*, p. 53.

22. Aarbakke, Vemund, *Ethnic Rivalry and the Quest for Macedonia, 1870–1913* (Boulder: East European Monographs, 2003), p. 97.

Η ΚΡΗΤΗ ΘΡΑΥΟΥΣΑ ΤΑ ΔΕΣΜΑ ΤΗΣ ΔΟΥΛΕΙΑΣ

FIGURE 6.1 "Crete Breaking the Chains of Slavery," published by G. Gavriotopoulos and G. Konstantinides, c. 1897. Courtesy of the National Historical Museum (Athens, Greece). Poster catalog number 4949/18.

Although often seen as "ungrateful" in Russian eyes, Greece was repeatedly able to request and receive substantial Russian support, especially in 1897, "when only the powerful word of our August Monarch had stopped the victorious march of the Sultan's army" on Athens and gave the island of Crete into the hands of the Greek prince under nominal Ottoman control and strong European tutelage. The decades of inconsistent Pan-Slav agitation had

BALKAN STATES

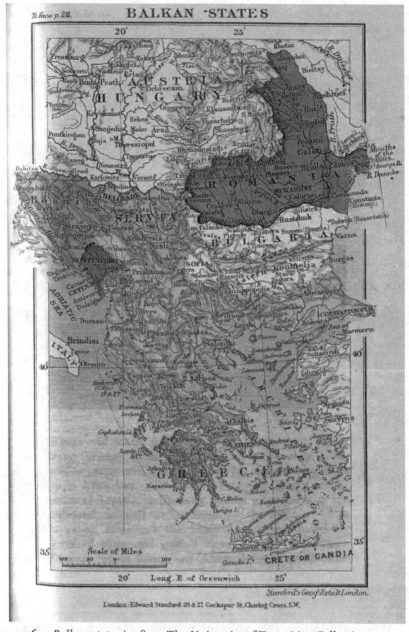

MAP 6.1 Balkan states in 1899. The University of Texas Map Collection.
http://www.lib.utexas.edu/maps/historical/balkan_states_1899.jpg

failed to turn Greece and the Patriarchate of Constantinople into Russian enemies. Just like other Balkan Christian groups, they were perceived as unreliable but still eligible participants of the traditional Russian patronage game. But as had been the case throughout the 1800s, Russia's main goal was not to indulge its Balkan clients but to prevent the partition of the Ottoman Empire for fear of instability that a drastic redrawing of the map would create in the Balkans and Europe as a whole.[23]

Pan-Orthodox activists like Nikolai Durnovo and the Russian Holy Synod in the press and from church pulpits called for donations for the benefit of suffering Orthodox Christians in Thessaly and Epirus affected by the hostilities of the Greco-Turkish War of 1897. The Patriarchate gratefully acknowledged the receipt of eight sets of priestly vestments that Durnovo had sent to help restore damaged churches.[24] The Russian Holy Synod sent from its budget 4,000 silver rubles for the purchase of liturgical wares and another 4,000 for distribution among the destitute. More funds were expected to come after Metropolitan Palladii of St. Petersburg authorized the collection of private contributions at Russian parishes.[25]

Although Greece snatched so many benefits out of the jaws of defeat, the humiliation of the 1897 war still produced a cultural crisis and even a malaise. Some intellectuals rejected seven decades of independent statehood as a failed imitation of ancient Hellas and of modern Western Europe. One of them, Ion Dragoumis, envisioned a new Greek civilization dominating the Balkans and mediating between East and West.[26] However, such non-Western alternatives never clearly articulated sophisticated theories and political agendas as in Russia.[27]

Greek nationalists were also worried by the greater assertiveness and aggressiveness of Bulgarian irredentism that came with the end of Stambolov's pro-Ottoman policy. By 1894, Prince Ferdinand was tired of being a European facade for his dictatorial Prime Minister Stambolov and helped organize

---

23. Russian Imperial Foreign Policy Archive (AVPRI), f. 151-482-3532, pp. 122–1220b, Secret Instruction to the Ambassador in Athens Baron Rosen, 5 August 1901.

24. The Patriarchate to Nikolai Durnovo, 4 November 1897, The Archive of the Ecumenical Patriarchate, A 69, pp. 352–353, Number 5748.

25. The Patriarchate to Ambassador Zinoviev, 21 January 1898, ibid., A 70, pp. 26–27, Number 411.

26. Augustinos, Gerasimos, *Consciousness and History: Nationalist Critics of Greek Society, 1897–1914* (Boulder: East European Quarterly; Distributed by Columbia University Press, New York, 1977), p. 115.

27. Exertzoglou, Haris, "Metaphors of Change: 'Tradition' and the East/West Discourse in the Late Ottoman Empire," in Frangoudaki, Anna, and Kedyer, Caglar, eds., *Ways*

his demise. A year later, Stambolov was brutally murdered by embittered Macedonian Slavic immigrants in Sofia, who considered Stambolov's pro-Ottoman policies as a betrayal of his Christian and national duty. In contrast to the IMRO, this bloodthirsty Macedonian lobby, also known as the Supreme Macedonian Committee (or the External Organization), advocated not autonomy for their home province but its outright annexation to Bulgaria. After Stambolov's assassination, they often demanded and received government support for their raids into Ottoman Macedonia in the form of money, arms, and army officers who trained and led the guerrillas across the border.[28]

Those freedom fighters were creating problems for the Exarchate. Using their "Byzantine skills," the Patriarchate's prelates had long tried to portray all ethnic Bulgarians as traitors to His Majesty the Sultan. Now they accused the Bulgarian Exarchate of being in cahoots with the Bulgarian nationalist bands. They encouraged the "Greco-maniac" Slavic villages in the Serres diocese to send petitions where the voices of the people drove that same point to the Ottoman authorities. In an official rebuttal, the Exarch naturally denied any connection to the bands and pointed out that it was not just Greeks and Turks but also ethnic Bulgarians who were victims of brigandage. But in the confidential letter to Sofia, the Exarch begged the Bulgarian Foreign Ministry to rein in the bands "who undoubtedly have their center in Sofia" and jeopardize many years of systematic work for the Bulgarian cause.[29]

A spoiled child of Mother Russia between 1878 and 1885, Bulgaria soon learned too well how to survive and prosper in a dangerous Balkan neighborhood. It is not surprising that Russian disillusionment with unredeemed Slavic brethren continued apace. To capitalize on those currents, the Greek ambassador in St. Petersburg suggested that his government should "cultivate our Orthodox bond to the great Northern Empire" to obtain Russian support for achieving Greek national interests. This Pan-Orthodox policy would not compromise Greece before the other Great Powers but like nothing else would increase Greek influence in Russia, "especially on the people."[30] Mavrokordatos also registered a marked decline in pro-Bulgarian sympathies

---

to Modernity: Encounters with Europe, 1850–1950 (London and New York: I. B. Tauris, 2007), p. 53.

28. Crampton, Richard, Bulgaria, 1878–1918: A History (Boulder: East European Monographs; Distributed by Columbia University Press, New York, 1983), pp. 158, 291.

29. Exarch Iosif to the Bulgarian Foreign Minister, 17 November 1900, Georgiev, Velichko, Trifonov, Staiko, eds., Ekzarkh Bulgarski Iosif I. Pisma i Dokladi, pp. 193–194.

30. Greek Archive for History and Literature (ELIA), collection 494 (Harilaos Trikoupes), folder 6, p.10b, Nikolaos Mavrokordatos to Harilaos Trikoupis, 5 July 1888.

in the Russian educated society, where "Bulgarians would never gain the same favor as before despite all the efforts of some fanatical Slavophiles."[31]

The forceful removal of the anti-Russian Prime Minister Stefan Stambolov coincided with the natural death of his august enemy Alexander III in 1894. The normal relations between two countries were restored in 1895 but "Russian attitudes on religious issues, primarily on the need to end the Schism, were far from welcome" among the leaders of the Bulgarian Principality and the Bulgarian Exarchate.[32] At Russia's insistence, Prince Ferdinand had his first-born son Boris chrysmated by Exarch Iosif in February 1896. After his birth in 1894, he had been baptized according to Catholic rites, which many Russians interpreted as a threat to Orthodoxy in Bulgaria.[33]

But when the Bulgarian delegation was invited to Moscow to attend the coronation of Nicholas II in 1896, the Russian diplomats excluded any Exarchist prelates to avoid irritating the representatives of the Eastern patriarchates who would be in the altar part of the cathedral during the ceremony.[34] Over-Procurator Konstantin Pobedonostsev summed up the attitude of the Russian Holy Synod at this point. By 1896, the Russian Church under his leadership continued to recognize the Bulgarian Schism of 1872: "to avoid a church conflict with the Greeks we do not allow the Bulgarian clergy to openly officiate with ours." Although the Russian Church secretly supplied the Bulgarian Exarchate with the Holy Myrrh, Pobedonostsev was opposed to any further rapprochement with the Bulgarian Church, fearing that the Russian government and the Holy Synod might get implicated in "all that turmoil, confusion, disorder going on in Bulgaria, Macedonia, and Serbia."[35]

Indeed, the report of Archbishop Panaretos of Strumica detailed some of the terror tactics the Bulgarian bands used to scare the ethnically undecided Slavic villagers into joining the Bulgarian Exarchate and to eliminate Patriarchist priests and prominent lay activists. The murders were sometimes preceded by long, savage torture sessions, as had been allegedly the case with Stephanos, the seventy-year-old priest from Myraftsa, the Gevgeli district. "The beasts in human form" doused him with kerosene and burned him

31. Ibid., N. Mavrokordatos to H.Trikoupes, 11/23 May 1888, p. 17b.

32. Crampton, *Bulgaria, 1878–1918*, p. 238.

33. Gerd, "Rossiia i greko-bolgarskii tserkovnyi vopros v 80-90-e gody XIX veka," pp. 289–291.

34. AVPRI, f. 192-527-30, p. 5, Lobanov-Rostovskii to Foreign Ministry, 10 April 1896.

35. State Archive of the Russian Federation (GARF), f. 543-1-623, pp. 5–6, Pobedonostsev's memorandum, 28 January 1896.

alive. His daughter-in-law had been told not to send her children to the Greek-language school. The inaction of the authorities was clear from the behavior of the deputy district governor (*muavin*). An Armenian Christian himself, he had been sent to Myraftsa to inspect the relations between the Exarchists and the Patriarchists. He spent the night of the murder in the home of the local Exarchist priest, entertained by the Exarchist teacher, who played some musical instrument for them.[36] According to Archbishop Ambrosios of Prespa-Pelagoneia (Monastir), many Orthodox and Muslim victims of "Bulgarian robber-rebels (*listandartes*)" were mutilated: "beheadings, gouged eyes, female bodies pierced with stakes, cut limbs, noses and male sex organs."[37]

The Balkans were clearly earning their notoriety as the powder keg of Europe, "the land of terror, fire, and sword." Nationalistic bands and common brigands were hard to tell apart, especially when both kidnapped Western travelers and missionaries for ransom.[38] The Great Powers observed with great concern how church and school rivalry among Greece, Serbia, and Bulgaria in Ottoman Macedonia rapidly spiraled into armed clashes between nationalist bands.[39] It was common knowledge that in the 1890s and the 1900s the Bulgarian and other Balkan governments more or less actively supported those bands.[40] In 1897, Russia and Austria-Hungary came to an agreement on the need to contain that turmoil in European Turkey so that "the Balkans should be kept on ice as long as possible."[41] Russia was happy to stop competing with the Habsburgs over influence there, because Tsar Nicholas II was embarking on an adventurous policy in the Far East that would lead to the disastrous war with Japan in 1904–1905.

Now Bulgarian nationalists could not easily play off Austria against Russia as they used to with the pro-Catholic Union blackmail. Instead, they came up with a trick to exploit Russia's desire to lift the Schism. But the ambassador in Constantinople, Ivan Zinoviev, saw through it when the chairman of the

---

36. Panaretos of Strumica to Joachim III, 11 December 1899, *Episima Engrafa Peri Tis En Makedonia Odyniras Katastaseos* (Thessaloniki: Kyriakidi, 1993, orig. 1906), pp. 21–25.

37. Ambrosios of Prespa-Pelagoneia (Monastir/Bitola) to Joachim III, 2 April 1903, ibid., p. 26.

38. Todorova, Maria, *Imagining the Balkans* (New York: Oxford University Press, 2009), p. 117.

39. Crampton, Richard, *Bulgaria, 1878–1918: A History* (Boulder: East European Monographs; Distributed by Columbia University Press, New York, 1983), p. 291.

40. Ibid., p. 232.

41. Ibid., p. 276.

Bulgarian Holy Synod, Metropolitan of Sofia Grigorii, put forward the initiative to reconcile the Bulgarian Exarchate with the Patriarchate.

In June 1898, Grigorii approached the Russian Consul General in Sofia Bakhmetev and promised to have Exarch Iosif recognize the supremacy of the Patriarch and move out of Constantinople to Ohrid. He was confident about the success of his project if Russia managed to secure the issue of two *berats* already promised by the Porte to Bulgarian bishops in the Macedonian dioceses of Polyani and Melenik.[42] Writing to his superiors in St. Petersburg, Zinoviev exposed Grigorii as an opportunist always siding with the powers that be. As the Metropolitan of Rushchuk, he prayed for Ottoman victory in the Russo-Turkish War of 1877–1878 and later sided with the anti-Russian party in liberated Bulgaria.

As Zinoviev saw it, "the Bulgarians" treated the Bulgarian Church Question as strictly political. Unable to secure desirable concessions from the Patriarch, "the Bulgarians themselves provoked the Schism to consolidate their influence in the expectation of the collapse of Turkey." If they secured the dioceses of Melenik and Polyani, "the area of the Bulgarian Exarchate would engulf the whole of Macedonia and coincide with the borders of Bulgaria of the Treaty of San Stefano—the aspiration of all Bulgarian patriots without exception." For the Bulgarians generally and Metropolitan Grigorii specifically, the reconciliation with the Patriarchate was secondary to the fulfillment of their national interests. Zinoviev argued that it was not in Russian interests to strip the already humiliated "Ecumenical Church" of the two dioceses it needed both for its prestige and for its material sustenance. Rather, the Patriarchate needed "our care and our moral as well as our material support."[43]

The Russian Foreign Minister and Tsar Nicholas II himself agreed with Zinoviev's skepticism of the sincerity of Grigorii's reconciliation project. They similarly believed that for its protagonists, the Bulgarian Church Question turned into an issue of "political ethnography." Thus, Russia would not help the Bulgarian nationalists to snatch two dioceses away from the Patriarchate and would instead continue to assist it.[44] The assumption underlying these criticisms of less-than-perfect coreligionists was the messianic self-image of Russia as the stalwart defender of true Orthodoxy.

Exarch Iosif's refusal to reach even a minimal accommodation with Serb nationalist aspirations was another irritant for Russian diplomats. From the

---

42. AVPRI, f. 151-482-3595, pp. 1–20b, A. N. Bakhmetev to I. A. Zinoviev, 23 June 1898.

43. Ibid., pp. 4–8, I. A. Zinoviev to the Foreign Ministry, 2/14 July 1898.

44. Ibid., pp. 90b–11, Foreign Minister to I. A. Zinoviev, 17 July 1898.

1890s, Belgrade had been working through the Patriarchate to appoint ethnically Serb bishops, priests, and teachers to help convince Macedonian Slavs that they were Serbs rather than Bulgarians. While denouncing the violence of Bulgarian nationalist bands, the Exarchate and the Bulgarian government predicted turmoil and bloodshed in reaction to the appointment of the ethnically Serbian Firmilian as the Archbishop of Skopje. Already uncomfortable about that veiled threat, Ambassador Zinoviev had to stop Exarch Iosif when he added that there were almost no Serbs in that city. "According to our data, there are 200 Serb families in Skopje and you can't deny the Patriarchate the right to appoint to a vacant post a prelate capable of communicating to the flock in their native language."

The agreement the Exarch was ready to make with the Serbs seemed totally unacceptable—there would be Slavic unity and brotherhood if the Serbs concentrated only on "Old Serbia" (Kosovo). In exasperation, Zinoviev ended the conversation, prophetically warning the Exarch, "The Bulgarians are too ambitious. I am afraid that in the future the Bulgarians will come to regret their excessive claims."[45]

To secure the cooperation of the Patriarchate with the Russian Pan-Orthodox policy, the embassy continued to use financial incentives—the conditional grant of 1,000 Ottoman pounds a year.[46] Not only did the Patriarchate appoint Firmilian to Skopje but it also gave the green light to the use of Old Church Slavonic and even reprimanded Archbishop Anthimos of Ohrid, who opposed it. At the same time, the Patriarchate was not ready to elevate this kind of practice into a general principle to discourage the resurgence of Albanian and Kutso-Vlach identity politics.[47] Abdulhamid II also promised to no longer block the appointment of Firmilian to Skopje when the danger of Bulgarian-sponsored turmoil was over. This delay displeased Ambassador Zinoviev: "since Turkey owes stability in Macedonia to our influence, I made it clear to the Sultan that I did not approve of this decision made without us being consulted about the issue in which we have a keen interest."[48]

In addition to Bulgarian double game, an increasingly active role of Serbia in the competition for the hearts and minds of Macedonian Slavs also cautioned Russian policymakers against sponsoring its traditional policy of

---

45. AVPRI, f. 151-482-3532, pp. 40b–50b, Zinoviev to the Foreign Minister, 9/22 January 1901.

46. Ibid., p. 160b, Lamzdorf to Zinoviev, 3 April 1901.

47. Ibid., p. 138, Zinoviev to Lamzdorf, 20 September/3 October 1901.

48. Ibid., pp. 32–320b, Zinoviev to the Foreign Minister, 27 March 1901.

reconciliation between the Bulgarian Exarchate and the Patriarchate around 1900. If they made "a deal" on territorial delimitation, the Patriarchate would recall its bishops from some disputed dioceses like Ohrid and Skopje. This limited agreement would still fall short of lifting the Schism, "would damage the integrity of the Church," and "would push the Serbs away from the Ecumenical Patriarchate." If the Patriarchate abandoned northern Macedonia to the Exarchate, then Serbia might organize a splinter pro-Serbian Orthodox community and pressure the Porte to recognize it on the model of the Bulgarian Exarchate itself. In that case, the Russian goal of Orthodox unity would not be achieved. Zinoviev managed to convince Patriarch Joachim III, just reelected for his second term in office (1901–1912), not to agree to any such plan.[49]

Even if any similar agreement with the Exarchate were adopted, militant Bulgarian irredentist factions were unlikely to accept any line separating them from any sizable coethnic population. After the abortive 1902 uprising, Prime Minister Danev made it more difficult to cross the border, officially closed all Macedonian committees, exiled many Macedonians into interior areas, and replaced War Minister Paprikov. The opposition immediately accused Danev's cabinet of being unpatriotic Russian stooges and threatened to assassinate Prince Ferdinand, who was interested in someone more loyal to him personally and more effective at dealing with the noisy nationalistic lobby. The new Prime Minister started "direct negotiations with Turkey doomed from the beginning" according to a Russian military analyst. Now the Bulgarian government could blame the Ottomans and stopped trying to control Macedonian freedom fighters on this side of the border.[50]

The Russian policymakers would have been overjoyed had they had a modicum of control over Balkan state and nonstate actors attributed to them in the popular American humor magazine *Puck*. Figure 6.2 features a racialized Russian man manipulating two fighting Orientalized puppets representing Bulgaria and Macedonia. Three more well-armed puppets on the wall are identified as "Roumelia, Servia, and Roumania." According to the caption, the Russian policy in the Balkans had not changed since Peter the Great.

Given the escalation of violence and the well-honed Balkan skills of playing the European embassies off against each other, all Great Powers increasingly felt the need to avoid something like the Eastern Crisis of 1875–1878. The Russian-Austrian joint project of legal and financial reform in Macedonia was presented to the Sultan after the approval by the ambassadors of England,

49. Ibid., 1180b, Zinoviev to the Foreign Minister, 6/19 July 1901.

50. RGVIA, f. 400-4-300, pp. 102–103, General-Major Protopopov, "A Brief Report on the Uprising in Macedonia," 22 September 1903.

FIGURE 6.2 "At Present He Works Bulgaria," by Udo J. Keppler (*Puck*, 1903). Library of Congress Prints and Photographs Division, Reproduction Number: LC-DIG-ppmsca-25783.

France, Germany, and Italy. Abdulhamid II could not go against united Europe but resorted to vintage Ottoman half-measures and delaying tactics. Thus, he created the new office of Inspector General of three Macedonian provinces of Thessaloniki, Kosovo, and Bitola (Monastir). But the other reforms remained on paper—half of the judicial and administrative offices to be reserved for Christians and abolition of hateful tax farming in favor of communal tax collection.[51]

To justify more pressure on the Sultan, the Russian Foreign Ministry subsequently published selected consular reports where the crisis in Macedonia appeared due not to the rivalry of various Balkan Christian nation-states but to the deeply ingrained anti-Christian policies and attitudes of the local Muslim population and Ottoman authorities. For example, Pot Aksentievich and Tacho Parafestich in Kosovo were badly beaten by some Muslims when the former had become a court member and the latter had applied to join the gendarmerie.[52]

The last major anti-Ottoman Christian uprising in the Balkans happened on Ilinden or St. Elijah's Day in August 1903 and gave the international community a sense of urgency to localize another dreaded explosion of the powder keg of Europe. Foreign diplomats took note of extensive preparations for the uprising coordinated from Bulgaria since January 1903. All Macedonians in Bulgaria were forced to contribute twenty francs or more to support the rebel groups. The Russian military attaché in Sofia also reported that the Ottoman government opened the border for them to provoke a premature uprising to have a legal pretext "to exterminate the unruly Bulgarians."[53]

Early in 1903, the French ambassador observed the change in the Exarch's views. Whereas he previously saw schools as the best way to advance the Bulgarian nation, now in a private conversation he praised the "courage" of rebellious acts. Although in public Iosif preached submission to the Sultan, the Exarchist communities were certainly getting ready for another insurrection.[54]

According to an Austrian vice-consul, Prince Ferdinand himself appointed the new Bulgarian trade representative in Bitola (Monastir). He took over the existing terrorist revolutionary network to prepare a revolt in Macedonia and its annexation to Bulgaria.[55] The Austrian Consul General in Thessaloniki did not see any revolutionary potential among Macedonian villagers. As before,

51. Isaeva, Olga, "Murzshtegskii opyt 'umirotvoreniia' Makedonii," in Grishina, Rita, ed., *Makedoniia: Problem istorii i kultury* (Moscow: Institut slavianovedeniia RAN, 1999), pp. 80–81.

52. Shcherbina to the Foreign Ministry, 3 February 1903, *Reformy v Makedonii, 1903–1905* (St. Petersburg: Russian Foreign Ministry, 1906), p.17.

53. RGVIA, f. 400-4-300, p. 53, Protopopov to the General Staff, 25 August 1903.

54. Constans to Delcasse, 7 January 1903, Chotzidis, Angelos et al., eds., *The Events of 1903 in Macedonia as Presented in European Diplomatic Correspondence* (Thessaloniki: Museum of the Macedonian Struggle, 1993), pp. 27–28.

55. Stepski to Goluchowski, 10 January 1903, ibid., pp. 28–29.

they did not subscribe to any high ideals and lent their support to Bulgarian-based bands only under pressure. Thus, many Patriarchists had to join the Exarchate and farmers of all religious and ethnic stripes had to deliver food to the hideouts in the mountains.[56]

In the fall of 1903, when the devastation of the Ilinden Uprising was still unfolding, Tsar Nicholas II visited King and Kaiser Franz Josef at the Styrian ski resort Muerzsteg. While the emperors were enjoying the scenery from a hunting lodge, their foreign ministers worked on a joint initiative of more extensive reforms for Macedonia but short of its separation from the Sultan. Although widespread discontent with administrative abuses especially among Christians seemed important, the chief cause of instability was now seen in the activities of the nationalist guerrillas. In addition to improving security generally, the main goal of the reforms was to prevent rivalry over the ethnic loyalties of the Macedonian Christians specifically.

One Austrian and one Russian representative, known as the Civil Agents, would chaperone the newly appointed Ottoman Inspector General Huseyn Hilmi Pasha around Macedonia, keeping an eye on everything and reporting back to their governments. European officers would be assigned to specific districts to train and control the Ottoman gendarmerie. The administrative boundaries would be changed to better suit ethnographic realities on the ground. More Christians would be admitted into administration. Over two hundred Christian villages that had been burned during the suppression of the Ilinden revolt would be tax exempt for one year. The Porte also had to agree to any reforms jointly proposed by the Powers in the future.

Abdulhamid II very reluctantly accepted this clear violation of his sovereignty rights under pressure from all the signatories of the Treaty of Berlin. Most of them (England, France, Germany, Austria, and Italy) had already been running Sultan's finances since 1881 through the Ottoman Public Debt Administration. Building on that experience, in late 1905, all the Powers set up the Financial Commission to partially rationalize taxation by eliminating tax farmers and to find revenue for the reforms. However, the salaries of European officers sent to Macedonia were paid by their home countries.[57]

According to the Austrian consul in Bitola, while "the Bulgarian circles" welcomed the appointment of the Austrian Civil Agent von Mueller, they were alarmed by the choice of Russian Civil Agent Demerik. In his tenure as the consul in Bitola, "he had showed little sympathy to them and is considered

---

56. Hickel to Goluchowski, 21 February 1903, ibid., pp. 37–38.

57. Lange-Akhund, Nadine, *The Macedonian Question, 1893–1908, from Western Sources* (Boulder: East European Monographs, 1998), pp. 148–200.

here to be an extreme Serbo- and Greco-phile."[58] But von Mueller was initially quite satisfied with the results of his cooperation with Demerik.

They made it clear to the Exarchist and Patriarchist spokesmen that the Great Powers would not allow their movements to develop. Coupled with reasonable concessions, "this cold treatment had a desirable effect"—violence decreased. Both Civil Agents and Hilmi Pasha agreed that the best solution in most cases would be to liberally grant Bulgarian requests for new church construction. Von Mueller suspected that "as a rule it seems that trigger-happy individuals are more interested in taking churches from 'the others' rather than in having one for themselves."[59]

The Muerzsteg reforms had a very noticeable positive impact at the beginning. The amnesty allowed many thousands of refugees to return to their homes or whatever was left of them. With a clearer chain of command, formal training, and higher wages, the Ottoman rural police became more efficient and respected. While the Great Powers managed to more or less hide their differences for a while, regional competition for influence in Macedonia increased. In part, it was fueled by the initial Russian-Austrian proposal to create more ethnically homogenous districts. Bulgaria, Greece, and Serbia rushed to stake more and more areas as their own.[60]

The earliest indication of where the best peace-keeping intentions were leading came in July of 1904, when Greek Foreign Minister Romanos shared with the Russian ambassador the reports of some Greek consuls. "In view of the coming ethnic-based population census," several Macedonian Bulgarian bands began to terrorize Patriarchist communities to force them to switch to the Exarchate. Romanos did not have reasons to suspect any direct involvement of the Bulgarian government. Seven such bands operated in the Thessaloniki province and four more were in the Kastoria district of the Monastir vilayet. The largest one had 150 men but most had 40 or less.[61]

As assassinations of prominent Patriarchist notables continued to terrorize their communities into joining the Exarchate and the noble cause of Macedonian liberation, the Greek diplomats urged the Porte to provide for the security of Orthodox Christians because vital Ottoman interests would suffer

---

58. Consul in Bitola to the Austrian Foreign Ministry, 21 December 1903, Bridge, F. R., ed., *Austro-Hungarian Documents Relating to the Macedonian Struggle, 1896–1912* (Thessaloniki: Institute for Balkan Studies, 1976), p. 115.

59. Von Mueller to the Foreign Ministry, 29 April 1904, ibid., pp. 132–133.

60. Isaeva, "Murzstegskii opyt," p. 9.

61. AVPRI, f. 151-482-3544, p. 36, Shcherbachev to the Foreign Ministry, 9 July 1904.

greatly "if they continued to become Bulgarians."[62] In spite of the skepticism of European diplomats, the European press and charities did what the rebels expected them to do and provided sympathetic coverage of the Ilinden Uprising and relief to Christian Slavs. This growing support for the Bulgarian movement led the Greek government to send army officers to reinforce less than impressive ranks of its own Robin Hoods in Macedonia in order to paralyze pro-Bulgarian bands.[63]

The core of the IMRO tried to keep a distance from predatory neighboring nation-states and sought to rely on local funding sources. In addition to more or less voluntary contributions of Macedonian farmers, the IMRO leaders extorted protection money from prominent businessmen of any ethnic background. Thus, Dimko Sarvanov wrote to six merchants with Slavic, Greek, and Muslim names demanding 200 Ottoman pounds for the security of their shops and employees.[64] Some IMRO fighters under Yane Sandanski remained committed to the idea of Macedonian autonomy within the Ottoman Empire and opposed outright incorporation into Bulgaria. That "left-wing" faction was open to negotiation and collaboration with the conspiratorial circles of the so-called Young Turks, who had plotted to overthrow the autocratic Sultan Abdulhamid II and to establish a more liberal regime.[65]

The Macedonian Question soured the normally cordial relations between Patriarch Joachim III and Ambassador Zinoviev, who "made clear the indecency of the escapade in the Patriarchate's official publication" (*Ecclesiastiki Aletheia*). It published a milder version of the report from Archbishop Stephanos of Vodena, who accused two locally stationed Russian officers of encouraging defections to the Exarchate and condoning targeted killings of Patriarchist notables by Bulgarian bands. To Zinoviev, the Greeks were spitefully scapegoating the Russian officers for something no one could control: "the gradual emancipation of the Slavic ethnicities of the Balkan

---

62. Evgeniadis to Rallis, 24 November 1903, Karabati, Persefoni et al., eds., *Aparhes tou Makedonikou Agona (1903–1904): 100 Engrafa apo to Ypourgeio ton Eksoterekon tes Elladas* (Thessaloniki: Mouseio Makedonikou Agonos, 1996), pp. 109–110.

63. Papoulas and Kolokotronis to the Bitola consulate, 23 April 1904, ibid., pp. 158–159.

64. Dimkos Sarvanov to Tomtson, Sifkon, Koltson, Ivan Yiontse, Tosion, Alet, 1907, Karabati, Persefoni, et al., eds., *I Televtaia fasi tis enoplis anametrisis sti Makedonia (1907–1908): 100 Engrafa apo to Ypourgeio ton Eksoterekon tes Elladas* (Thessaloniki: Mouseio Makedonikou Agonos, 1998), pp. 67–68.

65. Hacisalihoglu, Mehmet, "The Young Turk Policy in Macedonia: Cause of the Balkan Wars?" in Yavuz, M. Hakan, and Blumi, Isa, eds., *War and Nationalism: The Balkan Wars, 1912–1913, and Their Sociopolitical Implications* (Salt Lake City: University of Utah Press, 2013), pp. 104–105.

Peninsula was going to deal a death blow to the Greek ambitions of dominating Macedonia."[66]

In reaction to this controversy, on Zinoviev's recommendation, the Russian Foreign Ministry stopped disbursing the hefty annual subsidy of 1,000 Ottoman pounds from 1904 to 1909 to discourage "Patriarchate's policy towards non-Greek populations of the Orthodox East." In particular, the Russian embassy became increasingly dissatisfied by the treatment of the Romanian-speaking Kutso-Vlachs who had not been allowed to use their language in schools and churches.[67] Even the Patriarchate's legitimate protests against the persecution of the Greek Orthodox in Bulgaria in 1906 did not receive much Russian support. Joachim III's memo to all Great Powers explained the growing activity of the Greek bands in Macedonia as a self-defense against the predations of the Bulgarian bands. The Patriarch "failed to mention that the Greek bands are raging not just against the Bulgarian population but are just as vicious towards the Vlachs who had never taken up arms."[68]

The Russian officers reported about the Ottoman support for Greek bands as a counterweight to the IMRO. At least in 1905, this policy proved effective as it forced Bulgarian rebel groups to stop their activities. The Sublime Porte used force during the census to encourage the Exarchists to register as the Patriarchists not because it wanted to see any Christian group in the position of dominance but to keep all of them divided. As a weaker group, the Greeks were propped up. For the same crimes, they were tried by regular courts whereas the Bulgarians were tried in harsher extraordinary tribunals. According to a Russian inspector, the Muerzsteg reforms of gendarmerie did not protect the Christian population from the abuses of Ottoman authorities because they had not affected administrative and judicial structures.[69]

The defeat of the Bulgarian insurgency provoked quite a bit of agonizing soul-searching among Bulgarian leaders. Exarch Iosif could compare the persecution of Bulgarians only to the Armenian Massacres of 1894–1896. Ten years earlier, he foresaw and warned about this tragic outcome when the evolutionary cultural development had been interrupted and absorbed by the

---

66. AVPRI, f. 151-482-3544, pp. 113–117, Zinoviev to the Foreign Ministry, 16/29 October 1904.

67. AVPRI, f. 151-482-3549, pp. 6–60b, Zinoviev to the Foreign Ministry, 10/23 February 1907.

68. AVPRI, f. 151-482-3548, pp. 26–27, Svechin to the Foreign Ministry, 22 August/4 September 1906.

69. RGVIA, f. 450-1-124, pp. 700b–720b, Lieutenant Colonel Alekseev to the General Staff, 14 October 1905.

new revolutionary trend. Twenty more years of unimpeded Exarchate's work would have united Ottoman Bulgarians and would have crystallized their national identity to successfully assert their rights before the Sultan. While the Greeks, the Serbs, and the Romanians looked to one national center, changing Bulgarian cabinets and conflicting factions made any concerted policy impossible. Not only did the rebels fail to achieve autonomy for Macedonia but their actions led to the closure of many Bulgarian schools and churches. Bulgarian priests and teachers were forbidden to do their jobs. Bulgarian communities could not switch to the Exarchate and fell victim to the predations of Ottoman soldiers, Turks, and Albanians as well as of Serb and Greek bands. If Bulgaria was not going to intervene militarily to stop the extermination of its 1.5 million coethnics, it should announce its peaceful intentions and encourage Macedonian Bulgarians to fully participate in the European-sponsored reforms.[70]

In addition to the supervision and training of the Ottoman rural police by European officers, from 1906 Austria-Hungary and Russia developed a reform of the judicial system, which did not encroach on sharia courts but institutionalized a form of dual control of Ottoman civil courts. Based in Thessaloniki, both Austrian and Russian Civil Agents acted as a supreme oversight body and demanded information on any case from Ottoman legal officials of any level. Below the two Civil Agents were legal inspectors on the ground. The reform had not been fully implemented because the Great Powers broke their ranks in 1907. Germany and Austria-Hungary dropped the project after securing railroad concessions from the Sultan. Austria's effective withdrawal from the Muerzsteg system and the planned construction of the line from Sarajevo to Thessaloniki was widely seen as the beginning of a new policy aimed at annexing Macedonia as had happened with Bosnia-Herzegovina in 1878.[71]

Austria-Hungary's Foreign Minister Aehrenthal officially announced the railroad agreement in January 1908. It was assumed to have included the tacit understanding that Austria-Hungary would not insist on the full implementation of the Muerzsteg reform. The Russian press denounced Austrian duplicity since Russia had not been consulted. Both liberal and conservative publications urged the Russian government to consider the Muerzsteg program abrogated and to conclude a formal agreement on the Balkans with

70. Exarch Iosif to the Bulgarian Foreign Minister, *Bulgarski Iosif I. Pisma i Dokladi*, pp. 221–224.

71. Zaitsev, Victor, "Russia, Austria, and the Problem of Legal Reform in Macedonia in 1907," *Balkan Studies*, 36, 1 (1995): 31–37.

its French and British allies.[72] Outwardly, the Muerzsteg program continued in the spring of 1908 when the Russian and Austrian Civil Agents still accompanied Inspector General Hilmi Pasha as he traveled to Macedonian hot spots, listened to complaints of assembled notables, and received copies of their petitions.[73]

According to the Greek diplomats, Hilmi Pasha was able to "exploit the agendas of foreign organizers." He could typically count on the support of two Civil Agents and other European representatives when he proposed measures against those "who disturbed public order but in fact he encouraged Islamic fanaticism." His goal was to weaken the well-organized politically moderate Patriarchist communities. "The Ottomans began to arm themselves buying revolvers and munitions" while the number of murdered Christians was rising.[74]

Although the Muerzsteg reforms were supposed to prevent another Eastern Crisis and a very likely disintegration of the Ottoman Empire, its statesmen understandably saw them as an unwelcome outside intervention. The modest success of streamlining local administration was more than compensated by the spike in externally sponsored violence. One key part of the Muerzsteg program was deeply flawed. The idea of sorting out mixed populations based on modern ethnic categories was the product of the naïve modern bureaucratic mindset. This prospect invited intervention from Bulgaria, Greece, Serbia, and even Rumania to forcibly awaken their village cousins with traditional local and religious loyalties. Once this dynamic was under way, the Great Powers spent most of the time overcoming the effects of their own ill-conceived policy.

Still, it was probably the last time the Concert of Europe actually achieved anything. Its divisions and rivalries in the area were temporarily put on hold, which clearly benefited Russia before and during its war with Japan (1904–1905). European cooperation in the Muerzsteg program is all the more amazing at the time when the abyss between the Triple Entente and the Triple Alliance was rapidly growing.[75]

---

72. Bestuzhev, Igor', *Borba v Rossii po voprosam vneshnei politiki, 1906–1910* (Moscow: Academy of Sciences of the USSR, 1961), pp. 188–189.

73. A. Saktouris to the Foreign Ministry, 13 May 1908, *I Televtaia fasi tis enoplis anametrisis sti Makedonia (1907–1908)* , p. 235.

74. S. Polyhroniadis to the Foreign Ministry, 22 June 1908, ibid., p. 240.

75. Sowards, Steven, *Austria's Policy of Macedonian Reform* (Boulder: East European Monographs, 1989), p. 1; Rybachenok, I. S., "Poslednii bastion. V. N. Lamzdorf i Myurtsshtegskoie soglashenie 1903 goda," in Ignatiev, A. V. et al., eds., *Rossiiskaia diplomatiia v portretakh* (Moscow: Mezhdunarodnyie otnosheniia, 1992), p. 299.

European intervention was one of the main reasons for the so-called Young Turk Revolution, which in its turn led to the official end of the ambitious Muerzsteg program. The military coup d'état of 1908 started in Macedonia among Ottoman army officers who envied better-paid foreign inspectors and resented European control as clear proof of their homeland's weakness and backwardness. Their deep frustration explains many fatal steps in the radical modernization of the Ottoman Empire launched by the Young Turks.

Exorcising Ethnonationalism out of Pan-Slavism into Pan-Turkism, 1885–1908

The 1886 break between the "ungrateful" Bulgarian Principality and Russia led to the growth of negative attitudes to Bulgarian nationalism in the Russian educated society. The leading Pan-Slavs were worried by the tendency among both liberals and conservatives voiced by Prince Meshcherskii to forget about the Balkan problems and focus on domestic development. Professor Lamanskii reminded his readers that the "Eastern Slavic Question" had emerged long before the Turkish conquest of Constantinople at the time of Charlemagne when the Popes began to claim authority over the whole Church.[76]

For Pan-Orthodox commentators, it was an "I-told-you-so" moment. Nikolai Durnovo had warned about the danger of Bulgarian godlessness in his Vostok (1879–1886). In the 1890 collection of his articles, he did not think that Russia should leave its Balkan coreligionists to their fate. To fulfill its destiny, Russia had to ally itself with Greece, Serbia, and Romania, who had proved their right to Ottoman inheritance. In contrast, the Bulgarians cowardly stayed away from both the Russo-Turkish wars and the anti-Ottoman uprisings started by their neighbors. From a historical or an ethnographic viewpoint, Bulgaria had no legitimate claim on Macedonia and Thrace. Instead, those lands should belong to Serbia and Greece. If Russia helped Greece take control of Constantinople and the Straits, then the Greek navy would enable Russia to keep England out of the Eastern Mediterranean.[77]

Patriarch Constantine V praised Durnovo's Tserkovnyie Voprosy, where he defended the Patriarchate's supranational mission against those who accused

---

76. Lamanskii, Vladimir, "The Eastern Slavic Question," *Izvestiia Sankt-Peterburgskogo Slavianskogo Blagotvoritelnogo Obshchestva*, 9 (September 1887): 433–434.

77. Durnovo, Nikolai, *Gosudarstva i narody Balkanskogo poluostrova, ikh proshedsheie, na-toiashcheie i budushcheie, i bolgarskaia krivda* (Moscow: E. Lissner & Iu. Roman, 1890), pp. 1–2.

the Patriarchate of promoting only Greek interests.[78] Indeed, some Russian Pan-Slav commentators continued to describe Ottoman Bulgarians as victims of Greek-Phanariote oppression as before 1886. According to the Russian-educated Bulgarian journalist, whenever a Bulgarian priest tried to celebrate the Divine Liturgy in Old Church Slavonic, the Patriarchate allegedly reported him to the Ottoman authorities as a troublemaker and a Russian spy.[79]

But the post-1886 Russian mainstream was less willing to accept at face value the narrative of Bulgarian victimization by their Greek prelates. The same magazine reported about the festivities in Kiev in honor of the memory of Photios, the Patriarch of Constantinople in 857–867 and 877–886. He was respected in Bulgaria and Russia as the teacher of SS. Cyril and Methodius, who brought the Gospel to the Slavs.[80] Photios's relevance was highlighted by Ivan Pal'mov, the leading scholar of Slavic church history and a professor at the St. Petersburg Theological Academy. On 25 November 1890, he explained to the members of the city hall and of the St. Petersburg Slavic Benevolent Society that Patriarch Photios had helped convert Bulgarian King Boris to Christianity, thereby bridging the political gap between Byzantium and Bulgaria." The need to lift the ongoing Schism called for the spirit of Orthodoxy rather than of "pan-Bulgarianism or pan-Hellenism."[81]

While the image of the Patriarchate was improving, the Russian perceptions of their Bulgarian cousins deteriorated. At least one letter to the editor of the organ of the St. Petersburg Slavic Benevolent Society criticized the Bulgarians for treating Russia as "the milch cow." By violating the authority of the Patriarchate of Constantinople, the Bulgarians also became Protestant and Catholic agents.[82]

An anonymous Czech Pan-Slav chose that critical moment to encourage his Russian cousins to rethink the role of religion. He argued that national revival was the main reason why the South Slavs had parted ways with Russia in the mid-1880s. The pursuit of national happiness over anything else was

---

78. Constantine V to Durnovo, 30 July 1897, the Archive of the Ecumenical Patriarchate, A69, pp. 229–230, Number 3744.

79. Bobchev, Stefan, "Pis'ma o Makedonii i Makedonskom voprose," *Slavianskiie Izvestiia*, 27 (2 July 1889): 665.

80. "Chestvovanie pamiati Fotiia, Sviatogo Konstantinopol'skogo Patriarkha, 6 fevralia 1891 v Kieve," *Slavianskiie Izvestiie* 7 (17 February 1891): 107.

81. Pal'mov, Ivan, "Tsaregradskii Patriarkh Fotii i ego otnosheniie k sovremennomu emu slavianstvu," *Slavianskiie Izvestiia*, 13 (31 March 1891): 232–233.

82. Srutkovich, P., "Pismo k redaktoru," ibid., 12 (December 1887): 543–544.

due to Western rationalist secular influence. Thus, the decline of religious consciousness was "one of the main obstacles to the unification of Slavs and Russia." In the post-Christian context, Slavic solidarity was possible only on the basis of mutual support toward achieving national goals of individual Slavic nations.

The editor of the major Pan-Slav periodical, K. N. Bestuzhev-Riumin, took the hint but defended the traditions of Russian Pan-Slavism. He reminded that the early Slavophiles did not wish to impose Orthodox Christianity or Russian language on the Slavs. They also emphasized "the ethnographic foundation" on which to build Slavic unity. However, Bestuzhev did not agree with his Czech counterpart that Russian Pan-Slavs should emphasize ethnic affinity over religion. In his analysis of the situation, the main cause of the infighting among the Slavs and their hostility to Russia was not in the Slavic masses but rather in their power-seeking Westernized political elites. Although some of them studied in Russia, they too belonged to "the cosmopolites of the modern type for whom faith is an old prejudice and politicking is the peak of human wisdom."[83]

The same publication of the main Russian Pan-Slav society promoted a union of Orthodox churches, proposed by the Serbian newspaper *Dnevni List* as "the first step towards the creation of a Balkan Federation." Each of the Balkan churches would send one cleric and one layperson. That board would have its sessions preferably on Mt. Athos and chaired by the Patriarch of Constantinople.[84] Another article in the same issue saw more building blocks of "a Balkan confederation" in the growing number of student exchanges and political contacts between Balkan countries. The Greek champions of a Balkan federation had been publishing a journal in French to better spread their ideas. Former Greek Prime Minister Harilaos Trikoupis discussed them during his tour of Balkan capitals, where he met with an enthusiastic reception. "Such societies are opening in all Serbian cities."[85]

In his memoirs of the last Russo-Turkish war, General G. I. Bobrikov cautioned against excluding Bulgaria from a future Balkan federation. Russia should "coordinate" its political development and reduce mutual antagonism through concessions by all sides. In fact, this kind of policy was Russia's "historic obligation" as "the strongest Orthodox power, the leading

---

83. Bestuzhev-Ryumin, Konstantin, "Ot Redaktora," *Izvestiia Sankt-Peterburgskogo Slavianskogo Blagotvoritelnogo Obshestva*, 11 (1886): 499–507.

84. "Soiuz balkanskikh tserkvei," *Izvestiia Sankt-Peterburgskogo Slavianskogo Blagotvoritelnogo Obshchestva*, 24 (16 June 1891): 427.

85. Geris-v, "Balkanskaia Konfederatsiia," ibid., p. 423.

member of the Slavic family, and the representative of Eastern culture inherited from Byzantium."[86]

After 1886, some Pan-Slavs found a middle ground between religious and
ethnic sources of unity by embracing the idea of the Greco-Slavic world first
put forward by Professor Lamanskii in 1858. Anton Budilovich was a professor of Russian and Slavic studies at the University of Warsaw—the center of
attempted Russification of Poles, Byelorussians, and Ukrainians in the western provinces. In 1875, he warned about the dangers to "the Slavic element"
in Central and Southeastern Europe. In his list of the enemies of Slavdom,
shared Orthodoxy apparently did not make any difference: "Nowadays any
alien (*inorodets*) lords it over the Slav: be it the German, there the Magyar, or
the Rumanian, or the Italian, or the Greek, or the Turk, or the Jew."[87]

Budilovich's change of attitude toward the Greeks and Orthodoxy came as
a result of Filippov's influence. In a letter to Leontiev, Filippov took pride in
having convinced one of those "one-sided but smart Slav-lovers" "to acknowledge my views on the Greek-Bulgarian conflict."[88] As the editor and founder of
Slavianskoie Obozrenie, in 1892 Budilovich vigorously promoted closer unity of
the nations of the Greco-Slavic cultural type in the very midst of the mainstream
Russian Pan-Slav scholarly community. An important part of this agenda was
his advocacy of convening the Ecumenical Council of all Orthodox churches
as a solution to the Bulgarian Church Question. In this Pan-Orthodox project,
Professor Budilovich found inspiration in Filippov's publications.[89] But unlike
Filippov, he urged the Patriarchate to accept the accomplished fact of the independence of the Bulgarian Church and assigned the responsibility for the Schism
not only to Westernized Bulgarian nationalists but also to the Patriarchate.[90]

Politically, Budilovich promoted the concept of the Greco-Slavic cultural-
historical type to help stop internecine violence in Ottoman Macedonia. In
journal articles and separate pamphlets, he argued in favor of autonomy
rather than partition for that province as the birthplace of the civilization
founded by SS. Cyril and Methodius, the ninth-century sainted brothers and

---

86. Bobrikov, G. I., *V Serbii: Iz vospominanii o voine 1877–1878 godov* (St. Petersburg: St. Petersburg Military District Publications, 1891), pp. 179–180.

87. Budilovich, Anton, "O sovremennom polozhenii i vzaimnykh otnosheniiakh Slavian zapadnykh i iuzhnykh," in Strakhov, Nikolai, ed., *Slavianskii Sbornik*, vol. 1 (St. Petersburg: Second Department of His Majesty's Chancellery, 1875), pp. 593–595.

88. Russian State Archive for Literature and Art (RGALI), f. 290, op. 1, d.53, p. 3, T. I. Filippov to K. N. Leontiev, 3 October 1887.

89. GARF, f. 1099-1-1500, p. 37, A. S. Budilovich to T. I. Filippov, 17 March 1892.

90. Budilovich, Anton, "Letopis," *Slavianskoie Obozrenie*, 1, 2 (1892): 221.

Byzantine missionaries from Thessaloniki. Budilovich urged their feuding Greek and Slavic spiritual descendants to find reconciliation in the shared homeland and to serve as a model for a greater future Greco-Slavic union.[91]

In 1891, the same *Slavianskoie Obozrenie* started by Anton Budilovich saw the first publication of Professor Lamanskii's seminal article "Three Worlds of the Asian-European Continent" (*Tri Mira Aziisko-Evropeiskogo Materika*). Lamanskii used his earlier ideas of the Greco-Slavic world as the center-piece of proto-Eurasianism, which directly inspired Petr Savitskii's mani-festo of 1921.[92] Budilovich's successor as the editor of *Slavianskoie Obozrenie*, Professor Pal'mov, turned the monthly into a yearbook and carried on the commitment to provide information about academic and day-to-day life of "Slavs or nations of the Greco-Slavic cultural type generally" in fin-de-siècle Russia.[93]

Not all true believers in the Greco-Slavic world respected the Patriarchate of Constantinople. Professor Ivan Troitskii vigorously championed the ideal of the Greco-Slavic cultural type during the Eastern Crisis (1875–1878) in the major church periodical *Tserkovnyi Vestnik*, which met with Filippov's ap-proval at the time. But their lively and argumentative correspondence from 1877 to 1887 revealed significant differences between them. Troitskii refused to follow the tradition of supporting the institution of the Patriarchate of Constantinople as part of Russia's messianic role in the "Christian East." He continued to believe that the "East" and the Greeks generally exploited Orthodoxy for their nationalist agendas and left no room for Russia to fulfill its Pan-Orthodox destiny among its Balkan coreligionists. Troitskii blamed the perpetuation of the Bulgarian Schism solely on extreme Greek national-ist commentators and the anti-Slav public opinion they had created in Greek lands.[94] As a result, the Russian Church had nothing to learn from "Eastern churches" and "is the only one able to revive the fading church life of the East with the hot breath of its own healthy organism."[95]

---

91. Budilovich, Anton, *Znachenie Makedonii v sudbakh greko-slavianskogo mira (offprint from Izvestia Sankt-Peterburgskogo Slavianskogo Blagotvoritelnogo Obshestva)* (St. Petersburg: V. D. Smirnov, 1903), p. 19.

92. Glebov, Sergei, "Granitsy Imperii i Granitsy Moderna: Antikolonialnaia Ritoriaka i Teoria Kulturnykh Tipov v Evraziistve," *Ab Imperio*, 2003 (2): 282.

93. Palmov, Ivan, ed., *Slavianskoie Obozrenie: God vtoroi: Sbornik statei po slavianovedeniu*, (St. Petersburg: St Petersburg Slavic Benevolent Society, 1894), pp. II–IV.

94. GARF, f. 1099-1-2737, pp. 2–3, I. E. Troitskii to T. I. Filippov, 20 June 1885.

95. Troitskii, Ivan, "Nasha otechestvennaia tserkov zanimaiet pervoie mesto mezhdu vsemi pravoslavnymi tserkvami.' Otchet professora I. E. Troitskogo o komandirovke na Vostok. 1886 god," Gerd, L. A., ed., *Istoricheskii Arkhiv*, 4 (2001): 168.

Although flattering to Russian pride, Troitskii's views failed to persuade most Russian scholars and commentators interested in the Balkans. The growing respect for the Ecumenical Patriarchate is clear in the review of Russian publications on the Christian East by Alexei Lebedev, a professor of the Moscow Theological Academy. Criticizing Pan-Slav prejudices, he pointed out that "now only the blind are not asking themselves what countless troubles will befall the Bulgarian Church due to its separation from the Patriarch of Constantinople."[96] Lebedev praised Filippov's and Leontiev's writings for their crisp argumentation and solid sources. He even relied on them in his authoritative *History of the Eastern Greek Church under Turkish Rule*—it went through two editions (1896, 1903) in his lifetime and has not lost its relevance even today.[97]

Not all Russian intellectuals lost sympathy for the Bulgarian cause, but they had to acknowledge that disillusionment with all things Bulgarian had become mainstream. Even after the resumption of diplomatic relations after 1895, Bulgarian-Russian relations were not as cordial as before 1885. Pavel Miliukov, the famous Russian liberal historian and politician, spent over two years teaching and researching in Bulgaria (1897–1899). He was indignant about Russia's "one-sided support of Serbia to the detriment of Bulgaria."[98] The revived Slavophile magazine *Russkaia Beseda* praised Bulgarian Prince Ferdinand for having his son and heir baptized according to Orthodox rites in 1895 but urged him to prove the sincerity of that symbolic act by "normalizing the status of the Bulgarian national church."[99]

Although Konstantin Pobedonostsev as the Over-Procurator of the Russian Holy Synod assumed a cautious hands-off attitude in regards to the Ecumenical Patriarchate, Russian prelates as well as common parishioners remained intimately connected to their coreligionists in the Ottoman Empire. Between 1882 and 1914, the number of Russian pilgrims to the Holy Land rose from 2,000 to 15,000 a year. The Imperial Orthodox Palestine Society negotiated transportation discounts and improved facilities in Palestine to

96. Lebedev, Alexei, "Svedeniia i otzyvy o sovremennom sostoianii Khristianskogo Vostoka," *Chteniia v Obshchestve Liubetelei Dukhovnogo Prosvesheniia*, 4 (1893): 205.

97. Lebedev, Alexei, *Istoriia Greko-Vostochnoi Tserkvi pod vlastiu turok: Ot padeniia Konstantinopoliia v 1453 godu do nashi do nastoiashchego vremeni.* Vol. 1 (St. Petersburg: Oleg Byshko, 2004), pp. 74–75.

98. Miliukov, Pavel, *Vospominaniia.* Vol. 1 (New York: Chekhov Publishing House, 1955), p. 174.

99. Vasiliev, Afanasii, "Bolgarskiie dela," *Russkaia Beseda* (February 1896): 159. That magazine adopted the name and the ideas of the Slavophile journal started by A. I. Koshelev and T. I. Filippov in 1856.

make it possible for average Russians to walk in the footsteps of Jesus, Mary, and the Apostles.[100]

The holy relics also cemented Orthodox unity on both symbolic and physical levels through the centuries and across changing political boundaries. As in the 1500s, various monasteries in the Balkans and Asia Minor requested and received permission from the Russian church authorities to collect alms in the land of the Tsars. In 1893, the Holy Theotokos monastery fell into debt after rising taxation had combined with a series of bad harvests on its land in the diocese of Drama. Russian piety was a glimmer of hope in their dire economic straits if two monks with some holy relics were allowed to go to main Russian cities.[101]

The relics did not need to travel to Russia to be venerated by the Russian faithful. The stories of past and present miracles generated by the remains of ancient saints also created a powerful bond between two parts of the Orthodox world. When the Patriarchate and the Russian embassy bitterly argued over the conduct of Russian Muerzsteg inspectors, Patriarch Joachim III was deeply moved by the gift from a group of Russian prelates and laypeople. In 1904, Archbishop Antonii of St. Petersburg raised funds to commission a gilded and enameled silver reliquary for the remains of St. Euphemia preserved in the Patriarchate. She was a Roman martyr and a native of Chalcedon, which in the Middle Ages became an extension of Constantinople on the Asian side of the Bosphorus. The Russian-made reliquary with the relics of that saint still occupies a prominent place in the church of St. George (see Figure 6.3). As a token of appreciation for the beautiful present, Joachim III sent to Archbishop Antonii a reproduction of the rare Byzantine icon of the Blessed Theotokos.[102]

The radiance of Byzantine relics reached far east of Moscow. In January 1908, the Bishop of Perm' requested a piece of the remains of St. Haralambos from the treasury of the Patriarchate of Constantinople. Joachim III obliged him and added "May the Lord our God grant His grace, blessings, and fortitude to the Orthodox people of the said diocese through the relics of the holy martyr Haralambos."[103]

In addition to spiritual influence, the Ecumenical Patriarchate served as a model of discussed church reforms in Russia. As in earlier periods, the debate about the Bulgarian Question involved the issues of bishops' authority

---

100. Stavrou, Theofanis, *Russian Interests in Palestine, 1882–1914: A Study of Religious and Educational Enterprise* (Thessaloniki: Institute for Balkan Studies, 1963), p. 209.

101. Abbot of the Holy Theotokos Monastery to the Russian Holy Synod, 20 March 1893, The Archive of the Ecumenical Patriarchate, A63, pp. 68–69, Number 1130.

102. Joachim III to Antonii, 13 November 1904, ibid., A 76, p. 346, Number 7396.

103. Joachim III to Bishop Nikanor of Perm', January 1908, ibid., A82, p. 37, Number 60.

FIGURE 6.3 St. Euphemia's reliquary. The church of St. George, Fener, Istanbul (personal photograph with the blessing of Father Vissarion).

and of the restoration of the Moscow Patriarchate, which had been abolished by Peter the Great. By 1900, Bishop Antonii (first of Ufa, then of Volyn) emerged as the leader of that trend. Like Filippov, he saw the empowerment of the clergy in regards to the laity as the solution both of many Russian ills and of the Bulgarian Church Question.[104]

The Over-Procurator of the Holy Synod Pobedonostsev opposed restoring the Moscow Patriarchate, since that meant losing his job among other things, and considered Antonii a freethinker who was rocking the boat. According to Antonii's anonymous biographer, other Russian prelates supported him only to the extent that it did not damage their careers. Antonii's dream would come true only after the fall of the Romanovs in 1917 made it possible to restore the Patriarchate. Then Metropolitan of Kiev, Antonii would come very close to being elected Patriarch of Moscow and all Russia.[105]

104. Basil, *Church and State*, pp. 28–29; Cunningham, James, *A Vanquished Hope: The Movement for Church Renewal in Russia, 1905–1906* (Crestwood: St. Vladimir's Seminary Press, 1981), pp. 59–66.

105. *Pisma Blazhenneishego Mitropolita Antonia (Khrapovitskogo)* (Jordanville: Holy Trinity Monastery Saint Job of Pochaev Typography, 1988), pp. 16–18.

In the aftermath of the Revolution of 1905, Bishop Antonii voiced his views as the editor of the diocesan monthly, where he consistently criticized the notion of parish laity's control over clergy as inspired by "leftist newspapers" to further spread revolutionary agitation. Instead, he promoted the ideal of paternalistic "fusion of clergy with parishioners in a devoted and quiet prayer."[106]

In the 1890s, he began to take interest in the Balkans as the rector of the Moscow Theological Academy. Bishop Antonii favored Greek and Serbian students as "the representatives of those ancient Eastern Churches with which he strove wholeheartedly to communicate."[107] Antonii became active in the cause of lifting the Bulgarian Schism in his tenure as bishop of Ufa (1900–1902).[108] In a collection of sermons and articles, he denounced "the vain national ambitions" that produced in many Orthodox Greeks, Slavs, and Arabs "the madness of willingly separating themselves from the body of Christ to form a kind of Nebuchadnezzar's idol made of semi-Mohammedan Pan-Arabism, Uniate Serbism, schismatic Bulgarianism, and 'the Great Idea' of the Phanariots."[109]

While the Russian scholars and commentators were overcoming the temptation of Pan-Slavism, the Ottoman elites increasingly emphasized ethnicity—the concept totally out of touch with either traditional Islamic or civic Ottoman outlook. The ruling class had never before identified with "Turks," i.e., uncouth Anatolian peasants. The word "Turkey" had been used only by Europeans to designate the Ottoman Empire in general and lands populated by ethnic Turks specifically. But by the late 1800s, it was gradually borrowed in its French form into the Ottoman usage as "Turkiye," although the official name of the country remained "the Exalted State."[110]

Even more ominous was the spread of Pan-Turkism. Like the word "Turkey," it was also a product of Western modernity politicized by subaltern Muslim Tatar intelligentsia in the Russian Empire. They received European education in Russian schools and had easier access to modern ideas than their cousins under the less enlightened autocracy of Abdulhamid II. In both

---

106. *Volynskie Eparkhialnye Vedomosti*, 11 (9 March 1911): 241.

107. *Sbornik izbrannykh sochinenii Blazhenneishego Antonia, Mitropolita Kievskogo i Galitskogo* (Belgrad: Slovo, 1935), p. XXIII.

108. Ibid., p. 57.

109. Devteroksenos, *Vostochnaia Tserkov i narodnosti* (Kazan: Imperial Kazan University Press, 1900), p. 3.

110. Lewis, Bernard, *The Emergence of Modern Turkey*, 3d ed. (New York and Oxford: Oxford University Press: 2002), p. 333.

reaction to and emulation of Russian Pan-Slavism, their publications disseminated the awareness of the cultural unity of all Turkic peoples based on shared religion and linguistic affinity.

The latter was valued more than the former. Islam needed to be modernized, which meant that businessmen and intellectuals needed to take control of Volga and Central Asian Muslim communities from the Muslim clerics denounced as Russian collaborators. Traveling between Russia and the Ottoman Empire, Tatar and Azeri political entrepreneurs slowly propagandized the dreams of creating a Pan-Turkic state centered on Istanbul.[111]

Following a new Western fad, linguistic nationalism acquired strong pseudoscientific racist overtones. The discourse of Pan-Turkism sometimes shaded into Pan-Turanianism. Turan had been discovered by Turcophile European Orientalists who sought to bring the Ottomans closer to the West. In their accounts, Tanzimat reforms merely marked the natural turn of the Turks from the Semitic Arabic culture to the civilization of their Touro-Aryan kinsmen.[112] As such, racism was mixed together with liberal progressivism to create a heady cocktail for many educated ethnic Turks in underpaid state bureaucracy (especially among junior officers). When exiled abroad, they voiced those ideas to overthrow the old regime of Abdulhamid II, who carefully projected the image of a pious sultan-caliph to appeal to the Muslim majority tired of rampant Westernization. At the same time, he promoted foreign investment, improved modern infrastructure, and upheld the Tanzimat laws on legal equality to court Ottoman Christian bourgeoisie.[113]

Under Abdulhamid II, Christians did not have to build new churches behind high walls or disguised as residential structures. The largest church of the Patriarchate was constructed in 1880 (see Figure 6.4). It still dominates Taksim Square in the district of Pera—the most Westernized neighborhood of Constantinople with the majority of foreign embassies and banks. Not to be outdone by its main rival, the Bulgarian Exarchate chose an astonishingly modern design reminiscent of the Crystal Palace and the Eiffel Tower. Its main church (St. Stefan's) had its humble beginning in the home of Stefan Vogoridi in 1849. Between 1871 and 1898, it was rebuilt into a tall slender cathedral cast entirely in iron in Vienna and assembled on the shore of the Golden Horn harbor (see Figure 6.5).

---

111. Landau, Jacob, *Pan-Turkism: From Irredentism to Cooperation* (Bloomington: Indiana University Press, 1995), pp. 8–9.

112. Berkes, *The Development of Secularism in Turkey*, p. 316.

113. Zuercher, Erik Jan, *The Unionist Factor: The Role of the Committee of Union and Progress in the Turkish National Movement, 1905–1926* (Leiden: E. J. Brill, 1984), pp. 11–22.

FIGURE 6.4 Holy Trinity cathedral, Beyoglu (Pera), Istanbul (personal photograph).

Lost Opportunities: The Constitutional Regime of the Young Turks, 1908–1914

When threatened with disclosure and arrest by the sultan's secret police in July 1908, the conspiratorial army circles with links to the secret Committee of Union and Progress (CUP) staged a relatively bloodless coup in Macedonia. Their momentous decision was also triggered by the real fear of foreign

FIGURE 6.5 St. Stefan's Bulgarian church, Fener, Istanbul (personal photograph).

intervention. In June 1908, Edward VII of England and Nicholas II of Russia met aboard a yacht in the Bay of Reval to finalize a new round of the Muerzsteg reforms. European officers would have "a full measure of executive control" and the Ottoman governors would answer to the Great Powers.[114]

Mutinies in Macedonian garrisons spread like wild fire and forced Abdulhamid II to restore the suspended constitution of 1876. This undramatic takeover unleashed a torrent of profound political and cultural transformations, including women's activism and free press.[115] Despite its reservations about the Young Turks, the Patriarchate was actively preparing for parliamentary elections and asked the Greek embassy to use its consular network to ensure the success of the electoral campaign launched by Patriarchate's favorite candidates like Mikhail Theotokas, a Constantinople-based lawyer and a native of the island of Chios.[116]

114. Hanioglu, M. Sukru, *Preparation For a Revolution: The Young Turks, 1902–1908* (New York: Oxford University Press, 2001), pp. 233–235.

115. Brummett, Palmira, *Image and Imperialism in the Ottoman Revolutionary Press, 1908–1911* (Albany: State University of New York Press, 2000), p. 9.

116. The Patriarchate to the Greek Ambassador Gryparis, the Archive of the Ecumenical Patriarchate, 17 September 1908, A 82, pp. 403–404, Number 7035.

Outside the Ottoman capital, the reactions to the Young Turk Revolution were even more complicated. According to the Austrian consul in Bitola, the Macedonian Slavic peasants did not trust Bulgaria because of its narrow self-ish agendas. Although the IMRO was not a Bulgarian pawn, the locals were tired of its terrorism and extortions. Since the European-sponsored reforms had largely failed, the Macedonian Christians had high hopes for the Young Turks, who promised security, restored the Constitution, and pledged to en-force Christian-Muslim legal equality. The initial positive popular response to the Young Turk Revolution explains remarkable public order achieved in its aftermath.[117]

It made sense then for Yane Sandanski's left wing of IMRO to assist the CUP in the July 1908 coup in exchange for amnesty and recognition of their long fight against Abdulhamid II's tyranny. Envious of IMRO's new laurels, the Greek gov-ernment dismantled its network of costly and locally unpopular bands.[118]

The Young Turk Revolution clearly generated a lot of goodwill but the neighboring powers cynically took advantage of the turmoil. Austria-Hungary announced the annexation of Bosnia-Herzegovina on 6 October 1908 when the Ottoman Empire was preparing for free elections. The Treaty of Berlin left the Sultan a fig leaf of sovereignty when it legitimated the Austrian occupation of the province, ostensibly to promote stability and modernization. Encouraged by the Habsburg ministers, Bulgaria declared its complete independence a day earlier on October 5 (September 22 of the Julian Calendar). Shortly, the autonomous island of Crete began to call for union with Greece. Those blows disappointed the CUP leadership and made them less optimistic about saving the multiethnic and multireligious empire through liberal reforms.[119]

Having caught wind of Vienna's intentions, the Russian Foreign Minister Alexander Izvolskii and Tsar Nicholas II had made a secret agreement with the Austrian cabinet recognizing the annexation in exchange for its support in the revision of international treaties regulating the use of the Bosphorus and the Dardanelles. Russia's goal was to open them to the passage of warships belonging to the Black Sea countries. Austria-Hungary did not coordinate the timing of Bosnian annexation with Russia and did not use its leverage to change the Turkish Straits regime to Russia's advantage.

---

117. Consul in Bitola to the Foreign Ministry, 1 August 1908, *Austro-Hungarian Documents*, p. 397.

118. K. Dimaras to the Foreign Ministry, 18 July 1908, *I Televtaia fasi tis enoplis anametrisis sti Makedonia (1907–1908)*, pp. 248–250.

119. Yavuz, M. Hakan, "Warfare and Nationalism: The Balkan Wars as a Catalyst for Homogenization," in *War and Nationalism: The Balkan Wars*, pp. 49–50.

Most of the Russian press and the majority of the brand new Parliament (the State Duma) protested against what they saw as subjecting two Slavic provinces to the German yoke. But in March 1909, both Russia and Serbia had to recognize the annexation after the German ultimatum—an eerie prelude to the events of the summer of 1914. The implicit alternative would be the German-backed Austrian war on Serbia. After the Russo-Japanese war and the Russian Revolution of 1905, Russia could not risk getting involved in a major conflict. The Russian journalists often referred to that humiliating defeat of the Russian foreign policy as "the diplomatic Tsushima" (after the sinking of the Russian squadron in the Sea of Japan).[120]

One of the most popular monarchist dailies, *Novoe Vremia*, began to promote the idea of a Balkan union to compensate for Russia's defeat in the Bosnian Crisis. Ideally, it would include Serbia, Montenegro, Bulgaria, and the Ottoman Empire. Such a federation would reconcile Christian Balkan states with the Ottoman Empire and would snatch the Ottoman Empire away from the clutches of the Triple Alliance into the arms of the Triple Entente.[121] Veteran Pan-Slav commentators redoubled their efforts to remind the Russian readers of Nikolai Danilevsky's vision of saving Russia's coreligionists and coethnics from the German juggernaut.[122]

In response to the Bosnian Crisis, the embittered CUP quickly began to shed its liberal gloss. In late October of 1908, many Patriarchist communities complained about the increasing number of abuses during the election campaign. Joachim III submitted an official protest to the Grand Vizier and argued that the new regime broke more laws than autocratic Abdulhamid II. The Russian ambassador agreed that the Young Turk efforts "to create a pliable parliament" led to "the suffering of all Christians, not just the Greeks." Unwilling to confront the dominant political party, the Sublime Porte was indifferent to the protest and "accused the Christians, especially the Greeks, of fraud."[123]

The discontent was growing violent not just among the Christians. The Young Turk policy of centralization and homogenization triggered several uprisings among the Kurdish tribes in Eastern Anatolia in the name of their

---

120. Kostrikova, Elena, *Rossiiskoie obshchestvo i vneshnaia politika nakanune Pervoi Mirovoi Voiny, 1908–1914* (Moscow: Russian Academy of Sciences, 2007), pp. 25–95.

121. Bestuzhev, Igor', *Borba v Rossii po voprosam vneshnei politiki, 1906–1910* (Moscow: Academy of Sciences of the USSR, 1961), p. 229.

122. Sharapov, Sergei, *Blizhaisshie zadachi Rossii na Balkanakh* (Moscow, 1909); Surin, N., "Balkanskaia Federatsiia i Makedonskii Vopros," *Slavianskiie Izvestiia*, 1 (1910): 30.

123. AVPRI, f. 151-482-3549, p. 93, Zinoviev to the Foreign Ministry, 24 October/6 November 1908.

traditional privileges. Some of them turned to Russia for support across the border.[124] If there had been any "springtime of the peoples" in the summer of 1908, it did not last.

After the less than perfect elections, the Ottoman Parliament opened on December 17, 1908. It was packed with the CUP supporters eager to promote their understanding of liberalism and civic Ottomanism among all ethnic and religious groups. They turned the sultan into a figurehead by investing his prerogatives with the government answerable to the Parliament.[125]

But Abdulhamid II was going not with a whimper but with a bang. On 13 April 1909, several army units in Constantinople mutineered and supported the demonstrations demanding the restoration of the full powers of the Sultan and of the sharia law. Islamic extremists attacked Christians in many cities, culminating in the massacres of thousands of Armenians in Adana (Asia Minor). Luckily, the CUP was able to march the troops in Macedonia on the capital and to stop the counterrevolution. From that time on, the Young Turks used their control of the legislature to create Ottoman brotherhood by enforcing Turkish as the language of local courts, administration, and education. Even more controversially, the Christians no longer had the option of paying an exemption fee to avoid serving in the Ottoman army alongside the Muslims. To clear the way for unhindered growth of civic Ottoman nationalism, in 1909 the CUP outlawed all political associations based on ethnic affiliation.[126] The problem with this kind of "multicultural integration" was that it could be easily seen as little more than forced assimilation in disguise.[127]

Already in the summer of 1909, the CUP centralization drive had quickly borne fruit on the Orthodox tree. The Patriarchate of Constantinople turned to "its only powerful protector for support and sympathy," as had happened during the earlier Ottoman encroachments on its remaining vestiges of autonomy in 1884 and 1890. The new Russian ambassador in the Ottoman capital, Nikolai Charykov (1909–1912), embraced the Patriarchate's initiative and immediately secured his superiors' permission of the disbursal of the annual subsidy in the amount of 1,000 Ottoman pounds discontinued in 1904.[128]

---

124. Reynolds, Michael, *Shattering Empires: The Clash and Collapse of the Ottoman and Russian Empires, 1908–1918* (New York: Cambridge University Press, 2011), p. 27.

125. Yapp, Malcolm, *The Making of the Modern Near East, 1792–1923* (London and New York: Longman, 1987), p. 191.

126. Yavuz, "Warfare and Nationalism," p. 51.

127. Kymlicka, *Citizenship in Diverse Societies*, p.14.

128. AVPRI, f. 151-482-3550, pp. 10–100b, Charykov to the Foreign Ministry, 1 August 1909.

While on vacation in Sofia, Exarch Iosif reminded the Russian ambassador in the Bulgarian capital of another common enemy—as the Young Turks were increasing their pressure on Ottoman Christians, the Catholic bishop Menoni of Philippopolis and Sofia was very active trying to convert the Bulgarian Orthodox. The Young Turks were trying to separate the Exarchate from the church in the newly independent Bulgaria. Without the funding from the Bulgarian government, the Exarchate would not be able to counteract the Papacy's siren calls.[129]

More opposition to the CUP-dominated government came from the second congress of the main Ottoman Bulgarian political movement, with almost 10,000 active members: "the Bulgarian Constitutional Clubs." One hundred sixty delegates including two members of the Ottoman Parliament gathered in Thessaloniki in September 1909 and resolved to demand drastic reforms.

Tax collection and the relations between landlords and sharecroppers should be clearly regulated on the model of the 1863 law for Bosnia. The Christian farmers should have easier access to credit and regain the titles to land plots illegally taken from them under Abdulhamid II. The government should empower local communities based on the laws of 1864 and 1870. More local Christians should serve in the gendarmerie and some arms should be stored in the villages for self-defense. The CUP needed to stop fomenting conflicts among Christian groups in Macedonia. If Christians were to be conscripted, they should serve for only two years and only in their home provinces. One of the speakers went as far as to threaten, "we'd rather go back to the mountains than leave for Yemen as soldiers."[130]

To drive the wedge between the Exarchate and the Patriarchate, the Sublime Porte backed down on the issue of Patriarchate's autonomy. Ambassador Charykov observed with satisfaction that Grand Vizier Hilmi Pasha and the sensible Ministers of the Interior, Education, and Religious Affairs put pressure on the speaker of the Chamber of Deputies, Ahmed Riza, to block extreme anticlerical legislation inspired by French laicization models.[131]

To further divide Christian minorities, in July 1910 the Parliament adopted the law on school and church property. It should belong to a Christian community that could command a two-thirds majority. In effect, it meant enforcing Article X of the 1870 Exarchate decree on the local level. The government promised to provide funds to help the minority communities to build new

---

129. AVPRI, f. 151-482-3550, pp. 12–120b, Shtrandtman to the Foreign Ministry, 18 August 1909.

130. Ibid., pp. 16–17, Petraiev to the Foreign Ministry, 5 September 1909.

131. Ibid., pp. 22–220b, Charykov to the Foreign Ministry, 26 October/6 November 1909.

churches and schools, which did not sound realistic given the chronic crisis of Ottoman finances. The law clearly favored the Bulgarians (to take effect in October 1910) but they still hesitated to rally behind the CUP government. In Charykov's view, encouraged by the ill-informed public opinion of many European countries, "the proud nationalism of the Young Turk leaders increased the xenophobia of the masses of the Turkish people which in their mind always borders on savage hostility to Christian nationalities generally."[132]

Still, Charykov engaged in direct talks with CUP and their main European sponsor—the German envoy Marschall. Charykov argued that the reconciliation of the Bulgarian Exarchate and the Patriarchate would be in keeping with the official policy of "reconciliation of all population elements." Settling the Bulgarian Church Question would help consolidate the Young Turk regime by ending the protracted bloody conflict between the Greeks and the Bulgarians in Ottoman Macedonia, where the revolution of 1908 had originated.[133]

As Charykov saw it, the Exarchate was more willing to negotiate with the Patriarchate in October 1910 than in the previous thirty-six years from the advantageous position of the newly adopted law and earlier permissions to appoint archbishops to Skopje and Ohrid (1890), Nevrokop and Veles (1894), and Debar, Bitola, Melenik, and Strumica (1896).

But it was Joachim III who made the first move. He asked Charykov to find a copy of the 1873 draft agreement between Exarch Anthimus I and Patriarch Joachim II in the archives of the Russian embassy. In 1910, Joachim III insisted only on the rights of ethnically Greek communities to have their own priests in Ottoman Macedonia and inside Bulgaria. Charykov expected resistance from the Sublime Porte and Austria-Hungary "because both of them fear and oppose the reconciliation of two main population elements in European Turkey." Charykov's advice was to remember that no government could interfere with canon law or "prevent the Exarch from asking the Patriarch for forgiveness and recognizing him as his spiritual head."[134]

On the same day that the Russian ambassador described his conversation with Joachim III, Charykov visited the Exarch and wrote another report. Exarch Iosif was very interested in lifting the Schism because "all Christians regardless of nationality are suffering from Turkish atrocities in Macedonia." Iosif was already in contact with a Greek group, which included a member of the Ottoman Parliament. Working together, they managed to reduce

---

132. AVPRI, f. 151-482-3551, pp. 67–68, Charykov to the Foreign Ministry, 1 September 1910.

133. AVPRI, f. 180-517/2-3471, pp. 640b–65, N. V. Charykov to Foreign Minster, 10 November 1910.

134. Ibid., pp. 74–76, Charykov to the Foreign Ministry, 27 October 1910.

mutual hostility in the Bulgarian- and Greek-language newspapers published in Constantinople. Charykov was glad to find out that Exarch Iosif shared Joachim III's principle of reconciliation—the Greek- and Bulgarian-language minorities in specific dioceses should have communal and cultural rights.[135]

Another reason the Bulgarian Exarchate became interested in clearer territorial delimitation lay in the growing fear of Serbian competition. With Charykov's help, in the fall of 1909, Belgrade obtained from Joachim III the appointment of the Russian-educated Serb hieromonk Varnava as the archbishop of Debar-Kichevo. The ethnically Serb archbishops had already been installed in Prishtina and Skopje. As a result, "the position of Serb and generally Slavic church and culture has been consolidated in the most satisfactory fashion."[136]

In the Slavic areas of central and northern Macedonia, the Bulgarian nationalists found the Serbian efforts much more dangerous than the Greek ones. Having no national consciousness, the villagers could declare themselves to be either Serb or Bulgarian as long as the priest officiated "in an understandable Slavic language." With the end of violent rivalry between armed nationalist bands, the villagers found it advantageous to call themselves Serbs because the Serbian government actually paid them for that. According to the Russian consul in Monastir (Bitola), the Ottoman authorities also favored the Serbs, whom they saw as weaker than the Bulgarians.[137]

The ideas exchanged in 1873 pointed to the greater involvement of laity in the solution of the Bulgarian Question in the fall of 1910. In the conversation with Ambassador Ignatiev in December 1873, Patriarch Joachim II concluded that the very text of the declaration of the Schism included a possibility for reconciliation. The Bulgarian people represented by their notables or priests should address the Patriarchate in writing to reject the heresy of phyletism and announce their loyalty to Orthodoxy. That simple formality would open the negotiations.[138]

One such notable was Pancho Dorev, a representative of Bitola in the Ottoman Parliament. He and four Greek MP's visited Joachim III and talked for an hour and a half. Then Dorev shared with Charykov his positive impressions of that conversation and assured him of the success of the movement to lift the Schism. In fact, the Greek-Bulgarian rapprochement had already become reality in rural areas because "the Turks are equally hostile to both

---

135. Ibid, pp. 710b–720b, N. V. Charykov to Foreign Minster, 27 October 1910.

136. AVPRI, f. 151-482-3551, pp. 390b–40, Charykov to the Foreign Ministry, 29 March 1910.

137. Ibid., p. 51, Kal' to the Foreign Ministry, 12 May 1910.

138. Ibid., p. 670b, the 1st department of the Foreign Ministry to Charykov, 29 October 1910.

nationalities." Dorev's own brother had been condemned to fifteen years of hard labor as a member of the Bulgarian armed band. The Synod of the Patriarchate needed directions from Athens to be more receptive to Joachim III's ideas of reconciliation. Exarch Iosif received news through Sofia that the Greek government was going to encourage the Patriarchate to start negotiations with the Exarchate. Iosif himself gave "a very helpful interview" to the Ottoman Greek newspaper *Proodos*.[139]

The early result of those initial reconciliation efforts was a very considerable improvement for both Greeks and Bulgarians in Macedonia in the fall of 1910. The secret talks between Halil Bey, the CUP majority leader in the Parliament, and the Bulgarian consul in Thessaloniki led to revoking the martial law, court martials, and the extraordinary counterinsurgency law. Charykov learned about another hopeful development from the Greek Ottoman newspaper *Proodos*—the joint session of the Holy Synod and Lay Council of the Exarchate recommended local Bulgarian communities to reach agreements with the Patriarchists about the control of churches and schools instead of accepting the decisions of the Ottoman government based on the new law on communal property. According to the Russian ambassador, that local approach was the best way to implement Article X of the 1870 *firman*: "the main stumbling block."[140]

Two weeks later, Charykov was much less optimistic. The Exarchate had secret negotiations with the Greek mediators, including Mr. Karatheodori, a member of the Mixed Lay-Clerical Council of the Patriarchate, and some Greek members of the Ottoman Parliament such as Mr. Kallis. The Patriarchate could not accept the territorial division offered by the Exarchate where outside the coastal areas such as Karaferya, Kastoria, and Cavalla only three dioceses would remain in the Patriarchate—Thessaloniki, Serres, and Drama. The Exarch, in his turn, refused to agree to move out of Constantinople after lifting the Schism. Although all Orthodox autocephalous churches had their seats inside their jurisdiction, Iosif insisted that the Ottoman capital was the best place for him to serve as a spiritual leader of Macedonian Bulgarians.[141]

The Russian ambassador in Athens reported that the Greek and Bulgarian governments were not yet ready for an agreement on Macedonia. The Greek policymakers feared the possible unity of divided Exarchist and Patriarchist Slavs. The Greek press even raised the specter of a future Slav Patriarch in

---

139. AVPRI, f. 180-517/2-3471, pp. 63–64, Charykov to the Foreign Ministry, 10 November 1910.

140. Ibid., pp. 56–580b, Charykov to the Foreign Ministry, 17 November 1910.

141. Ibid., p. 51, Charykov to the Foreign Ministry, 1 December 1910.

Constantinople.[142] On the other hand, the Belgrade cabinet feared being left out in case of any agreement between rival churches on territorial jurisdiction. St. Petersburg had to reassure the Serb policymakers that the Russians put a premium on "fostering friendship between Slavic states" and did not expect the Schism to be resolved in the near future.[143]

As in earlier efforts to resolve the Bulgarian Church Question, in the 1910s, the Russian bureaucratic mindset curiously combined acute awareness of ethnic distinctions with age-old messianic ideas. Clearly, Russian foreign policymakers tended to be more consistently Pan-Orthodox rather than Pan-Slav. The low regard for Bulgarians as lacking discipline and devotion to Orthodoxy is also clear from the report by Charykov, where "the Bulgarians are unruly, everybody likes showing off, their masses are unstable and can fall an easy prey to Catholic and especially Protestant propaganda, always around and ready to act."[144]

Charykov involved the Russian Church in the peace process when he contacted Bishop Antonii of Volyn—the leading Russian prelate and an admirer of Joachim III. He hoped to draw on Antonii's ideas to help lift the Bulgarian Schism.[145] In his correspondence with Joachim III published in the Russian and Ottoman Greek press, Antonii considered it appropriate to treat the Exarchists like the Uniate clerics and laymen returning from the Catholic Church to Orthodoxy.[146]

Despite the reluctance of both Bulgarian and Greek governments, the cooperation of Christian minorities was rapidly developing in response to the renewed centralization policy pushed by the Young Turks. Modern Turkish historians are still bitter about the reluctance of non-Muslim communities to melt in the pot of Ottoman brotherhood and equate their demands for restoring *millet* autonomy with ethnic separatism.[147]

In early March 1911, the Armenian Patriarchate, the Patriarchate of Constantinople, and the Bulgarian Exarchate discussed the common action regarding the issue of schools and army service. The Armenian Patriarch

---

142. Ibid., p. 550b, Sverbeev to the Foreign Ministry, 21 November 1910.

143. AVPRI, f. 151-482-3617, p. 20, the Foreign Ministry to N. Hartwig, 20 November 1910.

144. AVPRI, f. 180-517/2-3471, pp. 360b–37, N. V. Charykov to Foreign Minister, 11 February 1911.

145. Ibid., p. 19, Archbishop Antonii to Ambassador Charykov, 14 August 1911.

146. "Perepiska Arkhiepiskopa Volynskogo i Zhitomirskogo Antoniia so Vselenskim Patriarkhom Ioakimom III," *Volynskie Eparkhialnye Vedomosti,* 6 (1911), in *Svet,* 21 November 1910 and 1 February 1911, *La Lloyd Ottoman,* 3 December 1910.

147. Atalay, *Fener Rum Ortodoks Patrikhanesi'nin Siyasi Faaliyetleri (1908–1923),* pp. 37–49.

urged his counterparts to jointly demand the official recognition of the status of legal persons for Christian communities to secure their property rights.[148] In mid-September 1911, all Christian-minority communities submitted identical memoranda to the Great Powers to force the Sublime Porte to recognize and secure their rights with international guarantees. The Greek Foreign Ministry instructed its embassy in Constantinople to invite to secret negotiations the representatives of the Patriarchate, the Exarchate, the Armenian Patriarchate, and the ethnically Greek, Bulgarian, and Serbian members of the Ottoman Parliament. The goal was to encourage "their own states" to move toward a defensive alliance.[149]

Thus, the joint petition of the Ottoman Christian communities was the first halting step toward the anti-Ottoman Balkan League. More conventionally, the turning point is placed earlier in 1910 (the effects of the new law on school and church property in Macedonia)[150] or later—the change in the geopolitical status quo during the Italo-Turkish War.[151] On 29 September 1911, Italy attacked the Ottoman Empire, occupying Libya and the Dodecanese islands in the Aegean. In this situation, the Young Turks could not afford antagonizing the neighboring Balkan states and satisfied the key demands of the Christian minorities. After this impressive show of Christian solidarity, Ambassador Charykov expected the Greeks to keep their promise made to Exarch Iosif and lift the Schism.

The Sublime Porte promised that Christian conversions to Islam would not be recognized during their military service. They would have the right to file official complaints about any commander. Christian chaplains would be permitted in every Ottoman army unit. Christian officer candidates would take the qualifying exam in their own language with only basic knowledge of Turkish. The Christian communities would have control over education (teachers' qualifications and curriculum) without Ottoman interference within certain limits. The diplomas could be written in any language but they would be recognized as equivalent to state-issued certificates if the student could read and write in Turkish. Charykov considered those concessions as the groundwork for a Balkan confederation supported by most Ottoman political parties. To capitalize on that emerging domestic compromise, Charykov

---

148. AYE, 1911, 21-7, Embassy in Constantinople (I. Alexandropoulos) to the Foreign Ministry, 8 March 1911.

149. Ibid., the Foreign Ministry to the Embassy in Constantinople, 17 September 1911.

150. Hacisalihoglu, "The Young Turk Policy in Macedonia," p. 121.

151. Rossos, Andrew, *Russia and the Balkans: Inter-Balkan Rivalries & Russian Foreign Policy, 1908–1914* (Toronto: University of Toronto Press, 1981), pp. 34–36.

initiated a flurry of negotiations to include Christian Balkan states into an Ottoman-led economic and political union.[152]

Instead of implementing the agreement with the minorities, the CUP government would soon renew its centralization drive.[153] This was understandable in the context of the difficult war with Italy but the broken promise of concessions clearly reduced the interest of non-Muslim communities in the survival of the increasingly intolerant Ottoman Empire.

It is important to note that the post-1908 fear of an Austrian drive to the Aegean was not the main motivation of another round of Russian efforts to solve the Bulgarian Church Question. Charykov stressed that his mediation would reaffirm Russia's traditional role as "the protector of Orthodoxy in the East."[154] In the 1910s, the Russian Pan-Orthodox publicists noticed the unusually high degree of Greek-Slavic political and ecclesiastical cooperation and argued for the relevance of Leontiev's ideas of the Byzantine-Slavic Union in the main right-wing Russian daily newspapers.[155]

Bulgaria, Serbia, and Greece never seriously considered the Russian plan of including the Ottoman Empire into an alliance against Austria. In September 1911, the Bulgarian policymakers despaired of a possibility of a privileged relationship with the Sublime Porte to increase their influence in Ottoman European provinces. When the clouds of the Italo-Turkish War were gathering, they approached the Serbs as their most dangerous rival in Macedonia. A full year later, in September 1912, after endless bickering over various villages and river tributaries, two fraternal South Slav governments had finally reached an agreement on military cooperation against the Ottoman Empire and even on the future partition of Macedonia. In case of any disagreements, they pledged to defer to the arbitration of Tsar Nicholas II.[156] Map 6.2 shows conflicting ambitions of the Balkan states that would haunt their alliance.

Only in February of 1912, when the negotiations with Serbia were clearly progressing, did the Bulgarian government turn to Greece. The Bulgarians expected to benefit from the Greek navy but had a very low opinion of the

152. AVPRI, f. 151-482-3552, pp. 16–170b, 14/27 November 1911.

153. AVPRI, f. 180-517/2-3471, pp. 11–130b, Girs to the Foreign Minister, 5 May 1912.

154. Ibid., p. 360b, N. V. Charykov to Foreign Minister, 28 February 1911.

155. Fudel, Protoierei Iosif, "Sudba K. N. Leontieva," *Moskovskie Vedomosti*, 262 (12 November 1910): 6; "Vostochnyi Vopros (pamiati K. Leontieva)," *Moskovskie Vedomosti*, 260 (12 November 1911): 2; Burnakin, A., "Tsargrad i Vseslavianstvo (prorochestva K. Leontieva)," *Novoe Vremia* (2 November 1911): 32.

156. Thaden, Edward, *Russia and the Balkan Alliance of 1912* (University Park: Pennsylvania State University Press, 1965), pp. 74–96.

MAP 6.2 Balkan aspirations (showing the boundaries of 1912). The University of Texas Map Collection.

http://www.lib.utexas.edu/maps/historical/balkan_aspirations_1914.jpg

Greek land forces after their dismal performance in the war of 1897. That is why the Bulgarians refused to discuss the partition of Macedonia with the Greeks. Prime Minister Elevtherios Venizelos reassured his cabinet that the area would be divided based on effective military occupation. He correctly predicted that by virtue of geography and the location of Ottoman armies in the coming war, Serbia would concentrate on Skopje, Bulgaria would push south toward Adrianople, and Greece would move its forces to Thessaloniki and Serres. After putting the divisive Macedonian Question on the back burner, Greece and Bulgaria concluded the agreement on 16 May 1912.

Although that alliance-building process was driven by local actors, the Russian ambassadors in the Balkan capitals were involved as well. St. Petersburg kept recommending the Balkan allies to include the Ottomans and to preserve the status quo. In the end, the Russian Foreign Ministry approved of the defensive clauses intended to contain Austria-Hungarian expansion and minimized the significance of the potentially offensive clauses directed against Turkey.[157]

---

157. Rossos, *Russia and the Balkans*, pp. 40–51.

All those plans and dreams were fueled by the deepening crisis in the Ottoman Empire. The lackluster Young Turk leadership during the ongoing Italo-Turkish War and their accelerated centralization policy antagonized most social and ethnic groups. Average Muslims and conservative elites generally were not happy to see their sultan-caliph relegated to being a constitutional monarch. Rural Turkish and urban Christian commercial bourgeoisie disliked extreme statism of the CUP and supported the new Liberal Party (*Hurriyet ve Itilaf Firkasi*) formed in November 1911. All non-Turkish groups and most economic elites were attracted to its program of federalization and reduction of government's role in economy. Only through considerable repression was the CUP able to secure its victory in the parliamentary elections in early 1912.[158]

The Christian communities now had to organize again to demand the same concessions they had seemingly won in November 1911. At the beginning of the parliamentary session, they submitted identical memoranda protesting three main issues—the provincial reform bill which would abolish any significant rights of religious organizations, military conscription, and electoral abuses. In June 1912, the Ecumenical Patriarchate, the Armenian Patriarchate, and the Bulgarian Exarchate were preparing a memorandum on education and a reminder about the earlier addresses ignored by the Sublime Porte. In case the CUP and both chambers of parliament took no action, the Greek diplomats were working on a joint appeal to the Great Powers on behalf of all main Christian groups.[159]

To defend their traditional autonomy, the Muslim Albanian clans did not mince words but occupied the towns of Prizren, Novi Pazar, and Skopje in May 1912. The general discontent was growing, Italy was clearly winning the war, and a new wave of nationalist terrorism and government reprisals was rising in Macedonia. All this chaos led to the dissolution of the Parliament, tainted by its association with the CUP. The new cabinet under Gazi Ahmed Muhtar Pasha was much more receptive to the opposition (22 July –29 October 1912).[160]

Unable to suppress the uprising, on August 20, the Ottoman government restored and, under Austrian pressure, even expanded the privileged status of Albanian lands while refusing to scale back centralization in other provinces. The Balkan states resented the Albanian control of four provinces (Yanina, Kosovo, Bitola, and Scutari) they regarded as their own inheritance.[161]

---

158. Hacisalihoglu, "The Young Turk Policy in Macedonia," p. 124.

159. AYE, 1912, f. 21-1, the Foreign Ministry to Gryparis, 27 June 1912.

160. Hacisalihoglu, "The Young Turk Policy in Macedonia," p. 124.

161. Rossos, *Russia and the Balkans*, p. 53.

Bulgaria led the other Balkan states to demand putting a stop to the oppression of the Christian communities and turning Macedonia into an autonomous province under a Christian governor from a second-rank European nation. Such ideas had been constantly discussed since 1878 based on the vague promise made in Article 23 of the Treaty of Berlin, but the Sublime Porte understandably blocked any such reform. All the Great Powers supported the decentralization project to avoid war and publicly insisted on the territorial status quo. But they were ready to accept a localized conflict even before the Sublime Porte declared general mobilization and on 14 October 1912 rejected the ultimatum issued by Bulgaria, Serbia, and Greece earlier.[162]

No one expected small fractious Balkan states to be so successful. Within a month, the Balkan alliance decisively defeated numerically superior Ottoman armies. By early November, the Bulgarian troops besieged Adrianople and reached the last defensive line barely forty kilometers away from Constantinople. This expansion greatly exceeded what Russia had been prepared to grant its Slavic brothers—the limits outlined in the preliminary Treaty of San Stefano of 1878. The Russian policymakers, not to speak of most Pan-Slav and Pan-Orthodox commentators, had made it very clear that in case of Ottoman dissolution, the area surrounding Constantinople should fall into Russian hands. But urged by its Entente partners, on November 6, St. Petersburg very reluctantly agreed to a possible temporary Bulgarian occupation of the Ottoman capital out of fear of Sofia's turn to the Central Powers for support in this delicate issue.[163]

A week earlier, anticipating the imminent triumph of the Cross over the Crescent, a secretary of the Russian embassy in Constantinople visited the Patriarch to inform him that the Bulgarians would soon liberate the city and take him to the Hagia Sophia cathedral, "where the Schism should be lifted." On October 29, Joachim III called an extraordinary session of the Holy Synod but it could not make any decision about the Schism. Exarch Iosif was ready to ask for forgiveness either orally or in writing to meet the conditions outlined in the declaration of the Schism of 1872. That act of submission should make it possible for the Exarch to join the Patriarch so that they could jointly celebrate the Divine Liturgy in the Hagia Sophia "next Wednesday"![164]

Obviously, that service was supposed to reconsecrate the most famous Orthodox church turned into mosque by Mehmet the Conqueror in May 1453.

---

162. Tokay, Gul, "The Origins of the Balkan Wars: A Reinterpretation," *War and Nationalism*, pp. 189–191.

163. Rossos, *Russia and the Balkans*, p. 89.

164. AYE, 1912, f. 89-3, Kanellopoulos to Athens via Zannetos, 31 October 1912.

The Greek government desperately tried to follow these momentous events, which were moving with breathtaking speed. Because of the war, the Greek embassy was closed and all wires from Greek undercover agents had to be sent via the consulate in Constanta, Romania. The Greek Foreign Minister consulted the Russian ambassador in Athens about the information the Russian representatives received from the Patriarch and approved Joachim III's decision not to rush the process of reconciliation with the Exarchate.[165]

The Patriarchate explained to the Exarch that his repentance was not enough to lift the Schism since his own residence in Constantinople continued to violate the principle of one bishop in one diocese. But if the Bulgarian army took over the city, shortly before the liturgy the Exarch could request Joachim III's permission to follow him into the cathedral.[166] The interests of the Patriarchate would greatly suffer if the Schism were to be abolished before reaching an agreement on the establishment of the autocephalous Bulgarian Church, on the status of the Exarch, and on the archbishops in the dioceses that the Ottoman Empire would have to cede to the allies.[167] When the news came that the Bulgarian army would not enter the city or would immediately withdraw from it, the Patriarch asked Athens to ensure the return of the Hagia Sophia to Orthodoxy in a special provision in the future peace treaty.[168]

Joachim III died at the end of November 1912 and did not know that the allies ignored his request—they were too busy dividing Ottoman provinces. In the Treaty of London of May 1913, under Austrian pressure, Serbia ceded the coveted Adriatic outlets to the newly created Albania and was determined to keep all of Macedonia under its military control. When Greece refused to surrender Thessaloniki, the Bulgarian government felt cheated out of its share of the spoils.[169] When the Bulgarian press began to demand ethnically Bulgarian areas in Macedonia, General Ovsianyi, the famous Russian Pan-Slav commentator and a veteran of the Russo-Turkish War of 1877–1878, urged the little Slavic brothers to be satisfied with effective occupation as the rule of all wars. The Bulgarians had conquered "a huge Turkish city of Adrianople with only 10,000 Bulgarians and all of the Aegean coast inhabited by the Greeks."[170]

---

165. Ibid., the Foreign Ministry to Zannetos for Kanellopoulos, 1 November 1912.

166. Ibid., Kanellopoulos to the Foreign Ministry via Zannetos, 2 November 1912.

167. Ibid., Kanellopoulos to the Foreign Ministry via Zannetos, 4 November 1912.

168. Ibid., Kanellopoulos to the Foreign Ministry via Zannetos, 7 November 1912.

169. Rossos, *Russia and the Balkans*, pp. 182–183.

170. Ovsianyi, Nikolai, "Beati Possidentes," in *Blizhnii Vostok i Slavianstvo* (St. Petersburg: Russko-Fratsuzskaia Tipografiia, 1913), p. 253.

In the Second Balkan War of 1913 (June-August 1913), Bulgaria turned on its allies in an effort to take possession of most parts of Macedonia but was defeated by Greece, Serbia, and a new player, Rumania. The Ottoman Empire joined them and retook Thrace with Adrianople from Bulgaria. Map 6.3 shows dramatic changes between the outcomes of the First and Second Balkan Wars.

In 1913, amidst defeats of the Balkan Wars, the CUP tacitly approved vigilante violence against Greek villagers perpetrated by Macedonian Muslim refugees in Thrace. That kind of ruthless manipulation served to further intimidate opposition and win popular support by presenting the problem of diversity in terms of non-Muslims' betrayal of the Ottoman caliphate.[171]

For CUP leaders, civic and ethnic nationalisms coexisted in a complementary relationship. The imperative of saving the only remaining Islamic state whose very existence seemed anomalous at the height of European imperialism made all options acceptable to many Ottoman intellectuals and statesmen in the early 1900s. Depending on the political contingency, the same person such as Russian-born Azeri Ahmet Agaev (Agaoglu) would alternately emphasize Ottomanism or Islamism to rally different Ottoman groups behind the state flag or Pan-Turkism to seek support or project influence abroad.[172]

In contrast, Russian Pan-Slavism was losing its ethnocentrism in the aftermath of the Balkan Wars. Both Pan-Slav and Pan-Orthodox scholars and commentators were disappointed in 1913 when "the Greco-Slavic crusade against the Crescent" had failed to produce an Eastern Confederation.[173] "The lack of culture and moderation among the winners" explains why that noble cause degenerated into "the disgraceful internecine war" among the allies.[174] Had they been more serious about Orthodoxy, they would have kept excessive nationalism at bay within their alliance; then, the Bulgarians would not have attacked the Greeks and their fellow Slavic Serb brothers.

The Pan-Orthodox publicists had the right to feel vindicated in the spring of 1914 when Exarch Iosif asked Russian diplomats in Sofia to mediate in his new attempt to lift the Schism. After the Balkan Wars, he had to move

---

171. Keyder, Caglar, "The Ottoman Empire," Barkey, Karen, and von Hagen, Mark, eds., *After Empire: Multiethnic Societies & Nation-Building* (Boulder: Westview Press, 1997), pp. 38–41.

172. Shissler, Holly, *Between Two Empires: Ahmet Agaoglu and the New Turkey* (London and New York: I. B. Tauris, 2003), pp. 38–39.

173. Sokolov, Ivan, *Pravoslavnyi Grecheskii Vostok*. Issue II (St. Petersburg, 1913), p 17.

174. Kriukov, Nikolai, *Slavianskiie zemli: Selskoie khoziaistvo v slavianskikh zemliakh v sviazi s obshchim razvitiiem etikh stran* (St. Petersburg: Kirshbaum, 1914), p. XXIV.

MAP 6.3 Territorial modifications in the Balkans—Conference of London (May 1913) and Treaty of Bucharest (August 1913). The University of Texas Map Collection. http://www.lib.utexas.edu/maps/historical/balkan_modifications_1914.jpg

to Sofia from Constantinople, where he had spent thirty-five years tirelessly defending and expanding the Exarchate. His life's ups and downs symbolized the ebb and flow of Bulgarian nationalist ambitions. During a personal interview with a Russian diplomat, the frail elderly prelate identified the reconciliation with the Patriarchate as "the most important issue for the country." The return to Orthodoxy would be a great consolation to the humiliated and embittered Bulgarian people, because "it would bring the Russian and Bulgarian Churches close together." According to the Exarch, at its sessions in January and March of 1914, the Holy Synod of the Exarchate unanimously voted to negotiate the end of the Schism with Russian mediation. After the end of the Schism, Iosif promised to the Russian diplomat to do his best to rebuild Serbian-Bulgarian relations as "the only way out of the intolerable situation which Bulgaria had itself created."[175]

The Russian ambassador in Constantinople, Mikhail Girs, was elated at the news from Sofia—Iosif's initiative was very timely and "in the interest of Orthodoxy." Patriarch Germanos V had already indicated on several occasions his willingness to end the Schism.[176] In 1913, the Russian government set the stage for the peace process by transferring 46,267.60 francs to the Patriarchate—the combined annual subsidy for two previous years.[177]

But in Bosnia, both the Austrian authorities and the Serbian "Black Hand" were already preparing in their own ways for the visit of Archduke Franz Ferdinand to Sarajevo. The penitential mood of Bulgarian elites would evaporate at the first glimmer of hope of regaining Macedonia with the help of some Great Power. In the First World War, Serbia, Greece, and Russia sided with France and England, whereas Bulgaria in both world wars followed Germany's lead.

Conclusion

The establishment of Bulgaria in 1878 profoundly transformed the Balkan political landscape. The Bulgarian annexation of Eastern Rumelia and victory over Serbia in 1886 dramatically raised the stakes for the other irredentist nation-states and greatly complicated the Russian task of rebuilding Orthodox unity. The Balkan statesmen inherited the old Ottoman habit of manipulating individual Great Powers, which carried more danger of a general European war at the time of the consolidation of the Triple Entente and the Triple Alliance into two hostile blocs.

The international response to the spiraling intercommunal violence was to impose reorganization of the Ottoman courts and gendarmerie in Ottoman Macedonia under the supervision of European officers from 1903 to 1908. The most fatal good intention was to redraw administrative boundaries to create

---

175. AVPRI, f. 146-495-3843, pp. 490b–500b, Fonvizin to Girs, 28 March 1914.

176. Ibid., p. 46, Girs to Sazonov, 3 April 1914.

177. Patriarchate's receipt issued to the Russian Embassy, 27 February 1913, the Archive of the Ecumenical Patriarchate, A87, p. 46, Number 1189.

more ethnically homogenous districts. The so-called Muerzsteg reform produced something like a land-run where state-sponsored Bulgarian, Greek, and Serbian armed nationalist bands began to compete even more frantically to force local villagers to identify with either the Exarchate or the Patriarchate.

In the summer of 1908, the situation in the Ottoman Empire changed drastically with the coup d'état inspired by liberal exiles and led by Westernizing army officers. The Young Turks ended Abdulhamid II's promising experiment at forging the sacred Ottoman nation based on the rallying of the Muslim majority around the symbolic figure and autocratic power of the successor to Prophet Muhammad. They forced the Sultan to move to a constitutional form of government. The advent of parliamentary politics opened new avenues for a peaceful solution to the problem of rival churches and competing Balkan nation-states lurking behind them.

An additional incentive for unity and reconciliation within the largest non-Muslim minority came from the increasingly centralizing policies launched by the Young Turk–controlled legislature and government. Unwittingly, the fear of assimilation had put an end to the clever divide-and-rule tactics used by all autocratic sultans. In fact, all non-Turkish minorities joined a parliamentary coalition with Turkish liberals to change the Ottoman Empire into a federation with significant communal autonomy rights. In that context, various visions of broader regional federations with or without the Ottoman Empire had been discussed and even tried.

Russian diplomats, bishops, and publicists encouraged this process and mediated between the Patriarchate, the Bulgarian Exarchate, and other groups. Russia had helped bring together the Sublime Porte, Bulgaria, Serbia, and Greece to stop Austrian expansion, but in the fall of 1912 their alliance attacked the crumbling Ottoman Empire instead. The Balkan Wars saw decisive victories both of the Cross over the Crescent and of nationalism over Orthodoxy and common sense. The allies put an end to the centuries of Ottoman domination and turned on each other, giving a bad name to the Balkans and "Balkanization." Devastated Bulgarian leaders were finally ready for Orthodox unity in the spring of 1914.

The period since 1886 was also a triumph of Pan-Orthodox views in Russia. Most Russian Pan-Slavs were shocked at the sight of "ungrateful" Slavic brothers exploiting Russia and murdering each other over some obscure Ruritanian places. Those disillusioned defectors stressed the Orthodox foundation of Russian Pan-Slavism or promoted a union of the nations of the Greco-Slavic world. The final chapter examines the role of ethnicity and religion in the changing Russian perceptions of Muslim Slavs.

7

Russians and Muslim Slavs

BROTHERS OR INFIDELS? (1856–1914)

"THERE STOOD OUT a flaky minaret. 'Ouch! Is it a Muslim village? But every-one knows that all Bulgarians are Orthodox Christians. And they are drink-ing wine which is forbidden by the Quran. But if the village is Christian, what is the minaret doing here? If it is a Muslim village, are they with us or with the Turks? I doubt they are with us."[1] This quote is not from an Orientalist nineteenth-century travelogue but from a best-selling historical spy novel published in 1998 and turned into a highly successful movie in 2005. It shows both the importance of ethnic kinship and its limits just like Russian reactions to the civil war in Bosnia-Herzegovina of the 1990s.

To be one with Mother Russia, it was not enough to speak a Slavic lan-guage as Bosniaks and Bulgarian Muslims (Pomaks) did and still do. One needed to be part of the Orthodox Christian commonwealth. From the mid-1800s to the early 1900s, the relationship between the Russians and Muslim Slavs went from religious hatred to unrequited ethnic love and dashed expec-tations of religious and political unity.

Brotherhood in the Shadow of Religious
Hatreds (1453–1856)

Balkan Christians, typically clerics, played a leading role in the Orthodox *millet*—an autonomous Ottoman institution based on religious affiliation. They were the main source of Russia's initial knowledge about Muslim Slavs. They often demonized the "Turks" to sensitize their patrons in Moscow to

---

1. Akunin, Boris, *Turetskii Gambit* (Moscow: Zakharov, 2001), p. 11.

their plight. Serbian Abbot Vasilii of the St. Sava and Ascension Mileshev monastery was not alone going as far as to say that "we live among Turkish people
like sheep among wolves ransoming Christian faith from godless Turks with
no helper other than the Lord, St. Sava of Serbia the Miracle-Worker, and you,
o righteous Sovereign."[2] Eleven years later, in 1658, the same monastery suffered even more at the hands of the "Turkish infidel Seydeotmit Ahmet Pasha
of Bosnia" because with St. Sava's help the monks converted some Turks into
Orthodoxy. Eight monks were imprisoned and tortured for several months,
two died, they lost one plot of land and had to pay a bribe of 4,000 silver talers.[3]

Based on such accounts, the Russians could have concluded that religion
was the only boundary between the "Turks" and the "Serbs." Later in the
1700s, such requests began to be occasionally made in the name of "the poor
Slavic nation" (*narod*), implying that only Orthodox Christians were true
Slavs.[4] Sometimes Serbs and Bulgarians were said to be part of "our Slav-
Russian nation" (*slaviano-rossiiskii narod*).[5]

After the Ottoman defeat in 1774, Russia had taken control of the northern Black Sea littoral but all Balkan areas remained in the Ottoman Empire.
Taxation and discrimination against Orthodox Christians seem to have increased because at least in Serbian lands they were seen as Russian puppets
and the fifth column in future wars. "Our main opponents and enemies are
Turks, the so called Boshnaks, who speak the same language as we do and
used to have the same religion but having renounced Christ the Savior gave
themselves to blasphemous Mohammad to follow him to eternal damnation."
It was Muslim Slavs who not only destroyed Orthodox churches and seized
Serbian property but also took Christian wives and children, inflicting "inde-
scribable pain and suffering."[6]

Thus, there was some information about ethnic affinity and fluidity among
religiously diverse Slavic populations but only the Orthodox addressed the
Russian government as its traditional clientele. In the dealings with the Porte,
Russian diplomats officially spoke only of coreligionists, for example, when

---

2. Abbot Vasilii of the St. Sava and Ascension Mileshev Monastery to Tsar Alexei I, 1647,
Dolgova, Svetlana et al., eds., *Moskva-Serbiia, Belgrad-Rossiia: Sbornik dokumentov i materi-
alov*. Vol. 1 (Moscow-Belgrade: Arhiv Srbije, Glavnoie arkhivnoie upravleniie, 2009), p. 256;
Archbishop Mikhail of Kratov to Tsar Alexei I, 26 December 1647, ibid., p. 263.

3. St. Sava and Ascension Mileshev Monastery to Tsar Alexei I, some time in 1659, ibid.,
p. 299.

4. Archbishop of Belgrade Vikentii to Empress Anna, April 1732, ibid., p. 396.

5. Serb Patriarch Arsenii IV to Empress Anna, 9 January 1738, ibid., p. 407.

6. Serbian headmen to Catherine II, February 1784, ibid., p. 433.

facilitating the issue of the permits required to rebuild or repair churches and monasteries in Herzegovina before the First Serbian Uprising (1804–1813).[7] Writing to Russian representatives, the Christian Slavs themselves often excluded their Muslim cousins, "Montenegro and the neighboring province of Herzegovina are populated by the Slavic nation (*narod*) whose courage and implacable hatred of the Mohammedan yoke as well as unbroken loyalty to the Russian throne are known across Europe."[8]

Local Orthodox leaders described Catholic Slavs almost as negatively as the Muslim Slavs, for example, those in control of the rich Ragusa Republic on the Dalmatian coast. A Montenegrin ruler praised the Russian Consul General Carl Fonton who stopped the persecution of Orthodox Greeks in that Catholic Slav city-state now known as Dubrovnik. This intervention "further strengthened the allegiance of Herzegovinian and Montenegrin Christians for whom faith (*edinoveriie*) is the strongest bond."[9]

Soon after the outbreak of the First Serbian Uprising in February 1804, one of Serb archbishops proposed to Tsar Alexander I to negotiate with the Sultan the creation of an autonomous tributary "Slav-Serb" state roughly within the borders of twentieth-century Yugoslavia where even Bosnian Turks and Dalmatian Catholics spoke almost the same language as Orthodox Serbs. This act would benefit not just the Russian Empire but also the whole "Slavic race" (*rod*).[10]

However, most of the time local Christians in their communications with the Russian government downplayed ethnic kinship. Bosnian Muslims remained infidel enemies especially when their forces joined the troops of Pasvanoglu of Vidin and of Ibrahim Pasha of Skutari operating against Serb and Bulgarian rebels. Early in 1806, Bosnian Muslims had taken many Serb women and children into captivity after killing most teenage and baby boys. The Serb rebel deputies in Vienna appealed for protection to Alexander I "as the divinely ordained protector of all Orthodox and Slavic nations on earth."[11] Herzegovinian community leaders asked to be liberated "from the heavy

---

7. Vice-Chancellor V. P. Kochubei to Ambassador V. S. Tamara, 15 July 1802, Narochnitskii, A. L. et al., eds., *Politicheskiie i kulturnyie otnosheniia Rossii s iugoslavianskimi zemliami v pervoi treti XIX veka* (Moscow: Nauka, 1997), p. 12.

8. M. Nikshich to Alexander I, 25 January 1803, ibid., p. 13.

9. Peter I Petrovich Negosh to State Chancellor A. P. Vorontsov, 12 February 1803, Russian translation from Serbian, ibid., p. 16.

10. Archbishop Stefan Stratimirovich to Alexander I, before 14 June 1804, Dolgova, Svetlana et al., eds., *Moskva-Serbiia, Belgrad-Rossiia*, pp. 448–449.

11. Serb deputation in Vienna to Alexander I, February 1806, Nikitin, S. A., Chubrilovich, V. et al., eds., *Pervoie Serbskoie Vosstanie 1804–1813 gg i Rossiia*. Vol. 1. *1804–1807* (Moscow: Nauka, 1980), pp. 217–219.

Hagarene yoke" and to become the subjects of the Russian crown because "our people are of one faith, one blood, and of one language with Russia."[12]

The Russian diplomats of non-Russian descent on occasions were themselves able to discern affinity between Orthodox Serbs and the so-called Turks. The consul in Bucharest L. G. Kirico observed that Belgrade Serbs revolted against the Turks "of the opposing party" who had murdered five of the Serbian headmen and massacred many Serbs in the fortress and suburbs. The Ottoman governor and the Porte were not involved in "the civil war" probably because they were interested in seeing rebellious Janissaries removed from Belgrade.[13]

The constant motif of forced Islamization also suggests that the Russian diplomats were reminded of blood ties between the "Serbian Slavs" and "Turks." In their pleas for Russian help, the leaders of the First Serbian Uprising emphasized this grievance immediately following the desecration of churches. Janissary captains "violated underage boys and deflowered teenage girls while forcing pretty girls and women to adopt Mohammedan faith. As a result, no father is a master of his children or a husband of his wife but each of them helplessly watches the violence of the Turks against his own children and relatives."[14]

But this process worked the other way too. In March 1807, after a long siege, the Serbs had finally stormed the fortress of Belgrade. According to the jubilant report of Archbishop Leontii, they killed the commandant "as well as all other Muslim inhabitants whose women and children gave themselves to our sacred religion and were immediately baptized."[15]

Before the Russo-Turkish War of 1806–1812, the Russian government avoided committing itself to the support of the First Serbian Uprising. Foreign Minister Prince Adam Chartoryiskii (himself of Polish descent) encouraged the Serb leaders to convince the Porte of their loyalty to the Sultan. As they fought against predatory provincial governors, they needed to refrain from mass killings of local Turks "for they know that those Turks are their co-ethnics (*sootchichi*) who have mistakenly changed religion in the past. Instead of oppression, love and tolerance would help to bring them back to truth." For example, Chartoryiskii suggested disarming Muslim Slavs and using them

---

12. Herzegovinian headmen to M. K. Ivelich, 22 March 1806, ibid., p. 41.

13. L. G. Kirico to A. A. Jerve, 13 March 1804, ibid., p. 14.

14. Georgii Petrovich et al. to A. Ia. Italinskii, 3 May 1804, ibid., p. 25.

15. Archbishop Leontii to K. Ipsilanti (who sent a copy to Russian Foreign Ministry), 9 March 1807, ibid., p. 330.

as farmhands in Serbian villages.[16] In his opinion, ethnic affinity was only a starting point of integration; its end was conversion to Orthodoxy.

But this relatively enlightened view did not square well with the logic of the holy war on the ground. In response to the attack by the "Karanovatsy Turks" on a Serb unit, Karageorgii's main forces stormed that place and "killed all Turks there sparing only women and children." Local Ottoman governors and commanders stepped up their recruitment of local "Turks" to fight against "the Serbs."[17]

In the Russian copy of his letter to the Ottoman governor of Herzegovina, the Montenegrin ruler, Archbishop Peter I Negosh protested against oppression of Herzegovinian Christians, "You know that every kingdom has religious and ethnic differences, especially the most glorious realm of my most gracious protector great Emperor and Autocrat of all Russia. No small number of the Turks of your faith live there in peace and prosperity."[18] The same leader made clear the priority of religious identity when he justified to Karageorgii the occupation of Bocca di Cotora as part of military cooperation with Russia against Napoleon, "in order to live in unity and freedom under the wing of the Christian Tsar where all of our Slavic Serb Illyrian nation (rod) is attracted (potezhe) by the same religion, language, and ethnicity."[19]

Thanks to the reports of their Serb and Montenegrin allies, Russian diplomats distinguished between Albanians and other Muslims, who were often lumped together as "Turks."[20] Some Albanian cavalrymen even joined the Russian expeditionary corps in Serbia and played an important role in the defeat of the Ottoman unit led by Mulla Pasha of Vidin.[21] This case of Russian cooperation with local Muslims does not seem typical as most of them remained loyal to the Sultan or at least too biased against Christian infidels. Thus, the Russian representative in Serbia considered Serb contribution to the Russian war effort very important. He had concerns about their internal divisions, lack of discipline, and the propensity for sectarian violence. "Supplied with Russian arms, all local leaders will be happy to fight in hopes of plundering Turkish towns and villages. Then our task will be to

16. A. A. Chartoryiskii to I. F. Bolkunov, 4 June 1805, ibid., p.136.

17. "Zapiska bukharestskikh i zadunaiskikh izvestii," 28 June 1805, ibid., pp. 142–143.

18. Peter I Negosh to Sinan Pasha, 30 September 1805, ibid., p. 165.

19. Peter I Negosh to Karageorgii, 15 February 1806, ibid., p. 214.

20. Peter I Negosh, 23 February 1807, ibid., p. 323.

21. I. I. Isaev to M. A. Miloradovich, 21 June 1807, ibid., p. 377.

organize them and if possible to discourage them from committing atrocities (*zla*)."[22]

Russian generals agreed with the diplomats that "the whole Serb nation is wholeheartedly committed to Russia based on the same ethnicity and religion (*edinozakonie*)."[23] But religion was not always seen as the guarantee for loyalty. At the time of the renewed Ottoman offensive, recent Muslim converts to Christianity became highly suspect. The Russian representative in Belgrade ordered 400 of them disarmed and locked up "to prevent the Turks from conceiving any evil plans."[24]

But locally recruited Albanian, Bosnian, and Herzegovinian Muslim units were in no rush to complete the destruction of the Serbian rebels to avoid the transfer to the main battle of the Russo-Turkish War on the Lower Danube.[25] With the impending invasion of Russia by Napoleon, Russia had to concentrate on that threat and agreed to the conditions that fell short of Serb expectations in the treaty of Bucharest of 1812. As the Russian expeditionary corps was leaving Serbia, the rebels had to abandon certain areas. In the town of Topola, "since the Turkish mosques were destroyed and many Turkish women had married the Serbs after adopting Christianity, the Serbs could not confidently expect Turkish mercy."[26]

Indeed, the Serb rebels refused to comply with the Article VIII of the Treaty to let Ottoman garrisons and civilians into fortresses and cities. The Russian representative in Belgrade was sympathetic to Serbian demands for autonomy—without "Turkish" troops and settlers Serbia would be more stable and prosperous thereby providing more revenue for the Porte.[27] But in the fall of 1813, with Russia totally preoccupied with Napoleon, the Ottoman armies finally suppressed the First Serbian Uprising "mercilessly massacring a great number of Serbs" in revenge for earlier atrocities against local Muslims.[28]

Forced conversions to Christianity were also invoked to justify the killings of Christians. In the town of Kladova, "several dozens of men and women were burned in a mosque where they hoped to find refuge. Babies were thrown into

---

22. K. K. Rodofinikin to A. A. Prozorovskii, 9 November 1807, ibid., pp. 431–432.

23. A. A. Prozorovskii to N. P. Rumiantsev, 30 April 1808, Dostian, I. S., Chubrilovich, V. et al eds., *Pervoie Serbskoie vosstanie 1804–1813*. Vol. 2 (Moscow: Nauka, 1983), p. 78.

24. A. A. Rodofinikin to A. A. Prozorovskii, 30 July 1809, ibid., pp. 108–109.

25. A. A. Rodofinikin to A. A. Prozorovskii, 1 August 1809, ibid., p. 110.

26. M. K. Ivelich to P. V. Chichagov, 1 August 1812, ibid., p. 270.

27. F. I. Nedoba to L. G. Kirico, 3 February 1813, ibid., p. 302.

28. A. Ia. Italinskii to N. P. Rumiantsev, 15 October 1813, ibid., p. 348.

boiling water. The Turks allegedly told the Serbs, 'You baptized our children in cold water. We'll do it in hot water.' Many were impaled or sold on the slave market."[29]

After months of repressions, Serbian agents made contact with the Russian representatives at the Congress of Vienna convened to rebuild Europe after Napoleon's defeat in 1814. They stressed the danger of wholesale Islamization of subdued Serbia—to avoid persecution, death, rape, and enslavement, many seemed prepared to convert.[30] Now Russia had the time to demand the enforcement of the Treaty of Bucharest, which promised a measure of autonomy to Serbia in 1812. The Second Serbian Uprising (1815–1817) added a sense of urgency to this process. As before, the rebels seized land from Muslim landowners and refused to compensate them. The only "Turks" they were prepared to see were small Ottoman garrisons who would not be in the position to challenge Serbia's effective independence.[31]

Muslim landlords who remained in control of their land in now autonomous Serbia did not always act wisely. Barely a year after the Uprising, in Uzhitsa, they raised the quitrent for their Christian Serb sharecroppers from 10% to 25% of the produce, which sparked intercommunal clashes. In his report, the Russian Ambassador in Constantinople concluded that "mutual hatred between two nations (deux peuples), the tyranny of one, and the subservience of the other have reached their limit."[32] Muslim Slavs in the neighboring Herzegovina were also seen as "tormentors" by their Christian cousins—not only because of preying on the locals but also because of raiding on Montenegro.[33]

In the aftermath of the Second Serbian Uprising (1815–1817), Russian diplomats supported Serbian demands to make their autonomous principality off-limits to all Muslims except Ottoman garrisons. The Serbian government would also manage "Turkish-owned" land and would send that income to the Porte along with the annual tribute.[34] In the early 1830s, the newly minted Serbian Prince Milosh Obrenovich tried to expel a few remaining Muslim

29. F. I. Nedoba, "O proisshestviakh v Serbii pered padeniem onoi opiate pod vlast Porty," 23 January 1814, ibid., p. 362.

30. I. A. Capodistrias to Alexander I, around 25 December 1814, Narochnitskii, A. L. et al., eds., Politicheskiie i kulturnyie otnosheniia Rossii s iugoslavianskimi zemliami v pervoi treti XIX veka (Moscow: Nauka, 1997), p. 94.

31. Russian Foreign Ministry's note about Serbian demands, 1 May 1816, ibid., pp. 130–131.

32. G. A. Stroganov to K. V. Nesselrode, 16 February 1818, ibid., p. 178.

33. Peter I Petrovich Negosh to G. A. Stroganov, 10 May 1817, ibid., p. 145.

34. Ribopier to Serbian deputies, 31 August 1827, ibid., p. 289.

civilians resident in the Belgrade fortress compound, to seize Muslim-owned land, and even to annex neighboring districts in the Vidin province. The Russian government had no desire to see more turmoil after the recent Russo-Turkish War of 1829–1830.

Foreign Minister Nesselrode sent a special envoy Colonel Budberg to remind Serbia's upstart ruler that his principality owed its very existence to the benevolence of the Russian Emperor. Turkish civilians in the Belgrade fortress compound should be considered as part of the garrison. It was fine to buy their shops and Muslim-owned land as part of the peaceful effort to cleanse the area of their presence. "Mohammedan national pride (*narodnoie samoliubie*) had been sufficiently hurt by the resettlement so there was no need to make them desperate through violence." Serbia's fragile status dictated avoiding the risk of infuriating Ottoman Muslims with the spectacle of "their compatriots and coreligionists, masters of that land, expelled, impoverished, and humiliated."[35]

Thus, Russian policymakers were occasionally aware of Muslim Slavs but that knowledge remained somewhat theoretical. All political connections to the Balkans were based on the support for Greek and Slavic Orthodox Christians. Russian commentators before 1856 rarely wrote about the Balkans. When they did, they focused on the Christians and discussed Muslim Slavs in passing. For example, in the seminal study of Bulgaria the Pomaks were not identified by that term. Bulgarian Muslims were mentioned as a very marginal group, a few converts in a desperate reaction to corrupt Greek church leadership and Turkish oppression.[36] A reviewer of the Serbian publication of Bosnian historical documents in the journal of the Ministry of Education exclaimed, "The hatred among the people of three different religions but of the same blood and ethnicity is unheard of and incomprehensible."[37]

Two Empires after the Crimean War: Ottomanism, Pan-Islamism, Pan-Orthodoxy, and Pan-Slavism (1856–1875)

After the Crimean War, Russian statesmen could no longer intervene unilaterally into Ottoman affairs but they could not just sit idle and defer to the

---

35. Nesselrode to Budberg, 13 August 1833, ibid., pp. 362–363.

36. Venelin, Iurii, *Drevneishiie i nyneshniie bolgare v otnoshenii k rossiianam*. Vol. 1 (Moscow: Universitetskaia tipografiia, 1829), p. 16.

37. Starchevskii, A., "Istoricheskiie i geograficheskiie zamechaniia o Bosnii," *Zhurnal Ministerstva Narodnogo Prosvesheniia*, 11 (1844): 119.

victorious Western powers all the time. As before the war, the Russian consuls received numerous petitions from local Orthodox Christians complain-
ing about the abuses and discrimination they suffered from Ottoman officials
and their Muslim neighbors.[38] Although Tanzimat reminds of Perestroika
in its literal meaning of "restructuring," even in the beginning there seems
to have been little or no expectation of a better future for Muslim-Christian
coexistence.

To maintain its prestige among local Christians, Foreign Minister
Gorchakov instructed the Russian ambassador in Paris to urge Napoleon III's
government to jointly inform the Sublime Porte about very serious obstacles
Tanzimat was running into in Bosnia and other areas.[39] For themselves
and local Christians, the Russian diplomats rationalized the European and
Ottoman promise of Christian-Muslim equality as Russia's only moral gain
in the Crimean War.[40]

After the Crimean War, the Russian consuls were much more aware of
ethnic ties to and among Balkan Slavs with the expansion of the consular
network and the growth of education and travel opportunities since the early
1800s. Konstantin Petkovich, the Bulgarian-born consul in Ragusa, proudly
noted that Bosnia-Herzegovina was the only Ottoman province where Turkish
had not taken roots. Instead, everyone spoke Serbian and even officials from
Istanbul had to assimilate into that environment.[41] A Russian military attaché
after his tour of the Balkans similarly observed that the Bulgarian Muslims
or Pomaks did not speak any Turkish even in mixed cities like Plevna. Despite
this strong ethnic affinity, "there was purely fanatical hostility between
Pomaks and Orthodox Bulgarians."[42]

In 1857, Alexander Gilferding, the Russian consul in Sarajevo, reminded
his superiors that "in the Slavic areas of Turkey, faith and ethnicity (*narodnost*) are synonymous. The Orthodox, Catholics, and Muslims considered
themselves to be three separate nations (*natsii*) although they spoke the same

---

38. For example, Kozarac district Christians to Alexander II, 30 October 1856, Pisarev, Iu.
A., and Ekmechich, M., eds., *Osvoboditelnaia borba narodov Bosnii i Gertsegoviny i Rossiia*,
1850–1864 (Moscow: Nauka, 1984), pp. 28–30.

39. Gorchakov to Kiselev, 5 March 1857, ibid., pp. 32–33.

40. Petkovich to Ignatiev, 19 February/3 March 1862, ibid., p. 386.

41. K. D. Petkovich's memo, no later than 18 January 1856, Pisarev, Iu. A., and Ekmechich,
M., eds., *Osvoboditelnaia borba narodov Bosnii i Gertsegoviny i Rossiia, 1850–1864*
(Moscow: Nauka, 1985), p. 24.

42. Russian State Military Historical Archive (RGVIA), 450-1-79, p. 1, A. V. Skalon,
"Dannyie dlia statistiki evropeiskoi Turtsii" (1867–1868).

language and belonged to the same ethnicity (*plemia*)."[43] With his training in Slavic studies and a penchant for journalism, Gilferding was in a great position to influence not just top bureaucrats but also the educated society. The Russian reading public discovered Bosnia-Herzegovina mostly through his scholarly and popular publications. The most colorful character in Gilferding's widely reprinted travelogue was Hanzi Beg Rizvanbegovich, described in terms of Nikolai Gogol's *Dead Souls* reminiscent of both Sobakevich and Nozdrev.

"The wild Herzegovinian aristocrat" was the head of the Stolac district, which also happened to be his hereditary domain. That big tall man immediately removed his uncomfortable Turkish uniform and had only his vest on for the rest of the evening. Skinny Gilferding and his friends fell short of Hanzi Beg's image of fabled fearsome Muscovites. Still, he threw a great party in their honor. He deeply impressed Russian travelers as a real Slavic hero (*iunak, molodets*) when he quickly drank several glasses of very potent plum brandy chased only with water before touching any food.[44]

Hanzi Beg was no exception among Muslim landlords. Everyone indulged in plum brandy but even intoxicated South Slavs were divided by pro-Muslim laws and policies—only the Christians had to pay the liquor tax.[45] Monogamy was another element of the genuine Slavic core behind a thin Islamic veneer.[46] However, even in Gilferding's account the Muslim Slavs were still "a foreign admixture" compared to the Orthodox Slavs who, east of Trebinje, were able to keep all Muslims out of their villages.[47]

The same attitude is clear in the report of the Russian military attaché in Constantinople on the Bosnian bashibazouk militia. The whole Muslim population was registered in those irregular units "assigned to maintain internal order and to monitor Serbian encroachments on the Slavic areas of Turkey."[48]

The first and the most successful Pan-Slav newspaper *Den'* (1861–1865) was even less sensitive to the distinctions between different varieties of South Slavs. Iavri Kadyn, a "Turkish" landlord from Leskovac, "felt like drinking

43. A. F. Gilferding to E. P. Kovalevskii, 16/28 June 1857, *Osvoboditelnaia borba narodov Bosnii i Gertsegoviny i Rossiia, 1850–1864*, p. 51.

44. Gilferding, Alexander, *Bosniia, Herzegovina, i Staraiia Serbiia* (St. Petersburg: Imperial Academy of Sciences, 1859), pp. 37–39.

45. E. R. Shulepnikov to A. B. Lobanov-Rostovskii, 25 October/6 November 1860, *Osvoboditelnaia borba narodov Bosnii i Gertsegoviny i Rossiia, 1850–1864*, p. 298.

46. Gilferding, *Bosniia, Herzegovina*, p. 79.

47. Ibid., p. 27.

48. RGVIA, 450-1-73, p. 54, Frankini to the General Staff, 10 March 1864.

some Christian blood" and in the middle of his house "shot a Christian who served him as a slave" with total impunity.[49] According to a "Bosnian Serb" correspondent, the "Turks" were determined to keep the whole Balkan Peninsula in "Asiatic ignorance" and the Bosnian landlords were fully complicit in this shameful act. Thus, Avdi Beg Gradachevich (a very Turkish sounding last name indeed!) tore down two schools and two churches in Obudovacka and Tserkvinska.[50] The Russians needed to wake up and understand how shameful it was for South Slavs to live as the slaves of "ferocious Turks" bent on not just exploitation but, most awfully, on destruction of Serbian cultural identity.[51]

There had been a very long history of such reports but in the 1860s they acquired an added urgency as they flew in the face of impossibly ambitious Ottoman reforms that aimed to implement legal equality for all subjects. The signal failure to transform discriminatory traditional Ottoman institutions made it hard for Muslim Slavs to see Christian Slavs not just as ethnic kin but even as fellow Ottomans. In Herzegovina, government-appointed judges in common courts were none other but Islamic hakims and qadis "who would consider it a mortal sin to decide a case in favor of a Christian."[52]

A popular Russian travel account claimed that Orthodox Slavs suffered more than "Negroes" but unlike them saw little sympathy from civilized Christian Europe. Western humanitarianism led to the creation of Liberia for freed slaves but Western Russophobia allegedly condemned Balkan Slavs to Muslim subjugation.[53]

It was not unusual to draw parallels between Islamic bifurcated states and racialized colonial regimes although religious barriers seem easier to cross. Thus, *Den'* sympathetically reprinted "A Balkan Plea to Europe," originally published in the Czech *Narodny Listy*, where a South Slav author compared Ottoman Christians to African-American slaves. European powers needed to stop supporting Muslim domination and to allow Christians to fight for their independence.[54]

---

49. Veleshanin, "Slaviansii otdel," *Den'*, 25 (22 June 1863): 17.

50. Serb Bosniiskii, "Pismo iz Bosnii," *Den'*, 38 (19 September 1864): 19.

51. Serb Bosniiskii, "Pismo iz Bosnii," *Den'*, 39 (28 October 1865): 936.

52. "Iz Mostara," *Den'*, 12 (1 January 1862): 18.

53. "Zamechaniia russkogo puteshestvennika o pravoslavnykh slavianskikh plemenakh, zhivushikh pod vladychestvom Turtsii," *Tserkovnaia Letopis "Dukhovnoi Besedy"* (18 March 1860): 352. Originally published in *Biblioteka dlia Chteniia*, March 1860.

54. "Golos k Evrope s Balkanskogo poluostrova," *Den'*, 21 (25 May 1863): 16.

Devoid of religious sympathies or hatreds, some Russian liberal publicists racialized all South Slavs, be they Muslim or Christian, in a very modern secular way, as in Nikolai Berg's controversial travelogue published in the influential Westernizing *Sovremennik* magazine (1836–1866).[55] In 1863, *Sovremennik* had a significant 6,000 subscribers among "progressive" elements of the educated society and, in the words of a Soviet source, "presented a great danger for autocracy as the focus of the propaganda of democratic and socialist ideas."[56]

Berg referred to South Slavs as "Negroes of Europe" and argued that the South Slavs were inferior to Western and Eastern Slavs and other Europeans not only as unhistoric peoples doomed to be subject to Austrian and Turkish domination but also as dark in coloring. In an editorial comment, *Den'* reminded the readers of the glory of medieval Bulgarian and Serbian kingdoms and took a particular issue with the term "Black Slavs." It was wrong for the author to call them black just "because of their dark eyes and hair and swarthy complexion. Had the author not explicitly referred to those traits, one could have been misled to think that those 'black' Slavic nations are none other but Negroes."[57] Although *Den'* sought to remove the "black" stigma from the South Slavs, it nevertheless implicitly acknowledged that they looked different from average Russians. Generally, these perceptions echoed Western European views of "the mongrel nature of the Balkans" as "a racial mixture."[58]

The anti-Ottoman and anti-Muslim tone of much of Pan-Slav press did not escape the attention of Ottoman authorities who translated many Montenegrin and Serbian inflammatory articles and encouraged a polemic in Bosnian newspapers such as *Saraevskii Tsvetnik*. The reaction of incensed local Muslims undermined modest Ottoman efforts to promote equality and reconciliation. Many Sarajevo Muslims organized by Hajji Lojo, Hajji Kaukchich, and Hajji Beg Rasnica through a local Sufi center successfully demanded that the government ban the use of hated church bells, threatening to launch anti-Christian pogroms. Symbolically, the church bells in Sarajevo rang only as long as the Tanzimat was seriously promoted at least in major cities from 1856 to early 1870s. The Sublime Porte and its officials

---

55. *Sovremennik*, 1 and 2 (1863): 63–119.

56. Dementiev, A. G., Zapadov, A. V., and Cherepakhov, M. S., eds., *Russkaia periodicheskaia pechat, 1702–1894* (Moscow: Political Literature, 1959), p. 252.

57. *Den'*, 9 (2 March 1863): 19.

58. Todorova, Maria, *Imagining the Balkans* (New York: Oxford University Press, 2009), pp. 18–19.

feared an uprising led by local notables in the name of Islamic principles and local autonomy.[59]

The Russian consul in Mostar was not at all enthusiastic about the resurgence of the power of Muslim Slav aristocrats in Herzegovina. The clans of Redzhepashichs, Lubushaks, Rizvanbegovichs, Sharichs, Chengichs, etc., were "selfish fanatics" stirring up discontent of the common folk against the authorities in Istanbul. It was preferable to have a stronger central government consistently imposing with an iron fist enlightened reforms approved by European Great Powers.[60]

However, administrative abuses and impoverishment sometimes led to collective actions involving both low-class Christian and Muslim Bosnians, who also began to respect Serbia for its more effective government and greater prosperity. They complained about violent extortions of tax farmers and corrupt officials to the Russian consul in Sarajevo. The latter concluded that common suffering would eventually help overcome religious divisions in the joint effort to get rid of the Ottoman government.[61]

The Russian consul in Ragusa also believed in the possibility of a united front based on his conversations with Christian notables from Herzegovina. "Muslim Serbs" (meaning Bosniaks) had some privileges (better treated in courts, eligible for army service, and not liable to army draft exemption tax) but not enough to ensure their loyalty to the Ottoman government. "They would have completely sided with the Christians, if local Turkish authorities had not fomented Islamic pride and fanaticism mainly by systematically humiliating Christians and allowing Muslims to commit crimes against them with impunity."[62]

For example, one frequent cause of Christian protests was the practice of taking Christian girls into Muslim harems. Christians, on the other hand, could neither marry Muslim women nor employ them as domestic servants. This complaint was included into the list of demands to be voiced by Christian Orthodox deputies in the new local representative institution—the Provincial Assembly in Sarajevo. The speech had no effect whatsoever—Governor Osman Pasha refused to consider the demands in writing to block any action at the local or central level.[63]

---

59. A. N. Kudriavtsev to N. P. Ignatiev, 22 February 1872, Pisarev, Ia. A. and Ekmechich, M., eds., *Osvoboditelnaia borba narodov Bosnii i Gertsegoviny i Rossiia, 1865–1875* (Moscow: Nauka, 1988), pp. 279–280.

60. V. A. Iakobson to A. M. Kumani, 10 September 1871, ibid., p. 265.

61. A. N. Kudriavtsev to N. P. Ignatiev, 4/16 June 1868, ibid., p. 123.

62. K. Petkovich to N. P. Ignatiev, 25 November/7 December 1868, ibid., p. 150.

63. A. N. Kudriavtsev to N. P. Ignatiev, 18/30 December 1868, ibid., pp. 154–155.

Traditional requests for financial aid from Orthodox clerics continued throughout the 1800s, but in the more liberal context of the post-Crimean Great Reforms they were addressed not only to the servitors of the Tsar but also to Slavic charitable societies—new private organizations with a special interest in non-Russian Slavs. According to the Sarajevo abbot Savva Sava Kosanovich, with many churches in disrepair and few inadequate schools, Orthodoxy in Bosnia kept losing about a thousand souls to Islam every year.[64]

Thus, not all conversions happened in harems but such stories had a certain prurience, which must have appealed to the readers of the Pan-Slav press.[65] Thick scholarly publications painted a more accurate picture. Based on extensive quotes from translated primary documents, Professor Nil Popov pointed to some signs of growing Slavic consciousness cutting across religious divides in Bosnia. On one hand, he agreed with Russian diplomats about the negative role of native Muslim Slavic barons. They treated their share-croppers like serfs and provoked widespread violent riots in 1859. Desperate Christian farmers appealed to the Porte for mediation because their main complaints were not about government taxes but about the exactions of their landlords who suddenly jacked up rents from 7% to 30% of the cash value of all produce.[66]

Popov became more hopeful about the prospects of Christian-Muslim Slavic brotherhood in an unlikely place. Interesting evidence came from his research in Bosnian prisons. They were unique institutions where average Bosnians closely interacted with each other free from traditional religious segregation. He discovered that Bosniak folk songs heaped abuse (*omerzenie*) on Muslim Turks, glorified "Muslim Serb heroes," and showed impartiality to Christian heroes.[67]

In prisons, Bosniak inmates found themselves treated on more or less equal terms with their Christian cousins. In fact, many native Christians who obtained a foreign passport were quickly released at the first intervention of their consuls. This privilege increased the prestige of European powers and undermined Muslim loyalty to the Sultan. They also learned

---

64. Savva Sava Kosanovich to Moscow Slavic Committee, 14 February 1873, ibid., p. 334.

65. *Den'*, 34 (2 June 1862): 17; *Den'*, 1 (5 January 1863): 16.

66. Popov, Nil, "Polozheniie raii v sovrmennoi Bosnii," in Strakhov, Nikolai, ed., *Slavianskii Sbornik*. Vol. 1 (St. Petersburg: Second Department of His Majesty's Chancellery, 1875), p. 355.

67. Ibid., p. 393.

from such well-traveled inmates that their coreligionists enjoyed tolerance in Russia.[68]

One of Nil Popov's Bosnian correspondents, abbot Savva Sava Kosanovich of Sarajevo, had earlier communicated the same idea after visiting Kazan— the main Volga Tatar center in Russia. "Seeing many magnificent Turkish mosques and Tatar equality in Kazan, I compared all this to the miserable situation of Bosnian 'reaya' in Turkish bondage who could not obtain permission even for repairing a single church."[69] Just a couple of years later, Russian Pan-Slavs and their local sympathizers would publicize such visions of an alternative future for Muslim Slavs to draw them closer to their Christian cousins and Mother Russia.

The same volume containing Popov's article also included a speech by Professor Anton Budilovich delivered at the session of the St. Petersburg Slavic Charitable Society on 3 November 1874. In his overview of the challenges and opportunities in the Slavic world, he stressed the treason of the Slavic upper class, which opened the gates to harmful foreign influences. In particular, he drew a parallel between Bosniak aristocrats and Polish nobility.[70] He lamented the loss of Slavic religious unity that existed at the time of SS. Cyril and Methodius. Yet, "Orthodoxy has some mysterious power over the Slavic spirit."[71]

In his travels across Slavic lands, Budilovich noticed the growing prestige of Russia because of its key contribution to the establishment and survival of Serbia, Greece, Rumania, and Montenegro. Local young intelligentsia realized that their people needed to rally around Russia to avoid extinction and assimilation into alien cultures. In every major city, Budilovich met some people who learned enough Russian to speak it fluently. Budilovich looked forward to the breakup of "Papism" as the Anglicans and Old Catholics were building close ties to the Russian Church. Slavs should be able to "free themselves from the Catholic Church" that had always been only "a stepmother" for them.[72]

---

68. Ibid., pp. 411–412.

69. Russian State Library Manuscript Division (OR RGB), 239-11-11, Savva Sava Kosanovich to Nil Popov, 18 June 1873, p. 290b.

70. Budilovich, Anton, "O sovremennom polozhenii i vzaimnykh otnosheniiakh slavian zapadnykk i iuzhnykh," in Strakhov, Nikolai, ed., Slavianskii Sbornik, p. 600.

71. Ibid., p. 601.

72. Ibid., p. 604.

The Russian military attaché in Constantinople was much less optimistic about any such cross-denominational solidarity, although he did not deny "the rudiments of national consciousness among Muslim Slavs and Albanians." They might eventually join a Christian uprising, if they stopped fearing the loss of their social and land rights with the fall of the Islamic government. It would also help if Slavic literacy spread among them. If more soldiers "recruited from among Asiatic Turks" were posted to the Balkans, then "linguistic and cultural differences despite shared faith would naturally produce a dissension between European and Asiatic Muslims. This would bring forth the idea of nationalism, so dangerous to the domination of the Porte."[73] Convincing as it is, this formula required a long time to work out in practice.

Muslim Slavs Between Three Empires and Five Nation-States

The situation changed drastically in 1875–1876 after the brutal suppression of the Christian uprisings in Bosnia-Herzegovina and Bulgaria by Ottoman troops and local Muslim irregulars—the notorious bashibazouks. Serbia, Montenegro, Russia, Austria-Hungary, and Rumania would intervene to drastically reduce the Ottoman dominion in the Balkans. After the dust had settled in 1878, most Muslim Slavs found themselves in Ottoman Macedonia, newly autonomous Bulgaria, and Habsburg-occupied Bosnia-Herzegovina.

In September 1875, two months into the uprising in the Western Balkans, a Russian consul met with some rebel leaders to get a better sense of their grievances. First and foremost, they could no longer bear the oppression by Muslim landlords, who treated their Christian sharecroppers as their slaves, "constantly dishonoring their wives and daughters." The extortions of tax farmers and "of Greek archbishops" came second and third on the list of their grievances. Finally, they rose against unending discrimination against Christians—the Ottoman authorities requisitioned horses only from Christians and pocketed compensation; impoverished Muslims joined the ranks of local gendarmes to improving their material well-being by fleecing Christian inhabitants; local courts did not accept Christian testimony against Muslims; and army draft exemption tax (*nizamiye*) was levied on all Christian males, including baby boys in their cradles.[74]

---

73. RGVIA, 450-1-94, pp. 200b–21, Colonel Zelenyi to the General Staff, 10/22 April 1875.

74. I. S. Iastrebov to the Foreign Ministry, 15 September 1875, Nikiforov, K. V. et al., eds., *Rossiia i vosstaniie v Bosnii i Herzegovine, 1875–1878* (Moscow: Indrik, 2008), pp. 118–120.

That is why it was not very convincing when some rebel groups called on the "Turks" to make common cause with the Christians and to liberate "our dear Bosnian fatherland" oppressed by Ottoman officials who did not know the local language and traditions. Christian rebels fought only for equality, promising to respect the ancestral religion and property of Bosnian "Turks." Their rights would be even more secure if Bosnia-Herzegovina were to be politically incorporated into culturally related Serbia.[75]

A Russian diplomat from the embassy in Constantinople on tour in the area reported that Serbian agents were spreading the leaflets to encourage Bosnian Muslims to join their Christian blood brothers (*edinokrovnyie*). If Serbia took over, the proclamation promised the broadest possible autonomy for Bosnia, with wide representation in a national parliament. The Russian representative was skeptical about any significant effect of that message because of entrenched Islamic fanaticism and the age-old habit of domination. At most, that appeal would attract some Muslim "proletarians" without clear political or religious views.[76]

Indeed, what followed was violence, destruction, and looting targeting rich Muslim landlords or Christian merchants. Landlords in particular would organize bands to recoup their losses at the expense of peaceful Christians. According to the Russian consul in Sarajevo, Ottoman authorities raised the banner of jihad because "the Slavs were rebelling against the Crescent." They gave out tens of thousands of rifles with ammunition. As a result, "every Muslim household is prepared for a massacre."[77]

From local Bosnian sources, Russian Pan-Slavs learned that even Catholics were siding with the Muslims against the Orthodox.[78] A little over three months later, Archbishop Mikhail of Belgrade, a key political figure in Serbia, in a private letter to the same Russian Pan-Slav organizer showed no solidarity with Muslim Slavs. "The reforms are not working out, are just irritating the Turks. The Christians are fleeing again. The Turkish authorities are not able to control the rabble."[79]

Most of the contemporary Russian press and brochures were similarly pessimistic about Christian-Muslim reconciliation through Pan-Slavism. Catholics and Muslims in Bosnia-Herzegovina "had completely forgotten

---

75. Brod committee to Bosnian Muslims, September 1875, ibid., pp. 137–140.

76. M. M. Bakunin to N. P. Ignatiev, 7/19 November 1875, ibid., pp. 158–159.

77. A. N. Kudriavtsev to N. P. Ignatiev, 10 December 1875, ibid., pp. 191–192.

78. OR RGB, 239-11-13, p. 270b, Savva Kosanovich to Nil Popov, 14 November 1875.

79. OR RGB, 239-13-48, Archbishop Mikhail to Nil Popov, 23 March 1876, p. 190b.

their nationality and had transferred their allegiance to religion." Muslim converts throughout history "had proved more fanatical than the Ottomans" in oppressing the Orthodox population and by 1876 "ethnic connection that used to provide a common tradition for Muslim aristocrats and the Christians had been broken."[80]

As many brochures were trying to unravel the complexities of the Eastern Crisis for the reading Russian public, they simply referred to the Christian struggle against Islamic oppression or "the battle between the Slavs and the Turks" without mentioning any Muslim Slavs at all.[81] A few commentators went beyond calls for a Crusade and discussed the future of Balkan Muslims as a whole.

In a speech to the Slavic Benevolent Committee in St. Petersburg, the main Bosnian-born coordinator of Russian relief for Bosnia-Herzegovina echoed the words of Father Savva Kosanovich to Nil Popov quoted above. When the Quran and the sharia formed the basis of the law of the land, non-Muslims were at best discriminated against and, more often than not, oppressed. "The Turks" treated Balkan Christians in the same way the Tatars had been treating the Russians in the 1200s and the 1300s. Thus, "after losing power, the Turks will become peaceful (*smiriatsia*) as the Tatars had done before." The humiliating status of Ottoman Christians negatively affected the Muslims themselves, "preventing them from getting accustomed to work and softening their manners (*nravy*)."[82]

But Ambassador Nikolai Ignatiev still had hopes for a joint Christian-Muslim uprising against the Sultan in Bosnia-Herzegovina. If the Porte

---

80. Anonymous, *Gertsegovina v istoricheskom, geograficheskom, i ekonomicheskom otnoshenii* (St. Petersburg: Tipografiia Departamenta Udelov, 1875), pp. 13, 33, 49; Khvolson, Daniil, *Vozmozhny li v Turtsii reformy v otnoshenii khristianskikh poddannykh?* (St. Petersburg: Imperial Academy of Sciences, 1877), pp. 1–3.

81. Anonymous, *Nastoiashee polozhenie Turetskoi Imperii* (Moscow: A. Tseissig, Iu. Roman, 1877); Anonymous, *Voina serbov, gertsegovintsev, i chernogortsev ili bitva slavian s turkami* (Moscow: Barbei, 1877), pp. 5–11; K. O., *Slaviane Balkanskogo Poluostrova: Bolgary, Serby, Bosniaki, Gertsegovintsy, i Chernogortsy* (St. Petersburg: 1876), pp. 3–4; Felkner, A., *Slavianskaia borba, 1875–1878: Istoricheskii ocherk vosstaniia balkanskikh slavian, chernogorsko-serbsko-turetskoi voiny i diplomaticheskikh snoshenii s iulia 1875 goda po ianvar 1877 goda* (St. Petersburg: I. P. Popov, 1877), pp. 4–7; Chemerzin, A., *Turtsiia, ee mogushestvo i raspadeniie: Istoricheskie i voennyie ocherki*. Vol. 1 (St. Petersburg: R. Golike, 1878), p. III.

82. Veseletskii-Bozhidarovich, Gavriil, *Publichnoie chteniie G. S. Veseletskogo-Bozhidarovicha o polozhenii slavianskikh semeistv Bosnii i Gertsegoviny, bezhavshikh po sluchaiu vosstaniia* (St. Petersburg: St. Petersburg Slavic Benevolent Committee Publications, 1876), p. 4.

satisfied even in part some of the Christian demands especially land redis-
tribution, then local Muslims would defend their property from government
encroachments. "The best result" of such "socialist" reforms would be "a rapprochement between Christians and Muslims to resist the arbitrariness of
the Porte."[83]

Ignatiev also reported about Slavic solidarity in the beginning of the ill-
fated April Uprising in Bulgaria in 1876. Surrounded by Christian population, the Pomak villages allegedly made clear their intention to surrender
their weapons in exchange for guarantees of security, saying that "their
sympathies naturally lay with their fellow Bulgarians (conationnaux) but
their religion forbade them to fight against other Muslims."[84] This expectation of cross-sectarian Slavic affinity was not confined to narrow circles of
diplomats. In 1877, the Moscow University press reprinted the memoirs of
I. P. Liprandi, the veteran of the Russo-Turkish War of 1829, mentioning that
Bulgarian Christians were treated better by "their co-ethnics who had adopted Mohammedanism" than by Ottoman Turks.[85]

But Russian diplomats close to the scene of action were quickly disappointed in their hopes. Two weeks after his report about the Pomaks, Ignatiev
wrote about "a war of extermination between two races" without any hint
at Slavic brotherhood. Local Muslim bashibazouk militias looted and massacred even peaceful Christians, forcing them to join the uprising to take
their revenge. "As they were leaving their homes in flames, there was no
hope of quick pacification."[86] This change of mind was a result of the report
of Ignatiev's subordinate, Prince Tseretelev, who had been sent from the
Embassy to learn of the facts on the ground. Tseretelev shared in a private
letter that "the Muslim population in its entirety is armed and is committing
atrocities with impunity."[87]

Sometimes-exaggerated press reports confirmed what the Russian educated public had already known in the 1860s. The subscribers spread the word
even further, "describing to the listeners the suffering inflicted on Christians

83. N. P. Ignatiev to A. M. Gorchakov, 29 March/10/April 1876, S. A. Nikitin et al., eds.
Osvoboditelnaia borba iuzhnykh slavian i Rossiia, 1875–1877. Vol. 1 (Moscow: Akademiia
Nauk SSSR, 1961), p. 194.

84. N. P. Ignatiev to Alexander II, 27 April/9 May 1876, ibid., p. 202.

85. Liprandi, Ivan, Bolgariia: Iz zapisok I. P. Liprandi (Moscow: Moscow University Press,
1877), p. 15.

86. N. P. Ignatiev to Alexander, 7/19 May 1876, ibid., p. 217.

87. OR RGB, 239-21-13, p. 50b, Alexei Tseretelev to Nil Popov, 27 May 1876.

in Herzegovina by the fanatical followers of Muhammad."[88] In addition to religious rhetoric, the Pan-Slav press and its readers often racialized the enemy but never mentioning any ethnic affinity to the oppressors who were referred to as "Asiatic bloodsuckers," "Asiatic Turkish barbarians," "cruel Asiatic horde,"[89] or even as "disgusting and despicable Arabs, of whom especially [infamous are] Bashibazouks and Circassians."[90]

On 24 October 1875, the commander of a military unit in the region of Kostroma who started a subscription to benefit Bosnians and Herzegovinians described his motivations as follows:

As one reads news reports and articles in the magazines about the Herzegovinian uprising and descriptions of today's condition in Bosnia and Herzegovina, one is inevitably struck by the horrors of our coreligionist Slavic brothers in the East. Fathers and sons are cut down by the ferocious followers of Islam who trample down the sacred human rights. Mothers and daughters with their babies flee to their kin in Montenegro and Serbia. On one hand, [we see] Mohammedan fanaticism torturing the non-Muslims with no regard for sex, age, and desecrating and destroying the shrines, on the other, the defenselessness of the Sultan's Slavic subjects with no opportunity to escape the oppression by the ferocious followers of Mohammedanism that drove the Slavs to despair. All this makes a striking scene.[91]

As in the press, in this letter "Christians" are synonymous with "Slavs." Hundreds of thousands of rubles were donated "to support Slavic families in Bosnia and Old Serbia suffering from the burdensome inhuman oppression of the Asiatic Turks,"[92] constantly "fearful for their freedom of religion, their property, the honor of their wives and daughters."[93]

The Imperial manifesto that accompanied Russia's declaration of war on the Ottoman Empire in March 1877 called on the Balkan Christians to make

88. State Archive of the Russian Federation (GARF), 1750-1-82, p. 29, priest Vladimir Obrash to I. S. Aksakov, 15 December 1875.

89. GARF, f. 1750, op.1, d.277, pp. 16, 57.

90. GARF, f. 1750, op.1, d. 278, p. 89.

91. GARF, f. 1750, op. 1, d. 81, p.79.

92. GARF, f. 1750, op.1, d. 276a, p. 110b (personnel of the Porkhov Police Department, 29 October 1875).

93. GARF, f. 1750, op. 1, d. 270, p. 12 (I. S. Aksakov to the Society of Merchants, 4 February 1876).

a common effort to help the Russians to liberate them from "Muslim oppression."[94] This message did not sound promising to Bulgarian Muslims,
Turkish and Slavic alike. Christian Bulgarians, locals and refugees, were
allowed and even required to temporarily use the homes and land of the
Muslims who had chosen to flee with the retreating Ottoman army. Village
headmen were to make sure that two-thirds of the grain and half of the
hay would be kept for absent Muslim owners.[95] Since the outbreak of the
war in March 1877, Russian authorities formed Christian Bulgarian militias but they quickly proved unable to keep order in occupied areas. Their
lack of discipline and extreme nationalism led to conflicts with Muslim
civilians, so the Russian governor had to request Russian troops from
the front.[96]

Some reserve battalions were diverted but the situation kept deteriorating—
"fires and looting in Turkish villages on a daily basis." The Russian administration realized that such turmoil would draw a lot of criticism and would
make it difficult to resettle returning Muslim refugees but could not do much
to stop the cycle of violence.[97] In fact, the Russian high command continued to arm local Christian Bulgarian population for self-defense against both
raiding Turkish irregulars and "attacks by armed Muslim neighbors."[98]

Some Christian militiamen operated completely independently and
turned from self-defense to protection rackets and indiscriminate looting
without any religious or ethnic bias. "It would be desirable that at least they
live off the Muslim population rather than the Christian population that
we have come to protect and not to expose to systematic violence." Militias
should not be led by former criminals or be allowed to stay in liberated areas.
Instead, they should be attached to forward reconnaissance units in the war
zone.[99]

The Russian high command understood that the only reliable way to discipline the militiamen would be to put them on the payroll. As late as fall of
1877, they were expected to rely on "war booty" to provide for their food and

---

94. Alexander II, Svishov, 19 June 1877, *Rusiia i vuzstanoviavaneto na bulgarskata
durzhavnost (1878—1885 g.)* (Sofia: State Archives Agency, 2008), pp. 34–35.

95. V. A. Cherkasskii to A. A. Nepokoichitskii, 29 June 1877, S. A. Nikitin et al., eds.,
Osvobozhdeniie Bolgarii ot turetskogo iga. Vol. 2 (Moscow: Nauka, 1964), p. 146.

96. V. A. Cherkasskii to Nikolai Nikolaevich, 4 July 1877, ibid., p. 155.

97. D. A. Miliutin to V. A. Cherkasskii, 23 July 1877, ibid., p. 194.

98. N. D. Artamonov to A. A.Nepokoichitskii, after 11 August 1877, ibid., p. 232.

99. V. A. Cherkasskii to A. A. Nepokoichitskii, 21 August 1877, ibid., p. 244.

clothes. But with the approaching winter there was a fear of more complaints from civilians.[100] Although the Russian high command did not systematically expel Muslims, they lacked the funds and the troops to stop the ongoing sectarian violence. They clearly favored the Christians and didn't distinguish between Turkish and Slavic Muslims mostly because locally religion trumped any other group identification.

Even the most liberal Russian reporters did not advocate any special treatment for Muslim Slavs and criticized the Russian authorities for not punishing Bulgarian Muslims from the villages, who were known for their cruelty to Christians.

> Numerous Turkish villages around us where the population returned after marauding in Lovcha are brimming with wealth in the midst of Bulgarian desolation. The thing is that our civilian administration is too protective of Muslims taking not a single sheaf of hay or a grain of wheat from them. There is too much flirtation and affectation of generosity to them. It is "what will Europe say?" again. I should add that this is being done to the same Turks who had repeatedly gone to Lovcha to kill and rob returning to "rest" in their villages like Akendzhilara, Kermenchi, and the like after our troops occupied that city.[101]

To many Pan-Slavs, it seemed that the Congress of Berlin that concluded the Russo-Turkish War of 1877–1878 did not justify the high cost of blood and treasure. Bosnia-Herzegovina was "lost" to Austria-Hungary and autonomous Bulgaria was smaller than envisioned in the preliminary peace treaty of San Stefano in February 1878 and the Constantinople conference of December 1876. The most active Pan-Slav committee—Moscow Slavic Benevolent Society—was closed because of its open criticism of Russian foreign policymakers as "the betrayal of the cause of Slavdom" to please "Europe."[102]

Nevertheless, Russia was able to exercise a protectorate over the autonomous Bulgarian Principality and Eastern Rumelia after 1878. Prince Dondukov, the Russian Imperial Commissioner, supervised Bulgaria's transition to self-government until late 1879. To stop sectarian blood feuds, he claimed that the Russian authorities punished Bulgarians more severely for

---

100. M. A. Khitrovo to A. A. Nepokoichitskii, 17 August 1877, ibid., pp. 298–299.

101. Nemirovich-Danchenko, Vasilii, *God voiny (Dnevnik russkogo korrespondenta): 1877–1878*. Vol. 2 (St. Petersburg: Novoe Vremia, 1878), p. 68.

102. Thaden, Edward, *Conservative Nationalism in 19th Century Russia* (Seattle: University of Washington Press, 1964), p. 139.

attacking the "Turks" than Muslim perpetrators of violence. Two Bulgarians were executed for killing two Turks, whereas no "Turks" including those implicated in the atrocities of 1876 suffered the same fate. This leniency to Muslims undermined Russian prestige.

Furthermore, since March 1878, the Russian administration diverted local resources to feed numerous "Turkish" refugees, for example, forty thousand of them concentrated in Adrianople. Throughout the month of Ramadan, the Russians paid for night illumination of mosques and traditional cannon salvoes in that city. They allowed those refugees to return gradually and only in small groups to avoid conflicts with the Bulgarians, who in the meantime moved into abandoned "Turkish" villages because their own homes had been destroyed. Generally, Muslim refugees were reluctant to return to the Christian-controlled lands, where they expected to be under political domination of the infidels and under their economic control "because of Turkish indolence and carelessness." Turkish fatalism and innate nomadism also explained why Muslims tended to leave newly independent Greece, Serbia, and Rumania in the past.[103]

Prince Dondukov suggested two measures to take advantage of this mood among Muslim refugees and to "completely remove" them from Bulgaria and Eastern Rumelia. First, the Russian government should encourage the Ottoman authorities to keep "Turkish" refugees in Ottoman Thrace and Asia Minor. Individual refugees should be allowed to travel to Eastern Rumelia to sell their property to "local Turks or Bulgarians." He also proposed land exchange—two hundred thousand Bulgarians from Ottoman Thrace would move into Muslim villages in Eastern Rumelia, ceding their homes to Bulgarian Muslims.[104] None of those schemes were tried in earnest but it is remarkable that the Russian High Commissioner never privileged Pomaks over other "Turks."

In contrast, Dondukov's later biographer, who was a junior Russian officer in Bulgaria in 1878, argued that the Pomak villages in the Rhodope mountains willingly accepted Russian occupation but "the bands of bashibazouks and Circassians from the defeated army of Suleiman Pasha" along with Muslim refugees forced the Pomaks to join the uprising and attack Christian Bulgarians.[105]

103. RGVIA, 846-1-29, pp. 280–282, The Report of Prince Dondukov-Korsakov, September 1878.

104. Ibid., pp. 286–286ob.

105. Ovsianyi, Nikolai, "Kniaz A. M. Dondukov-Korsakov," in *Blizhnii Vostok i Slavianstvo* (St. Petersburg: Russko-Frantsuzskaia tipografiia, 1913), p. 38.

As Russian occupation authorities were organizing local self-defense forces in Bulgaria and Eastern Rumelia, they allowed Muslim recruits to not wear the cross on the hat which was part of the uniform of their Greek and Bulgarian counterparts. The main motivation was clearly to maintain stability rather than to promote the awareness of ethnic affinity among Bulgarian Muslims—this report made no distinction between Muslim Turks and Pomaks either.[106]

In its annual report for Alexander II, the Foreign Ministry similarly saw only religious groups and concluded that in 1878–1879, the Austrian occupation of Bosnia-Herzegovina had led to nostalgia for Ottoman rule. Everyone was stunned by the brutal suppression of initial resistance. Muslim landlords received even more rights over their sharecroppers. The appointment of Catholics to most key posts, along with the active promotion of Catholicism and of Croat nationalism, alienated both the Muslim and the Orthodox populations of Bosnia. The Orthodox allegedly expected any improvement only from the Russian Tsar. Muslims were also attracted to Russia, based on the positive experience of Russian captivity among returning Bosnian POWs, among other reasons.[107]

This report was not a figment of bureaucratic imagination. It seems to be a faithful summary of diplomatic dispatches and of local sources such as Father Opatitch of Doubtzo in Bosnia.[108] Furthermore, the Ottoman ambassador in Belgrade confessed to his Russian counterpart that Bosnian Muslims had been lost to his government. On the other hand, Serbia was claiming them for itself. He suggested that Russia needed to moderate Serbian policy toward Muslims in Serbia, or else Bosniaks were not going to listen to the siren call from Belgrade.[109]

A year later, in 1880, a Russian consul published the same views in the important journal of the Ministry of Education. Muslim refugees who moved from Serbia to Bosnia-Herzegovina told him that they still missed their homeland and would have stayed there if the Serbian government had been

---

106. RGVIA, 846-2-17, p. 220, General Stolypin to Ambassador in Constantinople, 11 April 1879.

107. "Otchet MID za 1879 god," in Popov, Chedomir, ed., *Godovyie otchety MID Rossii o Serbii, Bosnii, i Gertsegovine (1878–1903)* (Novi Sad: Serbian Academy of Arts and Sciences, 1996), pp. 173–174.

108. RGVIA, 846-1-39, pp. 158–164ob, "The Report by the Orthodox Priest Opatitch," in Persiani to Giers, 15 July 1879.

109. Ibid., Persiani to Giers, 15 July 1879, p. 165ob.

more tolerant. "Would this have paved the way for Serbia to Bosnia better than propaganda and diplomatic maneuvers?"[110]

It seems that the ground had been prepared for Bosniak transition to Pan-Slavism. An encouraging sign of such a movement was the division among the representatives of Bosnia-Herzegovina in the fall of 1878. On their way back from Budapest, Catholics and rich Muslim landlords accepted the invitation of Croatian provincial authorities to make a stop in Zagreb, where they were welcomed as ethnic kinsmen. The Orthodox and Muslim gentry delegates refused to join this Austrian-sponsored celebration of South Slav unity because they were gravitating toward Serbia and Montenegro.[111]

Disappointed by the Russian gains, the Russian press highlighted any speed bumps the Austrian military machine was running into. Some reporters began to see a growing unity across sectarian lines, which disturbed the Russian Ambassador in Vienna, Evgenii Novikov. In October of 1878, he explained to the Foreign Minister that it was wrong to portray the Orthodox and the Muslims in Bosnia-Herzegovina "as children of the same race fighting against the foreign invasion." In his view, the Russian press forgot that the Orthodox had not been involved in armed resistance against Austria and just three years earlier had risen against the age-old Muslim oppression. That rebellion led to the Serbian-Montenegrin-Turkish War of 1876 and the Russo-Turkish War of 1877–1878. "To erase with a stroke of the pen this Christian memory would detract from the elevated and civilizing character of our war of liberation." In Novikov's view, this trend might suit Serbian interests but not traditional Russian policy in the area.[112]

Indeed, a month earlier the Russian embassy in Vienna reported that in Eastern Bosnia Muslim landlords had sought to organize "national and patriotic" resistance to the advancing Austrians but under the influence of fanatical imams it "degenerated into a purely religious anti-Christian movement."[113] It seems that the long-anticipated reunion of Muslim and Christian members of the Slavic family again failed to materialize.

---

110. Rovinskii, P., "Nabliudeniia vo vremia puteshestviia po Bosnii v 1879 godu," *Zhurnal Ministerstva Narodnogo Prosvesheniia*, 3 (1880): 23.

111. RGVIA, 846-1-31, p. 72, Russian consul in Fiume to the Foreign Ministry, 10 November 1878.

112. RGVIA, 846-1-30, p. 54, Novikov to the Foreign Ministry, 2/14 October 1878.

113. RGVIA, 846-1-29, p. 37, Fontan to Giers, 3/15 September 1878.

Indeed, average Russians remembered the Russo-Turkish War of 1877–1878 as a religious conflict rather than as the struggle between the Slavs and the Turks. 28 November 1887 saw the opening of the monument to the veterans of the Moscow Grenadier Regiment on one of Moscow's central squares. Funded by private donations and approved by public committees, the monument reflected the memory of the Eastern Crisis shared not just by direct participants but also by a large segment of the educated society. The monument is a small chapel shaped as a pyramid and topped with the Orthodox cross. One of the four bas-reliefs identifies the Christian victim and the Muslim victimizer—a Herzegovinian or a Bulgarian woman with a child attacked by a bashibazouk. Although his face is distorted with anger, his headgear and clothes are very similar to the attire of actual Muslim irregular militiamen in a contemporary Ottoman photograph (see Figures 7.1 and 7.2).

In the 1890s, Russian military experts considered Austria-Hungary as Russia's most dangerous rival in the Balkans and hoped to take advantage of ethnic affinity theoretically shared by all religious groups in Bosnia-Herzegovina. If the Habsburgs took over Ottoman Macedonia with the rich seaport of Thessaloniki, their economic and strategic standing would have greatly improved.[114] The manual on Balkan military statistics and geography described Bosnian population as ethnically Serbian but divided into three religions. Since for all practical purposes Austrian temporary occupation was equivalent to annexation, the population of older Habsburg Balkan provinces, Dalmatia and Croatia, should be analyzed together with that of Bosnia-Herzegovina. As a result, in terms of ethnicities (*plemena*), their combined population was predominantly Serbian (which included the Croats) with Italians as a distant second.[115]

Another leading General Staff analyst also stressed that the vast majority in Bosnia-Herzegovina belonged to "Serbo-Croatian ethnicity" (*plemia*). But he admitted that "Muslims are fanatically devoted to Islam and meticulously fulfill all the commandments of the Prophet." Similarly, "the Latins had long forgotten their ethnic ties to other Serbs and old folk traditions at the insistence of Catholic clergy."[116]

Russian army attachés in Vienna were in communication with local Pan-Slav activists but treated their information with a grain of salt. Thus, Ruthenian leader Adolf Dobrianskii shared "simply incredible things

---

114. Benderev, Anastas, *Voennaia geografiia i statistika Makedonii i sosednikh s nei oblastei Balkanskogo poluostrova* (St. Petersburg: Voennaia tipografiia, 1890), p. VII.

115. Ibid., pp. 105–106.

116. Ovsianyi, Nikolai, *Serbiia i Serby* (St. Petersburg: P. P. Soikin, 1898), pp. 289–290.

FIGURE 7.1 The monument to the veterans of the Moscow Grenadier Regiment (personal photograph).

regarding the mood of the Slavic units in the Austrian army who would definitely refuse to fight us in case of war."[117] There were plans to assign army intelligence officers disguised as secretaries to all four Russian consulates in Austria-Hungary—in Fiume, Trieste, Brody, and Chrernivtsi. Although the first two cities were close to the areas populated by the Slovenes, Croats, and Bosniaks, it was only in the last two cities situated in today's Ukraine that the Russian General Staff analysts expected to "find paid secret agents among pro-Russian Ruthenians."[118]

In their post-1878 research trips to the Balkan nation-states, Russian scholars of Slavic studies showed little sympathy for endangered Muslim Slav culture there. Thus, in a letter to Nil Popov, Professor Lavrov considered Nikshich "the best city in Montenegro." After the "Turks" had left, the old town was destroyed and "the Christians built a new city with wide streets, a broad square, and beautiful (compared to elsewhere in Montenegro) two-storeyed buildings."[119]

---

117. RGVIA, 401-4-16, p. 430b, Lieutenant-Colonel Zuev to the General Staff, 24 March 1887.

118. RGVIA, 846-4-26, p. 250b, General Staff memorandum, October 1892.

119. OR RGB, 239-11-12, p. 50b, Petr Lavrov to Nil Popov, 13 August 1884.

FIGURE 7.2 "Group portrait of three men, one smoking a nargile; possibly irregular cavalrymen (bashi-bazouks or bashibozuks)." Photographed by the Abdullah brothers between 1880 and 1900. Library of Congress Prints and Photographs Division, Reproduction Number: LC-DIG-ppmsca-03806.

Taking a broad view of the Balkans, Russian diplomats and military attachés increasingly stopped discerning the Slavs in the mass of Ottoman Muslim subjects, apparently because Muslim Slavs did not organize as a Russian-oriented interest group. At the same time, Christian-Muslim hostility was becoming more violent. From the mid-1890s to 1903, there was a spike in minor and major Christian insurrections in Ottoman Macedonia, culminating in the St. Elija's Day Uprising of August-September 1903. Since most local Greeks stayed out of it, some Russian observers saw that event as a Slavic revolt against the Turks, but as in 1875–1878 Muslim Slavs did not act on their ethnic bonds with the rebels. During the Ottoman suppression of the rebellion, hundreds of villages were totally destroyed. Their inhabitants were escaping into forests and mountains, forced by "extraordinary atrocities committed by both the troops and the mobs of armed Turks, Albanians, and Pomaks."[120]

The leading European states also relied on religious categories, especially when acting together in the Balkans. Russia and Austria-Hungary moved the other Great Powers to impose legal and financial reforms on the understandably reluctant Abdulhamid II. This intervention was justified as part of the ongoing European supervision over Ottoman implementation of Christian-Muslim equality. European governments were also supposedly responding to the growing concern over the treatment of Christian minorities in the European public opinion. The most significant part of the so-called Muerzsteg project was to send European officers to make the Macedonian gendarmerie less corrupt and more inclusive of the Christian population.[121]

Russian consular reports from Macedonia seemed to confirm that earlier Ottoman reforms, for example, those adopted in 1896 were simply a show to prevent European meddling. Handpicked Christian officials in the provincial administration and courts were simply stooges removed from any real decision-making process. Christians welcomed tighter European control over Tanzimat-style sequels, whereas Muslims feared an end to their domination if words of equality ever became a reality.[122]

The Russian representatives were acutely aware of ethnic divisions and conflicts among Orthodox Christians, especially when the Sublime Porte supported the weaker Greeks and the Patriarchate of Constantinople against the better-organized Bulgarian Exarchate and more subversive Bulgarian revolutionary committees.[123] But the Christian-Muslim differences seemed more important to most locals, especially in the areas where Christians were

120. RGVIA, 400-4-300, p. 940b, General-Major Protopopov, "A Brief Report on the Uprising in Macedonia," 22 September 1903.

121. Lamzdorf to Zinoviev, 7 November 1903, *Reformy v Makedonii, 1903–1905* (St. Petersburg: Russian Foreign Ministry, 1906), pp. 33–36.

122. AVPRI, 180-517/2-5670, pp. 34–41, A. Rostkovskii to the Foreign Ministry, Bitola, 2 December 1902.

123. AVPRI, 180-517/2-5672, p. 5, N. Kokhmanskii, Bitoli, 10 January 1905.

not ethnically mixed. During the Muerzsteg reforms, the senior Russian inspector in the Ottoman gendarmerie reported that in the Tikvesh (Kavadar) county, there were only Bulgarian Christians and Muslims. Far from embracing Pomaks as their Slavic brothers, "the people (*narod*) focus their entire existence on the hatred for Muslims, Turkish authorities, gendarmerie, in one word, for anything Turkish or remotely reminiscent of the hated yoke." The Pomaks in the Turkish army mistreated "Christians," who retaliated by killing several Muslims in the highlands and burning some property of Muslim landlords.[124]

"At least for some generations to come, the Muslim element in Slavdom is definitely a dead branch," concluded Alexander Bashmakov, a well-published Pan-Slav ethnographer and diplomat after traveling through Serbia and Macedonia in 1899. He was particularly disappointed in his attempts to elicit enthusiasm about close similarities between Russian and Serbian languages in a Bosnian aristocrat he met on the train.[125]

On the other hand, rapid Westernization renewed hopes for stronger ties among Bosnian Slavs in the early 1900s. Some Russian Pan-Slav travelers thought that before long Muslim Slavs would develop a sense of ethnic kinship with their Christian cousins. It was impossible to tell if Muslim leaders would side with Orthodox Serbs or Catholic Croats.[126]

A leading member of the St. Petersburg Slavic Benevolent Society urged all Russian Pan-Slav activists to mobilize the Russian society and government to stop "violence against the Serbian people in Bosnia-Herzegovina who are of the same blood and mostly the same faith," as they had done in 1875–1878. This protest against Austria's formal annexation of "subjugated Serbian provinces" in 1908 invoked the Crusading spirit of Russia's involvement in the previous Eastern Crisis. It was not a good sign for Muslim Slavs. War would be the last resort but Serbia, Bulgaria, and Russia should vociferously denounce the criminal act and make clear their ultimate goal—to form a Slavic union.[127]

As late as 1910, the Russian Pan-Slavs saw no need for a special approach to Muslim Slavs. "The Bosnian or Herzegovinian Mohammedan remembers

---

124. RGVIA, 400-3-2951, p. 20b, General-Major Shostak to the General Staff, Thessaloniki, 19 January 1907.

125. Bashmakov, Alexander, *Bolgariia i Makedoniia* (St. Petersburg: Slovo, 1903), p. 14.

126. Kharuzin, Alexei, *Bosnia-Herzegovina: Ocherki okkupatsionnoi provintsii Avstro-Vengrii* (St. Petersburg: Gosudarstvennaia Tipografiia, 1901), pp. 256–257.

127. Vasiliev, Afanasii, *Nash dolg v otnoshenii Bosnii i Herzegoviny* (Petrograd: Bussel, 1909), pp. 1–8.

well that Serbian blood flows through his veins" and also hated Austrian domination. Only Islamic fatalism explained why Bosniaks were less actively involved in the defense of their rights.[128]

These positive views of Muslim Slavs were inspired by some Serbian authors who reinterpreted history to create a vision of eternal ethnonational unity across religious divides. Reviewing two such books, Nikolai Ovsianyi cited published Russian and Bosnian Christian sources to debunk that new myth of benevolent Bosnian landlords with a true Serbian heart under a thin Islamic veneer.[129]

The references to Muslim Slavs disappeared from the Russian reactions to the First Balkan War of 1912, widely described as a Crusade. The Russian consul in Skopje sheltered many Muslim refugees and even the governor himself, but he clearly identified with "the limitless joy of the people liberated from the 500-year-long Islamic yoke."[130] During the siege of Adrianople, the Bulgarian troops accepted only Christian deserters and turned any fleeing Muslim soldiers back into the starving city.[131] When the holy alliance of Montenegro, Serbia, Greece, and Bulgaria was coming apart in the spring of 1913, the Russian government tried to save it and insisted that Bulgaria's role in the region should be based on "the feelings of solidarity with the coethnic and coreligionist states."[132]

Ethnic affinity was not enough for the Bulgarian government, the Exarchate, the Macedonian armed bands, and the regular troops. When the Bulgarian army reached the Pomak areas, it sponsored forced conversions often of whole communities in 1912–1913. As new Orthodox Bulgarians, they had to adopt Christian names, bite pork fat, and exchange fezzes for hats with crosses. The Pomak prisoners of war were always separated from the Turkish-speaking Muslim Ottoman soldiers and then were told to accept baptism if they wanted to see their loved ones again. The authorities encouraged the families of the captives to convert to expedite the release of their fathers, sons, husbands, and brothers.[133]

---

128. Vulfson, Emilia, *Bosnia-Herzegovina* (Moscow: A. S. Panafidina, 1910), p. 126.

129. Ovsianyi, Nikolai, "Iz istorii serbov-musulman," in *Blizhnii Vostok*, pp. 71–102.

130. Consul Kalmykov to the Foreign Ministry, 25 October 1912, *Sbornik diplomaticheskikh dokumentov kasaiushchikhsia sobytii na Balkanskom poluostrove (avgust 1912—iul 1913)* (St. Petersburg: Voennaia Tipografiia, 1914), p. 32.

131. Vice-Consul in Adrianople Klimenko to the Foreign Minister, 4 April 1913, ibid., p. 69.

132. The Foreign Minister to the Ambassador in Sofia, 3 May 1913, ibid., p. 119.

133. Myuhtar-May, Fatme, "Pomak Christianization (Pokrastvane) in Bulgaria during the Balkan Wars of 1912–1913," in Yavuz, M. Hakan, and Blumi, Isa, eds., *War and*

Other Muslim prisoners of war often suffered much more in Bulgarian hands. The case of one island camp on the Tundzha River in Thrace was extreme but indicative of the general attitudes and policies. A great number of Ottoman soldiers were left there to die "without shelter and food, under rain, in mud, on cold nights." A leading member of the commission sent by the Carnegie Endowment for International Peace photographed tree bark peeled and chewed by the captives.[134]

The First World War renewed the hopes and discussions of Slavic unity. An article in the official journal of the Russian Foreign Ministry left Muslim Slavs little choice. According to the author, some Bosniak aristocrats still kept charters of medieval Serbian and Bosnian kings to use as a proof of their lawful possession of landed estates in case their country came under Christian control. Muslim landlords allegedly made no secret that they would return to the church of their forefathers when Orthodoxy triumphed over the Crescent on the battlefield. Thus, the desire to keep wealth and power that explained the adoption of Islam in the 1400s was expected to work in the opposite direction.[135]

Conclusion

Since Slavic solidarity proved unable to cross religious barriers, Russia's main policy in the Balkans continued to focus on how to preserve viable Christian communities as pillars of its sphere of influence and outposts of beleaguered Orthodoxy. As a sideline, Russian diplomatic and military agents managed to build a close relationship with Muslim Kurds in Eastern Anatolia. Before 1914, cooperation with Christian Armenians there was often much more problematic. As early as 1877, some Ottoman Kurdish bands joined the Russian army operating from Transcaucasia in the capture of Kars and Erzurum. Some rebellious Kurdish chiefs found refuge and generous support in Russian Georgia. Those conspiratorial networks helped Russia to challenge Ottoman authority in the border areas both before and during the First World War.[136]

Nationalism: The Balkan Wars, 1912–1913, and Their Sociopolitical Implications (Salt Lake City: University of Utah Press, 2013), pp. 328–346.

134. Miliukov, Pavel, Vospominaniia. Vol. 2 (New York: Chekhov Press, 1955), p. 136.

135. Kutepov, G. N., "Bosnia-Herzegovina: Politicheskii i statisticheskii ocherk," Izvestiia Ministerstva Inostronnykh Del, 6 (1915): 141.

136. Reynolds, Michael, Shattering Empires: The Clash and Collapse of the Ottoman and Russian Empires, 1908–1918 (New York: Cambridge University Press, 2011), pp. 50, 115–123.

Thus, Russian policymakers were able to successfully work with Muslims inside both Russia and the Ottoman Empire. In contrast, Russia's relationship with Muslim Slavs at best remained platonic and unrequited because in the Balkans Christian and Muslim Slavs remained bitterly divided. In Ottoman and post-Ottoman identity politics, Muslim Slavs never organized as a separate constituency or joined Serbian and Bulgarian institutions. It takes two to tango, whereas a love triangle is rarely productive.

Some Russian and Balkan Pan-Slav commentators discussed the prospect of communitarian autonomy to attract their Muslim cousins to the prospect of Christian rule. This kind of structure worked for Russian Muslims but its appeal was probably lost in the plethora of publications where Muslim Slavs remained indistinguishable from the Turks or were expected to convert to Orthodoxy in the near future.

Conclusion

AT THE HEIGHT of the showdown over Ukraine, one of President Putin's advisers envisioned an alternative to the EU's Eastern Partnership in the integration of Greece, Cyprus, and Turkey into the Eurasian Union based on their common spiritual and economic ties with Russia, Belarus, and Kazakhstan.[1] A year later, during his press conference in December 2014, President Putin promoted a new gas pipeline project to connect Russia, Turkey, and Greece. He explained the historical background of that growing economic cooperation: "We have a special relationship with Greece because of our religious affinity." Historical conflicts between Russia and Turkey should not obscure common geopolitical interests. Both countries should learn from Germany and France, who were able to turn the dark pages of their past and to become the foundation of the European Union.[2] The specter of a Balkan federation is still haunting the Russian imagination.

After the Ottoman conquest of Constantinople in 1453, supranational Orthodox unity rested on shared faith, veneration of holy relics, Russian financial aid, pilgrimage, and the Ecumenical Patriarchate's role in Russian foreign policy. The Bulgarian Church Question put that relationship to the test in 1856 and provoked a heated debate among mostly right-wing Russian, Greek, Serbian, and Bulgarian clergy, scholars, and journalists. For the next sixty years of trial and error, they kept looking for ways to reconcile traditional religious institutions with new ethnocentric political claims. At the very least, that intense discussion in Orthodox lands demonstrates a strong political and cultural demand for new supranational visions of the union of the

---

1. Glaziev, Sergei, "Who Stands to Win," *Russia in Global Affairs* (27 December 2013) http://eng.globalaffairs.ru/number/Who-Stands-to-Win-16288.

2. President Putin's Press Conference, 18 December 2014, http://kremlin.ru/events/president/news/47250 Retrieved 3 September 2015.

Russian Empire and the Balkans with or without Turkey. It is amazing that Russian policymakers, Ottoman statesmen, Greek diplomats, and Orthodox prelates persisted in those efforts so hard and so long during the so-called Age of Nationalism. When they managed to work together, they succeeded in or came close to implementing some of those power-sharing and federative structures.

For over a year, the Ottoman Greek and Slavic delegates to the Community Assembly of 1858–1860 designed the reforms that gave laypersons greater control of the Patriarchate of Constantinople. In the late 1860s, Gregory VI and Nikolai Ignatiev conceived of the Bulgarian Exarchate with territorial and jurisdictional autonomy within the Patriarchate. They also proposed to convene an Ecumenical Council to legitimate novel solutions to new problems.

Between 1873 and 1876, the Russian and Greek diplomats facilitated Ottoman-sponsored plebiscites in several dioceses and made it possible for the Exarchate and the Patriarchate to reinterpret Orthodox canon law and to discuss concrete plans for lifting the Schism of 1872. Well ahead of their time, they included the agreement in principle on cultural rights and assistant bishops (*khorepiskopos*) for ethnic minorities in each mixed diocese. Those discussions served as the background for the joint European initiative that recommended decentralizing reforms to the Sublime Porte in December 1876. The Sultan's rejection of that proposal led to the Russo-Turkish War of 1877–1878.

In 1908–1912, the Patriarchate and the Exarchate prudently postponed a grand bargain on the thorniest issue of territorial delimitation. Instead, they cooperated in parliamentary elections and encouraged local communities to agree on the division or common use of schools and churches. That collaboration reflected and facilitated Russian attempts to forge a Balkan alliance or a federation with or without the Ottoman Empire.

All post-Enlightenment ideologies had to adjust to the entrenched religious and dynastic institutions and identities. Thus, mainstream Russian Pan-Slavism took onboard modern politicized ethnicity to navigate Russia not to some racial utopia but to the fulfillment of Russia's messianic destiny in the Christian East. Russian Pan-Slavs did not adopt the consistently secular ethnocentric logic spread by Bulgarian nationalist activists in the Russian press but produced an ethno-religious synthesis best formulated in Nikolai Danilevsky's system of cultural-historical types.

Pan-Slav revisions of the terms of traditional Russian irredentism toward Ottoman Christians did not go unchallenged. Pan-Orthodox commentators and diplomats maintained close contacts with their like-minded Greek counterparts and defended the Patriarchate of Constantinople as the font of Orthodoxy and the institutional bedrock of Russian influence in the Near

East. In response to Pan-Slavism, they accepted politicized ethnic distinctions but lashed out against the Westernizing trend of putting nation and ethnicity above religion. In their argument, the Pan-Orthodox commentators were fighting to preserve the original Slavophile ideal. This is how they saw Leontiev's recasting of Danilevsky's Slavic cultural-historical type into Byzantinism. Both rival theories were alternatives to Western civilizations but Pan-Slavism began to decline in the mid-1880s when "ungrateful" Bulgaria embarked on an independent policy of expansion in the remaining Ottoman Balkan provinces. Many Pan-Slavs were won over by the Pan-Orthodox critique of godless Western-inspired ethnocentrism in that period and especially in the aftermath of the Balkan Wars.

Greco-Slavism was a compromise between two main theories leaning toward one or the other depending on individual contributors. All three visions of a Russian cultural and political union with the Christian East contributed to formulating Russian cultural identity because they created a flattering image of powerful Russia saving oppressed or misguided Greeks and South Slavs from Westernization. Indeed, Greek and South Slav intelligentsia did not produce their own original sophisticated reinventions of Orthodox-Byzantine legacy but many individual Balkan prelates, scholars, and journalists welcomed Russian ideas. Some of those influences dominated local cultural discourse well into the twentieth century.[3]

All those intellectual constructs developed in the context of Russia's Great Reforms spurred by the defeat in the Crimean War. At the same time, the Tanzimat reforms provoked a variety of cultural and political responses in the Ottoman Empire. In part because of Russian Azeri and Tatar émigrés, Pan-Turkism, Pan-Islamism, and Ottomanism could also overlap and even morph into each other. Urged by international pressure and its own reformist bureaucracy, the Islamic bifurcated state was able to make significant strides toward a civic territorial nation which enjoyed the support of many Muslim and non-Muslim elites when it did not infringe on local and religious autonomy. To support the existing Christian institutions, Russian diplomats consistently advocated a federated structure for the Ottoman Empire. Another heady dose of Western liberalism and racism destroyed the Ottoman nation as the Young Turks more or less openly promoted centralization, Turkish supremacy, and militant irredentism, ultimately plunging their country into the Great War in the fall of 1914.

---

3. Buchenau, Klaus, *Auf Russischen Spuren: Orthodoxe Antiwestler in Serbien, 1850–1945* (Wiesbaden: Harassowitz Verlag, 2011).

Both Pan-Turkism and Ottomanism were Western-inspired products disseminated from the top without much success among the Muslim lower and middle classes. For nationalism to be believable, it has to resonate with previous popular traditions. Responding to that demand, Abdulhamid II promoted a communitarian majoritarian and relatively inclusive Ottoman nation, but the Young Turks derailed that promising project in 1908–1914.

Likewise, the deeply rooted traditions of Muslim and Christian conservative communitarianism made individual liberal citizenship largely irrelevant in the Ottoman context. Ottomanism captures the essence of contemporary debates on equality and difference in citizenship. The attempts to bring to life an Ottoman civic territorial nation should remind today's nation-builders that any majoritarian state should reassure its minorities of the protection of their communal rights. Both rival churches—the Patriarchate of Constantinople and the Bulgarian Exarchate—joined hands to defend the last vestiges of their autonomy in the face of centralization. With that goal in mind, they helped create an anti-Ottoman Balkan alliance and provided it with a pretext to attack the fragile realm of the Sultans. With divisive legacies of institutionalized discrimination, a national government should allow powerful outside states or international organizations to guarantee domestic solutions of the issues of citizenship.

The Russian involvement demonstrates that outside powers can heavily invest themselves into ethnic peace in a divided neighboring country—diplomatically, financially, and militarily. Although traditionally Russian policymakers targeted all Orthodox Christians, they learned how to take into account the role of ethnicity when they had to deal with the well-organized Bulgarian nationalist church movement and Greek and Serbian reactions to it from 1856 on. The Patriarchate of Constantinople was also flexible enough to adapt to the democratization of the autonomous institutions of the Orthodox *millet* started by the Tanzimat reforms in 1858. The mixed lay-clerical leadership was able to overlook certain regulations of the canon law and to give concessions to the newly politicized principle of ethnicity in various power-sharing arrangements tried between 1858 and 1912.

Those negotiations came tantalizingly close to success when the host state, i.e., the Sublime Porte, did not use divide-and-rule tactics as in 1858–1860 and in 1873–1876 or when it equally oppressed all non-Muslim and non-Turkish minorities in 1908–1912. Under this condition, the Bulgarian movement could not effectively play the main actors off against each other when Grand Viziers and Russian ambassadors worked hand in hand. The near solution of the Bulgarian Church Question was suspended by critical challenges that required absolute attention of all parties concerned—the year of three sultans in 1876 and the beginning of the rapid collapse of the Ottoman Empire in 1912.

Russia's cooperation with other major powers had a lot of potential to contain ethnic conflicts spawned by the Bulgarian Church Question in Macedonia. After the Austrian-Russian agreement of 1897 and the Muerzsteg reforms of 1903, rival nationalist movements and their government sponsors across the border found it hard to exploit the differences between the Great Powers to their advantage. Even the constant Russian fear of Catholic and Protestant proselytizing had become less acute and did not result in significant support for the Bulgarian Exarchate as in 1860–1861 and 1878. But the new district boundaries the European reformers had envisioned to better reflect local ethnic realities encouraged intense rivalry and covert armed intervention of neighboring nation-states.

Most importantly, the growing polarization between the Entente and the Triple Alliance eventually made international peacemaking in Macedonia impossible. Europe's powder keg exploded with the assassination of Archduke Franz Ferdinand. In the summer of 1914, Foreign Minister Sergei Sazonov convinced Tsar Nicholas II to declare general mobilization in response to the moves of Austria-Hungary and Germany. Otherwise, "Russia's historical influence on its natural allies in the Balkans would be destroyed."[4]

---

4. Miliukov, Pavel, *Vospominaniia*. Vol. 2 (New York: Chekhov Press, 1955), p. 179.

Index